Biko Lives:

CONTEMPORARY BLACK HISTORY

Manning Marable (Columbia University) and
Peniel Joseph (Brandeis University)
Series Editors

This series features cutting-edge scholarship in Contemporary Black History, underlining the importance of the study of history as a form of public advocacy and political activism. It focuses on postwar African-American history, from 1945 to the early 1990s, but it also includes international black history, bringing in high-quality interdisciplinary scholarship from around the globe. It is the series editors' firm belief that outstanding critical research can also be accessible and well-written. To this end, books in the series incorporate different methodologies that lend themselves to narrative richness, such as oral history and ethnography, and combine disciplines such as African-American Studies, Political Science, Sociology, Ethnic and Women's Studies, Cultural Studies, Anthropology, and Criminal Justice.

Published by Palgrave Macmillan:

Biko Lives!: Contesting the Legacies of Steve Biko
    Edited by Andile Mngxitama, Amanda Alexander, and Nigel C. Gibson

Biko Lives!

Contesting the Legacies of Steve Biko

Edited by

Andile Mngxitama, Amanda Alexander, and Nigel C. Gibson

palgrave
macmillan

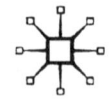

For Strini

BIKO LIVES!
Copyright © Andile Mngxitama, Amanda Alexander, and Nigel C. Gibson, 2008.

All rights reserved.

First published in 2008 by
PALGRAVE MACMILLAN™
175 Fifth Avenue, New York, N.Y. 10010 and
Houndmills, Basingstoke, Hampshire, England RG21 6XS
Companies and representatives throughout the world.

PALGRAVE MACMILLAN is the global academic imprint of the Palgrave Macmillan division of St. Martin's Press, LLC and of Palgrave Macmillan Ltd. Macmillan® is a registered trademark in the United States, United Kingdom and other countries. Palgrave is a registered trademark in the European Union and other countries.

ISBN-13: 978–0–230–60649–4 paperback
ISBN-10: 0–230–60649–0 paperback
ISBN-13: 978–0–230–60519–0 hardcover
ISBN-10: 0–230–60519–2 hardcover

Library of Congress Cataloging-in-Publication Data

  Biko lives! : contesting the legacies of Steve Biko / edited by Andile Mngxitama, Amanda Alexander, and Nigel C. Gibson.
    p. cm.—(Contemporary Black history)
  Includes bibliographical references and index.
  ISBN 0–230–60519–2—ISBN 0–230–60649–0
    1. Biko, Steve, 1946–1977—Influence. 2. Blacks—South Africa—Intellectual life. 3. Blacks—South Africa—Politics and government. 4. Anti-apartheid movements—South Africa—History. 5. Political prisoners—South Africa—Biography. 6. South Africa—Politics and government—1994– I. Mngxitama, Andile. II. Alexander, Amanda. III. Gibson, Nigel C.

DT1949.B55B54 2008
968.06'2092—dc22   2007048529

A catalogue record for this book is available from the British Library.

Design by Newgen Imaging Systems (P) Ltd., Chennai, India.

First edition: July 2008

10 9 8 7 6 5 4 3 2 1

Printed in the United States of America.

Contents

Series Editors' Preface   vii

Biko Lives   1
Andile Mngxitama, Amanda Alexander, and Nigel C. Gibson

Interview with Steve Biko   21
Gail M. Gerhart

Part 1   Philosophic Dialogues

1   Biko: Africana Existentialist Philosopher   45
    Mabogo P. More

2   Self-Consciousness as Force and Reason of Revolution
    in the Thought of Steve Biko   69
    Lou Turner

3   A Phenomenology of Biko's Black Consciousness   83
    Lewis R. Gordon

4   Biko and the Problematic of Presence   95
    Frank B. Wilderson, III

5   May the Black God Stand Please!: Biko's Challenge to Religion   115
    Tinyiko Sam Maluleke

Part 2   Contested Histories and Intellectual Trajectories

6   Black Consciousness after Biko: The Dialectics of
    Liberation in South Africa, 1977–1987   129
    Nigel C. Gibson

7   An Illuminating Moment: Background to the
    Azanian Manifesto   157
    Neville Alexander

8 Critical Intellectualism: The Role of Black
   Consciousness in Reconfiguring the
   Race-Class Problematic in South Africa   171
   Nurina Ally and Shireen Ally

Part 3 Cultural Critique and the Politics of Gender

9 The Influences and Representations of Biko and
   Black Consciousness in Poetry in Apartheid and
   Postapartheid South Africa/Azania   191
   Mphutlane wa Bofelo

10 A Human Face: Biko's Conceptions of
   African Culture and Humanism   213
   Andries Oliphant

11 Remembering Biko for the Here and Now   233
   Ahmed Veriava and Prishani Naidoo

12 The Black Consciousness Philosophy and the
   Woman's Question in South Africa: 1970–1980   253
   M. J. Oshadi Mangena

13 Interview with Strini Moodley   267
   Naomi Klein, Ashwin Desai, and Avi Lewis

14 Interview with Deborah Matshoba   275
   Amanda Alexander and Andile Mngxitama

Notes on Contributors   285

Index   289

Series Editors' Preface

Steve Biko and the International Context of Black Consciousness

This collection of chapters highlights the political genius and philosophical orientation of one of South Africa's greatest fighters—and martyrs—for freedom, Steve Biko. Biko emerged as a brilliant and provocative black writer during the 1970s, at a moment when the white minority apartheid government had convinced most of the world that mass, internal opposition to the regime had been silenced. The key forces opposing apartheid, notably the African National Congress (ANC) and the Pan Africanist Congress (PAC), had been brutally crushed and pushed underground, with their principal leaders imprisoned or exiled. But what the apartheid regime did not anticipate was the rise of new centers of opposition—from black churches, neighborhood centers in the townships, and school classrooms. Black schoolteachers, artists, and poets recognized that music and poetry could be effective resources for critiquing white racism, as well as affirming the integrity of African culture. These grassroots institutions gave birth to a broad, dynamic cultural and political movement by the mid-1970s called "Black Consciousness." Through his powerful use of language and his cultural philosophy of black pride and resistance, Steve Biko became the best-known voice for Black Consciousness, and consequently, apartheid's greatest foe.

The majority of the chapters here present a marvelous introduction to the philosophy, politics, and activism of Steve Biko, as well as mapping the broad outlines of the Black Consciousness movement of the 1970s and early 1980s. This brief preface, by contrast, seeks to explain Biko within the long memory and history of many African nationalist and black consciousness–oriented movements across the world throughout the twentieth century.

The twentieth century bore witness to the rise of a series of what Vijay Prashad has described as "Global Revolutionary Waves."[1] The first revolutionary wave produced the Bolshevik Revolution and established the

Soviet Union. The second wave, following the aftermath of World War II, was characterized by the achievement of independence first in India and Pakistan in 1947, anticolonial warfare in countries such as Vietnam and Algeria, the communist victory in China, and subsequently, the granting of nominal independence to countries across Africa, the Caribbean, and other regions of the third world. Sometimes lost or overlooked within this grand historical narrative is that many people of African descent, especially in colonial and semicolonial societies, did not take sides either with global Communism or with their imperialist masters.

What they sought was the realization of "self-determination," not simply the granting of "home rule" or local political institutions that should rule them and the organization of their economies. They questioned whether Europeans or colonial whites, even those who espoused antiracist and socialist views, could embrace the concept of black majority rule. They sometimes perceived the struggle for what Marxists termed "national-democratic revolution" in distinctly "racial" and ethnic terms, arguing that the generations of enslavement and suffering had produced among blacks a kind of consciousness of collective resistance that neither Marx nor Lenin had anticipated. One well-known example of black protest consciousness expressed as a mass movement was Marcus Garvey's Universal Negro Improvement Association (UNIA). In the turbulent period between 1919 and 1929, the UNIA established nearly two thousand branch organizations in the United States, the Caribbean, Central America and Africa, and claimed several million members and supporters. Garveyism spoke the militant language of "Race First" and "Africa for the Africans, at Home and Abroad," rather than "workers of the world, unite."

The majority of orthodox Marxists during the 1920s perceived Garvey's version of black consciousness as reactionary and dangerous. Appeals to "black pride" and racial separatism had the effect of dividing working people on racial lines, making it easier for both capitalist employers and politicians to exploit both groups. Marxists opposed appeals to black solidarity in favor of building multiethnic, multiclass coalitions that drew upon the resources of a broader social base, in order to challenge a country's ruling class. The black nationalist ideologies were derogatorily dismissed as a product of the rising black petit bourgeoisie, a fragile middle stratum especially in most African colonies that sometimes played a collaborationist role with white colonial elites.

During the military conflicts of World War II, it become crystal clear to most anticolonial black activists that the European colonial powers would be unable to reconstruct their old empires. Certain large colonial states like India clearly were destined to become independent. But for the independence process to succeed in colonial Africa, militant organizers such as Trinidadians George Padmore and C. L. R. James believed it would require the construction of transnational networks of organizers and individual colonies, mass democratic formations that had the popular support of black working people. The Fifth Pan-African Congress, organized by Padmore in Manchester, England, in October 1945, was a pivotal event in building momentum for the construction of successful anticolonial struggles across Africa and the British West Indies. What is also crucial to keep in mind, however, is that Padmore, an ex-communist, did not perceive his black liberation project as part of any global, proletarian struggle. Indeed, Padmore's most influential theoretical work, published during the height of the Cold War, was titled *Pan-Africanism or Communism?*

A generation later, in different regions of the African diaspora, African descendant peoples in the late 1960s through the early 1970s were launching a series of antiracist, social protest movements that were heavily influenced by both Pan-Africanist and black nationalist ideologies. This was most evident in the United States, with the striking emergence of Black Power. Black nationalist icons such as Malcolm X, Stokely Carmichael, and the Black Panther Party and the League of Revolutionary Black Workers advocated a militant, uncompromising politics of black identity and social protest. Elements within Black Power—leadership such as Angela Y. Davis and political prisoner George Jackson, and militant formations such as the League of Revolutionary Black Workers—were either communists, or were heavily influenced by Marxism-Leninism. The bulk of Black Power, however, was neither Marxist nor socialist. Its objective was twofold: the dismantling of white supremacy and institutions of white power; and the reconstruction of a positive black cultural identity, which was perceived as a necessary precondition to the building of a black united front capable of challenging white political and corporate elites. Many Black Powerites viewed the U.S. white working class as hopelessly reactionary. Only a politics of black consciousness could empower black people to struggle for power, in their own name.

It was inevitable that many of these same ideas about the politics of black identity, consciousness, and Pan-Africanism circulating in the United States would find a receptive home in South Africa by the early 1970s. Like Black Power in the United States, South Africa's "Black Consciousness movement" was grounded in the belief that African-descendant peoples had to overcome the enormous psychological and cultural damage imposed on them by a succession of white racist domains, such as enslavement and colonialism. Drawing upon the writings and speeches of Frantz Fanon, Aimé Césaire, and Malcolm X, advocates of Black Consciousness supported cultural and social activities that promoted a knowledge of black protest history. They actively promoted the establishment of independent, black-owned institutions, and favored radical reforms within school curricula that nurtured a positive black identity for young people.

In 1976, African high school students in Soweto, greater Johannesburg's largest segregated township, began a series of demonstrations against the compulsory assignment of the Afrikaans language. This issue, as well as other grievances, culminated in an unprecedented number of school strikes and street demonstrations involving tens of thousands of black children and teenagers. The proponents of Black Consciousness in the 1970s drew links between a positive African identity and solidarity. Like most of the U.S. Black Powerites, the Black Consciousness advocates rarely spoke in Marxist terms of "class struggle" and the "proletariat." They viewed apartheid as a distinctly *racial system* of oppression that denied the humanity of African people. Although the defenders of Black Consciousness rarely rejected coalition work with liberal whites and other nonwhites, they emphasized the importance of capacity-building among the most oppressed sectors of black civil society. These ideas paralleled those expressed by the most progressive wing of Marcus Garvey's movement of the 1920s, and the "African Nationalists" within the ANC a generation later.

The apartheid regime's repression of the Black Consciousness movement, and the students' protests of 1976–1977, was brutal and thorough. Thousands of young people were murdered, imprisoned, or in many instances simply disappeared. Steve Biko's bold personal example inspired thousands of young African nationalists to dedicate their lives to the anti-apartheid struggles. His tragic murder by the government created a vivid symbol of black resistance that continues to inspire new black activists. This reader presents the life and thought of an extraordinary intellectual activist, who was also representative of the rich tradition of Pan-Africanist and Black Nationalist protest.

MANNING MARABLE
PENIEL JOSEPH

Note

1. See Vijay Prashad, *The Darker Nations: A People's History of the Third World* (New York: New Press, 2007).

Biko Lives

*Andile Mngxitama, Amanda Alexander, and
Nigel C. Gibson*

This is one country where it would be possible to create a capitalist black society, if whites were intelligent, if the nationalists were intelligent. And that capitalist black society, black middle class, would be very effective...South Africa could succeed in putting across to the world a pretty convincing, integrated picture, with still 70 percent of the population being underdogs.

(Steve Biko, 1972)

Biko lives!!! Two words slashed across a ghetto wall. A phrase that haunts the nights of South Africa's rulers. Reactionaries and opportunists of every stripe hope and pray that it will disappear under a rain of blood and the white-wash of reform. But it remains, bold and powerful; not a tired and worn out slogan but a battle cry of a generation whose hopes and aspirations are for revolution, and end to all exploitation and oppression.

(Frank Talk, Editorial Vol. 2, 1984)

Although movements are typically larger than their individual spokespersons, it is hard to imagine the Black Consciousness movement without the towering figure of Stephen Bantu Biko, who would have turned sixty in December 2007. The Black Consciousness movement breathed life into a people who had been cowered into submission by the brutality of white oppression in apartheid South Africa. By borrowing from the resistance that came before it—the anticolonial struggles on the African continent, philosophers and thinkers, and the Black power movement in the United States—Black Consciousness made resistance not only imaginable but possible. South Africa—and the course of the country's liberation struggle—was never the same after Black Consciousness elicited the passion for a black-controlled, -defined, and -led project of liberation.

The thirtieth anniversary of Biko's murder in police custody (on September 12, 1977) comes almost fifteen years after the formal ending of apartheid in South Africa. This fact alone raises several fundamental questions: How do we remember Biko? What contributions did the Black Consciousness movement make to the course of black liberation in South Africa and the world? How does the conception of black liberation, as enunciated by Biko and his colleagues, square against the realities of postapartheid South Africa? In other words, are we now better able to articulate what must be done to attain black liberation in South Africa?

Indeed, Biko lives today in South Africa, but so do the material outcomes of colonialism, segregation, apartheid and—most recently—neoliberal economic policies. South Africa continues to be characterized by sharply contrasting realities. Under the terms of the negotiated settlement of the early 1990s, the African National Congress (ANC) won political—but not economic—power. Less than three percent of the country's land has changed hands from white to black since 1994 (over 80 percent is still held by white farmers, corporations and the state); and four white-owned conglomerates continue to control 80 percent of the Johannesburg Stock Exchange. Black Economic Empowerment (BEE) schemes have created black millionaires in the thousands, making South Africa the fourth fastest growing location for millionaires, after South Korea, India, and Russia. But the vast majority of South Africans remain at the other extreme—these are the 45 percent of South Africans who are unemployed, the one in four who live in shacks located in shantytowns without running water or electricity. This is the country Biko continues to haunt, and to inspire.

* * *

Black Consciousness did not evolve fully formed out of Biko's head. It was the product of a long process of discussion and action by a group of black students rejecting the politics of white liberalism (see Gail Gerhart's 1972 interview with Biko in this volume). Black Consciousness developed a new conception of blackness where "Black" is constructed—in reaction to the apartheid designation of "nonwhite"—as a positive, expansive concept including those designated as Coloured, Indian, and African.

But Biko was also a unique personality: an activist, strategist, and, above all, intellectual force who developed his ideas through long debates and discussions. Books were important to him. His decision to read Fanon, Senghor, Malcolm X, James Cone, or Paulo Friere was not a passive activity but a philosophical action grounded in practical necessities. "It wasn't a question of one thing out of a book and discovering that it's interesting," he says in the 1972 interview, but "also an *active search* for that type of book" (our emphasis). For Biko ideas are not academic but alive and books are active repositories that are part of ongoing discussions about philosophy and strategy. Equally important were discussions with his comrades that often went on late into the night as well as listening to the "uncommon people" in the townships. It is often forgotten that he wrote his first "Frank Talk" columns based on listening and talking with people going to work on the trains. More than the "orthodox" socialist texts of the ANC and South African Communist Party (SACP), the black masses offered a concrete notion of what the future society should look like and the problems it should address. Doggedly anti-imperialist and influenced by radical humanist thinkers, Biko rejected the models espoused by the Soviet Union and China as much as he rejected U.S. imperialism. He didn't want the future South Africa to be consumed by inter-imperialist rivalries.

Neither communist nor capitalist, Biko's vision of the future was neither liberal nor social democratic. Yet Biko's searing critique of white liberalism has sometimes been considered part of the liberal tradition. In other words, it has been portrayed as a critique of exclusion and a demand for full citizenship. There is some truth to this, but there is something more. Lewis Gordon argues that Biko's project was political, not ethical, because ethics presupposes the inherent justice of the political situation (which was hardly the case under apartheid). The prize of postapartheid South Africa, he continues, has come at the cost of an aggressive liberalism where white South Africans and a small group of the black rich can benefit without shame. Instead, Biko offered an idea of "Black Communalism," based on a nonstate concept of democracy indigenous to some parts of Africa. Contained in his conceptualization is an important critique of African nationalist politics that saw the goal as taking over the colonial state. Rather than taking over the apartheid state, Biko envisioned a fundamental decentralization of power based on the redistribution of land. Biko's nonstate idea of "communalism," often derided by Marxists at the time, is today mirrored in movements such as the Zapatistas in Mexico and found in current debates among activists who contest the direction of globalization.

Black communalism is an elemental aspect of Biko's Africanity and, in contrast to those who argued that Black Consciousness was a closed world, his conceptualization of Black Consciousness philosophy was open to change and development. The goal of the South African struggle was "a more human face," and Biko's radical humanism expressed a vital dialectic. In "White Racism and Black Consciousness," Biko took a quote from the conclusion of Fanon's chapter "The Pitfalls of National Consciousness" that summed up Biko's dialectic of self-consciousness: "As Fanon puts it, 'the consciousness of self is not the closing of a door to communication... National consciousness, which is not nationalism, is the only thing that will give us an international dimension'".[1]

Rather than a stage of psychological liberation, Biko considered "real needs"—the experience of "our common plight and struggle"—the challenge for Black Consciousness philosophy. At the same time he insisted that radical intellectuals not only reject the racist regime and its invention of "Bantustan" politics but play an important role by using what they have learnt in the apartheid schools and colleges against the regime itself. This of course meant a critique of "Bantu education," "tribal homelands," and any collaboration with the system and a liberation premised on "making it" based on the master's values. Moreover it demanded a rethinking and "return" to the source, which included African cultural concepts and a psychological liberation from all the inferiority complexes that had been produced by the years of living in apartheid South Africa that included the idea that theory could only come out of the intellectual's head.

Biko's concept of black liberation anticipates the postapartheid reality of black poverty and exclusion alongside white wealth, legitimized by a black presence in government. It has often proven difficult to describe this phenomenon, especially since the 1994 "miracle" destabilized discourses and ways of seeing that were rooted in the black experience, such as BC. How do we name a social political formation that is managed by former liberation fighters, but remains in the service of the apartheid status quo? In this volume, some contributors allude to this conundrum and provide suggestions. What is clear, though, is that Biko (as his writings show, and the 1972 interview emphasizes) had come to the logical conclusion that the kind of capitalism that emerged in South Africa was fundamentally antiblack and that it could not be reformed to serve black interests.

The Emergence of the Black Consciousness Movement

The Black Consciousness movement emerged in the mid-1960s in the political vacuum that followed the jailing and banning of the ANC and Pan Africanist Congress (PAC) leadership after the 1960 Sharpeville Massacre. BC entered a context where the most radical critique of the apartheid system had come in the form of the ANC's 1955 Freedom Charter, which would later be adopted as the platform of the Congress movement.[2] Broadly social democratic, the Charter's interpretation of the settler colony paradoxically denied the basis of a revolutionary challenge to the apartheid state. As Black Consciousness adherent Console Tleane wrote on the fiftieth anniversary of the Freedom Charter in 2005,

> The most ambiguous section in the Charter is its preamble, "South Africa belongs to all who live in it." This is not only ahistorical, it is illogical. The

very claim that the country belongs to all removes all claim to struggle itself. It is illogical to wage a struggle, call it a national liberation struggle, and yet deny or ignore the simple question about the very existence of the conquerors and the conquered, of the victors and the vanquished. The struggle in South Africa was not simply for equality between human beings. Nor was it simply, as others within our ranks want to argue, only about class. Failure on the side of certain sections of the liberation movement, especially the left, has led to a false analysis of the South African question where class has been privileged over race. It must be stated that this is an inverse of the same mistake committed by nationalists, who deny the existence of class. In the South African situation, then and now, race and class became intertwined as capitalistic development took a racial form and combined, wherein class became mediated through race.[3]

By the mid-1960s the brutality of the apartheid state had ensured that blacks only whispered their desires to be free, but those whispers, when they came, were further hobbled by the limited discourse of liberation that was on offer. Where was the analysis that took the psychological and material bases of racialized subjugation into account?

When BC appeared on the scene it loudly proclaimed its own name in its own language and created a new Black whose raison d'etre was the audacity to *be*, particularly in the face of white supremacist power. For this, the apartheid state charged many BC activists under the Terrorism Act, and locked them away. But when young activists of the Black Consciousness movement entered prison on Robben Island, they confronted the old political leaders who had been sitting in jail for decades with little hope and little fire for rebellion. The new Blacks appeared like a whirlwind, confounding the old leaders. Listen to Nelson Mandela recall the shock of this defiant quest to claim one's right to *be*:

> These fellows refused to conform to even basic prison regulations. One day I was at head office conferring with the commanding officer. As I was walking out with the major, we came upon a young prisoner being interviewed by a prison official. The young man, who was no more than eighteen, was wearing his prison cap in the presence of senior officers, a violation of regulations. Nor did he stand up when the major entered the room, another violation. The major looked at him and said, "Please take off your cap." The prisoner ignored him. Then in an irritated tone, the major said, "Take off your cap." The prisoner turned and looked at the major and said, "What for?" I could hardly believe what I had just heard. It was a revolutionary question: What for? The major also seemed taken aback, but managed a reply. "It is against regulations," he said. The young prisoner responded, "Why do you have this regulation? What is the purpose of it?" This questioning on the part of the prisoner was too much for the major,

and he stomped out of the room, saying, "Mandela, you talk to him." But I would not intervene on his behalf, and simply bowed in the direction of the prisoner to let him know that I was on his side. This was our first exposure to the Black Consciousness Movement.[4]

In an interview in this volume, BC leader and former Robben Island prisoner Strini Moodley describes such acts of defiance in prison as a practice of self-actualization, and a radical refusal to be a willing accomplice in one's own oppression. BC adherents thereby introduced a new ethic in the politics of resistance; from now onward the oppressor couldn't be allowed to freely determine the terms of engagement.

Outside prison, the new blacks told the white liberals who had arrogated unto themselves the right to speak for blacks to shut up and listen. The emergence of BC inaugurated a major displacement of the white left from black politics. For white liberals, BC challenged their relevance and in many ways "radicalized" them in the process. In search of relevancy they went from "libs" (liberals) to "rads" (radicals), often embracing the Marxism of the new left (see Ally and Ally), with some young white radicals playing a large role in the development of the Black trade union movement. But their turn to organizing black labor represented an embrace of class analysis that proved more comfortable than dealing with issues of race head-on. From here, white activists could continue to occupy positions of influence in black politics, and to speak for blacks. As Frank B. Wilderson III argues in this volume, the white left refused to "organize in a politically masochistic manner," as suggested by BC. They refused to go "against the concreteness of their own communities, their own families, and themselves, rather than against the abstraction of 'the system'—the target and nomenclature preferred by the UDF [United Democratic Front]." Instead of a "political masochism," which would have brought the white left to the brink of the "abyss of their own subjectivity," they shifted to Marxism and black labor. The irony of it all is that they wouldn't organize the white working class against capitalism and racism. (The investment of the white left bore fruit in the 1980s when they delivered organized black labor to the Congress movement.)

Confronted with the new blacks, apartheid went into overdrive. Those it couldn't incarcerate had to be killed. And they were so young. Some of the leading lights of the BC movement who were cut down include Onkgopotse Abraham Tiro, who was twenty-six years old when he was killed by a letter bomb sent by the apartheid regime. Tiro had delivered a short but powerful speech at Turfloop University in 1970, which got him expelled. His expulsion led to an explosion of student activity, as one black campus after another closed down in solidarity. Black university students began to reenter the townships, and they brought with them the new liberating ideas of BC. Tiro himself was a teacher in Soweto, playing a large role in molding the young men and women who protested against the compulsory use of Afrikaans as the medium of education in the 1976 Soweto uprising. Tsietsi Mashinini, who became a spearhead of the 1976 Soweto revolt, was taught for awhile by Tiro. Before Biko was killed in 1977, other BC militants had been murdered. Mapetla Mohapi (twenty-five years old), a close confidant of Biko, was killed in detention in 1976. Mthuli ka Shezi (twenty-nine years old) stood up against the harassment of black women by a white railway policeman and was thrown in front of an oncoming train. In her interview, Deborah Matshoba describes the sheer terror that the news of the murder of friends and comrades brought. She was in prison when she heard that Steve had been killed by his jailers: "I got scared now. If they can kill Steve, it means they are going to kill all of us who are still in prison."

Any movement that loses its key leaders at such a high rate will face great difficulties in trying to survive. But, even as nineteen BC organizations were banned in 1977, the movement was facing attacks beyond the apartheid apparatus. From the early 1980s, the BC movement's Azanian People's Organization (AZAPO) and the UDF, which developed as the new movement flying the banner of the ANC and the Freedom Charter, were locked in internecine violence. This violence has not been accounted for, nor has the role played by international solidarity organizations in the weakening of the BC movement. The Truth and Reconciliation Commission (TRC) did not have hearings on these atrocities. It is a well-known but unspoken fact that in places like Bekkersdaal township in the North West province and Wallmer in the Eastern Cape lie the graves of dozens if not hundreds of BC movement members who were killed because they dared to say "Biko is our father." The turf battle between the sections of the liberation movement, particularly AZAPO and the UDF, must account for a large part of the demise of the BC movement as a serious player in the politics of South Africa. So too the role of external interests in promoting one section of the liberation movement while denigrating the other still cries out for analysis and documentation. In a 2007 interview with Amanda Alexander and Andile Mngxitama, Lybon Mabasa, former executive of the Black People's Convention and current president of the Socialist Party of Azania, recalled the attacks on the body and soul of the Black Consciousness movement in the 1980s: "I think the 1985 Kabwe Congress of the ANC was a decisive congress. If you remember that statement: 'The Black Consciousness movement is fast growing in the country and it has the possibility of supplanting us in the minds of the people in South Africa.' And the last, most important, words: 'We should not allow it.' And from that moment we caught hell, *absolute hell*. In Port Elizabeth, more than 100 houses of our members burnt down and a whole lot of people were killed. The Black Consciousness movement was physically forced into recess... We were being killed at a rate of three to four a week. I used to go with blankets and collect the ashes of little boys, you can only identify them with a set of teeth or with a stocking that was not burned."[5]

Outline of the Volume

What you'll find in this volume of "conversations and contestations" is a thinker who is very much alive. His method with its "heterogeneous rhythms" makes him very much open to the here and now (see Naidoo and Veriava). As a work that seeks to critically reclaim Biko as a living thinker there are three areas of contestation that are central to this volume. First, a challenge to the increasingly standardized and orthodox history of the apartheid struggle, which includes contestations over historical memory and the activity of critical remembrance. Second, a discussion of the largely ignored consideration of Biko as a philosopher, as an original thinker. Third, there is Biko as cultural theorist and the importance of Black Consciousness to artistic productions.

The Historic Mirror

On the thirtieth anniversary of Biko's murder, *Biko Lives* begins by letting Steve Biko speak for himself. Thus the volume begins with Gail Gerhart's hitherto unpublished interview with Biko. What is clear in the interview is that by 1972, Biko had a highly sophisticated conceptualization of Black Consciousness. As well as tracing the South African Students Organization's (SASO) background, the politics of apartheid and its opposition and its intellectual sources, Biko talks about Black Consciousness as a concrete force in the South African struggle. Five years later, after a trip to the Cape to meet with Neville Alexander, Biko was dead.

In his chapter, Alexander remarks that victorious movements attempt to represent the past as a trajectory that inexorably and uninterruptedly lead to the moment of their victory. We always face history from the present. What surprises him is the speed of the "recasting and rewriting of South Africa's contemporary history." Indeed, soon after Biko was murdered, BC was already becoming conceptualized by different tendencies as a "passing stage" of psychological or mental liberation that would make way for the "real" political struggle, as if BC had only been the dress rehearsal for the "real" movement. Alexander, a Marxist and not a follower of BC, contends that "Biko died, literally, in quest of the unification of the forces of liberation in South Africa." Indeed, at the time, Biko was looking to build a principled united front against apartheid and had arranged to meet Alexander. On the way back he was stopped by the police.

The Azanian Manifesto (included as an appendix) was one of the products of the exploration of alliances between the BC movement and underground socialist groups. Born before the creation of the UDF, the National Forum did have some success such as campaigning against the Tri-cameral Parliament before it was occluded by the more populist ANC-backed organization. By the late 1990s, Alexander notes, the National Forum had almost disappeared from the "historical canvas." The same can be said in the shorthand history of the South African trade union movement that leaves out the work of BC activists and the importance of BC-inspired unions.

During the 1970s, but especially after Biko's death and the creation of a new BC organization in AZAPO, BC attempted to theorize the apartheid government's legalization of black trade unions[6] through a conceptualization of South Africa as a "racial capitalism" with race as the determinant of the class structure. While BC as an idea became an important element of the emerging mass organizations (most of whose leaders had been products of BC) as well as among workers in the fledgling black unions, the concept of "racial capitalism" remained an intellectual conceptualization. It might have been a useful response to new left Marxism as well as to the two-stage theories of the SACP but it did little to grip the masses (see Gibson). Whereas Nurina Ally and Shireen Ally consider the importance of BC in reconfiguring the race/class problematic in South Africa, Nigel Gibson argues that the BC turn to Marxism (often a crude materialism that went by the name of Marxism) constituted a turn away from Biko's conception of transforming South African reality.

At a time when the white liberals who had become radicals have in the postapartheid period once again become liberals, Biko's critique of white liberals remains relevant. Just as the turn to Marxism was not coincidental, argue Ally and Ally, the turn away from Marxism in postapartheid South Africa is equally not coincidental. Especially in as much as white liberals are now very much part of the nation's political, not only economic, decision making. By moving from apartheid to neoliberalism, postapartheid South Africa considers whiteness an economic problem only in as far as it is a barrier to black inclusion. The material legacies of racial capitalism are ultimately reduced to the liberal problem of equal access. As Lewis Gordon notes in his foreword to *I Write What I Like*, since white liberals are content with a system that maintains and creates the poor, liberals don't really care about poor people. Because Biko calls for the humanity of all blacks, his appeal to Black Consciousness is a call to get beyond such a system. Black Consciousness is thus an anathema to the BEE approach. Gordon writes, "Black liberation, the project that emerges as a consequence of Black Consciousness, calls for changing both the material conditions of poverty and the concepts by which such poverty is structured."[7]

The interviews with leading Black Consciousness activists Deborah Matshoba and Strini Moodley offer reflections on Biko from within the postapartheid context. Both recognized how profoundly Biko and Black Consciousness spoke to the present juncture, and Moodley offered a surprising rebuttal to those who lament BC's disappearance from the historical record: "From my point of view it's good BC has been written out of the struggle. Because if it was written in then we're part of the problem. Now we're still part of the solution."

Philosophic Dialogues

Why is it that although South Africa has produced acclaimed literary, political, and religious figures it has not produced well-known African philosophers and has no philosophical tradition of note, asks Mabogo More. Philosophy is embedded in the marvelous cultural work of BC poets and novelists discussed by Mphutlane Wa Bofelo in this volume. There is a strong tradition of existentialist philosophy in these genres, writes More, but he warns against the tendency of "locking" African thinkers in the biographical moment and political activism. This happened to Steve Biko and to the Black Consciousness philosophy he developed. The first section of this volume not only rescues Biko from such reductionism but is also a lively debate about his philosophy. Philosophical influences, such as Fanon's, Sartre's, Jaspers', and Friere's, are debated (see More, Turner, Gordon) and there is discussion of existential, ontological, and epistemological issues including notions of Africana existentialism developed in Lewis Gordon's work (see More and Wilderson).

Although it has been said that Biko did not have much access to nor read much Hegel, his understanding of dialectic is much more sophisticated than some think. In "Black Consciousness and the Quest for a True Humanity," Biko criticizes the synthetic thinking of the liberals who search for a "synthesis" between the two extremes of apartheid and non-racialism. He writes,

> The *thesis*, the *antithesis* and the *synthesis* have been mentioned by some great philosophers as the cardinal points around which any social revolution revolves. For the *liberals*, the *thesis* is apartheid, the *anti-thesis* is non-racialism, but the *synthesis* is very feebly defined... The failure of the liberals is in fact that their antithesis is already a watered-down version of

the truth whose proximity to the thesis will nullify the purported balance. (IW, 99–100)

The failure of the liberals is connected to their proximity to the system. In Biko's refashioning, "The thesis is in fact a strong white racism and therefore, the antithesis to this must, *ipso facto*, be a strong solidarity amongst the blacks on whom this white racism seeks to prey."[8] Yet he also rejects Sartre's idea that that black solidarity is *a priori* insufficient by itself. Indeed, rather than "class" as an external unifier, it is already embedded in the dialectic of negativity: "They tell us that the situation is a class struggle, rather than a racial one. Let them go to van Tonder in the Free State and tell him this."[9]

Black Consciousness set in motion a new dialectic, argues Lou Turner, based on the truth that the only vehicles for change are those people who have lost their humanity.[10] To speak of a new humanism is radical and Black Consciousness transcends the former (analytical moment) in order to achieve a new form of self-consciousness or new humanity.

And yet, Frank B. Wilderson III argues, this presence—based on absence—puts into question the very idea of liberal humanism. In a racist society human relations are unethical because the Black is positioned below humanity. To speak of a "Black Human," Wilderson argues, is an oxymoron. Wilderson locates the source of this absence in an inability to recognize that the "register of black suffering" goes beyond the "the political subject [as] imagined to be dispossessed of citizenship and access to civil society." It also goes beyond the SACP's formulation, which imagines the political subject as being dispossessed of labor power. Wilderson argues that "[N]either formulation rises to the temperature of the Black's grammar of suffering." BC on the other hand, he argues, accessed and articulated the possibility of speaking such a grammar. Different understandings and viewpoints of Fanon's critique of Sartre and Hegel and dialectical thought directly affect approaches to Biko. Turner notes a shortcoming in his own work, *Frantz Fanon, Soweto and American Black Thought*, written with John Alan in 1978. He argues that he emphasized Fanon's "deepening of the Hegelian concept of self-consciousness" but did not fully see the duality that Fanon posits in the dialectic of Black Consciousness, namely that alongside a will to freedom is a will to power that ends up emulating the white master. Gordon, at another register, argues that because antiblack racism structures blacks outside of the dialectics of recognition, contradictions are not only of the dialectical kind.

These positions are not mutually exclusive. The point here is that they are part of a larger conversation represented in this volume in which the retrospective on Biko is a perspective on the present. If Black Consciousness was a new stage of cognition that became generalized in the struggles of the 1980s, why didn't the total liberation that Biko envisioned come about? Although the movement was weakened by state terror and internecine violence, Gibson also highlights a failure of BC organizations to develop Biko's conception of Black Consciousness as a philosophy of liberation after his death.

Certainly Biko gestured to the problematics of a postapartheid society that would produce only partial freedom. But like Fanon and Amilcar Cabral, Biko died too young and too soon to see how the new stage of revolt, that he helped bring into being, would unfold. Whereas Fanon spoke of the laziness and betrayal of the nationalist middle class and intelligentsia, Cabral advised that such a class should commit suicide. These criticisms were muted in the period of negotiation and in postapartheid South Africa choices have been reduced to the market place. This is not the kind of liberation that Biko envisioned.

Culture

Do Biko's writings on Negritude, culture, and black communalism contain tensions and insights that have often been overlooked and might be of value to the present generation? Biko is critical of blacks who, mimicking white liberals, take an elitist attitude toward African cultures and thus fail to understand that the criticism of apartheid education coming out of rural areas is based on a fundamental truth: an elemental resistance to the destruction of African ways of life.[11] In rejecting the "tribal cocoons…called 'homelands' [which] are nothing else but sophisticated concentration camps where black people are allowed to 'suffer peacefully,'"[12] Biko was considering the experiences of people impoverished by apartheid as the ground of Black Consciousness philosophy.

For Biko, the liberation of the poor in South Africa is grounded in African cultural concepts of collectivity and sharing that resituates the human being at the center. Andries Oliphant relates Biko's idea of culture to Fanon and to Cabral's notion that anticolonial struggles are "acts of culture." Based on a number of fundamental aspects—human centeredness, intimacy, trust, cooperativeness, and sharing—Biko's conception of African culture is essentially anticolonialist and anticapitalist. In contrast to the possessive individualism of liberal humanism, the stress of Biko's humanism is not anti-individual but egalitarian. Like South American liberation theologians, Biko rejected the Christian homily that the poor are always among us.[13] As Tinyiko Sam Maluleke notes in his chapter, Biko was especially critical of a Christianity that played a role in the maintenance of subjugation. Dismissive of Marxism and critical of the church, Biko nevertheless acknowledged that the Christian-Marxist dialogue in South America had influenced his idea of "Black communalism." Biko also drew BC from the black revolt in the United States but, in contrast to Mandela's dismissive view that Black Consciousness is an American product (as Mandela quips, "in essence a rehash of Garveyism"),[14] Biko mainly located his thinking in Africa and saw Black Consciousness as part of the post–World War II anticolonial liberation movements.

Despite the importance of BC on Southern African literature and theatre (see Bofelo), Biko's writings on African culture are often regarded as lacking originality, yet as Prishani Naidoo and Ahmed Veriava argue, Biko's concepts continue to take on new life. Naidoo and Veriava engage a tension between Senghor and Fanon between a Negritude centered on an African past and Fanon's (and Césaire's) based on a dialectic of revolt. For Biko, unlike Senghor, culture is immediately political and so rather than "returning" to an idealized precolonial culture, Biko immediately reshapes it for the present. In this, Biko is akin to Fanon, but Naidoo and Veriava point to Biko's writings about American soul artist James Brown's black power anthem "Say It Loud. I'm Black and I'm Proud" as going beyond Fanon's concept of national culture by drawing from across the Black world and positing a "politics of his generation." On Negritude, Biko agrees with Fanon up to a point, argues Wilderson, but there is a split based on whether cultural empowerment can be comprehensive and sustainable or limited and provisional. Naidoo and Veriava remind us that since "Black" in Black Consciousness was not based on pigmentation but a matter of mental attitude and style of life, "Black and Proud" is a political statement founded on defiance. The notion of Blackness articulated by Biko is very different from the concept of race employed by the current South African government, which remains entangled in apartheid and colonial racial designations and, as Gordon puts it, "lacks the political understanding of Black Consciousness that [Biko] offered."

Black Consciousness and Gender

Because of its gendered language, Biko's thought has been considered oblivious to gender politics, if not outright sexist. Barney Pityana's statement "Black man you are on your own" is offered as proof that women were not included in the BC conception of liberation. Desiree Lewis has argued that the language of emasculation used to describe black men's condition under apartheid meant the marginalizing of women.[15] Pumla

Dineo Gqola has argued that BC discourse failed to recognize points of variation among blacks. She writes, "Due to its emphasis on racial solidarity as the only means towards the liberation of Black people, it promised complete freedom at the end from all oppressive forces despite its reluctance to acknowledge their existence. The experiences of gender, class, age, geographical location, and sexual orientation were not perceived as consequential enough to warrant inclusion into the discourse of the doctrine."[16] In addition to discursive problems, the experiences of women in BC organizations have been characterized by sexism. Akin to women's involvement in other nationalist movements in Africa (and in South Africa), it is argued that women in the movement were regarded mainly as supporters of the struggle with more assertive women becoming "honorary men." Perhaps the most famous woman in BC, Mamphela Ramphele, maintains that during the 1970s, the specificity of experience of sexism was utterly absent from the movement: "Women were important as wives, mothers, girlfriends and sisters, in fighting a common struggle against a common enemy." Scant regard was given to their position as individuals in their own right. As leaders in BC, women had to face the apartheid regime and the sexism of their comrades. As Ramphele states, "I soon learnt to be aggressive toward men who undermined women, both at social and political levels...A major part of the process of being socialized into activist ranks was becoming 'one of the boys.'"[17]

In this volume, Oshadi Mangena and Deborah Matshoba offer a complicated and contradictory picture of gender politics in the Black Consciousness movement of the 1970s and 1980s. Their accounts and analyses add to a small but significant body of scholarship in this area, but much work certainly remains to be done. Mangena highlights the fact that Winnie Kgware was elected the first president of the Black People's Convention when it was formed in 1972, making her the first black woman to lead a national political organization. But as we know, the presence of one person in a position of power hardly indicates the experience of a group within an organization as a whole. Matshoba also describes the objections to a proposal for a women's organization within SASO, on the argument that the contributions of women were essential to the main body, which would suffer if drained of their inputs. Matshoba recalls, "I remember we came with a name, made a proposal. We called it WSO—Women's Students Organization. They said down with WSO, they voted us down. And Steve blamed me and said 'Debs, you're coming with your YWCA mentality.' I worked at the YWCA office which was downstairs and the SASO office was upstairs... 'You guys have to admit you are very powerful,' that's how Steve would put it. 'You are very powerful.' And we asserted ourselves in the organization." As Matshoba explains, women asserted themselves by smoking, wearing hot pants and heels, speaking loudly, and adopting a tough walk. Becoming "one of the boys"—asserting oneself on a patriarchal pattern and through a male gaze—was undoubtedly both liberating in some ways and profoundly restricting in others. Matshoba describes how they began to take pride in themselves as black women, but simultaneously started to look down upon other women who chose not to adopt their dress, appearance, and attitudes.

Mangena argues, however, that far from recognizing women as "honorary men," the Black Consciousness movement leadership acknowledged that "a greater effort needed to be made to mobilize women's active participation." This led to the "launching of the Black Women's Federation (BWF) in Durban in December 1975...A total of 210 women attended the launching conference. People such as Fatima Meer, Winnie Mandela, Deborah Matshoba, Nomsisi Kraai, Oshadi Phakathi, Jeanne Noel and other prominent mature women from established groups such as YWCA, Zanele and church bodies were key participants in this conference." Mangena thus argues that Black Consciousness philosophy recognized women as equal participants and "colleagues" but not on the basis of "gender" considerations. There was a tacit recognition and acceptance of the idea, she argues, that women could be leaders in their own right.

The question of the link between women's emancipation and human liberation was being framed and debated in anticolonial struggles and postcolonial societies the world over and the Black Consciousness movement of the 1970s and 1980s did not articulate many answers in this regard. As Mangena writes, the question continued to haunt all factions of the antiapartheid struggle: "Does the transition to the 'new' South Africa warrant 'gender' acquiescence to patriarchal capitalism?" Biko's philosophy would reject such an acquiescence, but in engaging with Biko's thought in the present, it is vital to determine how it might help us understand the contours of patriarchal capitalism and sexism, and where and how it falls short.

Conclusion

At the turn of the twentieth century, Rosa Luxemburg predicted the future held either "socialism or barbarism." Perhaps she had seen the visage of barbarism before the carnage of World War I in the slaughter of the Herero people in the Kalahari. With apartheid we faced another barbarism—the logical conclusion of European colonialism in Africa. "Hitler was not dead," Biko said, paraphrasing Césaire, "he is likely to be found in Pretoria." Today we face a new age of absolutes: A South Africa of abundant wealth on one side and increasing pauperization on the other. The struggle has become more complicated and Rosa Luxemburg's slogan more appropriate. Masses of people live in desperate conditions and do not accept these conditions. The situation cries out for the widest possible debate and rethinking. An engagement with Biko's thought is part of this discussion.

As the frontispiece quotation shows, Biko was clear that a transformation agenda that fell short of a socialist experimentation based on not just the disabling of capitalist organization of society, but also the total rejection of the white value system upon which it is constructed would not emancipate the majority. In this conclusion, Biko's analysis and projection is apt to a fault. For sometime now, some analysts of South Africa and BC have argued that Biko's socialist inclination was not fully developed; some, using a single phrase or quotation out of context, have sought to project Biko as a liberal social democrat. Biko was against the social imperialism of Peking and, in particular, of Moscow, and he sought to build an indigenous anticapitalist reality for the emancipation of the black world. He clearly rejected "really existing socialism" but not a socialist path. In his refusal to provide a blueprint, Biko and his colleagues foretold a new kind of politics. "The quest of a true humanity" literally means changing the world. A new society required a profound change of value:

> [I]t is not only capitalism that is involved; it is also the whole gamut of white value systems, which have been adopted as standard by South Africa, both white and black so far. And that will need attention even in a postrevolutionary society. Values relating to all the fields—education, religion, culture and so on. So your problems are not solved completely when you alter the economic pattern, to a socialist pattern. You still don't become what you ought to be. There is a lot of dust to be swept off, you know, from the kind of slate we got from white society. (Gerhart interview, 34)

There are at least three main memories of Biko contending in South Africa today. The first finds expression in the black business class, through its claim to be entitled to the white wealth created from the exploitation of colonialism and apartheid. The BEE program mobilizes the common historical experience of oppression and exclusion by black South Africans to carve for itself a slice in the white world. The 1994 political settlement made it possible for those blacks most prepared to occupy the position of the whites in society to do so in the name of transformation without transforming the very structures of accumulation, production, and redistribution created by colonialism and apartheid. Moeletsi Mbeki, one of the foremost postapartheid analysts, has eloquently shown that BEE was conceived by white business to legitimate itself in the postapartheid era.[18] Apartheid started a similar program in the late 1970s and into the 1980s as a mechanism to build a buffer zone between itself and the hungry and angry oppressed black multitudes. The idea was that the black mass movement would have to contend with a layer of blacks who had vested interests in the prevailing economic system even if they disapproved of the political arrangement. This scheme was discarded by the militant mass mobilization that swept through South Africa in the 1980s and shook the foundations of apartheid to the core.

Biko advocated the rejection of such a scheme: "We believe that we have to reject their economic system, their political system, and values that govern human relationships... We are not really fighting against the government; we are fighting the entire system".[19] Biko had foreseen that an economic model that integrates blacks into the very structures of colonialism and apartheid would create an unhealthy and self-defeating competition amongst blacks: "It is an integration in which black will compete with black, using each other as rungs up a step ladder leading them to white values. It is an integration in which the black man will have to prove himself in terms of these values before meriting acceptance and ultimate assimilation, and in which the poor will grow poorer and rich richer in a country where the poor have always been black."[20]

The second contestation of Biko's memory comes from the state-linked political and bureaucratic classes. Their ascendance into the higher echelons of the postapartheid bureaucracy has in practice also mobilized a version of Black Consciousness which on the face of it privileges blackness. The discourse of "transformation," "representivity" and reflecting the "demographics" of society are the concepts employed in the process. However, the actual practice of power, as in the formal political system and its symbols, still employs colonial and apartheid forms. As a bureaucracy, this confronts the majority of blacks as a cold, arrogant, often violent and indifferent system. How could it be different, when democracy did not mean the establishment of new systems of relations?

The bureaucratic class at the higher levels shares a lot with the black business class. Often senior bureaucrats have left the administration for business after having laid out lucrative business possibilities from state institutions, often through privatization efforts. It must also be said that in the battle for the heart of the postapartheid bureaucracy, the black aspirant bureaucrat has not shied away from recalling the painful past of black exclusion as leverage in the battle against white position holders. But once the position is held, the behavior, vis-à-vis the black excluded, seldom changes.

In Biko's conception of liberation, "integration" into the white value system stands opposed to genuine "black liberation." The model of a black project promoted by the black business and political classes is integration, and in practice the experience of postapartheid has been the realization of the "integration" model that, as Biko had predicted, "... could succeed in putting across to the world a pretty convincing, integrated picture." This integrated picture chimes well with the ethic of reconciliation without justice that is associated with the TRC and the postapartheid version of nonracialism. The Biko that these two main postapartheid black classes have appropriated is a Biko who is mute in the face of continued black suffering, exclusion, and humiliation.

The business and political classes have nothing to say to the multitudes who live in the shacks and the Reconstruction and Development Programme (RDP) houses that have been described as dog kennels; who continue to suffer unacceptable infant mortality rates; whose hospitals are less than places of abandonment and death; who continue to die from AIDS. In a sense, Biko's thought has been reduced to slogans on T-shirts weaned of all radical content as a philosophy of black liberation, and images of Biko have come to adorn glossy magazines and fashion houses. As Prishani Naidoo and Ahmed Veriava put it in this volume, you might find Biko's face staring at you from a T-shirt selling for over R300. But they warn us not to be confused by

> "corporate Black Consciousness" and the importance of Black pride. Biko is big in Rosebank. So big that one can't help but be reminded of Walter Benjamin's warning: "not even the dead will be safer if the enemy wins. And the enemy has not ceased to be victorious."

Our struggle, Naidoo and Veriava continue, is to claim Biko against those who would "reduce his legacy to an affirmation of the political present." Biko lives but "BC is dead"? BC is a passing stage, useful to a certain point for the rising "bourgeois" class. But thus appropriated and institutionalized, Biko is no longer a threat. This is the Biko this volume is contesting.

The third contestation of Biko is the shout of the black majority for whom the formal ending of apartheid has not yet altered circumstances in any meaningful way. This living Biko finds expression in the everyday struggles of the black masses for dignity and freedom. As Imraan Buccus writes, "Since 2004 an unprecedented wave of popular protest has ebbed and flowed across the country. A number of protesters have been killed by the police and, recently, a number of ward councillors have been killed by protesters... The Minister for Safety and Security reported that there were more than 6,000 protests in 2005 and one academic has calculated that this makes South Africa 'the most protest-rich country in the world.'"[21] It is the explicit contention of editors that Biko lives in these spaces of resistance that now appear and disappear and are revived in different forms and different parts of postapartheid society. The legacy carriers of the BC philosophy are the excluded majority who continue to make life under extreme conditions and who, as Frantz Fanon once put it, cannot conceive of life otherwise than in the form of a battle against exploitation, misery, and hunger. An array of movements and organizations are demanding a dignity and a recognition that fundamentally challenges neoliberal postapartheid South Africa. Every election cycle since the 2004 national election has seen movements across the country lift cries of "No Land! No Vote!" or "No Land! No House! No Vote!" signaling their refusal to participate in an unsatisfying "ballot box democracy." Instead, they demand a genuine reciprocity, a different notion of politics, "a true humanity," as Biko puts it "where power politics will have no place."[22]

Still, it must be noted that much of the postapartheid resistance and social movements that receive press attention is characterized by white left dominance, particularly as strategists and spokespersons. It is almost as if it were South Africa before the emergence of SASO in the late 1960s. It is this dynamic that inspired poet Vonani Bila to write in 2004, "We think the ghost of Apartheid is long dead/ Comrades, Don't We Delude Ourselves?"[23] The new black resistance does not yet fully speak for itself; it relies in major ways on the white left for illuminating its voice, often with the consequence that this resistance's demands are reduced to the most basic necessities to keep body and soul together and constitute a residual insult of colonialism and apartheid. If resistance is allowed to be stopped at blacks simply gaining access to water, adequate shelter, electricity, and food (little more than the basic needs of animals), it will not succeed in countering apartheid and neoliberalism's dehumanization of blacks. But there are sparks of hope as popular movements have begun to challenge the influence of largely white dominated NGOs, thus breaking with a form of second class participation brought about by virtue of skewed access to money and networks. If a politics that transcends the current reality is to emerge, it would in all likelihood emerge as these new movements and forms of self-activity continue to develop their own voice.

A note on why the editors' names are not listed alphabetically: It is customary to list names alphabetically unless there is a senior or "lead" author/editor who takes precedence. We worked collectively and equally on this volume but we also understand that just as a book about Biko is political, the listing of names is political. We decided that Andile Mngxitama's status as the sole black South African editor had to be named first. It was an important political reason to change the order. Such a move is, of course, symbolic, but it does indicate our wish to ground *Biko Lives* on South African soil. Finally, we dedicate this volume to the memory of Strini Moodley, who remained stubbornly unsatisfied with the postapartheid present, living Biko's Black Consciousness until his death in 2006.

Notes

1. Steve Biko, *I Write What I Like* (Chicago, IL: Chicago University Press, 2002), 72.
2. The Congress movement consists of all organizations under the political leadership of the ANC, including the SACP and the Congress of South African Trade Unions (COSATU).
3. Console Tleane, "Is There Any Future in the Past? A Critique of the Freedom Charter in the Era of Neoliberalism," in Amanda Alexander, ed., *Articulations: A Harold Wolpe Memorial Lecture Collection* (Trenton, Durban: Africa World Press/Centre for Civil Society, 2006).
4. Nelson Mandela, *Long Walk to Freedom: The Autobiography of Nelson Mandela* (Boston, MA: Little Brown Company, 1994), 577–578.
5. Interview with Amanda Alexander and Andile Mngxitama, Braamfontein, January 2007.
6. The Wiehahn Commission was set up by the apartheid government in 1977 in an attempt to control the increasing militancy of the emerging black trade unions, recommending union registration, and recognizing collective bargaining.
7. Lewis Gordon, foreword to Steve Biko, *I Write What I Like* (Chicago, IL: Chicago University Press, 2002), xi.
8. Biko, *I Write What I Like*, 89–90.
9. Ibid., 89.
10. Ibid., 29.
11. Ibid., 69–70.
12. Ibid., 86.
13. Similarly, James Cone argued that the Christian message of liberation of the poor in the United States must be a black theology.
14. Nelson Mandela, "Whither the Black Consciousness Movement" (1978) reprinted in Mac Maharaj, ed., *Reflection in Prison* (Cape Town: Zebra and Robben Island Prison, 2001), 40.
15. Desiree Lewis, "Women and Gender in South Africa," in Vincent Maphai, ed., *South Africa: The Challenge of Change* (Harare, Zimbabwe: SAPES Books, 1994).
16. Pumla Dineo Gqola, "Contradictory Locations: Blackwomen and the Discourse of the Black Consciousness Movement in South Africa," *Meridians* 2, no. 1 (2001): 136.
17. "The Dynamics of Gender Within Black Consciousness Organizations: A Personal View," in N. Barney Pityana, Mamphela Ramphele, Malusi Mpumlwan, and Lindy Wilson, eds., *Bounds of Possibility: The Legacy of Steve Biko and Black Consciousness* (Cape Town, SA: David Philip, 1991), 218.
18. Moeletsi Mbeki, "Concepts of Transformation and the Social Structure of South Africa," in Xolela Mangcu, Gill Marcus, Khehla Shubane, and Adrian Hadland, eds., *Visions of Black Economic Empowerment* (Johannesburg, SA: Jacana, 2007).
19. Interview with Greg Lanning, June 5, 1971.
20. Biko, *I Write What I Like*, 91.
21. *The Mercury*, August 16, 2007.
22. Biko, *I Write What I Like*, 106.
23. Vonani Bila, *In the Name of Amandla* (Elim, Limpopo Province: Timbila Poetry Project, 2004), 82.

Interview with Steve Biko

Gail M. Gerhart

In October 1972, Steve Biko was employed by the black division of the Study Project of Christianity in Apartheid Society (SPRO-CAS), which had its office in the same building as the South African Student Organization (SASO) at 86 Beatrice Street, Durban. American political scientist Gail M. Gerhart interviewed Biko in those offices on October 24, 1972, amid a constant flow of SASO people in and out. The interview is published here for the first time. It has been edited for length; a full transcript is available in the Historical Papers division of the Cullen Library at the University of the Witwatersrand in Johannesburg, and on microfilm in the Karis-Gerhart Collection, available through the Cooperative Africana Microform Project (CAMP) of the Center for Research Libraries in Chicago.

What can you tell me about the intellectual origins of the black consciousness movement?

We have to see this evolution of black consciousness side by side with other political doctrines in the country, and other movements of resistance. I think a hell of a lot of this is attributable to the sudden death of political articulation of ideas within black ranks, which came about as a result of the banning of all the political parties. And here I think, the operative feature is that the only people who were left with some sort of organizations from which to operate were white people. Between 1912 and 1960 blacks could speak through one form of organization or another, be it ANC, trade union movements, or later the CP [Communist Party] and other political parties. So when they were banned in 1960, effectively all black resistance was killed, and the stage was left open to whites of liberal opinion to make representations for blacks, in a way that had not happened in the past, unaccompanied by black opinion.

Between 1960 and 1967, the only strong elements of dissent came from groups like NUSAS [National Union of South African Students], the Progressive Party, particularly the Young Progressives, and elements of the Liberal Party that had diffused into other organizations like Defense and Aid—which were in fact white organizations, white dominated in terms of members but open in terms of membership. The best blacks could do was just to be there, and to allow whites to speak on their behalf. And all blacks were doing all this time was just to clap and say "amen."

In '67 the [NUSAS] conference had some inroads. We went there expecting to stay on the campus. As we were leaving we got word that the conference was in fact going to be segregated, in the sense that although we would be at the university, whites would stay in one residence and we would stay in another. Our immediate response was that conference must close; this was my own response—until the organizers can find a proper venue. It was my first year within the movement, and I had sort of sorted out a few ideas, from friends and from reading. The conference proceeded, but I had made up my mind at that stage that this was a dead organization; it wouldn't listen to us, and that no useful and forthright opinion can be expressed from the aegis of this organization. So what I began to do even at that conference was to begin to caucus with the blacks.

And then the next move we made was the following year [at the NUSAS conference in July 1968]. What we ultimately did was to use an occasion that arose over this permit law. There was a big argument. Africans can only stay for 72 hours within a white area. So at the end of the first 72 hours a debate was introduced as to what should be done. Do we take a walk out of the magisterial area and come back for a new 72 hours, or do we defy the law. Now the whites were claiming that no, we should just take a walk. Some of the blacks from the very restrictive campuses were also agreeing with this; they didn't want to do anything dramatic that would reveal their presence there. A few of us were claiming that this was nonsense: we stay right here. Now what made the whites hysterical about what we were saying was that we said all right, when the vans come to collect us, whites should all lie in front of the vans so that they don't move. Then we'll allow the police to do what they like with blacks. You just lie there and don't move. The whites could not accept this. They saw it as an extremely irresponsible, radical line that didn't take into account the interests of the students on the restricted campuses. Our approach was: good, you whites are now bullshitting us into accepting your logic and your analysis of the situation. In fact this decision should be ours, because we are the only people who are affected; we are the only people who carry passes; we need permits—you don't need them—so this is one time you should learn to listen.

Then there was a huge two-hour debate on this thing. The whites were saying "Bull! You are introducing racialism"; and we were saying "Bull! You are introducing *baasskaap* [white supremacy]." So eventually we realized that if we subjected the issue to a vote we might lose because of the fringe number of blacks who might vote with the whites. So we said even this decision to vote depends on us. And as far as we see it, there is no need to vote; we blacks are just having a meeting 1 o'clock tomorrow. All blacks must come. Now at this stage we were only arguing about the people who need to have the permits, and these were only Africans, you see? But we had agreed already in our analysis of the other groups, like the Indians and Coloureds who didn't need to have permits, that they were also part of the oppressed camp.

The discussion on the 72 hour law took exactly ten minutes. We came there and we said listen, it's a waste of time to even argue this. We don't want to participate in protest politics like these guys have been telling us to do for these many years. We are here for constructive purposes. So this 72 hour law must be left aside, and we just walk across the border. Now let's begin to talk about our business as blacks.

So then I had introduced a whole new trend of thinking, and I had to do this by asking questions and by using this particular example, this recent debate. By drawing the attention of the crowd to the fact that we are taking a back seat in our own battle. We are making ourselves watchers—we are watching the match from the touchlines, whereas it's a match in which we ought to be participating, primarily. I spoke a lot about the influence of white thinking in blacks' attempting to make viable decisions, in their struggle. And I pointed out several examples from the same conference where if we were alone we would have taken one decision, but because we were there with those other guys we take another decision. And people saw this, you know; it was so simple. And it was dramatized a hell of a lot by the debate on this same 72 hour law. So people just accepted this. They said right; we put up a committee to call a conference in December for blacks to talk about themselves.

[By 1968] we were receptive to other influences, influences much more from Africa, guys who could speak for themselves. This was a novelty in the country which many people couldn't see. That blacks in this last ten-year period had been subjected to so much suffocation by representation by whites, representation by this, by that—that to speak for themselves was a novelty. Again, now, talking primarily about the young group. The older people might perhaps have accommodated this. We couldn't accommodate this.

Now the influence from Africa was very important at that time. People like Fanon, people like Senghor, and a few other poets, Diop and company. They spoke to us, you know. These people obviously were very influential.

What I'm trying to say here is that it wasn't a question of one thing out of a book and discovering that it's interesting. In a sense it was also an active search for that type of book, for the kind of thing that will say things to you, that was bound to evoke a response.

There was a bit of influence from groups like the SNCC [Student Nonviolent Coordinating Committee], you know—statements from Stokely [Carmichael] and a few others. I'm talking about SNCC primarily because of the similarity in terms of organizational arrangement. And then later, of course, from books like this one by Stokely and [Charles] Hamilton [*Black Power*], it made a hell of a lot of sense in one way, but people were shocked to see the differences primarily around the area of what is the end-goal. You know in the United States one almost accepts the inevitability of a common society, on the basis of what the white man says. And all the black man can hope to get there is recognition for himself within the whole society. Whereas in a country like this one, there is a hell of a lot of value system to be changed, changes in the common order of society, to make the general order of society truly black, and reflective of the fact that this is in Africa, you see. Unlike in the United States. So there are these differences. But there's no doubt that reading all those kind of background books sharpened people's articulation of their own standpoint, and where they wanted to go.

A hell of a lot of people who were peripheral to the movement joined the movement on the strength of what they read. Those who were in the so-called leadership, whatever their different aptitudes for reading—personally, I do very little reading. I rarely finish a book, I always go to find something from a book. Otherwise I read a book over a long period, when I'm going to sleep and so on. I'm talking about books that relate to people's philosophies, people's strategies and so on. I've been having Stokely's book now for I don't know how many years, since '68, '69. I haven't finished it. Or others, like [James] Cone's book; I've read parts of it, on black theology.

But others of course are much more avid readers than I am. They do a lot of reading, they do a lot of writing, interpretation, and so on. So that element has that kind of effect. What I'm saying is that it's a complementary effect upon a basic attitude formed primarily from experience, from an analysis of the situation as one sees it. And it helps to sharpen one's focus, it helps to make the guy much more confident about whatever he's actually articulating. The common experience of the Third World people.

Do you think that without this literature the ideology would have developed to the same degree of sophistication?

Inevitably yes, but perhaps at a much slower pace. But I think, one must remember again, even without the literature the most important element is the small insights we are given into Africa by the conservative press that we have in this country. A hell of a lot of them have what they regard as Africa series, or Africa columns, depicting what is said by so many different people in Africa, so many people in other parts of the Third World, Asia and Latin America, particularly China. This creates a focus for identification. So I would say the direction was inevitable. Perhaps what one might say is that the pace might have been slower. Its accuracy might have been much greater if the pace was even slower—accuracy in the sense that it was going to be a movement with the people, rather than a situation where one conceives an idea and actually addresses it very neatly, and then transposes it onto a situation. This was inborn, in a sense. Some people have found great difficulty in being able to analyze and see the difference between Fanon's France versus Algeria, or Stokely's white America versus black America, and our situation of whites versus blacks. Because people tend to do very little homework.

But that's not so much from our ranks. That's much more from hangers-on who come in, people who could not be convinced by indigenous argument. People who had to respect somebody else first from outside, read him, understand him in that situation and then say "Yah, those boys are right! Now this is what we should be saying!" The people who analyzed Nyerere and his works begin to see these things, then having accepted them [ask] what about the situation at home. So, you do get this kind of broad spectrum which differs in the sense of attaching different importances to little nuances—little nuances about post-revolutionary society, others opting for socialism, others opting for a nondescript type of nonracialism. You might say there is nonracial capitalist, nonracial socialist. Others might be opting for some kind of bantustan type of thing, like Gatsha's [Buthelezi] thing of black federation, or the adoption of a kind of black consciousness within the type of amorphous situation we have now. So there is this wide spectrum. But broadly speaking the authentic movement one could say talks of a non-exploitative, egalitarian, nonracialist society. And they're not prepared to expound on this any further. One knows why they will not do this.

Liberals decried apartheid and segregation and discrimination so that people refused to talk in any terms which in any way either simulated apartheid or segregation or discrimination. In fact it became a sine qua non that before you even started entering the arena of politics and fighting for social change you must be a nonracialist. And this explains why in fact it became necessary for SASO to mount such a heavy attack on liberals. They did a quick and good job. In one year, I think the campuses obliterated any strong trace of liberalism. And in the larger society, now going out of campus, blacks began to see that in fact it was a fallacy to think that before you fight you need to have a white man next to you, for the sake of depicting a non-racial society.

At the December 1968 conference was the name SASO coined?

Yes, we coined it right there. In fact the major ideas regarding a constitution, and so on were coined there. And what the conference was to do the following year was to give the thing a proper mandate in the various student areas. In one year, we had thrown NUSAS off the campuses and we had firmly entrenched SASO. Our first campus was Turfloop, and then came ours [University of Natal Non-European Medical School]—ours was a very developed campus—we were facing, as I said, two sides, the pro-NUSAS and the pro-PAC. Those PAC guys saw us as an extension of NUSAS.

On my campus I had been a NUSAS man the first year, so they tended not to trust this kind of approach. They were friends, you know, people we could talk to: we were in the same discussion circles. But they were very sensitive to plots, liberal plots. They knew there was a possibility that this just could be a liberal plot. And they used this argument about Indians and Coloureds a hell of a lot. Now we ultimately resolved it the following year and their camp was heavily defeated. They had organized there very heavily, they had called their people. And at that meeting they were very insulting. They used good tactics, insulting Indians and Coloureds, and Indians and Coloureds walked out, they thought they could now force the issue to a debate. We beat them thoroughly in the debate, we won a hell of a lot of their friends, and we beat them in the vote and the campus was affiliated. And they died at that moment.

Our attitude was that we are involved in a struggle, each group has got grievances, and we will work with people who are committed to work for a removal of the source of those grievances, be they African, Indians, or Coloureds. We're not going to operate on a liberal stance that there must be one Indian for one Coloured, etc. But if Indian and Coloured people are as much committed as obviously as some African people are committed to the struggle for our liberation—this is not a movement for Africans, not a movement for Indians, for Coloured people; it's a movement for people who are oppressed. And those who feel the oppression are going to join it. And that argument weighed very heavily. And we won.

In our preparation for the '71 conference, between '70 and '71, I went into a very extensive study of political movements in this country. This we did for our leadership training courses. Concentrating on the early so-called religious breakaways of 1890, the Ethiopian movement; concentrating on the foundation of ANC and reasons for the foundation of ANC; concentrating on the ICU [Industrial and Commercial Workers' Union], its operation, its growth, its cause of growth and its death, its cause of death. And concentrating on the foundation of the CP, its growth and its so-called death. That type of early history, right up to the time of the Congress Alliance and ANC; in fact this is when I began to reject definitely elements of ANC. And a lot of the so-called socialist crap that used to come from CP and its ranks. Now the operations of CP as I saw it were highly suspect. I referred to this earlier on. Highly suspect, much more in terms of their observance of a strict code of discipline and adherence to Moscow's wishes than to the normal evolution of the movement toward social change. One couldn't blame them for wanting to maintain some degree of ideological purity amongst their ranks, but I think they had to adapt this a hell of a lot to the wishes of the people down here.

You remember, for instance, there were times when guys like S. P. Bunting went to the Transkei and organized very efficiently and had to cancel and break down all the structures there had been in the Transkei, purely on the strength of instructions from Moscow.

Looking at the operations of all political parties you'll notice that SASO doesn't lay too much stress on so-called post-revolutionary society. This is very deliberate. It's deliberate for a number of reasons, the most important one being the extent to which it divides people. PAC, ANC, CP, all these other groups had a lot of different slants to what they called post-revolutionary society. And as much as they sold their policies to people on the basis of what they were working for. In the same way white parties do. We see this as being much more to enunciate a common cause to which people should respond together and immediately, there's a need for a sense of identification with what's happening. Then once they come together, they can begin perhaps to play around with ideas. But one finds it terribly dividing to attach a lot of importance to the detail of the post-revolutionary society, before you actually attach people to the idea of fighting for the social change.

[In SASO] there is a common ideology which everybody accepts, and now it is a matter of different slants, different stresses on several points, within the common strategy. So you would say there is this gradual—one guy for instance is going to be radical on one point and rightist on one point—and they would mix (overlap). You get for instance a guy who is committed to violence and at the same time not so committed to socialism; you get another who is committed to socialism but not so committed to violence. So it's difficult to say in straight ideological terms there exists this kind of movement. But broadly speaking there is unity. There is unity primarily because there is the tacit recognition of a certain leadership.

What's interesting about the leadership ranks in SASO is precisely their informal nature. We go to conference every year, we've got a fast-changing executive. No president has stayed for more than a year, since we started. But the organizational leadership in an ideological sense is not necessarily the same. There are people who are regarded as ideological leaders; there are people who are regarded as political leaders in the sense that they can plan ahead for the organization in a given context. There are those who enunciate what we will stand for; there are those who say okay, we will do this, we will go so far and no further. And there are people who are student leaders.

And there's a very, very great faith, I must say, in the leadership. For instance, there are decisions taken in SASO with the cooperation of the house which the house is not fully aware of. Let's just take the question of leadership. We have an executive in existence, and we have a means of substituting another executive at a moment's notice. And the people with which we would substitute that executive are elected by the house, but the house doesn't know the results. There is a secret ballot and the result is not announced. So the house knows that there is in existence a shadow executive, to fill up positions at any moment of crisis.

The people themselves are told that they are on the list, but where on the list they don't know. Because you see you've got to get their consent. For a given year you'll have so many people, let's say three or four, in a certain order, and all of them are supposed to say yes or no to their being nominated as a stand-by executive. Each man will say yes or no for himself, but he doesn't know where on the list he falls. It is the Secretary-general who knows, as well as the chairman of the Planning Commission. And the house has voted those people in that order. There's a completely democratic but not quite democratic system.

This is to guard against the possibility of—

Banning orders, arrests, passports—sorry, deportations. The kind of trust one finds in SASO is such that if a president were to do anything drastic, or rather if I were to hear tomorrow that the present president has been deposed, the natural reaction is to know that something has happened—the house will expect an explanation at the right time. In the meantime they commit themselves to whatever is given by the executive. That kind of trust.

There've been rumblings about a political party talking for blacks for quite a time now, coming from non-student ranks as well as from student ranks. SASO has participated in all discussions that led to—in fact, SASO initiated the discussions among society organizations, and promoted the idea of BPC [the Black People's Convention]. Time wise, SASO pressed for a shorter time limit than other people were prepared to accommodate. They were prepared to work on a longer basis. And SASO guys—I guess had been convinced of their own strength in their own movement. They were of the opinion that people were ready to begin to move into—whereas other groups were beginning to imbibe this idea of black consciousness and so on and were really moving at a much slower pace, because of a slower acceptance of the ideology in their own ranks.

There is in South Africa an over-riding idea to move towards "comfortable" politics, between leaders. And they hold discussions among themselves about this. Comfortable politics in the sense that we must move at a pace that doesn't rock the boat. In other words people are shaped by the system even in their consideration of approaches against the system. Not shaped in the sense of working out meaningful strategies, but shaped in the sense of working out an approach that won't lead them into any confrontation with the system. So they tend to accommodate the system, to censure themselves, in a much stronger way than the system would probably censure them.

For instance, there's no automatic ban on political movements in this country. But you get common talk to that effect amongst people, that any political agitation is banned. Which is nonsense. It's not banned. And our attitude is that the longer the silence, the more accustomed white society is going to be to that silence. And therefore the more stringent the measures are going to be against anybody who tries to undo that situation. Hence there must be some type of agitation. It doesn't matter if the agitation doesn't take a fully directed form immediately or a fully supported form. But there must be, in the minds of the people, in existence the idea that somewhere, somehow along the line we have our own thing going, and our own thing says this. And it must be only a matter of time before they are fully committed to it.

It's not a question of whether people are ready or not. It's a question of whether people should be made ready or not. You see when you talk of people being ready, I'm looking at it from a different sense. Are people ready for the final action, you see? Now the political party that is formed may not necessarily be the final form that we need to take, but it is some kind of measure, right? It needs to be there anyway to promote us towards the final step. So that whether people were ready or not is irrelevant. The point is is what's happening right or wrong. If it's wrong, then we need some kind of platform that's going to tell us what is right. And what to do in order to get towards that right. This is our justification for the existence of a political party.

And it becomes much more necessary and much more urgent when in fact people are being made by the system accustomed to be ineffective, phony telephones, that are meant to communicate with the white society, as if on behalf of blacks, when in fact they are against blacks. I'm referring here to these institutions of apartheid life—the bantustans, the CRC [Coloured Representative Council], the Indian council. All of which are set up by the system as "answers"—quote unquote—to our problems. They are part of the same system that has created the problem.

And this is where we come in. We want to come in at a stage when people have not been so thoroughly affected by the system and its little cocoons of racialism and oppression as to make them believe that in fact our solution lies in that system. If the silence is continued any longer this is inevitable. It has become a big problem already.

So this justifies the need for the emergence, the creation of a political party at this stage, as a constant reminder to the people that there's something wrong in this system. Something everywhere; what is right is *this* kind of thing.

We'd like to stop, first of all, the people from moving into the system and get them into our system. I'm talking about the people who are not in the system now. People who don't believe in the system. The urban African, for instance: the Asian and Coloured sectors have not been followed up completely. The rural Africans participate in a sense that people cannot fully understand at the moment. In Natal out of a sense of commitment, the old generation of kings and so on—and to what extent this implies an acceptance of the bantustans idea one doesn't completely know. The Cape African, this is true in the Cape particularly, has rejected chiefs and all that kind of nonsense. So there's minimal participation there. In Transkei there's a confused picture. Now this will become an interesting area to work in some time, but I think one needs to concentrate and work hard on the so-called urban people.

Rural people have a much more understandable group orientation than urban people, and hence it's faster to work among rural people than it is to work amongst urban people. But at the same time, what goes on in the rural area becomes heavily influenced by what goes on in the urban area, because of migratory labor. This is the importance therefore of conquering urban areas, because all of us go home for a certain while... You know, so many things that attach to [migrant laborers] because of this old axis between the rural and urban person. Although the rural community is a closed community, it includes him in the sense that he belongs to it. All of them are not completely urban in a sense. They are open to influences once they're here, but a number of them still see their roots as being there. And there is a constant traveling between home and the work situation. It's useful.

The whole operation of SASO in black-power type of politics, fists and slogans, you know, has incidentally caught up much, much more readily amongst workers—it's interesting to see the NIC [Natal Indian Congress] operating and SASO, again, where BPC is only really in its rudimentary stages. This is an area of Indian workers mainly. The NIC organized, or somebody organized, a meeting and there were several speakers, amongst whom there were several speakers from NIC. There was almost a unanimous rejection of people like [Arthur] Grobbelaar and these white trade unionists. And then Rajab and a few other Indian Congress people. And this was done on the basis of this so-called black power slogan "white man, go home," you Europeans here, we don't want you—that type of thing. So that even looking at the Indian community, for instance, which a lot of people would say is likely to be resistant to say complete involvement in BPC programs; this only applies to the rich areas. When you go to the area where there are workers, to them it's not a problem, to identify with that kind of salute, that kind of coming into black power ranks. A feeling of oneness, basically, with the rest of the oppressed community. Viewing it from the same basis, a bunch of workers, like the dock workers have got the same sort of orientation basically. And any kind of demonstration of that kind of symbol is so much more meaningful to them than any number of speeches by people.

SASO see their role as being supportive to a political party. It would be difficult and I think stupid to try to make people identify with a student movement which is not going to play the leadership role in community affairs. Rather it would be more meaningful for people to identify with a political party in which students can then play a role, a supportive role. Because the dynamics of political change in an oppressed community revolve a hell of a lot around who your leader is. And your leader must be a man who can carry you right through. Now students can't do that.

People just won't look to students as their leaders.

That's right, yes. This has been our problem; even now it's still our problem. There is a hell of a lot of attachment to SASO in some quarters, and people tend to want to read more in to SASO than SASO ought to be. Obviously the same people in SASO are going to be much more active in another capacity in BPC, for instance. But here it is much more logical for it to be so, because then people can identify with a political party, which they can join or work in. It would be difficult to prompt the same identification with SASO and at the same time want to exclude people from joining because it's a student movement.

Isn't there a contradiction here, given the fact that older people are always more conservative? Isn't there some chance that these two bodies [SASO and BPC] will come to clash with one another?

No, for two reasons. Firstly, primarily because BPC is mainly made up of young people, and of course a few older sympathizers. And secondly because we have not seen all that much ideological difference between say middle-aged people and us, on this question of blackness. There will be differences, I agree, on specific issues. Like if all of us black people are now voting regarding action on a specific issue, the younger ones are going to opt for more violent, more militant action, and the older ones for less militant action. But on the broad question of blackness and the need to cooperate, that sort of thing, there's no real disagreement. Saths [Cooper] was telling me about a meeting in Chatsworth [Durban] where NIC spokesmen, who are basically opposed to black consciousness, had to use that approach because that was the only message that could carry weight in Chatsworth, it's the only language people are going to listen to seriously.

In a sense I think the older generation has also given leadership status to the younger generation, in this particular field. If you go to a guy like [Curnick] Ndamse he'll say without any possible doubt that "those boys are right." He might put a few "buts." Primarily he sees himself not as a propagator of the idea. Whenever he speaks in public meetings, he is defending—if this is a hostile camp, like whites—what the younger generation is saying. Although he doesn't quite say it himself.

But we have very little faith in old people, and we don't think we have a lot of dependence on them. Although we are committed to totality of involvement, I think another very important aspect of our movement is to retain as much purity as we can. We wouldn't like to carry with us any hangers-on. We're happy with them saying that we are right, and following on behind, but not come interfere with us.

What about [Robert] Sobukwe?

I have never heard him express an opinion about the details of the ideology, which makes him again a very admirable guy. Unlike ANC ranks and other ranks, his major concern is about continued opposition to the system, and continued direction being given to the people. And from that angle he sees the whole new move as being important and valuable. The other guys—there's a whole host of priests and other fellows of that nature who are now in London, some in Europe anyway, who are of the older rank, well, say 42. I'd regard them as some of the most vociferous proponents of this whole ideology. And their stance has been much more affected by their being where they are now. They'd been talking, whilst they were here, in much more subdued tones than they are now that they're out. And this is occasioned, I think, by the ability for anybody from a struggle to view it much more critically when he's outside. He can see much more intelligently what role he could play there. And they're doing a hell of a lot of P.R.O. [public relations] work for this kind of ideology, particularly with groups from the country, ANC groups, PAC groups and so on, trying to make those fellows accept that in fact there's a new swing at home now. There's no more PAC, there's no more ANC; there's just the struggle. And this is the kind of ideology that they're talking.

I find this particularly valuable, precisely because of the existence of this long debate—silent debate in some quarters, noisy in some quarters—about the slant that SASO is taking. You know, is it a PAC slant or an ANC slant? Are they anti-communist or are they pro-communist? A lot of people attach meaning to some things we say, either in private or public; we have written or we have said on some platforms, very bad things about the Communist Party of South Africa, but that doesn't mean necessarily that we are not socialists. According to South African communist-oriented people we are anti—... you know. That's a problem with people who are in the struggle; they are so keyed-up, screwed up with this kind of nonsense: are you pro-this or pro-that. And we have refused for three years now, four years, to identify ourselves in any direct sense with any group.

People don't commit themselves to ANC or PAC these days. You get people who commit themselves to the struggle. The distinction between ANC and PAC, incidentally, in the eyes of the masses is terribly thin... And the nuances of whether one is socialist, one is nationalist, one is this, one is that, never got down through into their minds. So that it's an intellectual debate that is meaningless. At home, some guys are emotional about the ANC. But okay, what is ANC? "It's a party for Africans!" You know? It's all he knows about ANC. He might know a leader and admire one—Mandela is the darling of ANC people, and Sobukwe of course darling of the PAC people. But you ask them what the difference is; they don't know. The radical difference that people see at the moment between those groups and us is this solidarity approach we're adopting. ANC people, on a mass basis, see this as different from ANC, primarily because ANC in its organization concentrated a hell of a lot on enunciating the policy for the top, but not for the bottom. And yet spent a lot of time quarreling with other groups because of their policies. In spite of the fact that in the eyes of the masses the difference was not so sharp.

In your view, is a white communist and a liberal white just basically the same thing?

No, not in terms of their ideologies, but in terms of their significance for the black struggle. They're pretty much the same when you consider their operations in the past, and their control measures, even down to the present day actually. They're different if you look at their slants. The liberals, Alan Paton and so on, one would reject at any stage, any stage be it now on up to the revolution. There are some leftist whites who have attachment to say the same rough principles of post-revolutionary society, but a lot of them are still terribly cynical about, for instance, the importance of value systems which we enunciate so often, from the black consciousness angle. That it is not only capitalism that is involved; it is also the whole gamut of white value systems which has been adopted as standard by South Africa, both whites and blacks so far. And that will need attention, even in a post-revolutionary society. Values relating to all the fields—education, religion, culture and so on. So your problems are not solved completely when you alter the economic pattern, to a socialist pattern. You still don't become what you ought to be. There's still a lot of dust to be swept off, you know, from the kind of slate we got from white society.

Do you mean that a person schooled in left-wing ideology won't accept that?

A number of them are defensive. You must remember they exist in South Africa, and they see themselves as threatened. A number of whites in this country adopt the class analysis, primarily because they want to detach us from anything relating to race. In case it has a rebound effect on them because they are white. This is the problem. So a lot of them adopt the class analysis as a defense mechanism and are persuaded of it because they find it more comfortable. And of course a number of them are terribly puritanical, dogmatic, and very, very arrogant. They don't quite know to what extent they have to give up a part of themselves in order to be a true Marxist.

But white society is quite agreed, in terms of the liberal-leftist axis, that blacks are being denied here and that blacks have to come up, they have to be lifted. A lot of them don't see that this entails them coming down. And this is the problem. We talk about that, and we get a whole lot of reaction and self-preservation mechanisms from them.

I would say it's submerged by a greater wish, I think, to see international cooperation on a pan-black basis. Which is essentially really a long-term war with the so-called first and second worlds; fighting exploitation, and arising out of exploitation, fighting oppression of the third world. This is the preoccupation of blacks now, and it's in line with black feelings in so many other parts of the world. The United States of Africa issue is not such a hot issue as it was in '65, '64–'65. There is no more unanimous approval of what happens in Africa, as there was at that time. There is criticism of India, for its refusal to move in a faster manner towards a much more mass-oriented economic system. So that it's difficult now to tie people's attention completely to Africa as in the past. Remember in '65 all these countries who achieved freedom for their countries were hailed as heroes by everybody, Nkrumah, Kenyatta, Banda, the whole lot. This was normally the case. People are much more critical now. So the commitment has changed now, I would say, to the appreciation of the importance of international cooperation.

What is a "formation school?" Or what sort of leadership training do you have?

The pattern is normally to pick out an area and concentrate on it, an area within our broad concern. On this particular occasion [referring to document on black consciousness] we were concentrating on the whole ideology of black consciousness. It was in three parts. The rationale behind it was to make a definition, and some practical application of black consciousness.

On other occasions, like in December this year the topic we picked was education, attitudes to education, as the key area around which it was structured, our leadership training course. To analyze exactly what students see as meaningful education, to analyze the whole classroom approach, and perhaps spill over to methods of literacy training. The areas are vastly different. As I said, last year and the year before, they picked the history of the black struggle here. That's when we went through the evolution of the religious movements, trade union movements of the past, political movements of the past.

It's normally a four or five day training period, during which all the discussions are closed discussions. There's no public participation at all. And people go into in-depth discussions around major inputs by one or two picked people, depending on the topic. We have a regular set of so-called student leadership, and this one is merely meant for efficiency at the student committee level. People who are coming in to serve on student committees at the beginning of the year; they are subjected to some amount of training, technical approach to the problems of student leadership. So it's a two-way process.

There's a branch virtually in every university and college; at the last conference there were about ten campuses represented. There's been a drastic increase in the number of branches not based on campuses too, primarily because of the May [1972] student revolts. A lot of them have gone out to open branches in their respective areas. Before, there were four main branches outside campuses. Now there are more than double that number, in smaller towns—Kroonstad, Kimberley, Vryheid, Springs. Set up by students who left university during the disturbances. At the last conference there were six towns represented and eight campuses.

Is there any particular advantage to having the headquarters here in Durban?

No, it's just a historical aberration. Perhaps there is, in the sense that Durban is not so easy to categorize in terms of group areas. Jo'burg is mainly white in the middle, and the other areas are demarcated and separate. Whereas in Durban there is this whole meeting ground of this half of town. It is supposed to be an Indian area, and it is accessible therefore to all groups. There are no restrictions attached to Africans regarding Indian areas, whereas this does happen if we were to say establish an office in an African area. An Indian would have to get permission to be there. Because of this type of arrangement it is easier to get people to allow us to be sub-tenants.

What do you think the attitude of the government is toward SASO?

It's obviously watching. You see, unlike the old movements, which they could easily associate with communism—or violence, which they still define as communism—their initial analysis of SASO was that it sounded like an organization which was going to function along the kind of lines they wanted to see. But the pronouncements are obviously unabashedly anti-government. They haven't outlawed black consciousness as a philosophy in the same way that they've outlawed socialism. So that nobody can be held to ransom for preaching black consciousness. In any case it would be extremely untenable for them to preach white power and outlaw what they regard as black power.

Now a few of their very intelligent people have suggested that before the government can do anything, it would have to outlaw black power in one form or another. But the less intelligent of the Nationalist government officials are still attempting to explain away the existence of SASO in terms of a rejection of liberals. Primarily because they see their war as being primarily against whites who side with blacks, rather than blacks. They accept it ipso facto that blacks are going to be satisfied, but they have always regarded the whites who work with blacks as more dangerous. As agitators, and in terms of technical know-how and so many things. They simply don't believe that blacks are intelligent enough to enunciate their own ideas properly on their own. So this whole SASO game they're still watching. One would like to feel that they have made up their minds that there's a link somewhere between SASO and some white-oriented group. And they think time will tell. I think that's the kind of rationale they have. Because they've done nothing drastic. They've made a few inroads, but they normally make it possible to provide another explanation for what they do.

Why would they so quickly go to destroy UCM, while leaving SASO?

It's the same link again. They believe it's much more dangerous. What I'm saying is that the government hasn't taken us seriously at all.

Because it's all black?

Yes—it's not intelligent, no expertise, and so on. And all the time just watch out to see if this is really all black, that there aren't any sideline connections with whites. Obviously in time they're going to be increasingly more vigilant; they're going to take much more definite action. Except that it is too late in a sense. We don't need an organization now to push the kind of ideology we are pushing. It's there; it's already been planted. It's in people. They could ban five of us; it makes no real difference. It might delay things in some quarters; it might confuse people for a while. But it can have no lasting effect.

We've got a very broad front which is completely unintimidated. And this is one of the things I ought to have mentioned, talking about lessons from history. This constant change in leadership in SASO is partly to accommodate a very quick graduation of people into a certain level. To effectively silence SASO, they'd have to ban no less than 20 people, that is to effectively silence the leadership ranks. But even there, having banned the 20 people, there'd still be more. Unlike in some of the old movements, where leadership was concentrated around individuals.

I believe security has also made up its mind that they should deal with us court-wise for as long as we are manageable. To actually try to catch us breaking laws. So they are playing a watching-game on all those fronts. And it's a long watching game, because all of them are wrong.

Security does come out with a pretty insightful analysis of what they think we think. Like when they question some of us they will say "so-and-so is infiltrating the movement." And by saying this—although it's meant to be a question—it gives you the idea that they've made up their minds that there must be somebody who is the main force. And they always make the statement that SASO is alright, were it not for—then they go into the influences by [Strini] Moodley and Saths [Cooper] here in Durban or they'll quote other figures, individuals that they feel they can associate with something else away from SASO.

Particularly the non-Africans?

Yes. The strategy of security is also to create alienation between Africans and Indians in Durban and between Africans and Coloureds in the Western Cape. The least affected people, or the least terrorized people in a sense are leadership, the very, very top leadership. But the lower echelons will make it possible for whole chunks of campuses to affiliate, are the ones who are persecuted so that link can be broken. The students at Durban-Westville, for instance; their leadership ranks there were in SASO. Pressure was very heavy there, both from security and from their university, which has been given definite instructions to cut this link. And the same thing happens in the western Cape, the guys who are links between that campus and SASO are the ones who are being chopped.

Otherwise, on the African campuses there's an interesting phenomenon. The universities are always against SASO, definitely, we feel very uncomfortable. But there is apparently an order that they must observe some measure of acceptance of SASO. And hence they cannot victimize SASO personnel on African campuses. What they do is to find small little technical things to break the link between SASO locally in the campus and SASO national. They'll say, for instance, as at Fort Hare, "Your president has attacked this university, and therefore we cannot pay fees to SASO on your behalf"; and they don't pay fees. But they don't go on to say disaffiliate from SASO or anything like that.

Or at Turfloop, after the SRC had been thrown away, and various students had been expelled for participating in the strike, we thought when the SASO men come the principal is going to say, "Oh, SASO is quite welcome"—and they start operating as soon as we restore order, or as soon as we restore the SRC amongst the student ranks. So they're playing a sort of double game, in the sense that they've been given this mandate to accommodate SASO, but they can also see, being on the spot, most of the problems vis-à-vis students and staff arise primarily because of the impetus coming from SASO ranks.

It still seems inconsistent to me. If they really do want to destroy SASO, why bother with the lower echelons? Why not just ban the top twenty or the movement itself?

Their whole philosophy is directed at (1) sounding sincere to the white electorate about apartheid and so many other things. They don't really bother about us. Now if they ban anything which is not inconsistent with apartheid, then the opposition jumps in, in the same way the opposition was against SASO, or the SASO ideology. When SASO becomes banned, the liberals, the Progressives and the United Party are going to unite to say the Nationalist government is insincere about apartheid. Here you are, with these people having this thing on their own campuses—you see. This is a problem. And they know this. So that they are quite happy with containing the movement, if they can contain it, and allowing it to exist. Because of another fact also: it also gives credibility. If SASO can speak out and at the same time remain harmless, well and good.

The Helen Suzman effect.

That's right. The calculation they have made—it's a dangerous calculation, but I think they are prepared to gamble with it. If it turned out in a major conference of Afrikaners that there was some major discontent because of the growth of black power or black consciousness in this country you would get within one week the Prime Minister ordering a complete arrest or ban of the leadership. Then they defy the world at that point. Because they try the other way first, of appeasing the world, appeasing the opposition, appeasing the general electorate by containing the blacks for as far as it is possible. When it is impossible, then they use drastic—to assure now their own electorate, which is mainly Afrikaner, that they are still in power.

In your own mind, do you project forward any probable timetable for when this stage might be reached? Do you think there's a very finite amount of time involved?

I wouldn't be able to say in a precise way. One thing is when you make calculations or assumptions about white society, you must make the observation that it is deaf to black opinion, very deaf, deliberately. And when that does happen, it is likely to be too late. Too late for them to stop whatever has started. This is the only calculation I can make, but how long it will take, I don't know. They still listen to the debate about the Broederbond right now. Those are very insignificant questions, but it's a major thing within their ranks. They are so busy talking among themselves they're too busy to think about the other guy.

Just English versus Afrikaner politics.

Yah. They are convinced of one thing: the power of their security. Even the average white man who is anti-system, when he thinks of any possible threat from blacks, he relies very heavily on the existence of a very powerful security. And none of us would doubt that it's a very powerful security in terms of weapons, in terms of so many things. But it's also a stupid security. They depend a hell of a lot on gadgets for detecting information. But they are limited in the extent to which they can analyze whatever information they get: limited by their own prejudices against blacks.

PAC, quite frankly, was banned for its show of strength more than anything else. They were happy when PAC broke off from ANC, but it was a very short-lived happiness. Suddenly PAC began to demonstrate that it could move people in certain ways. And the PAC approach was a very emotional approach, which could lead to short-term action. Now whites feel uncomfortable against that. You look at the marches that led to Sharpeville and the Langa incidents. Any intelligent person would know that this is a very impotent lot of people. They were unarmed people. But white society can't stand that kind of thing. To them it always signals what they expect in their subconscious: a major revolt. They would have to shoot at some stage. Because blacks just can't take a beating without fighting back. Once you're in that type of mood, I don't care who says what, whether we're three or four or five, I don't see a policeman hitting me and me standing there and not doing anything. Because to me he's an enemy, all the time. He couldn't be doing that on my behalf.

The student revolts were directed at the black community to demonstrate (a) solidarity, and (b) determination, on the part of black students to reject what they don't want, and to be prepared to suffer for that. And it worked, insofar as that's concerned. It didn't work with the individual parents of the individual children. But the black community as a whole has learnt a fantastic lesson from that. You used to get this kind of thing before: the students are great talkers. But with that kind of background they couldn't say it any more. Here were students marching out of varsity, offering to march out of varsity, and knowing that they've got no ready-made society that they're walking into. A lot of them are still outside. So that it has heightened the receptivity of the community to student opinion. But as for what step two is, we don't know. It's subject to so many forces and interpretations and so on. We have individual opinions, that may not be well formulated either. One doesn't know or wouldn't like to say anything about it.

As you look at the economy of this country, what trends or factors in it to do you feel are working toward the fulfillment of the long term ends of blacks?

One can only say this in comparison to something else. If you look at the system managed and run by Nationalists it's preferable to the system as managed and run by the United Party, and still more preferable to the system as managed and run by the Progressive Party. In the sense that Nationalists have not perfected their capitalist system. One of the elements of capitalism for instance is to create a discontented middle-class group among the ranks of those you are excluding from the mainstream of the country's economy. In other words, if you are dealing with a group of people who identify through one fact, for example the color of their skins, if you want to then exclude the bulk of those people, you have to give something back to a few of them in order to create amongst them a middle-class which is going to be a buffer zone, so to speak, between you and the masses who you are exploiting. So what's happening in this country is that blacks don't have a very strong or large middle-class.

So that the one effect of apartheid in a sense is that it is a great leveler. Blacks don't have a very strong or large middle-class. It's concentrated to mainly the Indian community, that is the black middle-class, so to speak. Most black people are about the same on an urban basis. And most black people are about the same on a rural basis. Out in the country, for example, each family is allowed a maximum say of seven cows, and five sheep, one pig, that type of thing. And people can only improve up to that point. And at that point they remain steady, there's a sort of a similarity in the community.

If you look at the housing scheme of the Nationalists, it's a four-roomed basis for everybody in a township. The means of transport is bus and train for everybody. So the people participate in the same things, they share so many common interests. It's a perfect system for identification, common identification. So what I'm trying to suggest is that there is this constant jarring effect of the system on the people, which makes it possible for quick organization around certain central issues.

Now whereas if you were working under a Progressive [Party] system, then you would get stratification creeping in, with your masses remaining where they are or getting poorer, and your cream of leadership, which is invariably derived from the so-called educated people, beginning to enter bourgeois ranks: admitted into town, able to vote, developing new attitudes and new friends for their movements. So you'd get a completely different tone. And this is one country where it would be possible to create a capitalist black society. If whites were intelligent. If the Nationalists were intelligent. And that capitalist black society, black middle-class, would be very effective at an important stage. Primarily because a hell of a lot of blacks here have got a bit of education—I'm talking comparatively speaking—to the so-called rest of Africa, and a hell of a lot them could compete favorably with whites in the fields of industry, commerce, and professions. And South Africa could succeed to put across to the world a pretty convincing, integrated picture, with still 70 percent of the population being underdogs.

But the whites are terribly afraid of this. You see now, they've built up this race yardstick beyond all proportions, and it is beginning to scare them, even in their own little nice world. Hence the separate doors, separate entrances, separate toilets, separate this—rubbish. My own interpretation of the system is, therefore, that we have the best economic system for a revolution. And the evils of it are so pointed and so clear, and therefore make teaching of alternative methods, more meaningful methods, more indigenous methods even, much easier under the present sort of setup. And the growth of the townships in the pattern that they are now growing makes communication also all that much easier. Communication not necessarily through shared platforms, shared meetings and so on, but communication of ideas through a shared, common stimulus. Because everybody has to stay in a specific area. I'm talking here mainly about the African population. If I go to Jo'burg I know automatically, I don't have to choose: I just have to go and stay in Soweto, whether I could afford a house in Lower Houghton or not.

So this thing of talking for or on behalf of the masses is nonsense, because you live with them, you stay with them; you make your inputs primarily because you are there, and no physical distance or intellectual distance is ultimately created. A guy who's a priest or a teacher or something like this in an area is forced by circumstances to relate to the neighbors that society has created for him. He doesn't choose neighbors. So that he carves his place in that community. Alright, he might be regarded as a man of major import, primarily because he can put several words together much faster than anybody else, but the important thing is that even he himself sees himself as a member of that community. And in this whole conscientization program, this is what makes ideas so easily flow across amongst people; this common ghetto experience that blacks are subjected to.

Part I

Philosophic Dialogues

1

Biko: Africana Existentialist Philosopher

Mabogo P. More

> The thing about Biko that appealed to me is that he doesn't conform to the standard Freedom Fighter image. Mandela might have been more typical but...he is very much in the tradition of Kenyatta or Nyerere, leaders of political movements. Steve Biko was much more of a philosopher.
>
> *(Richard Fawkes, cited in* The Sunday Star, *May 31, 1992)*

Introduction

One of the curious features of African intellectual life in South Africa is, as is the case with Afro-Caribbean philosophy, "the near absence of an explicitly cultivated philosophical tradition."[1] South Africa has produced a number of internationally acclaimed African literary, social, religious, and political figures whose works are full of philosophical insights and arguments. Yet this country has apparently not produced African philosophers of the same calibre and comparable to internationally well-known African philosophers such as Kwame Nkrumah, Julius Nyerere, Paulin Hountondji, Kwasi Wiredu, Odera Oruka, Kwame Anthony Appiah, or V.Y. Mudimbe.

If Africans in South Africa and those in diaspora were able to produce poetry, literature, political theories, or theological doctrines, why not a philosophical tradition of note? It is indeed among the very same literary, political, or theological figures that African philosophical minds are embedded. One major reason for their invisibility is that African philosophy has mainly been "an intertextually embedded discursive practice, and not an isolated or absolutely autonomous one."[2] From this intertextuality, African philosophy becomes an open but diverse discursive field in which ontological, epistemological, ethical, moral, social, political, and especially existentialist traditions emerge. These traditions, defined by the peculiarities and actualities of the South African lived experiences, have been fashioned and sustained in, for example, the novels, the protest literature (especially of the 1970s and 1980s), autobiographies and poetry of many African writers. It is in these genres that the existentialist tradition as a strong philosophical tradition may be found.[3]

There is an ongoing tendency in certain quarters of locking African thinkers and their productions in the biographical moment and political activism. Biko was to some extent a victim of this practice.[4] But he defies the simple reduction to a politician or activist by assuming other equally important identities. He also combines the cultural, the political, and the philosophical in the same person. He and his comrades espoused what has normally been described as a philosophy. Hence Biko himself, together with commentators, spoke of "the philosophy of Black Consciousness,"[5] the "Black Consciousness philosophy."[6] Paradoxically, very few people referred to Biko, popularly known as "the 'father' of the Black Consciousness Movement"[7] in South Africa, as a philosopher. Themba Sono, for instance, describes Biko as "a formidable and articulate philosopher,"[8] a philosopher not in the usual academic sense of a university professor, but more precisely a man of theory and action, an "organising philosopher"[9]; perhaps a sort of social and political lay philosopher. But to merely describe someone as a philosopher, as Sono or Richard Fawkes in our epigraph do, is merely to state a generality without specificity. Therefore, this paper, following on Lewis Gordon's extensive phenomenological work on Frantz Fanon,[10] seeks to locate Bantu Steve Biko within the philosophical terrain, more pointedly, the Africana existentialist tradition. The aim, in short, is to constitute Biko as part of what Benita Parry describes as the attempt "to disclose the dead victim's... [philosophical] claims."[11]

Africana Existential Philosophy

What is Africana existential philosophy? To understand what this philosophical tradition is we need first to explain what the broader term Africana philosophy is. The phrase "Africana Philosophy" was coined and popularised by Lucius Outlaw as:

> [A] "gathering" notion under which to situate the articulations (writings, speeches, etc.) and traditions of the same, of African and peoples

of African descent collectively, as well as the sub-discipline—or field-forming, tradition-defining, tradition-organizing—reconstructive efforts which are (to be) regarded as philosophy.[12]

In other words, Africana philosophy is for Outlaw an "umbrella" term "under which can be gathered a potentially large collection of traditions of practices, agendas, and literature of African and African-descended peoples."[13] Under this umbrella may thus be included literature, poetry, political writings, philosophical texts, art, or proverbs of Africans on the continent and Africans in diaspora. It is an intertextually embedded philosophy that draws from a multiplicity of sources of black intellectual production. Such a philosophy, as Lewis Gordon explains, "addresses problems across a wide range of philosophical and social issues,"[14] a shared concern by Africans and peoples of African descent over issues such as imperialism, colonialism, slavery, racism, and resistance to them.

By virtue of the historical fact of racial oppression, colonization, and slavery, Africana philosophy raises questions of identity and liberation by focusing on the reality that African people are a black people and hence are affected by the significance of race and racism. The raising and articulation of the existential questions of identity and liberation within the context and framework of the situation of black people, constitutes what has recently come to be known as "Africana existential philosophy." This tradition deals with issues of the emergence of black selfhood, black suffering, embodied agency, freedom, bad faith, racism, and liberation; in short, it deals with *being-black-in-the-world*.[15] In Gordon's view, these questions of problematic existence and suffering animate the theoretical dimensions of black intellectual existential production.[16] Africana existential philosophy, therefore, consists in reflections, rooted in black experience, on the boundaries of human existence and the utilization of such reflections to challenges confronting African and African-descended people in diaspora.

As part of Africana philosophy, Africana existential philosophy raises questions concerning primarily two themes: identity and liberation. Identity questions are in the form: "Who are Africana (Black) people?" or "What are Africana people?" In other words, at the subjective level, the questions combined may become "Who or what am I?" The *who* of identity, Gordon argues, generates questions about selfhood: "Who am I?" The *what* in identity takes on an ontological demand about questions of *being, essence,* and the existential question of meaning, namely: "What am I?" This is the ontological question about black identity in an antiblack world.

Liberation, on the other hand, is purposive or teleological in nature. Its concerns are directly connected to the demands of "ought" or "why."

Accordingly, as Gordon points out, whatever we may be, the point is to focus energy on what we ought to become. There is, therefore, a convergence between questions of identity and questions of liberation; they intersect at the question: "*Who* is to be liberated?" Put differently, an epistemological turn constitutes the intersection between the ontological and the teleological. To know what we ought to do requires knowing who we are, and to know who we are we frequently have to discover what we ought to be doing. These concerns are symbiotic concerns which point values at the heart of *being* and forms of being at the heart of value. It is within this discursive field of Africana existential philosophy that Biko claims his philosophical space.

Philosophical Influences

As a philosopher, Biko's concern was not with theoretical abstractions, but with the concrete and existential struggles which shape human—especially black—existence, what Fanon discussed in chapter five of *Black Skin, White Masks*, "The Fact of Blackness." Indeed, Fanon constitutes the pillar of Black Consciousness. Both Fanon's classics, *Black Skin, White Masks* and *The Wretched of the Earth*, became the grounding texts of the Black Consciousness philosophy in South Africa. Biko's text *I Write What I Like* testifies to Fanon's influence on him. Besides the numerous references to Fanon in the text, some of the chapter titles of Biko's work directly echo Fanon, for example, "Black Souls in White Skins?," "Black Consciousness and the Quest for Humanity," or "White Racism and Black Consciousness." When asked by Gail Gerhart about the thinkers who influenced his thinking, Biko responded: "people like Fanon, people like Senghor... They spoke to us, you know. These people were obviously very influential."[17] Hence, as Turner and Alan observe, it was no accident that Fanon's philosophy proved to be relevant to the liberation struggles of the Black Consciousness movement, for, "It was Fanon who had... deepened the Hegelian concept of self-consciousness and in his sharp *critique* of 'reciprocity,' denied that there is any reciprocity when the relationship of Master and Slave has the additive of color."[18]

Fanon was of course not the only dominant existentialist figure in Biko's thinking; Sartre's name and other existentialists also featured quite regularly in the thinking of Black Consciousness advocates. Sartre's influence on Biko, in particular, is evident in the latter's thinking and writings. Barney Pityana—a very close comrade of Biko—states that Biko "laid his hands on some philosophical writings like Jean-Paul Sartre and made ready use of them."[19] For instance, alluding to Sartre's concept of freedom and its implications for speaking out without fear, Biko himself notes: "There is no freedom in silence, Sartre discovered this to his dismay."[20] Invoking Sartre's concept of freedom and responsibility, Biko writes:

> We have to imprison ourselves in the ideal of humanity. Humanity is beyond freedom. To be human is to be more than free. Freedom is subservient to humanity although Sartre believes that man is *condemned* to freedom; but I would hastily add that he is condemned to responsibility too, which is a human attribute.[21]

As we shall see later, Biko appropriates Sartre's interpretation of the black/white dialectics in an antiblack world. Thus, Sartre's influence on Biko was not only a Fanonian mediated influence but also direct from Sartre's writings.[22]

Unfortunately, as in our epigraph, Sam Nolutshungu's claims, for example, about Biko, Black Consciousness and philosophy were mere assertions rather than demonstrations of the philosophical content of Biko's ideas. In what follows an effort is made to tease out some existentialist categories from Biko's writings. Within the confines of an essay such as this one, it is impossible to pay attention and do justice to all the categories contained in Biko's thinking. Hence, the focus will mainly be on the following themes that best articulate the concerns of Africana philosophy of existence. First, is the articulation of Biko's conception of antiblack racism; second, and connected to the first, will be his conception of black identity within the context of the antiblack apartheid society; third, the question of liberation from racism; then finally and closely connected to the question of liberation, is the Sartrean category of bad faith.

Biko, Black Consciousness, and Racism

The fundamental categories in Biko's thinking are *racism, Blackness, consciousness, freedom,* and *authenticity.*[23] These categories get interwoven to constitute a set of ideas that came to be called the Black Consciousness philosophy. For Biko, there is the primordial human being-in-the-world of pre-reflective consciousness. Arising from this ontology are two modes of human existence in an antiblack society such as South Africa, which are products of reflective consciousness: being-white-in-the-world (white consciousness) and being-black-in-the-world (black consciousness), what, according to Gordon is the "qualitative...knowledge of each consciousness' situation in a given society."[24] These two modes of being or "ways of life" are dialectically related in such a way that they are contradictory yet dependent upon each other for their existence. Through various means—economic, religious, social, political, and legal—white self-consciousness subjugated and controlled black self-consciousness thus denying blacks their existential freedom.

But, as Sartre points out, human reality *qua* consciousness is by definition free; that is, consciousness *is* freedom. The emergence of Black Consciousness was therefore a response to a white consciousness that sought to appropriate and dominate the consciousness and thus the freedom of black people. It was and still is a struggle for a new consciousness, a reawakening of a self-consciousness, a re-appropriation of black self-consciousness from the clutches of an appropriative and dominating white consciousness, a rediscovery of the black self which lay buried beneath white consciousness imposed on blacks by cultural, political, economic, linguistic, and religious domination. It is, so to speak, an "affirmative action" on the self by the self, an affirmation not from the Other but from and by the self. Odera Oruka captures the essence of Black Consciousness thus:

> (1) a black man's [sic] awareness or realization that the world is infested with an anti-black social reality, (2) the black man's recognition of himself as black, as a Negro and to be proud of the fact, (3) the black man's urge to explain away or annihilate this social reality, and (4) move toward the creation of a new reality, a fair social reality as a condition for universal humanism.[25]

Central to Biko's thinking is first and foremost the problem of racism, especially of the apartheid type. His thoughts on racism then reflect that reality and should be understood within that context. This concern with the racial problematic fully situates Biko in the tradition of Africana existential philosophy. As Gordon points out: "[R]acial problems serve a dominating role. In Africana existential philosophy, this reality has meant detailed explorations of this dominating factor in the lived experience of African people. It has meant an exploration of their lived experience of blackness."[26]

Echoing Fanon and Stokely Carmichael (Kwame Toure), Biko defines racism as "discrimination by a group against another for the purpose of subjugation or maintaining subjugation."[27] First, to "discriminate" involves acts of exclusion and inclusion—that is, certain practices; in this case, discriminatory practices. Accordingly, it is not enough to characterize racism as simply ideological. And, to "subjugate" entails the notion of power. This leads to a conception of power which "entails conflicts of vested interests."[28] To have power according to this conception, therefore, is to have "power-over" or to have control over someone both of which are predicated on or originate in separation. "This is because [power] secures compliance or control, or is a relation of dependence or a hierarchical relation of inequality."[29] A definition of this kind then is obviously one that indicates that power, by controlling and dominating, establishes and maintains exclusionary relations of superiority and inferiority: racism. Taken within the context of apartheid and the extant power relations between blacks and whites within that system, Biko's definition restricts all acts or expressions of racism to white people. Biko constantly refers to whites as a group that "wields power"[30] or the "totality of white power."[31] Thus, black people cannot be racists because "we do not have the power to subjugate anyone... Racism does not only imply exclusion of one race by another—it always presupposes that the exclusion is for the purpose of subjugation."[32]

Power, as Goldberg indicates, "involves control that can be exercised—at least in principle—over a person(s) or over resources—often over the former to effect the latter, or vice versa."[33] Racism, therefore, is not discrimination alone, but also the power to control the lives of those excluded. This power found its concrete exercise in apartheid white subjugation of the blacks through acts of control, domination, conquest, or defeat. In all these acts, power is also exercised in the promotion, execution, and maintenance of discriminatory practices. Indeed, Biko enjoys a lot of good company in restricting racism to the powerful: Stokely Carmichael, Manning Marable, and A. Sivanandan, among others.[34] The latter, for example, defines racism in such a way that the focus is on practice and power: "It is the acting out of racial prejudice and not racial prejudice itself that matters... Racism is about power not about prejudice."[35]

The main concepts in Biko's definition of racism—racial "discrimination" (exclusion/inclusion), "subjugation" (domination and control)—were informed and echoed by the main architect of apartheid, Prime Minister Hendrik Verwoerd, in an attempt to justify apartheid or "separate development" as he preferred to call it:

> Reduced to its simplest form the problem is nothing else than this: We want to keep South Africa White... "keeping it White" can only mean one thing, namely White *domination*, not "leadership," not "guidance," but *"control," "supremacy."* If we are agreed that it is the desire of the people that the white man should be able to protect himself by retaining White *domination*, we say that it can be achieved by separate development.[36]

Biko's definition, therefore, without pretension to universality, captures apartheid racism as it is articulated by Verwoerd in the statement just cited. However, to the extent that apartheid was "settler-colonialism" or "colonialism of a special kind" this definition captures the kind of racism that one finds in a colonial situation. Power as conceived in this definition is not abstract and anonymous, but functions through state apparatuses and social and economic agencies.

Verwoerd's justification of apartheid racism above expresses one significant element of a racist consciousness: the idea of the "opposite race." In his racist consciousness, the black race is believed to be the absolute Other, an enemy, and threat to the white race (Swart gevaar/Black danger) against whom all whites must unite. It was therefore in the context of such racist consciousness that Biko, in a similar fashion as Sartre, in relation to Negritude, articulated his conception of Black Consciousness in term of the Hegelian triadic dialectic of thesis, antithesis, and synthesis. Biko writes, in a tone reminiscent of Sartre's phenomenological description of Negritude:

> The overall analysis therefore, based on the Hegelian theory of dialectic... is as follows... The thesis is in fact a strong white racism and therefore, the *antithesis* to this must, *ipso facto*, be a strong solidarity amongst the blacks on whom this white racism seeks to prey. Out of these two situations we can therefore hope to reach some kind of balance—a true humanity.[37]

Black Consciousness as the negative moment of the dialectical progression in the struggle for black authentic existence, was for Biko a necessary stage, a means toward freedom rather than an end in itself. Black Consciousness, he declared, "would be irrelevant in a colourless and non-exploitative egalitarian society."[38]

Biko's characterization of Black Consciousness in Hegelian terms notably and deliberately recalls Sartre's famous essay, "Black Orpheus," in which Negritude is described as an antithesis, the weak upbeat of a dialectical progression, a negative moment responding to white racism; in short, an "antiracist racism."[39] Even though Fanon launched a serious critique of Negritude, he also took exception to Sartre's view of Negritude. "Jean-Paul Sartre," he lamented, "has destroyed black zeal... The dialectic that brings necessity into the foundation of my freedom drives me out of my myself."[40] Unlike Fanon, Biko endorses Sartre's conclusion because he probably realized that Sartre was speaking in methodological terms when he used the expression "the moment of separation or negativity:... antiracist racism" which is not, in this context, pejorative at all.

Taking their cue from Sartre's "antiracist racism," and placing a heavy accent on the last word "*racism*," many of those opposed to Negritude and Black Consciousness or any form of race loyalty or solidarity labelled them racist. Ruch, for example, interprets the antithetical moment (Negritude/Black Consciousness) as racist. Referring to the blacks who espouse blackness, he writes: "In order therefore to find their identity as a race, they become racialist in their turn, belittling their former superiors, burning what they used to adore, and showing by all means at their disposal that they themselves and not their oppressors are in fact the superior beings."[41]

What distinguished racialism from racism is that in the latter, the superiority of one race over another is asserted. A racist, in other words, would not only say that there are different races, but also that certain races—especially one's own—are superior to other races. In other words, racism adds to racialism a hierarchically discriminating value judgement.

Sartre himself is guilty of causing this error by describing the "moment of separation" as a kind of racism instead of racialism. For, it is evident from the context of "Black Orpheus," that his intention was not to label the Negritude thinkers "racist" in the usual derogatory manner. If he had meant to suggest that they are racist, that would imply that they not only had the power to dominate Europeans but also that they consider themselves superior to them; a claim neither Sartre nor the Negritudinists would defend. He makes this point clear when he asserts about Negritude: "But there is something even more important in it: the Negro himself, we have said, creates a kind of antiracist racism. *He wishes in no way to dominate the world: he desires the abolition of all kinds of ethnic privileges; he asserts his solidarity with the oppressed of every color.*"[42]

It is clear from the above that to describe Negritude as "racism" is inappropriate. Not all separatisms are necessarily racist. In the context of the situation of the blacks within an antiblack white world, black solidarity may not necessarily amount to racism. At best, it may be correctly described as "racialism" which in and by itself is not dangerous, pernicious, or racist. Indeed, Sartre's idea would make more sense if it were to be rephrased from "antiracist racism" to "antiracist racialism."

The Question of Identity

Sartre's "antiracist racism" idea also introduces two fundamental challenges confronting black particularistic doctrines such as Black Consciousness. In Gordon's terms, the challenges amount to: "First, can the struggle against racism avoid being racist? And second, can the achievement of black liberation avoid the elimination of the black race."[43]

Biko is acutely aware of these challenges and attempts to confront them head on. As early as his tenure as the president of the South African Student Organisation (SASO), Biko responded:

> The fact that the whole ideology centres around non-white students as a group might make a few people to believe that the organisation is racially inclined. Yet what SASO has done is simply to take stock of the present

scene in the country and to realise that not unless the non-white students decide to lift themselves from the doldrums will they ever hope to get out of them.[44]

Again he observes: "Some will charge that we are racist."[45]

To Gordon's first question: Can the struggle against racism avoid being racist?—the answer for Biko is affirmative. His first and immediate response to this question is an echo of his conceptualization of racism as predicated upon power relations of exclusion and inclusion. Racism, in terms of Biko's conception, is about power; hence, "One cannot be a racist unless he has the power to subjugate."[46] Racism, Biko argues, is a prerogative of white people because the "order of things" is such that white people throughout the entire world are in power. Since black people in South Africa had no power whatsoever, they could not be racist. As a matter of fact, Black Consciousness has never been espoused as a credo for subjugation and domination of whites. In this respect it differs tremendously with apartheid.

This might mean that an individual or a designated racial group A treats an individual or a designated group B in a racist manner only if A holds power over B and uses that power to discriminate against B on the basis of biological and physical differences. Since in South Africa whites hold power over blacks, then only whites can be racist and not blacks because the latter lacks power. This conception of racism is unacceptable to some people on the basis that "The bitter, solitary old [white] bigot, alone in her room, is a racist for all her powerlessness."[47] The appropriate response to this objection would be the question, "powerless" in relation to whom and as a member of which group? If she belongs to the dominant group, powerless as she may seem to be at that particular time, she however belongs to a group designated as a race that at that particular point in time possesses power. Therefore the power she wields is the power derived from her membership in the powerful and dominant group. This power is expressed succinctly by Margaret Mead in her discussions about race with James Baldwin:

> But you see, I've been on a plantation in New Guinea where I was responsible for a labor line. Now they were indentured labourers; they were grown men. You had two hundred men out of the bush. Some of them had been cannibals. Some of them weren't cannibals; some of them had just been good, fiery fighters. But they came out of a very, very primitive technical level of society....
>
> Now, when I was temporarily alone, I had to run that labor line. I had to give them orders based on *absolutely nothing but white supremacy. I was one lone white woman.* Any one of them could have killed me, and it was

my business not to get killed. *If anything happened to me, maybe twenty of them would have been killed.*[48]

White power in an antiblack world means that the life of a single white woman is worth more than two hundred black lives. This is precisely what racism means for Biko, that one single white woman can control and have the power of life and death over thousands of black people. We see this phenomenon even in our media: the blood of one single white farmer in Zimbabwe or South Africa, for example, makes the headlines of the press and is reflected on TV throughout the whole world rather than the blood of a thousand black workers in the same country. In short, Biko's concept of power translates into a demand by a single white woman that the black other justify his existence. Her existence is justified by the existence of the black other whose existence depends on her. In other words, she is her own justification, her own foundation, a Sartrean in-itself-for-itself, God.

Second, Black Consciousness for Biko was not racist because race does not play a part in the concept of "blackness" as it was conceived. All people defined as races other than whites were negatively referred to as non-whites. Their non-whiteness was their common identity within the antiblack racism of the apartheid regime that confronted them. It was this common identity and experience of racism and exploitation that led to the adoption of the term "black" as a political identity to be worn with pride against a color-conscious apartheid regime. African, Indian, and Coloured medical students at the University of Natal were forced to share common university facilities different from their white counterparts. Because of this common experience—even though Africans, Indians, and Coloureds in South Africa are perceived and still perceive themselves as racially different—the concept "Black" was used as part of a set of constitutive ideas and principles to promote collective action. Defining "blacks," Biko and his comrades in the South African Students' Organisation, insisted that the term refers to those "who are by law or tradition politically, economically and socially discriminated against as a group in the south African society and identifying themselves as a unit in the struggle towards the realisation of their aspiration."[49]

Black Consciousness was therefore not racial or racist in content but a socially and politically constructed identity in an antiblack society that perceives color as the central marker of inferiority and superiority. In other words, "black" became transformed to what in William R. Jones' terms is "a designation of an antagonist."[50] There is a sense, therefore, in which to formulate a Black Consciousness philosophy is a consequence and a tacit recognition of the fact that a philosophy that reflects or endorses a white consciousness dominates our experience. Thus, to call for Black

Consciousness from this perspective is to launch an implicit attack on white racism. Besides, the term "black," as a socio-political rather than a biological concept, was for Biko not necessarily all-inclusive. "The fact we are all *not white* does not necessarily mean that we are all *black*... If one's aspiration is whiteness but his pigmentation makes attainment of this impossible, then that person is a non-white."[51]

In Biko's dialectic, black consciousness is not only a response to white consciousness but also its product. The core of black identity, therefore, must be rooted in the same quality that is the basis for black subjugation and oppression, that quality which is the focus of the dominant group's perception: blackness. Black identity needed to be grounded in a concrete consciousness of the situation of being black in an antiblack world. "What blacks are doing," he asserts, "is merely to respond to a situation in which they find themselves objects of white racism" and he continues, "We are in the position in which we are because of our skin. We are collectively segregated against—what can be more logical than for us to respond as a group?"[52] This is a call for black solidarity and unity, a solidarity the kind of which Appiah would call racist.

Appiah posits two kinds of racisms, "extrinsic" and "intrinsic." Extrinsic racism is a belief that people of different racial groups possess certain characteristics that warrant differential treatment. Intrinsic racism, on the other hand, involves loyalty and preference of one's own racial group based on racial solidarity. Given Biko's insistence on the solidarity and unity of the black oppressed, that "all blacks must sit as one big unit... We must cling to each other with the tenacity that will shock the perpetrators of evil,"[53] Black Consciousness seems to fit Appiah's designation of intrinsic racism which is predicated on racial solidarity. The basis of Biko's black solidarity, on the contrary, lies in shared or common collective historical experiences rather than on shared biological or genetic characteristics.

Even supposing Black Consciousness was "intrinsic racism" as defined by Appiah, is "intrinsic racism" really racism? One of the salient features of racism as understood by Biko is not only power but also the belief in the given superiority of the racist group and the supposed inherent inferiority of the excluded and discriminated against racial group. It is this supposed inherent inferiority that provides the foundation of the power to subjugate. Black Consciousness, on the contrary, was black solidarity in the face of subjugation and domination, a solidarity of those and by those who were subjugated and certainly did not regard themselves as inherently superior to whites. Such solidarity cannot possibly be called racist even of the "intrinsic" type.

If Biko's Black Consciousness is not racist, how then do we explain the exclusionary practice against whites as a race in the struggle for justice?

He rejected integration. Was he then a racial separatist? Biko was both a (non)separatist and a (non)integrationist. As a separatist, Biko's argument was consequentialist because he strongly believed that given the apartheid circumstances, the only practical means to achieve freedom for blacks was through separation from whites. Hence the slogan: "Black man, you are on your own!" Separatism, it is obvious, is for Biko merely a means to an end rather than an end in itself. Biko himself warns us of the conflation of the means-ends nexus that afflicts popular perception of Black Consciousness philosophy. In this respect, Biko's views resonate with the Pan Africanist Congress (PAC) policy. For both these tendencies, separatism is construed as a necessary strategic phase towards integration.[54] Biko, as I indicated, was both a non-integrationist, as we have just seen, but also an integrationist. How is this possible?

Liberation

To Gordon's second concern: Can the achievement of black liberation avoid the elimination of the black race? Put differently: Can blacks become subjects instead of objects without losing their identity as blacks? Once again, Biko's response to this question is instructive. When Biko speaks of a "synthesis" in the white/black dialectic, is he articulating a position that would lead to the elimination of both the white and black races? How would the "synthesis" manifest itself; through assimilation or integration? Biko launches a scathing attack on liberals, for confusing the antithetical moment of the dialectical progression with the synthetic moment, which they interpret as an expression of integration or assimilation: "For the *liberals*, the *thesis* is apartheid, the *antithesis* is non-racialism, but the *synthesis* is very feebly defined. They want to tell the blacks that they see integration as the ideal solution."[55] But this integration, Biko insists, is a liberal ruse to foist white norms and values upon blacks and thus to achieve black assimilation into white culture, norms and values. The logical point here is that nonracialism cannot both be the antithesis and the synthesis of the dialectical process. The synthetic moment is a product of and therefore must be a higher expression of both the thetical and antithetical moments. To equate the antithetical moment and the synthetical moment is to arrest the process of change at a particular stage and thus to reproduce the status quo in a veiled and masked form. For, in this kind of integration as envisaged by liberals, the "in-built complexes of superiority and infcriority...continue to manifest themselves even in the 'nonracial' set-up of the integrated complex. As a result, the integration so achieved is a one-way course."[56]

While Biko's view may not have been derived from Sartre's analysis of the liberal democrat in *Portrait of the Anti-Semite*, it is however close to it in many respects. For Biko, just as for Sartre, the real target is precisely the liberals, the "do-gooders" who in their defence of blacks or Jews, rescue them as (Western) human beings, but annihilate them as blacks. The liberal is as a matter-of-fact an assimilationist, one who wants blacks to be full members of humanity only if they renounce their blackness. In other words, black liberation would therefore mean the elimination of the black race. Speaking of the liberal democrat in relation to the Jew, Sartre writes:

> "There is no such thing as a Jew, there is no such things as a Jewish question," he [liberal democrat] says. Which means that he wishes to separate the Jew from his religion, his family, his ethnic group, in order to plunge him in the democratic crucible, out of which he will emerge single and naked, an individual and solitary particle, just like all the other particles. This was known in the United States as the policy of assimilation.[57]

Integration for Biko does not mean the assimilation of blacks into an already established set of values set up and maintained by whites. By assimilation generally, is meant the attempt to have one racial or ethnic group absorbed, physically and/or culturally, by another. The absorbed group takes on the defining characteristics of the absorbing group and renounces its own racial or ethnic uniqueness and singularity. The black assimilation project is however limited because, unlike the Jew who can physically disappear within a white world, the black body is overdetermined from without. At the ontological level, therefore, as Gordon points out, assimilation, especially black assimilation, is easily classifiable with hatred, for, "[i]t manifests a desire to eliminate the Other *as* Other—in other words, to create a world of only one *kind* of human being."[58] The liberal "myth" of integration, which is, in fact, a form of progressive assimilation, Biko insists, "must be cracked and killed"[59] because it ultimately turns out to be an attempt to deny the culture of black people. To this extent, Biko was, in the words of Howard McGary, also a "cultural separatist" like Amiri Baraka and Moulana Karenga in the United States who believed that "integration deprives black people of a culture that they already have or that they ought to regain because it involves the grafting of black people onto the white culture."[60] Biko, just as Baraka and Karenga, urged blacks to recover and maintain the positive aspects of their culture.

There is at a deeper level the means/ends problem that finds expression in the antithetical/synthetical moments at play. It is precisely this means/ends problem that ultimately sets Biko apart from both the liberals and the now ruling African National Congress party policy. For both the liberals and the ANC, integration *qua* nonracialism is both a means and an end. As a means integration (nonracialism) fails on two accounts. First, such integration is infested by inbuilt apartheid complexes of superiority and inferiority, which continue to manifest themselves in any such "nonracial" movements, organizations, or situations. As a result of such integration, power relations remain untouched. Second, this type of integration quite often suffers from internal strife generated by "the lack of common ground for solid identification."[61] To overcome these complexes resulting from 300 years of oppression, "a very strong grass-roots build-up of black consciousness"[62] is necessary.

What kind of liberatory synthesis then does Biko conceptualize? It is suggested that this synthetic moment in Biko's dialectics is nonracialism. What does nonracialism mean? Does it imply the obliteration or elimination of blacks and whites as "races"? Is it a negation of the existence of "races"? But to negate something is on the one hand to implicitly recognize its presence, in whatever form it may take. On the other hand, to deny the existence of "races" is, in a significant sense, to posit the unity and sameness of humanity.

The Bikoan synthesis is a kind of what in Lucius Outlaw's terms is a "pluralist integration,"[63] an economically, politically, and socially integrated society, but racially and culturally distinct whilst not threatening the integration of the social whole by cultural distinctness. That is, integration for Biko "means there shall be free participation by all members of a society, catering for the full expression of the self in a freely changing society."[64] In a sense, Biko would reject Sartre's Hegelian invitation to look "to the end of particularism in order to find the dawn of the universal." This invitation would be tantamount to giving a negative answer to Gordon's question: Can the achievement of black liberation avoid the elimination of the black race? Instead, Biko insists on a synthetic moment that preserves the interplay of unity and diversity, that is a recognition of difference within sameness, of the universal, and the particular. Incidentally, this synthetic view would seem to avoid the "bad faith" which Biko sees as one of the major problems emanating from racism; the full identification with my past to the exclusion of my future possibilities, my facticity to the exclusion of my transcendence, my body to the exclusion of my consciousness, or my universality to the exclusion of my particularity, or vice versa.

If nonracialism *qua* integration means the elimination of blacks as a race then, Biko emphatically declares, he would be totally against it. If integration means "a breakthrough into white society by blacks, an assimilation and acceptance of blacks into an already established set of norms and code of behaviour set up and maintained by whites... YES I am against it."[65] For Biko, assimilation *qua* integration is not only to be rejected because it is the project of the liberals, but also because it leads to bad faith and alienation in blacks who strive for it. The black who tries to assimilate is inauthentic because s/he wants to deny her racial and social identity.

Bad Faith

Fundamental to Black Consciousness is the problem of bad faith (inauthenticity) and its necessary consequence, alienation. In the antiblack apartheid world, bad faith is an "effort to evade one's humanity" by asserting this "humanity as what it is not."[66] That is, as either black or white consciousness. This view is a consequence of the principle in dialectical thought according to which a being realizes itself in direct proportion to the degree of its opposite, such that interiority, for example, is realized in direct proportion to exteriority, transcendence to facticity, or whiteness to blackness. So black consciousness is posited as the antithesis of white consciousness, a purging from black people of a consciousness that alienates them from who they are, not essentially but situationally. As Biko succinctly declares: "I think Black Consciousness refers itself to the black man and to his situation."[67] This alienation has its origin in the antiblack racism that affects the black person from the cradle to the grave. Because of the injustices, differential treatments, inequality "you begin to feel that there is something incomplete in your humanity, and that completeness goes with whiteness."[68]

"What is the being… of human reality in an antiblack world?" Gordon asks; the answer, he declares in a single phrase, is *bad faith*. The concept of bad faith, popularized by Jean-Paul Sartre, basically refers to different modes of human existence characterized by self-deception, self-evasion, flight from one's freedom and responsibility, and the acceptance of values as pre-given. Without delving deeper into the complexities of the concept as articulated by Sartre, and the different patterns bad faith normally assumes, suffice it to say with Gordon that located within the context of an antiblack world, bad faith is "an effort to deny the blackness within by way of asserting the supremacy of whiteness. It can be regarded as an effort to purge blackness from the self and the world, symbolically and literally."[69] Bad faith, therefore, has to do with self-identity in the sense of one's reflective consciousness of who one is and what one is like. Such reflection is however unavoidable given that, as Sartre puts it, a human being is "a being such that in its own being, its being is in question."[70]

Apartheid racism, Biko emphatically declared, is obviously evil. However, the tragedy of it all is that the victims of this vicious system, black people, not only acquiesce in it but also participate in their own oppression. This is because they deceive themselves into believing in the naturalness and givenness of their situation. "What makes the black man fail to tick?" Biko asks in earnest. Because, "reduced to an obliging shell, he looks with awe at the white power structure and accepts what he regards as the 'inevitable position.'"[71] However, deep inside, the black person knows that he is lying to her/himself for "In the privacy of his toilet his face twists in the silent condemnation of white society but brightens up in sheepish obedience as he comes out hurrying in response to his master's impatient call."[72] In the presence of the white person, the black person assumes an attitude of pure facticity. He plays the role assigned to him by the master. He lives his situation by fleeing it; he chooses either to deny it or to deny his responsibility.

One of the tragedies arising from racism for Biko is the effect of self-negation which characterizes the black person's situation: "[T]he black man in himself has developed a certain state of alienation, he rejects himself, precisely because he attaches the meaning white to all that is good, in other words he associates good and he equates good with white."[73] Part of the source of this alienation, Biko believes, is the education system as whole, a system whose content a black child does not recognize herself in. This is a system that teaches the black child about Europe and Europeans to a point where "we don't behave like Africans, we behave like Europeans who are staying in Africa."[74] Fanon makes the same point: "The black schoolboy in the Antilles, who in his lessons is forever talking about 'our ancestors, the Gauls,' identifies himself with the explorer, the bringer of civilization, the white man who carries truth to savages—an all-white truth. There is identification—that is, the young Negro subjectively adopts a white man's attitude."[75] In the South African case, "the explorer, the bringer of civilization, the white man who carries the truth to savages" was the supposed discoverer of the Cape of Good Hope, Jan van Riebeeck.

Also because of a developed sense of self-hatred, black alienation involves an attempt to flee one's black body, "the way they make up and so on, which tends to be a negation of their true state and in a sense a running away from their colour; they use lightening creams, they use straightening devices for their hair and so on."[76] This attempt to play at not being black condemns them to a perpetual struggle of what Sartre calls "impression management" which becomes a mark of the oppressed. The desire of the slave, the Jew, or the colonized to become like the master, the anti-Semite, or the colonizer, is an avoidable consequence of the master-slave relationship, anti-Semitism, or colonialism.

Oppression often makes blacks turn against their own in an attempt to flee and evade their blackness. They assert a white consciousness by adopting an antiblack standpoint on human reality. This they attempt to achieve in several ways. For example, seduced by the seeming nonracialism and equal treatment in liberal organizations, mixing with whites at wine, beer, and tea parties in white suburbs, "[t]his serves to boost up their own ego to the extent of making them feel slightly superior to those blacks who do not get similar treatment from whites."[77] What these blacks try to forget is that even in those "mixed" circles it is as blacks that they are received. In doing so they lie to themselves because they know perfectly well that they cannot cease being black. They conceal from themselves the truth, which, despite their futile attempts to deny, they nevertheless carry in the depths of their being. By assuming an antiblack consciousness, by trying to flee from the black reality, by attempting to cut themselves off from the mistakes of their race, by making themselves judges of other blacks, they evince a consciousness in bad faith and lack of authenticity.

The other way in which antiblack consciousness manifests itself in blacks is when a black, because of the accumulation of white insults in his being, "vents it in the wrong direction—on his fellow man in the township."[78] This is normally called "black-on-black violence." Several reasons may be advanced for this phenomenon but one of them is certainly the fact that such a black "may either be displacing his anger toward whites—he may be hiding from his own desire for white recognition... [a clear example of bad faith]—or he may be avoiding the unbearable sense of humiliation of not being recognized by even the lowest denominator [black people]."[79]

What should blacks do to be authentic and avoid bad faith? The authentic black, in terms of Biko's Black Consciousness, should be *conscientized*—what Heidegger might term the "call of conscience"[80] or Sartre the "radical conversion"—to choose to be black in the face of an antiblack racism. Conscientization is that process which brings to the consciousness of black people the task of taking charge of their destiny, of resolutely taking responsibility for who they are and the choices they make, of committing themselves to authentic possibilities, taking over their freedom, uniqueness, and resolutely engaging in the projects through which they create themselves. Black Consciousness thus becomes the quest (vehicle) for authenticity.

By Way of Conclusion

This portrait of Biko as an Africana existential philosopher is neither exhaustive nor by any means an attempt to encase his identity within a single determinate essence. That indeed would be both difficult and unfair. The focus of this essay has been to break with the prevailing tendency of interpreting Biko's thinking singularly as political to the almost total exclusion of the philosophical. It is suggested therefore that as a radical Africana existential philosopher, Biko was simultaneously, like most radical Africana existentialists such as Fanon and Sartre, a critical race and liberation theorist.

Some people, especially mainstream and traditional philosophers, have contemptuously pointed out that Africana philosophers seem to be preoccupied with race, and that for them to make race their primary subject is in the long run counterproductive, for it harms their image by portraying them as perpetual "one-themers."[81] Indeed, some of these critics even go to the extent of rejecting race as a legitimate philosophical problem by locating it in sociological or anthropological terrains. Undeniably, a considerable number of Africana philosophers are indeed "pre-occupied" with race. But this is because, following on Nkrumah's observation, philosophy always arises from a social milieu such that a social content is always present either explicitly or implicitly. The social milieu affects the content of philosophy, and the content of philosophy seeks to affect the social milieu, either by confirming it or by opposing it. Philosophy therefore is a product of the lived-experience of social beings. The reality of the social milieu of Africans and African-descended people is a racialized reality. Hence the primacy of the racial problematic among black philosophers. A further problem about this objection is the assumption on the part of the critics that Africana philosophy is the sole preserve of a racially distinct group, namely, people of African descent. Not all contributors to Africana existential philosophy are black. "'Africana philosophy' is meant to include, as well, the work of those persons who are neither African nor of African descent but who recognize the legitimacy and importance of the issues and endeavors that constitute the philosophizing of persons African or African-descended and who contribute to discussions of their efforts."[82] Besides Sartre, among the leading contemporary non-black Africana philosophers are: Robert Bernasconi, David Theo Goldberg, and Nigel Gibson.

As though responding to the above critics, Sartre—a paradigmatic case of a non-black Africana philosopher—in his *What is Literature?* responds to the question "For whom does one write?" by giving as an example the writings of the African-American novelist Richard Wright:

> If we consider only his condition as a *man*, that is, as a Southern "nigger" transported to the North, we shall at once imagine that he can only write about Negroes or Whites *seen through the eyes of Negroes*. Can one imagine for a moment that he would agree to pass his life in the contemplation of the eternal True, Good, and Beautiful when ninety per cent of the negroes in the South are practically deprived of the right to vote?...
>
> If we want to go further, we must consider his public. To whom does Richard Wright address himself? Certainly not the universal man. The essential characteristic of the notion of the universal man is that he is not involved in any particular age, and that he is no more and no less moved by the lot of the negroes of Louisiana than by that of the Roman slaves... He is a pure and abstract affirmation of the inalienable right of man. But neither can Wright think of intending his book for the white racialists of Virginia or South Carolina whose minds are made up in advance and who will not open them.[83]

The dilemmas of a black philosopher are therefore different from the dilemmas of, say, a white philosopher. The black philosopher's problem is about recognition as a human being, denied precisely because she/he is not regarded as a full person. This recognition matters to the black philosopher precisely because the Other exercises power over her/him thereby limiting her/his possibilities. Had it not been for this power relation, the Other's recognition would certainly not matter at all. So the black philosopher's preoccupation is to attempt to convince the Other that s/he is not merely a sub-being or thing but a person and therefore deserves to be treated as such. The "*I AM*" of the black philosopher will thus be different: "it will be relational, not monadic; dialogic, not monologic; one is a subperson precisely because *others*—persons—have categorized one as such and have the power to enforce their categorization."[84] Africana existential philosophy is therefore inherently oppositional and liberatory.

Even though Biko nowhere provides a sustained and systematic articulation or treatise of a traditional philosophical nature, his writings contain numerous philosophical insights and ideas from which it is possible to draw together an account of a philosophical outlook. Such a philosophical outlook, we have suggested, is an Africana existentialist preoccupation with "being-black-in-an antiblack-world" and questions of "black authenticity" and "black liberation." He realized that liberation of any kind required an authentic consciousness of self, for, as he avers, "we cannot be conscious of ourselves and yet remain in bondage."[85] Like Fanon, Biko recognized one right only, a right that led to his untimely death: "That of demanding human behavior from the Other."[86]

Notes

This chapter originally appeared in 2004 in *Alternation*, Volume 11.

1. Paget Henry, *Caliban's Reason: Introducing Afro-Caribbean Philosophy* (New York: Routledge, 2000), xi.
2. Ibid., 2.
3. In his classic, *The African Image* (1962), E'skia Mphahlele, for instance, strongly rejects Leopold Sedar Senghor's concept of "Negritude" from a literary perspective. However, he agrees with Senghor's philosophical interpretation of "African humanism," a theme that occupies pride of place in his literary texts and constitutes the basis of his epistemology in his *Towards a Humanistic Philosophy of Education* (1982). In 1977 Mazisi Kunene gave a lengthy interview on the meaning and practice of African Philosophy in South Africa that was followed by a publication on "The Relevance of African Cosmological Systems to African Literature." See C. Luchembe, "An Interview with Mazisi Kunene on African Philosophy," *Ufahamu* 7, no. 2 (1977): 3–27, and Mazisi Kunene, "The Relevance of African Cosmological Systems to African Literature Today," in E. D. Jones, ed., *African Literature Today: Myth and History*

(London: Heinemann, 1980). Mathole Motshekga published a monograph entitled, *An Introduction to Kara Philosophy* (1983) that in a profound way anticipated Martin Bernal's *Black Athena* (1987).
4. A substantial number of writings on Biko focus mostly on the political aspect of his thinking and a few on his thoughts on culture and politics. In this respect, see for example, Robert Fatton, *Black Consciousness in South Africa* (Albany, NJ: State University of New York Press, 1986); N. Barney Pityana, Mamphela Ramphele, Malusi Mpumlwana, and Lindy Wilson, eds., *Bounds of Possibility: The Legacy of Steve Biko and Black Conciousness* (Cape Town, SA: David Philip, 1991); C. R. D. Halisi, *Black Political Thought in the Making of South African Democracy* (Bloomington: Indiana University Press, 1999); Thomas K. Ranuga, "Frantz Fanon and Black Consciousness in Azania," *Phylon* 47, no. 3 (1986): 182–191; Chris J. Nteta, "Revolutionary Self-Consciousness as an Objective Force Within the Process of Liberation" *Radical America* 21, no. 5 (1987): 55–61; Nigel Gibson, "Black Consciousness 1977–1987: The Dialectics of Liberation in South Africa," *Africa Today* (1980): 5–26; David Hemson, "The Antimonies of Black Rage," *Alternation* 2, no. 2 (1995): 184–206; Pal Ahluwalia and Abebe Zegeye, "Frantz Fanon and Steve Biko: Towards Liberation," *Social Identities* 7, no. 3 (2001): 455–469.
5. Steve Biko, *I Write What I Like: A Selection of his Writings* (Randburg: Ravan Press, 1996), 92; Ranunga, "Frantz Fanon," 186.
6. C. R. D. Halisi, "Biko and Black Consciousness Philosophy: An Interpretation" in N. Barney Pityana, Mamphela Ramphele, Malusi Mpumlwana, and Lindy Wilson, eds., *Bounds of Possibility: The Legacy of Steve Biko and Black Consciousness* (Cape Town, SA: David Philip, 1991), 100–110; Ranuga, "Frantz Fanon," 182.
7. P. Ahluwalia and A. Zegeye, "Frantz Fanon and Steve Biko: Towards Liberation," *Social Identities* 7, no. 3 (2001): 460.
8. Themba Sono, *Reflections on the Origin of Black Consciousness in South Africa* (Pretoria: HSRC Press, 1993), 90.
9. Ibid., 102.
10. For more on Fanon, the existential phenomenologist, see Lewis R. Gordon, *Fanon and the Crisis of European Man: An Essay on Philosophy and the Human Sciences* (New York: Routledge, 1995); *Her Majesty's Other Children* (Lanham: Rowman and Littlefield, 1997), especially ch. 2; Lewis R. Gordon, T. D. Sharpley-Whiting, and R. T. White, eds. *Fanon: A Critical Reader* (Oxford: Blackwell, 1996), especially ch. 5, 8, 9, and 10.
11. Benita Parry, "Reconciliation and Remembrance," *Die Suid Afrikaan* (February 1996): 12.
12. Lucius Outlaw, *On Race and Philosophy* (New York: Routledge, 1996), 76.
13. Ibid., 77.
14. Lewis R. Gordon, *Existence in Black: An Anthology of Black Existential Philosophy* (New York: Routledge, 1997), 6.
15. For the existentialist category of "being-black-in-the-world" see, for example, Chabani Manganyi, who has over the years articulated a humanist existentialism that found its most profound expression in his seminal text, *Being-Black-in-the-World* (Johannesburg: Sprocas/Ravan, 1973). See also his other existentialist texts, *Mashangu's Reverie and Other Essays* (Johannesburg: Ravan, 1977); *Alienation and the Body in Racist Society* (New York: Nok, 1977); and *Looking Through the Keyhole* (Johannesburg: Ravan, 1981).
16. Lewis R. Gordon, *Existentia Africana: Understanding Africana Existential Thought* (New York: Routledge, 2000), 8.
17. Steve Biko, interview with Gail M. Gerhart, Durban, October 24, 1972.

18. L. Turner and J. Alan, *Frantz Fanon, Soweto and American Black Thought* (Chicago, IL: News and Letters, 1986), 38.
19. Barney Pityana, 2002. "Steve Biko: An Enduring Legacy." www.unisa.ac.za/contents/about/principle/docs/Biko.doc–.
20. Steve Biko, "I Write What I Like: By Frank Talk," *SASO Newsletter* 2, no. 1 (1972): 10.
21. Ibid., 7.
22. More than Biko, Sartre's influence on other Black Consciousness movement proponents was even more explicit and direct. A case in point is Chabani Noel Manganyi in whose work Sartre's philosophy proliferates and is even evident in his choice of the titles of his essays. For example, his seminal text, *Being-Black-in-the-World* (1973) prods anyone with knowledge of existential phenomenology to Heidegger's and Sartre's category of "Being-in-the-world." His subsequent text *Looking Through the Keyhole* (1981) clearly recalls Sartre's famous example of a man who, driven by intense jealousy, is caught peeping through the keyhole in the section "The Look" of *Being and Nothingness*. Some other chapter titles with a Sartrean flavor include "Us and Them," "Nausea," "The Body-for-Others," and "Alienation: The Body and Racism." These are to be found in his other texts such as *Alienation and the Body in Racist Society* (1977) and *Mashangu's Reverie and Other Essays* (1977). Considering himself as having been influenced by "a philosophical orientation which may be described as existential-phenomenological" (Chabani Manganyi, *Alienation and the Body in Racist Society* [New York: NOK, 1977], 8). The text that appears to have had the most impact on his thinking is Sartre's *Portrait of the Anti-Semite*.
23. Freedom and authenticity will be dealt with, derivatively, in the sections on "Liberation" and "Bad faith" respectively.
24. Lewis R. Gordon, *Bad Faith and Antiblack Racism* (Atlantic Highlands, NJ: Humanities, 1995), 131.
25. Odera H. Oruka, *Trends in Contemporary African Philosophy* (Nairobi, Kenya: Shirikon, 1990), 71.
26. Gordon, *Existentia Africana*, 8.
27. Biko, *I Write What I Like* (1996), 25.
28. T.B. Dyrberg, *The Circular Structure of Power* (London: Verso, 1997), 2.
29. Ibid.
30. Biko, *I Write What I Like* (1996), 65.
31. Biko, interview with Gerhart.
32. Biko, *I Write What I Like* (1996), 97–98.
33. D. T. Goldberg, "Hate, or Power?" *APA Newsletter* 94, no. 2 (1995): 13.
34. For detailed conceptions of racism as power relations see, for example, A. Sivanandan, "Challenging Racism: Strategies for the '80s," *Race and Class* 26, no. 2 (1982): 1–12; A. Hacker, *Two Nations: Black and White, Separate, Hostile, Unequal* (New York: Scribner, 1992); M. Marable, *Speaking Truth to Power* (Boulder, CO: Westview, 1996); S. Carmichael and C. V. Hamilton, *Black Power: The Politics of Liberation in America* (New York: Vintage Books, 1967).
35. Sivanandan, "Challenging Racism," 3.
36. Quoted by B. Bunting in A. La Guma, ed., *Apartheid* (New York: International Publishers, 1971), 28. Emphasis added.
37. Biko, *I Write What I Like* (1996), 51 and 90.
38. Ibid., 87.
39. Jean-Paul Sartre, "Black Orpheus," in John MacCombie, trans., *"What Is Literature?" And Other Essays* (Cambridge, MA: Harvard University Press, 1988), 296.

40. Frantz Fanon, *Black Skin, White Masks*, trans. C. L. Markmann (New York: Grove, 1967), 135.
41. E. A. Ruch and K. C. Anyanwu, *African Philosophy* (Rome: Catholic Book Agency, 1981), 201. Besides the obvious inaccuracy of the claim, "showing by all means at their disposal that they themselves and not their oppressors are in fact the *superior beings*," a distinction rarely made by most people like Ruch, is the one between "racism" and "racialism." (For similar distinction between racism and racialism see Albert Mosley, *African Philosophy: Selected Readings* [Englewood Cliff, NJ: Prentice Hall, 1995], 216–235; Alain de Benoist, "What is Racism?" *Telos* 114 [1999]: 11–49; Lucius T. Outlaw, *On Race and Philosophy* [New York: Routledge, 1996], 8 and 18.) These are often conflated to mean one thing, namely, the belief that one's race is superior to others and, therefore, has the right to dominate others. The two are however distinct and do not necessarily entail each other. A racialist believes in the existence of races and that these races are different, both physiologically and even behaviorally. Racialism by itself does not posit racial hierarchical value judgments about one race or another. It limits itself merely to distinguishing between races without attribution of negative or positive valuations. In this sense, racialism is not necessarily, certainly not always practically, pernicious and to be opposed automatically. Even Appiah, a great opponent of the concept of race acknowledges that "Racialism is not, in itself, a doctrine that must be dangerous." (A. K. Appiah, *In My Father's House: Africa in the Philosophy of Culture* [Oxford: Oxford University Press, 1992], 13.)
42. Sartre, "Black Orpheus," 326. Emphasis added.
43. Gordon, *Bad Faith*, 4.
44. Biko, *I Write What I Like* (1996), 5.
45. Ibid., 97.
46. Ibid., 25.
47. J. L. A. Garcia, "'Current Conceptions of Racism': A Critical Examination of Some Recent Social Philosophy," *Journal of Social Philosophy* 28, no. 2 (1997): 13.
48. Margaret Mead and James Baldwin, *A Rap on Race* (London: Michael Joseph, 1971), 21. Emphasis Added.
49. B. Langa, ed., *SASO on the Attack: An Introduction to the South African Student Organisation* (Durban, SA: SASO, 1973), 9.
50. William R. Jones, "The Legitimacy and Necessity of Black Philosophy: Some Preliminary. Considerations," *The Philosophical Forum* 9, nos. 2–3 (1977–1978): 53.
51. Biko, *I Write What I Like* (1996), 48.
52. Ibid., 25.
53. Ibid., 97.
54. For different kinds of separatists, see Howard McGary, "Racial Integration and Racial Separatism: Conceptual Clarifications," in Leonard Harris, ed., *Philosophy Born of Struggle* (Dubuque, IA: Kendall/Hunt, 1983).
55. Biko, *I Write What I Like* (1996), 90.
56. Ibid., 20.
57. Jean-Paul Sartre, *Portrait of the Anti-Semite*, trans. Erik de Mauny (London: Secker and Warburg, 1948), 46.
58. Gordon, *Bad Faith*, 153.
59. Biko, *I Write What I Like* (1996), 64.
60. Amiri Baraka and Moulana Karenga, quoted in Harris, *Philosophy Born of Struggle*, 202.
61. Biko, *I Write What I Like* (1996), 21.
62. Ibid.

63. Outlaw, *On Race and Philosophy*, 81.
64. Biko, *I Write What I Like* (1996), 24.
65. Ibid.
66. Gordon, *Existence in Black*, 124.
67. Biko, *I Write What I Like* (1996), 100.
68. Ibid., 101.
69. Gordon, *Bad Faith*, 6.
70. Jean-Paul Sartre, *Being and Nothingness: A Phenomenological Essay on Ontology* (New York: Philosophical Library, 1956).
71. Biko, *I Write What I Like* (1996), 28.
72. Ibid.
73. Ibid., 100.
74. Ibid., 131.
75. Fanon, *Black Skin, White Masks*, 147.
76. Biko, *I Write What I Like* (1996), 104.
77. Ibid., 23.
78. Ibid., 28.
79. Gordon, *Bad Faith*, 111.
80. Martin Heidegger, *Being and Time*, trans. John Macquarrie and Edward Robinson (Oxford: Blackwell, 1962), 317.
81. For interesting discussions of this attitude and events involving them see, for example, George Yancy, ed., *What White Looks Like: African-American Philosophers on the Whiteness Question* (New York: Routledge, 2004), especially the intro. and ch. 2 and 6; George Yancy, ed., *African-American Philosophers: 17 Conversations* (New York: Routledge, 1998); Charles W. Mills, *The Racial Contract* (Ithaca, NY: Cornell University Press, 1997); Charles W. Mills, *Blackness Invisible* (Ithaca, NY: Cornell University Press, 1998). On the marginalization of "race" as a legitimate philosophical concern see, for example, Jones, "The Legitimacy and Necessity," 149–160 or Outlaw, *On Race and Philosophy*.
82. Outlaw, *On Race and Philosophy*, 76.
83. Sartre, "Black Orpheus," 80.
84. Mills, *Blackness Invisible*, 9.
85. Biko, *I Write What I Like* (1996), 49.
86. Fanon, *Black Skin, White Masks*, 219.

2

Self-Consciousness as Force and Reason of Revolution in the Thought of Steve Biko

Lou Turner

We here recognize one of the laws of the psychology of colonization. In an initial phase, it is the action, the plans of the occupier that determine the centers of resistance around which a people's will to survive becomes organized.

It is the white man who creates the Negro. But it is the Negro who creates negritude.

(*Frantz Fanon,* A Dying Colonialism)

By Black consciousness I mean the cultural and political revival of an oppressed people. This must be related to the emancipation of the entire continent of Africa since the Second World War. Africa has experienced the death of white invincibility…

The call for Black consciousness is the most positive call to come from any group in the Black world for a long time. It is more than just a reactionary rejection of Whites by Blacks. The quintessence of it is the realization by the Blacks that, in order to feature well in this game of power politics, they have to use the concept of group power and to build a strong foundation for this. Being an historically, politically, socially and economically disinherited and dispossessed group, they have the strongest foundation from which to operate. The philosophy of Black consciousness, therefore, expresses group pride and the determination by the Blacks to rise and attain the envisaged self.

At the heart of this kind of thinking is the realization by the Blacks that the most potent weapon in the hands of the oppressor is the mind of the oppressed. Once the latter has been so effectively manipulated and controlled by the oppressor as to make the oppressed believe that he is a liability to the White man, then there will be nothing the oppressed can do that will really scare the powerful masters. Hence thinking along lines of Black consciousness makes the Black man see himself as a being, entire in himself, and not as an extension of a broom or additional leverage to some machine...

It is often claimed that the advocates of Black consciousness are hemming themselves into a closed world, choosing to weep on each other's shoulders and thereby cutting out useful dialogue with the rest of the world. Yet I feel that the Black people of the world, in choosing to reject the legacy of colonialism and white domination and to build around themselves their own values, standards and outlook to life, have at last established a solid base for meaningful cooperation amongst themselves in the larger battle of the Third World against the rich nations.

As Fanon put it, "the consciousness of the self is not the closing of the door to communication...National consciousness, which is not nationalism, is the only thing that will give us an international dimension..."[1]

(*Steve Biko, Quoted in Lou Turner and John Alan,*
Frantz Fanon, Soweto and American Black Thought *[1986]*)

Man's cognition not only reflects the objective world, but creates it.

(*V.I. Lenin,* Philosophic Notebooks on Hegel's Science of Logic)

Any narrative of the life and death of Steve Biko is replete with references to "section 6 of the Terrorism Act." From August to December 1976, Biko was held under the ubiquitous "Terrorism Act," and again, for the last time as it would turn out, he was detained from August to December 1977 under the "Terrorism Act." There is nothing hyperbolic about the white South African government's rhetoric of "Terrorism." Its underlying assumption is that any form of black protest to the racialized social order of apartheid is, in the Parsonian terms with which Edward Feit assesses insurgent revolt in South Africa, a form of disorder whether for purposes of reform or in order to make the system "ungovernable."

Protest has always walked in the shadow of massacre in South Africa. Order is the hegemon that made "terrorists" of nonviolent protestors and armed insurrectionaries alike. And because "order" exerts social as well as political hegemonic power over the mind of elites, black opposition to the apartheid racial order was, for white South Africans, tantamount to bombs growing out of black heads. That is why, today, the only difference between the rhetoric that castigates the criminogenic "pathologies" of South Africa's black working-class poor as terroristic and the rhetoric used to demonize the mass antiapartheid movement that called itself "Black Consciousness" is that a black elite has now been added to the chorus.

Today, of course, there is an epidemiological intersection of these rhetorics of terrorism with the biological terrorism of HIV/AIDS in South Africa. In the underpsyche of political elites charged with maintaining "order," each of these three forms of "terrorism" takes its turn as the rhetorical signifier for the others:

- Black political protests are viewed as symptoms of the supposed social pathology of the working-class poor;
- Disease pathology becomes a metaphor for the deep racial and class crisis of South African society;
- The HIV/AIDS epidemic is hypostasized as a tragic consequence of a social disorder that had its genesis in the political turmoil that made apartheid society ungovernable.

"Order," in Feit's positivistic view, "is the normal state of things and... disorder is very difficult to sustain."[2] In the calculus of social forces of the South African state, the state pursued the perfectibility of the social system, wherein prediction got privileged over spontaneity and the ungovernability sought by the insurgency through a sustained campaign of disorder. The so-called "normal state of things," attributed to order, is also supposed to be the state of things preferred by the people, even oppressed people. Presumably, because the urgency that people attribute to their mundane concerns "constitute[s] an obstacle for both government and insurgents, [t]he people, like the jungle, are neutral. They will side with whoever can best protect them. Protection means order. Disorder makes life difficult. Order is, therefore, the crucial issue."[3]

It is perhaps understandable that someone, in 1971, would write about the black struggle in South Africa in these terms, following a decadelong nadir of post-Sharpeville repression. By 1986, however, following a decade of continuous revolutionary struggle after the Soweto revolt, it became possible to write that "the unemployment consequences of disinvestment pressures are a price that blacks—having suffered so much already for so long—would be quite prepared to pay..."[4] It is not the contention then that "...the 'minds of the people'...are 'won' by the side that can maintain order"[5] that was demonstrated by nearly two decades of continuous black revolt in South Africa. On the contrary, the white apartheid government maintained a repressive order "without any hope of 'winning the minds' of the majority—the blacks—who are denied most political and many economic rights."[6]

It is here that the two terms—terrorism and mind—intersect to form the dialectic of Black Consciousness. To the white South African mind, Black Consciousness was a formation of domestic terrorism that could not be countenanced in any form, whether reformist or revolutionary, neither African National Congress (ANC) nonracialism, nor Pan Africanist Congress (PAC) black nationalism. White hysteria that the African community was, in its own land, the "internal enemy" of domestic order and tranquility represented a tacit acknowledgment of the right of the antiapartheid movement to totally reject white authority over black life and labor. The logic of white hysteria over "internal enemies" and "terrorism" was also tacit recognition of the nonviability of racial apartheid masquerading as racial pluralism.

Black Consciousness—The Negation of the Negation of Pluralism

What was distinctive about Black Consciousness, especially as espoused by Steve Biko, was its unabashed avowal of being a *philosophy* of liberation. The need for philosophy arose out of this dialectic of terrorism and mind: black South Africans, especially students, in deciding to think for themselves slipped the noose of white liberalism and became, in the eyes of their white friends and the apartheid state, "militants." "It seems sometimes that it is a crime for non-white students to think for themselves," observed Biko in his inaugural address as president of the South African Students Organization (SASO), December 1969. "The idea of everything being done for the blacks is an old one and all liberals take pride in it; but once the black students want to do things for themselves suddenly they are regarded as becoming 'militant.'"[7]

The apparent anomaly that Black Consciousness is nonracialist in its intent and purpose makes a philosophic, indeed a dialectical, approach to it necessary. The problem is, as Biko understood, a question of the "competence of pluralistic groups to examine without bias problems affecting one group especially if the unaffected group is from the oppressor camp."[8] Black Consciousness is a response to the violent contradictions of racial pluralism in a decidedly racist society. It is not that apartheid makes pluralism illusory, it is that apartheid confronts liberal pluralism with its totalitarian foundations. We may, in other words, be dealing with nothing more than Slavoj Žižek's contention that "Fascism, to take a worn-out example, is not an external opposite to democracy but has its roots in liberal democracy's own inner antagonisms."[9]

To this dialectical transformation into opposite, that is, of pluralism into apartheid or apartheid into liberal pluralism, Biko posed the transformation of Black Consciousness as nonracialist in intent and purpose. Consequently, when Biko states that the "time had come when blacks had to formulate their own thinking, unpolluted by ideas emanating from a group with lots at stake in the *status quo*,"[10] it does not merely announce the assumption of a black mind of one's own. It signifies that pluralism is but the first negation of the racist apartheid ethos and that Black Consciousness is the negation of that negation, insofar as it preserves the nonracialist moment posited by pluralism.

This is where Black Consciousness overcomes the limitations of the ANC's pluralism and the PAC's black nationalism; it is the transcendence uniting them both. The problem of integration was part of the policy formation of SASO: "We reject...integration as being based on standards predominantly set by white society. It is more of what the white man expects the black man to do than the other way around. We feel we do not have to prove ourselves to anybody."[11] Biko saw that there was nothing contradictory in blacks demanding freedom from racial restrictions at the same time refusing to renounce black politics; that is, it is by no means contrary to the political freedoms they demand to divide their social ontology into nonracial citizenship rights, while maintaining the particularity of their racial-historical individuality.[12] In Biko's view,

> ...a lot of time and strength is wasted in maintaining artificial and token nonracialism...—artificial not in the sense that it is natural to segregate but rather because even those involved in it have certain prejudices that they cannot get rid of and are therefore basically dishonest to themselves, to their black counterparts and to the community of black people who are called upon to have faith in such people.[13]

Oliver Cromwell Cox observes that pluralism, specifically legal pluralism, often involves the "urban privileges of special citizens."[14] In rethinking Horace Kallen's concept of "cultural pluralism" as "structural pluralism," wherein racial apartheid operates as a kind of estate system, Milton Gordon argues, "It is not possible for cultural pluralism to exist without the existence of separate subsocieties, but it's possible for separate subsocieties to exist without cultural pluralism."[15] Pluralism in these terms is indicative of a kind of liberal cosmopolitanism in which the ethnoracial segregation of urban areas and enclaves goes by the political fiction of pluralism, with or without the empowerment of subordinate racial or ethnic elites in the state.

A more materialist, though not necessarily a more Marxist, view than Cox's is offered by two Dutch theorists of social pluralism, John Furnivall and Julius Boeke. Furnivall and Boeke contend, *apropos* of our consideration of the capitalist development of South African apartheid society, that "pluralistic society derived from the disintegration of native cultures under the impact of capitalism."[16] In short, all colonial societies disintegrate under the impact of the forces of capitalist accumulation into systems of social pluralism. Furnivall and Boeke's concern is with European colonialism's impact on non-European peoples of the so-called "third world." In their view, the critical question concerns capitalist-imperialistic forces and organization, and the manner in which their disruption of native life and archaic self-sufficient rural formations express themselves in their most concentrated form in the development of *the city*. Whether in the colonial periphery or in the capitalist center, it is the process of concentration and centralization of capital "which brings pluralism into being."[17]

These processes of capitalist accumulation and urbanization of space (and time) are coextensive at times when questions of pluralism surface and express the ethnoracial crises of modernity and postmodernity. Disruption of the native economy fed the pluralism of the city, whether it was the rural production relations that maintained the authoritarian race relations of the Jim Crow U.S. South, or construction of the system of apartheid, originally in Namibia at the turn of the twentieth century, and later in post-World War II South Africa. The emphasis on capitalist accumulation in our consideration of pluralism has less, however, to do with the entrepreneurial impulses of subordinate group elites than with capitalism's critical need for the cheap, disposable labor of subordinate group working classes. So, although ethnoracial pluralism may exist, it nonetheless exists on the basis of the structural assimilation of subordinate racial groups into the functions of capitalist production (i.e., according to an ethnoracial division of labor).

Owing to this bifurcation, there is no common general will under pluralism. Social standards were not established for the national welfare but instead for the efficient exploitation of labor-power, whether nationally or globally. All questions of economic opportunity, social status, immigration, and racial and gender equity are "left to the play of economic forces."[18] Pluralism arises where *laissez faire* exempts capitalism from control by the general will. Although nationalism produces group solidarity under capitalism,[19] in international situations such as war and trade, it is just as likely that nationalism also produces counternationalisms in pluralistic societies, with one community set against another, in a kind of Hobbesian cultural war of all groups against each other.

Black Consciousness—"Movement from Practice Which Is Itself a Form of Theory"

All of this, of course, raises serious questions of theory and practice, as well as problems of comprehending the relationship between the material and the ideological. For instance, Gail Gerhart states that the PAC adopted Nkrumahism in the 1960s, and that SASO "began to actively shop for ideas in the black world outside of South Africa."[20] This neither does credit to the PAC or to the Black Consciousness Movement, nor does it catch the dialectic between ideas and social movements, wherein concepts are made concrete at any particular historical moment as they are indigenous to the objective-subjective conditions of the masses of people independent of the theoretical interests of intellectuals. This is precisely the duality inherent in what the late revolutionary philosopher Raya Dunayevskaya called theory as a movement from practice[21] versus theory as mere phenomenological description because it is separated from practice. The former leads to philosophy, whereas the latter leads to the organizational formalism of party intellectuals or to the state. The PAC, for instance, emerged out of the ANC Youth League at a time when South Africa underwent post-war industrialization that broke up old capitalist, mostly agrarian, production relations and brought tens of thousands of workers into urban industrial areas. The pan-Africanism that swept Africa in the same period gave a new impetus to the ideological strivings of the black working class; an impetus that was, given the historical context of previous stages of the black South African liberation movement, indigenous.

One is reminded of Nat Turner's response to his captors, following his 1831 slave insurrection in Southampton, Virginia, who charged him with also fomenting rebellion in neighboring territories: "Cannot you think that the same idea [freedom] prompted others as well as myself to this undertaking."[22] In short, the identity between the various articulations of pan-Africanism that revolved around what Nkrumah called the "African personality" was an attempt by each to comprehend a notion of the African mind as a revolutionary response to Western colonialism.

The point that escapes so many historians and social theorists of black liberation movements, like black South Africa's, is that the freedom of the black mind could not have arisen on so hollow an abstraction as "western democracy" or "pluralism." Black mind had of necessity to have a very different actuality for its freedom. The only freedom black South Africans had for the expression of their minds was resistance, rebellion, and revolution. Historically, black resistance, rebellion, and revolution confronted the racialized violence of South African society as the very force of reason that white South Africa's masquerade of ethnoracial pluralism monopolized as its moral ideal, but that it was woefully incapable of making real. It is according to this dialectic that reason, resistance, and revolution form the historical material life of the black South African mind.

Steve Biko's reference to "[m]aterial want...coupled with spiritual poverty"[23] is no mere "man does not live by bread alone" homily. It accounts for the phenomenological, no less than material, deprivation of black folk. Biko explains that at the output end of the machine of white supremacy "a kind of black man who is man only in form"[24] is produced. Biko's characterization of white supremacy as a "machine," taken in conjunction with the Hegelian notion of the state as machine, suggests that white domination never appears without a state apparatus. The further suggestion, on the other hand, is that states are machines that produce men and women in something other than a human form. It is the form itself that apartheid dehumanizes. The racism of this state machine involves a productive process of dehumanization of black people. Black men and women as products of this machine are men and women in form only.

That Biko views this in historical terms, inasmuch as he contends that "Black people under the Smuts government were oppressed but they were still men [and women],"[25] raises the question: What were the prevailing historical conditions at the time of his dire diagnosis of black humanity in South Africa, in the early 1970s? The anomaly is that Biko posits his dread assessment of "defeated people" in South Africa during the heyday of the worldwide revolutionary upsurges of the late 1960s–early 1970s, especially among peoples of color. The historical conditions in South Africa then *appeared* to be anything but revolutionary. Instead, the material laws of historical development prevailed. As Frantz Fanon noted, in his 1956 speech before the First Congress of Negro Writers and Artists, in Paris:

> Progressively... the evolution of techniques of production..., the increasingly necessary existence of collaborators, impose a new attitude upon the [occupier]. The complexity of the means of production, the evolution of economic relations inevitably involving the evolution of ideologies, unbalance the system. Vulgar racism in its biological form corresponds to the period of crude exploitation of man's arms and legs. The perfecting of the means of production inevitably brings about the camouflage of the techniques by which man is exploited, hence of the forms of racism.[26]

The decadelong post-Sharpeville nadir, that left a whole generation of "defeated people" in its wake, corresponds to such a period in the development of South Africa's capitalist production relations. As Frantz Fanon concluded at the beginning of the 1960s of third world revolutions:

> Each generation must, out of relative obscurity, discover its mission, fulfill it, or betray it... It needed more than one native to say 'We've had enough'; more than one peasant rising crushed, more than one demonstration put down before we could today hold our own, certain of our victory. As for us who have decided to break the back of colonialism, our historic mission is to sanction all revolts, all desperate actions, all those abortive attempts drowned in rivers of blood.[27]

Black Consciousness issues from the nadir of the black South African liberation struggle, not from the surge of a revolutionary perfect storm. The logic of white domination did not only produce the empty shell of black humanity that Biko diagnoses, that is, a phenomenology of black alienation, it is also discernible in its arrogant, self-confident, security grown large on its defeat of the black liberation movement at the beginning of the 1960s, led by the ANC and the PAC. Black Consciousness *as a movement* set in motion a new logic that seemed to come out of nowhere, its dialectic unbalancing the state machine. In fact, the logic of the previous decade of racial and political repression formed the historical conditions for a new dialectic of liberation to emerge. "It becomes more necessary," Biko writes, "to see th[is] truth as it is if you realize that the only vehicle for change are these people who have lost their personality."[28] This is Biko's epistemological turn—his new way of knowing black humanity and its phenomenological condition. What, however, makes this a dialectical moment, that is, what makes it a dialectic of liberation, is its self-reflexive character. "This is what we mean by an inward-looking process. This is the definition of 'Black Consciousness.'"[29] In other words, the very theory of analysis of the black phenomenological condition equally involves a synthetic "inward-looking" moment that transcends the former (analytical moment) in order to achieve a new form of self-consciousness and a new, "true humanity."

Throughout his "Frank Talk" articles, particularly "Black Souls in White Skins" and "We Blacks," Biko makes liberal use of Frantz Fanon's phenomenological treatment of black alienation, but concretized for the specific conditions and terrain of post-Sharpeville apartheid society. It is interesting, here, that Biko contends that the Indian community is well along the path of cultural decolonization, both in terms of reclaiming its past from colonial incursion and in reasserting Indian cultural communality. He, furthermore, contends that Black Theology (BT) is the form that spiritual recovery of black people from spiritual poverty will take. BT, however, has only an instrumental use here, in that "the bible," Biko believes, "must continually be shown to have something to say to the black man to keep him going in his long journey towards realization of the self."[30] It is, in other words, not Christianity but the "long journey towards realization of the self" that is essential.

Black Consciousness—A Revolutionary Journey toward Realization of the Self

What we wrote in 1978, during the revolutionary maelstrom in South Africa sparked by the 1976 Soweto rebellion, was that "Steve Biko brought forth the re-discovery of self-consciousness as an objective force within the process of liberation."[31] The 1968 high point of the '60s was already a decade past when, in collaboration with the Marxist-Hegelian philosopher Raya Dunayevskaya, John Alan and I saw in South Africa's Black Consciousness Movement and the revolutionary activities of students, workers, and women a powerful concretization of Dunayevskaya's dialectical-historical concept that ours is an epoch in which revolutionary movements from practice are themselves a form of theory. So open to the multilinear pathways to revolution in our age was Dunayevskaya that the theorist that we saw reflected in the Black Consciousness Movement was not so much Marx as Fanon. Moreover, the philosophical ground that we discovered in Biko's thought was of a Frantz Fanon, an original thinker and world revolutionary, breaking with Marxian orthodoxy on the one category of the Hegelian dialectic that even the most anti-Hegelian Marxist was willing to acknowledge Marx's debt to Hegel, namely, the famous Lordship and Bondage or Master-Slave dialectic in Hegel's *Phenomenology of Spirit*. We wrote then, less than two years into what was to become nearly two decades of continuous revolt:

> It is not accidental that Fanon's thoughts are relevant to the liberation struggles in South Africa, as manifested in the Black Consciousness movement. It was Fanon who had, in *Black Skin, White Masks*, both deepened the Hegelian concept of self-consciousness and in his sharp *critique* of "reciprocity," denied that there is any reciprocity when the relationship of Master and Slave has the additive of color. Quite the contrary. He made that the foundation of revolutionary action. In the dialectical relationship between the oppressed and the oppressor, the oppressed gains the idea of his or her own being—one's own self-consciousness—and the desire of being for self, and not for "other."
>
> Fanon's philosophy of revolution has the quality of actuality in the brutal life-and-death struggle between the Black masses of South Africa and the arrogant white ruling class that would, if they could, reduce Black humanity to a thing—an object among other objects.[32]

The contours of this category of self-consciousness were not fully visible thirty years ago, despite the uncompromising totality of Fanon's divergence from Hegelian dialectic to posit a Slave who instead of finding the source of his liberation in his labor turns from the object of labor toward an identification with the Master. What was crucial back then, in 1978, was that nonreciprocity in the dialectic of black self-consciousness made gaining a mind of one's own a revolutionary act. Then, we articulated the duality that Fanon posits in the dialectic of black self-consciousness, one in which historical conditions may just as well provide the basis for black self-consciousness to manifest a will to power that emulates the white master as manifest a liberatory will to freedom. The former, of course, is a more visible outcome of the dialectic of black self-consciousness in today's South Africa (and, it might be added, in the United States) than the latter.

What Fanon illumined was the logical consequence of race intervening in a dialectic of class consciousness: The self-consciousness that emerges from a struggle over lordship and bondage is driven back to the foundations of material desire whence the Ego arises. For Fanon, the black slave preempts Hegel's substantiation of the class consciousness of the master-slave dialectic. Fanon's black slave is not the slave of the lordship and bondage discourse found in Hegel's discussion of the dependence and independence of self-consciousness. Fanon's slave is instead one burdened by the double impasse of his own material desire to be like the master and the material instrumentality of his labor as the pathway out of the master-slave relationship. In other words, Fanon's racializing of Hegel's master-slave dialectic, by preempting the class moment inherent in Hegel's self-consciousness discourse, disclosed class differentiation *within* black self-consciousness.

Self-consciousness determines itself in relationship to an object, or in the case of white racialized consciousness, in relationship to an other that it makes an object for itself. This is a rational movement insofar as self-consciousness determines its relationship to its object vis-à-vis the formation of its *own* conception and certainty of the object. The dissolution that threatens consciousness on the threshold of its moment of experiencing the object, that is, consciousness's intuition that it is about to enter into an immediate relationship with its object, impels consciousness to make *certainty* itself its object. In Hegel's "Truth of Self-Certainty" discourse, which remains the foundation of Fanon's master-slave dialectic, certainty is the "simple unity or Ego" that both distinguishes the object/other, in terms that Fanon explores in the "fact of blackness" in *Black Skin, White Masks*, and abolishes such distinction. It is precisely here that Fanon locates the actuality of a dialectic of race.

The advantage that certainty provides to consciousness, over its more empirical relationship to objectivity, is that consciousness can make the object correspond to its conception of it. And insofar as certainty is nothing more than the sum total or unity of concepts that consciousness has formed of its object(s) from its (consciousness's) subjective understanding, certainty comes to know that not only its origin but its very process of relating *is* its self or ego. In the Ego's conception of blackness, the object/other's being-in-itself and being-for-another are one and the same, by virtue of the fact that their identity *is* the ego that posits it. This *fact* represents the bare subsistence of life and desire whence self-consciousness arises. Fanon's concept of other, that is, an otherness without reciprocity, instead of the otherness of another self-consciousness struggling for recognition, originates in this fact of blackness. Fanon's concept of otherness does not vitiate Hegel's. On the contrary, it accomplishes in the most powerful terms Hegel's contention that "Ego is the content of the relation and itself the process of relating. It is Ego itself which is opposed to an other and, at the same time, reaches out beyond this other, which other is all the same taken to be only itself."[33] The closed circuit of Fanon's master-slave dialectic means that even the barest human reciprocity has been subsumed by racial oppression. Fanon's point of departure is clear: On the one hand, he claims that "at the foundation of Hegelian dialectic there is an absolute reciprocity," on the other, he maintains however that "if I close the circuit, if I prevent the accomplishment of movement in two directions, I keep the other within himself. Ultimately, I deprive him even of his being-for-self."[34]

This, of course, is what Biko comprehends of the dialectic of racial domination in apartheid South Africa. It could not be otherwise, not only for a system of absolute racial separation and domination but at a time when that system of white supremacy had achieved absolute and total hegemony over black social, political, and cultural life, as the apartheid state had in the post-Sharpeville nadir. The sociopolitical consciousness of white South Africa literally replicates the moves of Hegel's self-consciousness discourse: White South African consciousness, at one and the same time, constituted an absolute distinction from blackness (*qua* otherness) and determined that such distinction per se has no being and hence was mere appearance. However—and this is the real point—the opposition of its appearance to its truth "finds its real essence... only in the truth—the unity of self-consciousness with itself."[35] No real black consciousness has any being before white self-consciousness, for this white consciousness is taken up with its conceptions and certainties, whether conservative or liberal, of blackness. The essential truth of self-consciousness, that is, of the identity of its various concepts and "certainty," is that it is patently incapable of reciprocity with black consciousness, simply because reciprocity exists only with an other held to have the selfsame desire for unity with itself. Black consciousness is apperceived as being without the being of such a desire and is instead held to be no more than the bare being of the unreflected natural world whence self-consciousness has reflected itself.

Arguably, Fanon was right to suppose that at the moment that self-consciousness constitutes itself, it also constitutes the "fact of blackness" as its other; an other that falls outside of any truly reciprocal relation with self-consciousness simply because it is self-consciousness that posits it. Locating the "fact of blackness" at this point, that is, prior to the struggle of self-consciousness for recognition and independence, intensifies the determination of black consciousness to gain a mind of its own, or, as Biko declared, "the determination by the Blacks to rise and attain the envisaged self."[36]

It is often the case that Fanon's critical appropriation of the Hegelian categories of self-consciousness is misconstrued, due in part to the willful ignoring of Fanon's critique of Sartre. This has constrained Fanon's notion of freedom within the undetermined categories of Sartrean existentialism, which bear an uncanny resemblance to the liberalism that Biko criticized for constraining black consciousness. Fanon's critique of the exteriority of freedom found in Sartrean existentialism resonates, profoundly, with Biko's critique of liberal pluralism. The existentialist attitude toward the "dependent self" was formulated in works such as *Being and Nothingness* and in *Anti-Semite and Jew*, works that had a profound influence on Fanon's thinking and on the question of the liberation of women in Simone de Beauvoir's *The Second Sex*. In each of these works the liberation of the "dependent self," that is, of Jewish consciousness and woman's consciousness, is made the task of the "independent other," namely, the Western white male.

Although Fanon's philosophic point of departure was similar, his recognition that such freedom is only conferred externally was not, as it was for Sartre and de Beauvoir, in order to declare it the resolution of the contradiction. Quite the contrary, he saw that "the dialectic that brings necessity into the foundation of my freedom drives me out of myself."[37] Far from accepting a so-called existentialist resolution of the contradiction of race, Fanon recognized existentialism as a pseudo-dialectic that merely resulted in a form of black alienation that necessitated a real revolution. That is why one sees, in the revolutionary thought of Steve Biko and the two decades of continuous Black Consciousness revolt in South Africa that more than anything brought an "end" to apartheid, Frantz Fanon's far-reaching prognosis for Africa:

> Africa will not be free through the mechanical development of material forces, but it is the hand of the African and his brain that will set into motion and implement the dialectics of the liberation of the continent.[38]

Notes

1. Such a long frontisquote to a chapter surely begs the indulgence of the reader. Although in an anthology devoted to the life and thought of Steve Biko, I might be forgiven such an indulgence. In fact, the purpose of so long a frontistext is not merely to hear Biko speak for himself, but to serve the discursive aim of providing at a single textual site a distillation of the philosophic ground of Biko's thought that will be examined in this chapter.
2. Edward Feit, *Urban Revolt in South Africa, 1960–1964: A Case Study* (Evanston, IL: Northwestern University Press, 1971), 73.
3. Ibid., 74.
4. Mark Orkin, *Disinvestment, the Struggle, and the Future: What Black South Africans Really Think* (Johannesburg: Ravan Press, 1986), 19.

5. Feit, *Urban Revolt*, 74.
6. Ibid.
7. Steve Biko, *Steve Biko—I Write What I Like*, ed. Aelred Stubbs (San Francisco, CA: Harper and Row, 1978), 4.
8. Ibid., 10.
9. Slavoj Žižek, *For They Know Not What They Do: Enjoyment as a Political Factor* (London: Verso, 1994), 180.
10. Biko, *Steve Biko*, 10.
11. Ibid., 13.
12. Lou Turner, "The Young Marx's Critique of Civil Society, and the Self-Limiting Emancipation of Black Folk: A Post–Los Angeles Reconstruction," *Humanity and Society* 19, no. 4 (1995): 91–107.
13. Biko, *Steve Biko*, 17.
14. Oliver Cromwell Cox, "The Question of Pluralism," in Herbert M. Hunter and Sameer Y. Abraham, eds., *Race, Class, and the World System: The Sociology of Oliver C. Cox* (New York: Monthly Review Press, 1987), 107.
15. Ibid., 108.
16. Cox, "The Question of Pluralism," 109.
17. Ibid., 110.
18. Ibid., 112.
19. Ibid.
20. Gail Gerhart, *Black Power in South Africa: The Evolution of an Ideology* (Berkeley, CA: University of California Press, 1979), 271.
21. Raya Dunayevskaya, *Philosophy and Revolution: From Hegel to Sartre and from Marx to Mao* (Atlantic Highlands, NJ: Humanities Press, 1982).
22. Nat Turner, cited in ibid.
23. Biko, *Steve Biko*, 28.
24. Ibid.
25. Ibid.
26. Frantz Fanon, *Toward the African Revolution (Political Essays)*, trans. Haakon Chevalier (New York: Grove Press, 1969), 35.
27. Frantz Fanon, *The Wretched of the Earth*, trans. Constance Farrington (New York: Grove Press, 1966), 167–68.
28. Biko, *Steve Biko*, 29.
29. Ibid.
30. Ibid., 31.
31. Lou Turner and John Alan, *Frantz Fanon, Soweto and American Black Thought* (Chicago: News and Letters, 1986), 23.
32. Ibid., 38.
33. G. W. F. Hegel, *Phenomenology of Mind*, trans. J. B. Baillie (London: Allen and Unwin, 1931), 219.
34. Frantz Fanon, *Black Skin, White Masks*, trans. Charles Lam Markmann (New York: Grove Press, 1967), 217.
35. Hegel, *Phenomenology of Mind*, 220.
36. Biko, quoted in Turner and Alan, *Frantz Fanon*, 21.
37. Fanon, *Black Skin, White Masks*, 135.
38. Fanon, *Toward the African Revolution*, 1973.

3

A Phenomenology of Biko's Black Consciousness

Lewis R. Gordon

Mabogo Samuel More (also known as Percy Mabogo More) has pointed out the philosophical importance of Steve Biko's thought in the areas of Africana existential philosophy, and social and political philosophy. In the latter, Biko's thought is distinguished by his critique of liberalism and his discussions of the political and epistemic conditions for black liberation. As for the former, much is offered from his readings of Hegel, Marx, Sartre, and Fanon, and Biko's own creative understanding of social identities formed by political practice, that is most acutely formulated in his theory of Black Consciousness. This gathering notion has generated discussion in terms of its existential dimensions in the work of Mabogo More and the resources of psychoanalysis and deconstruction in the writings of Rozena Maart. This short essay will add some thoughts on its phenomenological significance.

Why phenomenology? Phenomenology examines the formation of meaning as constituted by consciousness where the latter is relationally understood as always directed to a manifestation *of* something. That Black Consciousness refers to a form of *consciousness* already calls for a phenomenological analysis. Biko is explicit about its inclusiveness, that Black Consciousness is not premised upon biology or birth but social and political location. Under the brutal system of apartheid in South Africa, whole categories of people were positioned below those who counted most—namely, whites. That system generated lower layers of subhuman existence ranging from Asians and Coloureds to blacks. The Coloureds were designations for mixed offspring of Afrikaner (white South Africans of Dutch descent) and indigenous blacks. The racial schema made British and indigenous black offspring a problematic category. Among the Asians, the East Indian population was the largest, although Northeast Asians were also included below whites (except, at times, for the Japanese). As with American apartheid, Jews complicated the schema as they were generally seen as Eastern European and German Caucasian immigrants to the region. The South African Jewish story is complicated as there was also a group of descendants of Yemenite Jews who migrated there at least 1,000 years prior to the influx of Ashkenazi and small numbers of Sephardi during the last quarter of the nineteenth century. The work of Neil Roos has offered additional complications to the South African schema, since there were few white women (and in some communities none) among the Boers who eventually became the Afrikaners, which meant that the growth of their community had to be through sexual relationships with indigenous women. It is clear, argues Roos, that children who could "pass" made their way back into the Boer community and contributed to the line of contemporary whites, and those who could not assimilate fell into the world that became Coloureds.

Among Biko's contributions is a generation of political mythos that both offered a critique of racial formation through actively *constructing* an expanded and new conception of one of its categories. For him, East Indians, Coloureds, and indigenous blacks in South Africa all became *blacks*, a designation that reflected the reality of their political situation.

Biko's addition offers a politically situated understanding of consciousness that lends itself at first to a Hegelian-affected model of racial relations and a semiological and, ultimately, existential phenomenological model that suggests more than the Hegelian one. The Hegelian narrative, as articulated in his *Phenomenology of Spirit* and with some additional considerations in his *Philosophy of Right*, is familiar. The self is not a complete formation of itself but a dialectical unfolding of overcoming through which selves and correlated concepts of domination, bondage, and freedom emerge. The self, so to speak, is always struggling with its own fragmentation and incompleteness in relation to a world that resists it and through which other selves emerge through such struggles. A point of realization is the understanding that the self cannot be a self *by itself*. In transcendental terms, the only meaningful understanding of selfhood and freedom is that manifested in a world of others. The semiological addition points out that the relations of meaning accompany such an unfolding, which manifest a fragile balance at each point of identification. The matrix of such a system is often binary and it offers seductions in relation to each binary point. Consequently, much of the semiological discussion is about what happens between white and black, which everyone occupies always at a point short of an ideal. Hence, whiteness by itself is never white enough except in relation to its distance from blackness, which makes this domination also a form of dependency. Blackness is always too black except in relation to its distance from itself, which means that one is always too black in relation to white but never white enough. Coloured, Asian, and brown function as degrees of whiteness and blackness. The slipperiness of these categories means a system of unceasing conflict the subtext of which is a teleological whiteness. Biko's notion of Black Consciousness demands shifting such a telos. To aim at becoming black undermines the legitimacy of whiteness, but it does so with an additional consideration. Whiteness, in spite of the historic and empirical reality of mixture (as pointed out by Roos and many other scholars in recent scholarship on white formation), works on a presumption of purity. Blackness, however, is a broad category that includes, as is the case in the New World from the Americas to North America—a mixture. Consequently, Biko was able to work with a range of peoples under the rubric of blackness that ironically includes some of those listed under old racial designations as "white." The old racial designations supported absolute interpretations of such identities, but Biko argued for their permeability.

As a semiological notion, Black Consciousness is thus fluid. It becomes a term that can be understood as an identity of most people. It also brings under critical reflection the question of the formation of whiteness—there was not always, for instance, a Europe. That geopolitical notion emerged from the process that succeeded the expulsion of the Moors from the Iberian Peninsula in 1492 in the name of Christendom. The consequent unfolding of a political anthropology of hierarchical racial formation brought along with it the transformation of what was, in reality, the western peninsula of Asia into "Europe" as literally the home of white people, of Europeans. (I will leave aside the current political dynamics in the formation of a European Union in the face of the multiraciality of nearly all of these countries.) The Hegelian challenge returns here through the fragility of these relations by virtue of their dependence on dialectics of struggle for recognition. There was no reason for Christendom to have considered itself white nor for Moorish Islam to have considered itself black, except for the unique consequences that led to the formation of Europe as the place of whites and Africa as the place of blacks. The Hegelian model affirms their mutual role in the formation of their modern identity. This point could be illustrated through the etymology of the word "race." The term has immediate roots in the French by way of the Italian word *razza*, which in turn suggests origins in Spain or Portugal through the term *raza*, which, according to Sebastian de Covarrubias in 1611, referred to "the caste of purebred horses, which are marked by a brand so that they can be recognized...Raza in lineages is meant negatively, as in having some raza of Moor or Jew."[1] Yet, if we consider that Spain and Portugal were under

Moorish (Afro-Arabic) rule for 800 years, a continued etymology suggests the Arabic word *ra's*, which is related to the Hebrew and Amharic words *rosh* and *ras*—head, beginning, or origin. One could push this history/genealogy further and go to the Coptic or to the ancient Egyptian/Kamitan considerations in the word *Ra*, as in the god Amon-Ra, which refers to the sun and, at times, the King of all gods or located in the origin stories of the gods. In short, the theme of origins, beginnings, and the rising sun, even when connected to animals such as horses and dogs, suggests the following narrative. The Moors introduced *ra's* into the Iberian Peninsula (Andalusia) to articulate origins and to differentiate even themselves from the Christian Germanic peoples (Visigoths) they conquered and colonized. By 1492, the by then hybrid (Germanic-Afro-Latin-Arabic) peoples who pushed out the Moors (mostly Afro-Arabic, but by this point probably Afro-Arabic-Latin-Germanic) in the name of Christendom, used the term that by then became *raz* and eventually *razza* to designate the foreign darker peoples within a theologically oriented naturalistic episteme who, in a holy war, were pushed further southward back to the continent of Africa and into (as they imagined it) the Atlantic Ocean and the New World. Although both uses of the word and its mutation refer to foreigners, the indexical point is what has shifted in the transition from the Middle Ages to the Modern World. Where *ra's* may have once meant "I" and "we" who are from elsewhere, it became "they" who are not from here and who exemplified a deviation from a theological order in which being Christian located one in a normative and natural relationship with God. The discursive shift into what is often referred to as the "other" took shape. We see here the compatibility with the Hegelian model, since the term emerged, through struggle, to the effect of a mutual formation. But, as we will see, its slope was a slippery one, so its movement went beyond the threshold of "self" and "other."

At this point, a connection between Biko and Frantz Fanon might prove useful. In his critique of Hegel and the question of recognition, Fanon argued in *Black Skin, White Masks*, which he elaborated further in *The Wretched of the Earth*, that antiblack racism structures blacks outside of the dialectics of recognition and the ethical struggle of self and other. In effect, the semiological structure of oppositions pushes the poles to a continued extreme in racist situations. The result is a struggle *to enter* ethico-political relations, ironically to establish the self both as "self" and "other." The not-self-and-not-other is characterized by Fanon as "the zone of nonbeing" in his early work, and in his final one, it simply means to be the damned of the earth. For our purposes, this racialized schema below the Hegelian model, when mastery/Lordship and enslavement/bondsman have been issued as overcoming, demands an approach that addresses contradictions that are not of a dialectical kind. The call for Black *Consciousness* already demands addressing a "lived reality," as Fanon would say, a meaning-constituting point of view, that requires acknowledging, although at the same time structured, as lacking a point of view. In effect, it is the point of view from that which is not a point of view. The consequence is the retort: At least the other is an other. To become such initiates ethical relations.

To arrive at such a conclusion, additional phenomenological considerations are needed. One must not only take into account the lived-reality of consciousness, but also how reflection itself already situates a relationship with contingent forces in a dialectics of freedom. Put differently, the self is posed as the self through the realization of others, which means that a social framework for selfhood is that upon which even identity (an effort to recognize the self) relies. Linked to all this is the communicative dimension of every process of recognition. At the basic level of conscious life, which we share with other animals, this communication is primarily signification for activities at the level of signs, but the human being also lives at the level of meaning wrought with ambiguity, as Ernst Cassirer and Maurice Merleau-Ponty have argued. This other level is governed by symbols more than signs, of meanings more than signification. At this level, which is a fundamentally social level, the organization of meaning does not only affect life but also construct new forms of life. Fanon characterized this phenomenon as sociogenesis. Biko explored in more detail its *political* dimensions.

Political phenomena are those governed by discursive opposition. To understand this, one should think about the etymological roots of politics in the *polis* or ancient city-state. Although the term is Greek in origin, the activity is much older. Walls to protect them surrounded ancient cities. This encirclement established a relationship between those within and those without, and in each instance different governing norms emerged. The relation to without is primarily one of war; this relationship within would dissolve the city, since it would be a civil war. It is not possible for people within the city to live without disagreement, however, which means that opposition, short of war (between states), is needed. The shift to the discursive, recognized in ancient times through to the present as "speech," initiated or produced new forms of relations, identities, and ways of life that became known as politics. The question asked by Fanon and Biko (and most modern revolutionaries, but especially so by African ones and their Diaspora) is the role of politics in the context of political formation. In other words, what should one do when the place of discursive opposition has been barred to some people? What should those who live in the city but are structurally outside of it do if they do not accept their place of being insiders who have been pushed outside? Their questions pose the possibility of politics for the sake of establishing political life. It is an activity that is paradoxical. They must do politics in order to establish politics, where politics is recognized according to norms that will always respond to them as illegitimate—as violent—by attempting to change what is already recognized as the discursive limits. Put differently, one group wants to claim benevolence to those whom they dominate, and the other must seize its freedom. Echoing Frederick Douglass, Biko writes:

> We must learn to accept that no group, however benevolent, can ever hand power to the vanquished on a plate. We must accept that the limits of tyrants are prescribed by the endurance of those whom they oppress… The system concedes nothing without demand, for it formulates its very method of operation on the basis that the ignorant will learn to know, the child will grow into an adult and therefore demands will begin to be made. It gears itself to resist demands in whatever way it sees fit. When you refuse to make these demands and choose to come to a round table to beg for your deliverance, you are asking for the contempt of those who have power over you.[2]

We see here, then, a conflict not simply between politics (in the city) and the nonpolitical (beyond the walls of the city), but also about the very notion of politics itself. There are those within the city who are structured as though outside of it, which means the city has to explain why discursive opposition with certain inhabitants is not the continuation of politics instead of the feared attack on social order. Biko's pseudonym "Frank Talk" situated this opposition in apartheid South Africa: Why was the response to him, as the embodiment of speech, the brutal assertion of the state? His assassination was not simply one of a man but also an effort to suppress an activity and an idea, of political entities outside of the narrow framework of those defined by the state in terms with more political consequences than political activities. In other words, the apartheid state was not only a war on people of color, it was also a war on politics.

Biko understood this. His genius included rendering politics *black*. By fusing the apartheid state's opposition to blacks with its opposition to politics, he was able to pose a genuinely revolutionary question of social transformation. The question of *citizenship* instead of rule, as Mahmood Mamdani has formulated for the opposition, became a question, as well, that interrogated white legitimacy *in political terms*. I stress political terms here because of the bankruptcy the antiapartheid groups found in the assertion of *ethical* terms. Recall that the ethical already presupposed the self/other dialectic. Biko's (and Fanon's) challenge was to show that much had to have been in place for ethics to be the dominating factor. To assert the ethical, consequently had the effect of presupposing the inherent justice of the political situation when it was circumstance itself that was being brought into question. The political conflict with ethics in this sense, then, is the reality that colonialism has left us with a situation that requires political intervention for ethical life. In Biko's words: "In time we shall be in a position to bestow upon South Africa the greatest gift possible—a more human face."[3] What Biko also showed, however, is that such a structure and encomium render politics black.

Black Consciousness is thus identical with political life, and those who are willing to take on the risk of politics in a context where a state has waged war on politics are, as their opposition mounts, blackened by such a process. As a political concept, this makes the potential range of Black Consciousness wide enough to mean the collapse of the antidemocratic state. The moving symbol of this was the expansion of that consciousness in apartheid South Africa and its spilling over into the international community with the consequence of a response that required more than the question of inclusion instead of the construction of *a different state*. The new state, as Fanon would no doubt argue, now faces *its* political struggles, and, as scholars such as Ashwin Desai, Richard Pithouse, and Nigel Gibson have shown, *the poors* have emerged as a new dimension of that struggle in the postapartheid government's effort to put the brakes on democratic expansion; a move from possible socialism and de facto liberalism to neoliberalism has brought with it renewed tension between citizenship and rule.

I would like to, at this point, explore further in phenomenological terms the significance of the gift of "a more human face." The phenomenological dimensions of politics are that discursive opposition requires communication, that in turn requires intersubjectivity. There is, thus, a social dimension of political life, and much of the oppression has been an effort to bar social life and hence political life to certain groups of people. Phenomenology also demands that one examines consciousness as a lived, embodied reality, not as a floating abstraction. What this means is that consciousness must always be considered as indexical and in the flesh. Speech should not, from this perspective, be considered an expression of consciousness but instead as symbiotically related to the bodies by which, through which, and in which it is made manifest. In human beings, this phenomenon is manifested in our entire bodies, but it is most acutely so in our face and hands, our primary sites of signification, although the entire body is symbolic. It is no accident that oppression often takes the form of forcing its subjects downward, to look down, so their faces cannot be seen, and even where there is nothing they can do, their hands are often tied. In these instances, oppression is an effort to erase the face and eliminate the gesticulating capacity of hands; it is an effort to render a subject speechless. In antiblack societies, to be black is to be without a face. This is because only human beings (and presumed equals of human beings) have faces, and blacks, in such societies, are not fully human beings. By raising the question of Black Consciousness, Biko also raises the question of black *human beings*, which is considered a contradiction of terms in such societies. A conflict comes to the fore that is similar to the one on politics. Just as the state was shown to have been waging war on politics, and that politics was black, so, too, one finds a war against the human being, and in it one against humanity, in which looking at the human being in black face becomes crucial to looking at the human being *as a human being*. This requires transforming the relationship of I–it ("them blacks") to I–You (with blacks) in which an "us" and a "we" could be considered *from the point of view of blacks*. When "I" could see being "you," even when it is impossible for me to be identical with you, there is possibility of transparency even at the level of conflict. In effect, the movement is the ethical responsibility of a shared world.

The phenomenology of Black Consciousness suggests, then, that such a consciousness cannot properly function as a negative term of a prior positivity. Its link to the political is such that its opposition would have to be the chimera, appealed to in retreats to neutrality and blindness. Should we consider, for instance, the popular liberal model of cosmopolitanism? The conclusion will be that such claims hold subterranean endorsements of white normativity. This is because white consciousness is not properly a racial consciousness. It is that which does not require its relative term, which means, in effect, that it could simply assert itself, at least in political terms, as consciousness itself. The effect would be an affirmation of status quo conditions through an appeal to an ethics of the self: The cosmopolitanist fails to see, in other words, that politics is at work in the illusion of transcending particularity. To point this out to the cosmopolitanist would constitute an intrusion of the political in the dream world of ethical efficacy. It would mean to blacken the cosmopolitan world, or, in the suggestive language of Biko's critique, to render it conscious of political reality, to begin its path into Black Consciousness.

We are living in the period of postapartheid in South Africa. That is a good thing. What is unfortunate is that the prize has come along with an aggressive assertion at a global level of the kinds of liberalism Biko criticized in *I Write What I Like*. The path of this development has been a world situation in which the war on politics has also returned as forces of destruction have pushed regimes more to the right. As the right-wing in liberal democracies and theocratic states has ascended, the dissolution of civil liberties has been such that political life is in even greater jeopardy. In this global order, Biko's thought has come full circle, where even liberalism finds itself in increasing need of political solutions to political problems and therein faces the possibility of its own Black and hopefully far less naïve Consciousness. As the South African example reveals, neoliberalism has meant the construction of procedural structures that enable, as Mamdani has argued, the shining example of a deracialized state in the sullied interests of a radically unequal and more rigorously racist civil society. In spite of the gripe and anxieties over the black middle class and small exemplars of black wealth, which is still more an exception than a rule, in the new South Africa, the fact remains that white South Africans can now benefit from white supremacy without shame in the global arena. The structures that now more rigorously subordinate groups of South Africans in poverty ("the poors") present themselves in ways that at first seem to make Biko's appeal to a *black* consciousness problematic. Nevertheless, the blacks who now represent blackness in the South African government are clearly not based on Biko's political designation, but the old South African racial designations. But the fact remains that the liberalism they exemplify clearly also lacks the political understanding of Black Consciousness that he offered. In effect, they have taken the reins from the whites and have presented a more rigorous means of disarming the political voice of excluded populations.

Biko's critique of liberalism ultimately challenged appeals to blindness. If politics itself is what is at stake in the failure to address blackness, then there is the ironic conclusion that the contemporary South African state is also an antiblack one. The places for speech, for protest, avowed by the efforts of a liberal state in the African context, requires challenging claims of homogeneity in African societies and the reflexive appeals to a communitarian consciousness. In effect, it means that sites of opposition must be protected, but such communities are genealogically linked to Biko's formulation of blackness. In effect, the struggle of politics itself has returned. But at this moment, since it is an avowed liberal democracy in power, it now faces the contradictions of its claims. For its claims of transcending the pathologies of many of its neighbors rests on possessing what many of them lack. Some liberalization would be welcomed in central Africa, as Kwame Gyekye and Elias Bongmba have recently argued, but the contemporary South African situation is revealing that such an achievement, if wedded to *neo*liberal demands for state-level equality and a radically unequal, market-centered economy, brings liberalism in conflict with the political promise it was supposed to exemplify.

Biko did not consider Black Consciousness a fixed category. Whether as the poors or the blacks, the political itself now faces global challenges that reveal the continued significance of Biko's foresight on the dialectics of its appearance. Freedom continues to demand a face.

Notes

1. Sebastian de Covarrubias Orozsco, *Tesoro de la lengua* (1611), quoted in and translated by David Nirenberg, "Race and the Middle Ages: The Case of Spain and Its Jews," in *Rereading the Black Legend: The Discourses of Religious and Racial Difference in the Renaissance Empires*, eds. Margaret R. Greer, Walter D. Mignolo, and Maueen Quilligan (Chicago: University Of Chicago Press, 2007), p. 79.
2. Steve Bantu Biko, *I Write What I Like: Selected Writings*, ed. Aelred Stubbs (Chicago: University of Chicago Press, 2002), 91.
3. Ibid., 98.

Bibliography

Biko, Steve Bantu. 2002. *I Write What I Like: Selected Writings*, ed. with a personal memoir by Aelred Stubbs. Preface by Desmond Tutu. An intro. by Malusi and Thoko Mpumlwana. A new foreword by Lewis R. Gordon (Chicago, IL: University of Chicago Press).

Bongmba, Elias Kifon. 2006. *The Dialectics of Transformation in Africa* (New York: Palgrave Macmillan).

Comaroff, John L. and Jean Comaroff. 1997. *Of Revelation and Revolution*, vol. 2: *The Dialectics of Modernity on a South African Frontier*. Chicago, IL: University of Chicago Press).

———. 1991. *Of Revelation and Revolution*, vol. 1, *Christianity, Colonialism, and Consciousness in South Africa* (Chicago, IL: University of Chicago Press).

Desai, Ashwin. 2002. *We Are the Poors: Community Struggles in Post-Apartheid South Africa*. (New York: Monthly Review Press).

———. 2000. *South Africa: Still Revolting* (Johannesburg: Impact Africa Publishing).

———. 2000a. *The Poors of Chatsworth: Race, Class and Social Movements in Post-Apartheid South Africa* (Durban, SA; Madiba Publishers).

Dussel, Enrique. 2003. *Beyond Philosophy: Ethics, History, Marxism, and Liberation Theology*, trans. and ed. Eduardo Mendieta (Lanham, MD: Rowman and Littlefield).

———. 1995. *The Invention of the Americas: Eclipse of "the Other" and the Myth of Modernity*, trans. Michael D. Barber (New York: Continuum).

Fanon, Frantz. 1967. *Black Skin, White Masks*, trans. by Charles Lamm Markman (New York: Grove Press).

———. 1963. *The Wretched of the Earth*, trans. Constance Farrington. An intro. Jean-Paul Sartre (New York: Grove Press).

Gibson, Nigel, ed. 2005. *Challenging Hegemony: Social Movements and the Quest for a New Humanism in Post-Apartheid South Africa* (Trenton, NJ: Africa World Press).

———. 2003. *Fanon: The Postcolonial Imagination* (Cambridge, UK: Polity Press).

Gordon, Jane Anna. 2007. "The Gift of Double Consciousness: Some Obstacles to Grasping the Contributions of the Colonized," in *Postcolonialism and Political Theory*, ed. Nalini Persram (Lanham, MD: Lexington Books), 143–161.

Gordon, Lewis R. 2008. *An Introduction to Africana Philosophy* (Cambridge, MA: Cambridge University Press).

———. 2007. "Problematic People and Epistemic Decolonization: Toward the Postcolonial in Africana Political Thought," in *Postcolonialism and Political Theory*, ed. Nalini Persram (Lanham, MD: Lexington Books), 121–141.

———. 2000. *Existentia Africana: Understanding Africana Existential Thought* (New York: Routledge).
Gyekye, Kwame. 1997. *Tradition and Modernity, Philosophical Reflections on the African Experience* (New York and Oxford: Oxford University Press).
———. 1995/1987. *An Essay on African Philosophical Thought: The Akan Conceptual Scheme*, revised edition (Philadelphia, PA: Temple University Press).
Hegel, Georg Wilhelm Friederich. 1989. *Hegel's Science of Logic*, trans. A. V. Miller (Amherst, NY: Humanity/Prometheus Books).
———. 1979 [1807]. *Phenomenology of Spirit*, trans. A. V. Miller (Oxford: Oxford University Press).
———. 1967. *Philosophy of Right*, trans. with notes by T. M. Knox (Oxford: Clarendon).
———. 1956. *The Philosophy of History*, with prefaces by Charles Hegel. Trans. J. Sibree. A new intro. C. J. Friedrich (New York: Dover Publications).
Maart, Rozena. 1990. *Talk About It* (Ontario, Canada: Williams-Wallace Publishers).
———. 2004. *Rosa's District Six* (Toronto, Canada: Tsar Publications).
———. 2006. *The Politics of Consciousness, the Consciousness of Politics: When Black Consciousness Meets White Consciousness*, vol. 1, *The Interrogation of Writing* (Guelph, Canada: Awomandla Publishers).
———. 2006a. *The Politics of Consciousness, the Consciousness of Politics: When Black Consciousness Meets White Consciousness*, vol. 2, *The Research Settings, the Interrogation of Speech and Imagination* (Guelph, Canada: Awomandla Publishers).
Mamdani, Mahmood. 1996. *Citizen and Subject: Contemporary Africa and the Legacy of Late Colonialism* (Princeton, NJ: Princeton University Press).
More, Mabogo P. Samuel. 2004. "Philosophy in South Africa Under and After Apartheid," in *A Companion to African Philosophy*, ed. Wiredu (Malden, MA: Blackwell Publishers), 149–160.
———. 2004a. "Albert Luthuli, Steve Biko, and Nelson Mandela: The Philosophical Basis of their Thought and Practice," in *A Companion to African Philosophy*, ed. Wiredu (Malden, MA: Blackwell Publishers), 207–215.
———. 2004b. "Biko: Africana Existentialist Philosopher," *Alternation* 11, no. 1: 79–108.
Nirenberg, David. 2007. "Race and the Middle Ages: The Case of Spain and Its Jews," in *Rereading the Black legend: The Discourses of Religious and Racial Difference in the Renaissance Empires*, eds. Margaret R. Greer, Walter D. Mignolo, and Maueen Quilligan (Chicago: University Of Chicago Press, 2007), 71–87.
Pithouse, Richard. 2006. *Asinamali: University Struggles in Post-Apartheid South Africa* (Trenton, NJ: Africa World Press).
Robinson, Cedric, 2001. *An Anthropology of Marxism* (Aldershot, UK: Ashgate).
Roos, Neil. 2005. *Ordinary Springboks: White Servicemen and Social Justice in South Africa, 1939–1961* (Aldershot, UK: Ashgate).
Van Sertima, Ivan, ed. 1992. *Golden Age of the Moor* (New Brunswick, NJ: Transaction Publishers).

4

Biko and the Problematic of Presence

Frank B. Wilderson, III

Let us assume that black people receive the value of Absence. This mode of being becomes existence manqué—existence gone wrong. Their mode of being becomes the being of the NO.

(Lewis Gordon)[1]

The biggest mistake the black world ever made was to assume that whoever opposed apartheid was an ally.

(Steven Biko)[2]

Black Recognition?

When I first arrived in South Africa in 1989, I was a Marxist. Toward the end of 1996, two and half years after Nelson Mandela came to power, I left not knowing what I was. This is not to say that I, like so many repentant Marxists, had come around to what policy wonks and highly placed notables within the African National Congress (ANC) National Executive Committee (NEC) called for then, a so-called "mixed economy"; a phrase that explained less than nothing but was catchy and saturated with common sense, thus making it unassailable. No, I had not been converted to the "ethics" of the "free" market, but I was convinced the rubric of exploitation and alienation (or a grammar of suffering predicated on the intensification of work and the extraction of surplus value) was not up to the task of (a) describing the structure of the antagonism, (b) delineating a proper revolutionary subject, or (c) elaborating a trajectory of institutional iconoclasm comprehensive enough to start "the only thing in the world that's worth the effort of starting: the end of the world, by God!"[3]

In June 1992, not long after the massacre at Boipatong, Ronnie Kasrils cochaired a Tripartite Alliance Rolling Mass Action meeting with a Congress of South African Trade Unions (COSATU) central committee member and an ANC NEC member. They sat together at a long table on the stage in the basement auditorium of the Allied Bank Building in Johannesburg. One hundred delegates of the Tripartite Alliance had been sent there to plan a series of civil actions designed to paralyze the urban nerve centers of South African cities ("the Leipzig Option" as some called it). I was one of the delegates. Out of 100 people it seemed as though no more than 5 to 10 were White or Indian. There were a few Coloureds. One Black American—me; and eighty to ninety Black South Africans.

We began with songs that lasted so long, and were so loud, and so pointed in their message ("Chris Hani is our shield! Socialism is our shield! Kill the Farmer Kill the Boer!"), that by the time the meeting finally got underway one sensed a quiet tension in the faces of Kasrils and his cochairs. An expression I'd seen time and again since 1991 on the faces of Charterist notables; faces contorted by smiling teeth and knitted brow, solidarity and anxiety; faces pulled by opposing needs—the need to bring the state to heel and the need to manage the Blacks, and it was this need that was looking unmanageable.

Planning for a mass excursion was on the table: An armada of buses, filled with demonstrators, was to ride to the border of the "homeland" of the Ciskei, that was ruled by the notorious General Joshua Oupa Gqozo. We would disembark, hold a rally, then a march, then, at one moment in the march, we would crash through the fence, thus liberating the people of the "homeland" by the sheer volume of our presence. Kasrils and his cochairs looked at one another. Yes, things were indeed getting out of hand. As a round of singing and chanting ensued, they leaned their heads together and whispered.

Comrade Kasrils rises; he exits, stage right; he returns with a small piece of paper. An important intelligence report, comrades, news that should give us pause. Reading from the slip of paper, he says he has just received word that, were we to actually *pass* the motion on the floor to cross the Ciskei border en masse, to flood the "homeland" with out belligerent mass, General Joshua Oupa Gqozo would open fire on us with live ammunition. To Comrade Kasrils' horror the room erupts in cheers and applause. This, I am thinking, as I join the cheering and the singing, is not the response his "intelligence" was meant to elicit.

Had Comrade Kasrils been hoisted by his own petard or was there dissonance between the assumptive logic through which he and the Tripartite Alliance posed the question: What does it mean to suffer? and the way the question was posed by—or imposed upon—the mass of Black delegates? The divergence of our joy and what appeared to be his anxiety was expressed as divergent structures of feeling that I believe to be symptomatic of a contrast in conceptions of suffering and to be symptomatic of irreconcilable differences in how and where Blacks are positioned, ontologically, in relation to non-Blacks. In the last days of apartheid, we failed to imagine the fundamental difference between the worker and the Black. How we understand suffering and whether we locate its essence in economic exploitation or in anti-Blackness has a direct impact on how we imagine freedom; and on how we foment revolution.[4]

Perhaps the bullets that were promised us did not manifest within our psyches as lethal deterrents because they were manifested as gifts; rare gifts of recognition; gifts unbequeathed to Blackness; acknowledgment that we *did* form an ensemble of Human capacity instead of a collection of kaffirs or a bunch of niggers. We experienced a transcendent impossibility: A moment of Blackness-as-Presence in a world overdetermined by Blackness-as-Absence.

I am not saying that we welcomed the prophesy of our collective death. I am arguing that the threat of our collective death, a threat *in response to the gesture of our collective—our "living"—will*, made us *feel* as though we were alive, as though we possessed what in fact we could not possess, Human life, as opposed to Black life (which is always already "substitutively dead," "a fatal way of being alive")[5]—we could die because we lived. It was as though we had penetrated three layers of Absence in the libidinal economy; an economy that organizes the structure of reality in ways that were too often eschewed by South African Marxists, and Charterists more broadly, in favor of the "verifiable" data of political economy; an economy that in many respects was at the center of Steven Biko's meditations and the foundation of Black Consciousness. Like Steven Biko before him, Lewis Gordon, also a close reader of Frantz Fanon, reminds us of the serious pitfalls and "limitations [in] excluding the evasive aspects of affect from interpretation of reality."[6] Building on Lewis Gordon's ontological schema of Absence and Presence, that is a reconstruction and elaboration of Fanon's ontological arguments in *Black Skin, White Masks*, I designate three layers of Black Absence, *subjective, cartographic,* and *political,* through which we might read the cheering that erupted as affective (rather than discursive) symptoms of an ontological "discovery."

Absence of Subjective Presence

The world cannot accommodate a black(ened) relation at the level of bodies—subjectivity. Thus, Black "presence is a form of absence" for to see *a* Black is to see *the* Black, an ontological frieze that waits for a gaze, rather than a living ontology moving with agency in the field of vision. The Black's moment of recognition by the Other is always already "Blackness," upon which supplements are lavished—American, Caribbean, Xhosa, Zulu, etc. But the supplements are superfluous rather than substantive, they don't unblacken. As Gordon points out, "there is 'something' absent whenever blacks are present. The more *present* a black is, the more absent is this 'something.' And the more absent a black is, the more *present* is this something." Blackness, then, is the destruction of presence, for Blacks "seem to suck presence into themselves as a black hole, pretty much like the astrophysical phenomenon that bears that name."[7]

The inverse is even more devastating to contemplate vis-à-vis the dim prospects for Blacks in the world. For not only are Whites "prosthetic Gods," the embodiment of "full presence," that is, "when a white is absent *something* is absent," there is "a lacuna in being," as one would assume given the status of Blackness but Whiteness is also "the standpoint from which others are seen"; which is to say Whiteness is both full Presence *and* absolute perspectivity.[8]

> [T]o look at a black body is to look at a mere being-among-beings... [But] the white body, being human (Presence), doesn't live as a mere-being-among-beings. It lives with the potential to be a being that stands out from mere beings. Its being-in-itself ironically enables it to be a being-for-itself.[9]

Human value is an effect of recognition that is inextricably bound with vision. Human value is an effect of perspectivity. What does it mean, then, if perspectivity, as the strategy for value extraction and expression, is most *visionary* when it is White and most blind when it is Black? It means that "to be valued [is to] *receive* value outside of blackness."[10] Blacks, then, void of Presence, cannot embody value, and void of perspectivity, cannot bestow value. Blacks cannot *be*. *Their mode of being becomes the being of the NO.*

Absence of Cartographic Presence

In a passage richly suggestive of maps, Gordon writes, "The worlds of the black and the white become worlds separated by Absence leading to 'fate' on the one hand and Presence leading to 'freedom' on the other. Put differently, the former lives in a world of WHEN and the latter lives in a world of WHETHER."[11] Here the Absence of cartographic Presence resonates in the libidinal economy in the way Black "homeland" (in this case, the Ciskei) replicates the constituent deficiencies of Black "body" or "subject." The Black "homeland" is a fated place where fated Black bodies are domiciled. It is the nowhere of no one. But it is more—*or less*—for "homeland" cartography suffers from a double inscription. The "homeland" is an Absence of national Presence drawn on the Absence of continental Presence; a Black "nation" on a Black "continent"; nowhere to the power of two. Lamenting Africa's status as *terra nullius* in the Human psyche, Sartre wrote, "A great many countries have been present in their time at the heart of our concerns, but Africa...is only an absence, and this great hole in the map of the world lets us keep our conscience clean."[12] Just as the Black body is a corpus (or corpse) of fated WHEN (when will I be arrested, when will I be shunned, when will I be a threat), the Black "homeland," and the Black "continent" on which it sits, is a map of fated WHEN "battered down by tom-toms, cannibalism, intellectual deficiency, fetishism, racial defects, slave ships, and above all else, above all 'Sho good eatin.'"[13] From the terrestrial scale of cartography to the corporeal scale of the body, Blackness suffers through homologies of Absence.

Absence of Political Presence

The third manifestation of Black Absence that our ecstasy assailed, or perhaps simply *recognized*, that afternoon, was Black Absence from the political hegemony of the Charterist grammar of suffering; a grammar of suffering that ran from tepid—the ANC/UDF formulation in which the political subject is imagined to be dispossessed of citizenship and access to civil society, to lukewarm—the South African Communist Party's (SACP) formulation in which the political subject is imagined to be dispossessed of labor power. Neither formulation rises to the temperature of the Black's grammar of suffering. How, inside the Charterist Movement, would it have been possible to articulate a political line that was essential, as opposed to supplemental, to the suffering of Blacks; a grammar of suffering in which the subject is not simply dispossessed of labor power but is a sentient being dispossessed of being? The second question implied here is whether or not Steve Biko's presence on that stage, instead of Ronnie Kasrils and the Charterist generals, would have been sufficient to transpose our *felt* recognition of a Black grammar of suffering (Absence in a world of Presence) into discourse, and from there into a new political hegemony? Were the seeds of this articulation and transposition in Black Consciousness? If not, why not? And if so, why did they not take root? Such questions have great bearing upon our thinking about the political past, present, and future of South Africa, if for no other reason than the fact that the presence of Ronnie Kasrils (as the prototypical White, Charterist, radical) on stage that afternoon had been vouchsafed by the absence of Steve Biko from that stage and others like it.[14]

As we roared, toyi toyied, and sang, we had the feeling that we'd rent the three layers of Absence. It was exhilarating; a shattering of the WHEN of Black Absence; a breaking through to the WHETHER of Human Presence—recognition of ourselves as beings void of the inertia of objects; endowed at last with the force of subjects.

It was, I suspect, that burst of desire for recognition, and the shocking realization of what Blackness as Presence would *really* entail—the violence necessary to enact one moment of Black recognition—that gave comrade Kasrils pause. It would have given us pause as well had we *thought* it instead of *felt* it—had it been transposed from affect into discourse. For turning Absence into Presence is not the same as turning waged workers into free workers. The latter reorganizes the world; the former brings it to an end.

Unlike the delegates, Comrade Kasrils' answer to the question—What does it mean to suffer?—was predicated on economic exploitation and not on anti-Blackness. As a Marxist, Ronnie Kasrils could not imagine a fundamental difference between the worker and the Black. *Kasrils could think historically, politically, and economically, but not ontologically.* Or maybe he did know the difference, as we knew it, intuitively; and was compelled all the more to manage it.

It may seem sacrilegious to accuse White antiapartheid Charterists of anti-Blackness. People like Ronnie Kasrils, Derrick Honnekom, and Albie Sachs risked their lives and ostracization from their families and communities—they gave blood and spilt blood. To imbue them, or the structure of feeling through which they conducted their political life, with the same anti-Blackness that they fought against appears, at first blush, to impose upon them an injudicious form of double jeopardy. The record, however, indicates that anti-Blackness cannot be disentangled from the story of their political ascent.

After the 1976 Children's Revolution, the multiracial ANC absorbed thousands of young cadres who'd been politicized by Black Consciousness and who'd been driven out of the country. The Black Consciousness Movement had no organizational infrastructure outside of South Africa. In short, the ANC was the only viable home in exile. Although the ANC absorbed BC sympathizers into the camps, it simultaneously launched a successful campaign to "prevent any international financing of, and recognition for, BC activities."[15]

The marginalizing efforts of the ANC did not unfold in a vacuum. International aid agencies in the West and state sponsors in the Communist

Bloc (CB) had never been predisposed to aiding political and social uplift efforts that were in fee ideologically to Black psychic and political empowerment, first, and coalition politics, second. Western agencies that "were willing to fund the nationalist cause would balk at supporting a movement with...socialist sympathies." CB states that "might have supported radical political initiatives would not do the same for an organisation that emphasised the significance of colour."[16] And within South Africa, White intellectuals and organizations wielded hegemonic power resulting in an equally effective crowding out scenario of Black Consciousness. The hydraulics of state repression allowed for a situation whereby "the [White South African] progressives *came up*," according to a BCM activist at the time. "White organisations...are taking over black-initiated organisations. U.D.F. has whites and gets money from whites."[17] This is not a conspiracy theory, but an institutional analysis. As David Hirschmann explains, Left-leaning Whites in South Africa:

> ...have had a powerful influence in integrating class analysis and socialist strategies into the domestic South African anti-*apartheid* debate...at universities, research and support agencies, and in trade unions. [They] have also contributed to the development of the trade union movement which [became] a strong competing political force... [W]hites opposed to the Government have contributed in various ways—organisationally, financially, intellectually, and in terms of personnel and research—to strengthening the non-racial groupings opposed to the B.C.M.[18]

Within six years of the state's murder of Biko, the United Democratic Front (UDF) had "emerged...as the most popular internal South African opposition movement." By 1987 the UDF "had an annual budget of two million rands and over eighty full-time employees, with affiliated organizations estimated to be receiving approximately 200 million rands in the same year."[19]

In the late 1960s and early 1970s, White politicos had been radicalized by Black Consciousness' criticism of their liberal hypocrisy. But in the 1980s and 1990s they responded to this radicalization with sullen resentment of the "rejection" they had experienced at the hands of Black Consciousness— the movement that had radicalized them. Rather than explore—and surrender to—the assumptive logic behind their radicalization, and allow Blacks to continue to lead, even if it meant that they (Whites) would be sidelined politically for another ten or twenty years—or, follow Biko's demand that they work with and against Whites *right where they lived*—they instead attached themselves to trade unions such as COSATU, and to the UDF, and rode back into the center of political life on the wings of a "nonracial" class analysis.[20] They "had returned to...opposition politics with a sense of revenge and vengeance towards the B.C.M." and through "their access to financial resources and their influence over the media, academia, and publishing houses...they...succeeded in stifling the Movement..."[21]

Even if these White radicals had been persuaded by Biko and Black Consciousness that the essential nature of the antagonism was not capitalism but anti-Blackness (and no doubt some *had* been persuaded), *they could not have been persuaded to organize in a politically masochistic manner*; that is, against the concreteness of their own communities, their own families, and themselves, rather than against the abstraction of "the system"—the targetless nomenclature preferred by the UDF. Political masochism would indeed be ethical but would also bring them to the brink of the abyss of their own subjectivity. They would be embarking upon a political journey the trajectory of which would not simply hold out the promise of obliterating class relations and establishing an egalitarian socius (what less articulate and more starry-eyed White activists in the United States refer to as "vision"), but they would be embarking upon a journey whose trajectory Frantz Fanon called "the end of the world."[22] The "new" world that class-based political "vision" is predicated on (i.e., the dictatorship of the proletariat) isn't new in the sense that it ushers in an unimaginable episteme; it is really no more than a reorganization of Modernity's own instruments of knowledge. But a world without race, more precisely, a world without Blackness, is truly unimaginable. Such a world cannot be accomplished with a blueprint of what is to come on the other side. It *must* be undone because, as Biko, Fanon, and others have intimated, it is unethical, but it cannot be refashioned in the mind prior to its undoing. A political project such as this, whereby the only certainty is uncertainty and a loss of all of one's coordinates, is not the kind of political project Whites could be expected to meditate on, agitate for, theorize, or finance. And though it might not be the kind of project that Blacks would consciously support, it is the essence of the psychic and material *location* of where Blacks *are*. Caught between a shameful return to liberalism and a terrifying encounter with the abyss of Black "life"— caught, that is, between liberalism and death—some White activists took up the banner of socialism, others espoused a vague but vociferous anti-apartheidism, and most simply worked aimlessly yet tirelessly to fortify and extend the interlocutory life of "the ANC's long-standing policy of deferring consideration of working class interests...until after national liberation had been achieved."[23]

There was no respite from the crowding out scenario elaborated by disaffected White politicos and Charterist stalwarts on the Left, because the hydraulics of outright repression from the Right was just as debilitating. "[I]n the aftermath of the 1976 uprisings the South African Government proscribed BC organisations and persecuted their leaders—many were banned, imprisoned, and tortured, and some died while in detention," culminating in the brutal murder of Biko himself. Black Consciousness was caught in a pincer move between White power in what Gramsci designates as "political society," state coercion, and White power in civil society, benign hegemony of the Left, which culminated in its "removal from the scene, [and] facilitated, at least to some extent, the return to dominance of the A.N.C."[24]

It is not my intention to cathedralize the legacy of Steve Biko, nor the analytic framework of Black Consciousness. The archive is as replete with critical analysis of the BCM's penchant for attracting Black students at the expense of Black workers, its preference for self-help initiatives such as schools and clinics over political mobilization (a preference that can also be seen as a necessity given the swift and uncompromising response to mass mobilization on the part of the state) and its impoverished institutional analysis, as it is with examples of the hydraulics of White backlash. Nonetheless, in the basement of the Allied Bank Building when 100 delegates cheered at Ronnie Kasrils' news, an impromptu encounter was suddenly staged between Karl Marx and Frantz Fanon—an encounter that caught Kasrils and the leadership by surprise that afternoon in 1992. Perhaps, with a living Steve Biko and a longer shelf life for Black Consciousness, that encounter could have been more coherent and elaborated a more sustained debate between Marx's worker's paradise and Fanon's end of the world. But for this to happen, Black Consciousness would have also had to undergo adjustments in its assumptive logic. Adjustments that would have moved it away from its pragmatic interpretation of Fanon's dream of disalienation; adjustments that would have allowed it to comprehend those moments in Fanon's work when Fanon could not make the dispossession of the colonial subject jibe with the dispossession of the Black object or slave: Fanon's revelations (albeit often more symptomatic than declarative) that Black colony is an oxymoron, for Blacks are not, *essentially*, dispossessed of land or labor power, but dispossessed of being. The Black Consciousness Movement would have had to make adjustments that allowed it to embrace not just the hope of Fanon's psychoanalytic dream of disalienation, but the abject dereliction implied in Fanon's unflinching paradigmatic analysis.

Steve Biko and Black Consciousness were compelled to read *Black Skin, White Masks* pragmatically rather than theoretically; thus denying their analysis the most disturbing aspects of *Black Skin, White Masks* which lay in Fanon's capacity to explain Blackness as an antirelation; that is, as the impossible subjectivity of a sentient being who can have "no recognition in the eyes of" the Other.[25] (Fanon himself seems to stumble, accidentally, into much of his paradigmatic analysis.) Black Consciousness latches on to (fetishizes?) the very antithesis of Fanon's paradigmatic analysis and does so in the name of Fanon—or, more accurately, in the name of the Fanon it prefers the Fanon of disalienation, the Fanon who heals.

This theoretical slippage within Black Consciousness stems from the fact that although its structure of feeling attends to the abject dereliction that characterizes Black dispossession, *its actual discourse imagines Black dispossession through the rubric of decolonization*: this is to say, Black Consciousness *feels* the distinction between the postemancipation subject and the postcolonial subject, but it is unable (or unwilling) to *be elaborated by* the grammar of accumulation and fungibility, rather than the grammar of exploitation and alienation.[26] This slippage in Black Consciousness can be traced to both its selective and utilitarian reading of Fanon, as well as to the hydraulics of state terror, that were acutely draconian during the time of Steve Biko (making any form of reflection a miracle). It should be remembered that not only was it treasonous to call for an end to apartheid but it was also treasonous to call state terror "terror." Every enunciation had to function like a feint, a slight of hand, part call to arms, part allegory. That anything at all was said under such conditions is a testament to the will and courage of Biko and his comrades. I proceed, therefore, in full recognition that the power of understanding (analysis) is sometimes incompatible with the need to empower (struggle).

Like Marxism, Black Consciousness was also hobbled in an essential way. Fundamental to Marxism is the notion that the world is unethical due to its subsumption by relations of capital. What we learn from Fanon and others is that the world is unethical due to its subsumption by the slave relation. The slave relation, then, relegates the capital relation (the irreconcilability between the position of the worker and the position of the capitalist) to a conflict, and not the antagonism that Marx (and the South African Charterists) perceived it to be. The worker/capitalist relation can no longer be perceived as an antagonism because were it to be "solved" (were it to cease to exist as a relation, after the victory of the proletariat), the world would still be subsumed by the slave relation: an antagonism not between the position of the worker and that of the boss, but between the Human and the Black. One of the more lasting contributions of Orlando Patterson's *Slavery and Social Death* has been his thesis that work, or forced labor, is not a *constituent element* of slavery, but an incidental (though commonplace) *experience* of the slave. Patterson's corrective involves seeing slavery, first and foremost, as a *structuring relation* that constitutes the paradigm of human interaction. The slave overdetermines Human relationality because without the slave there would be no foundation for Human exchange. In other words, humanity can only occur at the place and in the time where the slave is not; but the slave, however, must be present (whether figuratively or literally) if humanity is to experience its time and place imbued with coherence. To properly define slavery, Patterson elaborates "three sets of constituent features corresponding to...three sets of power." First, naked might—what I refer to as gratuitous violence. This violence is akin to an ontological first moment—or a point of paradigmatic origin, in that, once inside the paradigm one feels (experiences) its timelessness and its boundless cartography. "This act of violence constitutes the prehistory of all stratified societies," Welskopf argued, "but it determines both 'the prehistory and (concurrent) history of slavery." The second element in the slave relation is natal alienation, "that aspect of [slavery] which rests on authority, on the control of symbolic instruments... [T]he definition of the slave, *however recruited*, as a socially dead person." Finally, Patterson points out, slaves are "dishonored in a generalized way... due to the origin of his status, the indignity and all-pervasiveness of his indebtedness, his absence of any independent social existence, but most of all because he was without power except through another."[27] The homologies between Patterson's slave and Gordon's Black, are striking; and they subtend two points fundamental to my argument: (1) that exploitation and alienation is not the essential rubric of suffering for a being who is a "being for the captor"—this rubric must be replaced by accumulation and fungibility; and (2) that it is impossible to disentangle both Blackness and Africanness from the constituent elements of slavery since their emergence and legibility are inextricably bound with the centuries old process through which subjects were turned into objects.[28]

In much of Biko's work, one finds a structure of feeling that *senses* this fundamental antagonism and seems to know, though without analytic rigor, that an analysis based primarily on resource dispossession is not underwritten by the Black's grammar of suffering. But the literature also exhibits a repeated disavowal of the paradigmatic analysis which would seem to be foundational to its structure of feeling: namely, that there can be no calibration between the Black and the Human without the world literally and figuratively coming to an end; that is say, without the destruction of all that makes relationality possible in Modernity. Put another way, Black Consciousness *knows intuitively* that the only way Humanity can maintain both its corporeal and libidinal integrity is through the various strategies through which Blackness is the abyss into which Humanness can never fall; but it *disavows this knowledge intellectually* in an attempt to entify that which cannot be entified.

I borrow the concept of entification from psychoanalysis in order to connote a process through which the analysand collapses the signifier with the signified and, in so doing, *fills up*, entifies the signifier and makes it appear to be identical with itself. Thus, the analysand is able to represent her/his subjectivity as an undivided, present, and unified self. Of course, the myth of a present and unified subject is deconstructed by both Marxism and psychoanalysis—and the analysand who persists in this delusional speech predicated on this collapse of the signifier and signified will suffer the neurosis of what Lacan calls "empty speech," the speech of entification, or egoic monumentalization, until s/he reaches the end of analysis wherein s/he accepts and learns to live with the inevitable chasm between her/his *being* and the symbolic strategies s/he uses to represent *being*.[29] Psychoanalysis must bring the analysand to the realization "that he is nothing, absolutely nothing—and that he must put an end to the narcissism on which he relies in order to imagine that he is different from the other 'animals.'"[30]

But entification would seem to be a precondition of a political project. There is a type-persona for whom a movement fights and there is corresponding loss that a movement seeks to regain for this type-persona. A movement cannot be built, let alone sustained, on behalf of "nothing, absolutely nothing"—a nonentity. What would the politics of a dead relation, a slave, look like? Again, a political movement must be built and sustained on behalf of *someone* who has lost *something*. Necessity may have required Black Consciousness to monumentalize the ego of a dead relation. "In the words of Barney Pityana [Biko's successor as SASO President], it was essential 'to pump life into his empty shell... to infuse him with pride and dignity.'"[31] Black Consciousness sought "to infuse the black community with a new-found pride in themselves, their efforts, their value systems, their culture, their religion and their outlook on life."[32] But for Black pride to become a tangible goal, something at the level of understanding had to be scuttled with respect to a paradigmatic analysis of Black positionality.

Will the "Real" Fanon Please Stand Up?

There are three Fanons, maybe more. There is the Fanon who heals the psyche, a psychoanalyst who disalienates his analysand. There is the Fanon who rebels against society, a revolutionary whose call to arms speaks of the cleansing properties of violence and the strategies through which social structures can be upended. Finally, there is the Fanon who explains the paradigm, by subordinating Marx's wage relation and Freud's Oedipal relation to the Human relation—a relation guaranteed by the slave. Neither of these three Fanons are neatly tucked away in separate volumes, nor do individual chapters compartmentalize them. The (sometimes conflicting) echoes of all three can be found in a single book, or woven disturbingly into a single sentence. The sign of the three Fanons in *Black Skin, White Masks* attends to three levels of subjectivity: *Preconscious interests, unconscious identifications,* and *structural positionality.*

The level of *preconscious interest* comprises those aspects of the divided subject that can be brought into speech; that the subject can enunciate about her/himself. The level of preconscious interests encounters contradictions (sometimes of crisis proportions) when it is confronted with the level of *unconscious identifications*, or desire. Positive affirmations of *interest* are often not in compliance with desire's affective destinations (i.e., I may *claim* to be Black but I may *want* unconsciously to be White). Unconscious identifications are never quite so tangible and resolute, nor can they be "known" at the moment of identification.

The level of unconscious identifications is where Frantz Fanon began his interventions. His attempts to root out a neurosis that yearns for "lactification" or, in clinical terms, "hallucinatory whitening," are at the heart of his quest for psychic disalienation.[33]

> If [my patient] is overwhelmed to such a degree by the wish to be white, it is because he lives in a society that makes his inferiority complex possible [and]... derives its stability from the perpetuation of this complex... [Thus] he will find himself thrust into a neurotic situation... As a psychoanalyst, I should help my patient to become *conscious* of his unconscious and abandon his attempts at a hallucinatory whitening...[34]

Like Fanon the healer, Biko also believed that "the first step in the process of disalienation and decolonization is the eradication of Western values... [which] make it difficult for blacks to reverse their position of subservience and dependency."[35] "At the heart of this kind of thinking," Biko wrote, "is the realisation by blacks that the most potent weapon in the hands of the oppressor is the mind of the oppressed."[36]

Finally, *Black Skin, White Masks* is attentive to the subject's *structural positionality*. This is the level of subjectivity that bears most essentially on political ontology. It is the level of subjectivity that most profoundly exceeds and anticipates the subject. It literally positions him/her paradigmatically. For example, one is born pregendered, which is to say a place, a position, boy or girl, son or daughter, literally *waits for* (anticipates) one, and *envelopes* (exceeds) one upon arrival. As one evolves, one can "challenge" one's position within this filial, gendered, and often Oedipal paradigm.[37] That is to say, one can be positioned as a boy and claim effeminacy (assert "identity" at the level of preconscious interests); or one can unconsciously desire effeminacy, but one cannot dismantle the filial economy through which one is always already positioned as boy or girl.

The economic paradigm (political economy), which also exceeds and anticipates (positions) the subject, according to Marx and his political heirs, is even more intransigent than the filial paradigm. Leopoldina Fortunati argues that there is no exchange of filial affection (i.e., the nurturing of children by parents, the nurturing of parents by children, or sexual encounters between parents) that is not in service to the reproduction of labor power and therefore to the valorization of capital.[38] In light of this, she argues that in order to destroy relations of capital and not simply democratize networks of distribution (à la the ANC's early Reconstruction and Development Program and subsequent "initiatives" by the Government of National Unity), community itself must be subverted and destroyed, that means the destruction of filiation, as it is currently constituted.

But Fanon reveals a structural relation that is more comprehensive, more devastating, more essential, and therefore more unethical than either the filial relation or the capital relation—namely, the Human relation. The filial relation is unethical because it is overdetermined by the Name of the Father and because it is parasitic on the position known as female. It subsumes the world in asymmetrical power relations predicated on gender. The capital relation is unethical because it is parasitic on the worker's labor power. It subsumes the world in asymmetrical power relations predicated on class.

At a glance, it would appear as if Fanon's meditations coalesce around the following postulate: The Human relation is unethical because it relegates Blacks to the lowest rung of Humanity; and because it subsumes the world in asymmetrical power relations predicated on race. In point of fact, Fanon's revelations are more severe than that. Race is a vertical distribution of values *within* Humanity. But a Black is a sentient being positioned below, or beyond, Humanity's distribution of values. The Black/Human dyad is essential to the Human relation(s), or to relationality as an ensemble of capacities (i.e. Gordon's perspectivity) through which one knows one is among the living. For without the Black, Human relationality would be illegible. Put the other way round, were the Black to become legible, that is acquire Human value (even low Human value), Humanity would expand into a shapeless, worthless, and incoherent mass. The unethical structure of political economy lies in the fact that its Other is the worker. The unethical structure of filiation lies in the fact that its Other is the woman. The unethical structure of Humanity lies in the fact that its Other is the Black. Fanon illustrates this in his famous rejoinders to Jean-Paul Sartre. Biko applauded the first rejoinder and elaborated it in the discourse of Black Consciousness.

Sartre attempts to applaud Negritude (and its poetic revival of Africanisms) with one hand, celebrating it as a powerful cry of anticolonial rage and with the other hand he condescends, suggesting that Negritude is no more than a minor term on the dialectic. The works of Fanon and Biko are united in their orientation toward Negritude, but only up to a point. Both agree that Negritude is an important tool for finding meaning and self-worth in an anti-Black world. But Biko seems to think of Negritude as being vital to the foundation of a disalienated Black identity. For Fanon, Black identity is a provisional, if not suspect, category whose points of reference are at turns unknowable and unattainable.

For Biko, Negritude (and cultural Pan-Africanism) had all the accoutrements of a discourse that can aid and abet the reconstitution of the Black's subjective integrity as well as "teach the Westerner a lesson or two."[39]

> Thus, in its entirety the African Culture spells us out as a people particularly close to nature. As [former Zambian President Kenneth] Kaunda puts it, our people may be unlettered and their physical horizons may be limited yet "they inhabit a larger world than the sophisticated Westerner who has magnified his physical senses through inverted gadgets at the price all too often of cutting out the dimension of the spiritual." This close proximity to Nature enables the emotional component in us to be so much richer in that it makes possible for us, without any apparent difficulty to feel for people and to easily identify with them in any emotional situation arising out of suffering.[40]

But for Fanon, these ideas run the risk of reversing racist stereotypes by celebrating them, or worse, reinforcing a delusion that Blacks were made to rule the world with their intuition.[41] He responds with sarcasm to the "Nature" Biko celebrates.

> I was told by a friend [that], "The presence of the Negroes beside the whites is in a way an insurance policy on humanness. When the whites feel that they have become too mechanized, they turn to the men of color and ask them for a little human sustenance." At last I had been recognized, I was no longer a zero.[42]

This split between Biko and Fanon vis-à-vis Negritude and the place of African culture in disalienation and political struggle, however, is not predicated on a difference regarding the truth claims of what is or is not Negritude or African culture; but on whether or not cultural empowerment can enable a comprehensive and sustainable liberation or a limited and provisional one. Fanon's skepticism, as regards the former, is based on the argument that no program of self-worth can bring the Black into Human recognition, upon which relationality is predicated.

Despite his key departure from Biko as regards Negritude (and African cultural revival), Fanon does not join the Marxist chorus that asserts that Negritude is a minor term on the dialectic. Fanon was incensed by Sartre's assertion that, as a moment of negativity in the Marxist-Hegelian dialectic, Negritude was no more than a predetermined stage in fee to the victory of the proletariat and to Negro political maturity, when "the subjective, existential, ethnic idea of *negritude* 'passes,' as Hegel puts it, into the objective, positive, exact idea of the proletariat."[43]

Forty years later, Sartre's assessment of Negritude was echoed in Left wing scholars' postmortem examinations of Black Consciousness, as exemplified in David Hirschmann's pronouncements:

> As the antithetical stage of the revolutionary dialectic the Black Consciousness Movement was bound to work for its own abolition...Once black people have engaged in revolutionary activity and erected the foundations of a new society, the Black Consciousness Movement will be superseded, since the clash between the polar opposites will have resulted in a new synthesis.[44]

Biko's response to such White Leftist assessment of Black Consciousness exhibits a stunning mutuality to Fanon's response to Sartre:

> They tell us that the situation is a class struggle rather than a racial one. Let them go to van Tonder in the Free State and tell him this...The *thesis, the antithesis* and the *synthesis* have been mentioned by some great philosophers as the cardinal points around which any social revolution revolves. For the *liberals*, the *thesis* is apartheid, the *anti-thesis* is non-racialism, but the *synthesis* is very feebly defined...The *thesis* is in fact a strong white racism and therefore, the *antithesis* to this must, *ipso facto*, be a strong solidarity amongst the blacks on whom this white racism seeks to prey.[45]

And Fanon's outrage at Sartre resulted in this famous rejoinder that was later recouped in the literature of Black Consciousness:

> [B]lack consciousness is immanent in its own eyes. I am not a potentiality of something, I am wholly what I am. I do not have to look for the universal. No probability has any place inside me. My Negro consciousness does not hold itself out as a lack. It *is*. It is its own follower.[46]

Here, Fanon and Biko's support for Black consciousness, and their disparagement of Sartre's strange rendering of Hegelian dialectics (his crude materialism), run along parallel lines.

But through Fanon's extended rejoinder to Sartre (in which he draws a sharp and controversial distinction between the grammar of Jewish suffering, as elaborated in Sartre's *Anti-Semite and Jew*, and the grammar of Black suffering) we witness Fanon's point of departure from Biko's assumptive logic. By now, Fanon's penultimate claim in his rejoinder is well known: "ontology—once it is finally admitted as leaving existence by the wayside—does not permit us to understand the being of the black man. For not only must the black man be black; but he must be black in relation to the white man."[47] Fanon is arguing that, though Blacks are indeed sentient beings, the structure of the world's entire semantic field—regardless of cultural and national discrepancies, that is, "leaving existence by the wayside"—in other words, the Modern episteme, is sutured by anti-Black solidarity. This is a dialectic of negativity, that offers no imaginable synthesis—not Sartre's dialectic through which the oppressed worker becomes the proletariat, nor Biko's dialectic through which the Black becomes a "man" [sic].

The importance of this for our meditation on Biko's Black Consciousness can be stated simply: empowerment predicated on Black Consciousness can only impact/liberate the Black at the level of preconscious interests and at the level of unconscious identifications; but not at the level of structural positionality. Psychic disalienation is therefore a problematic conception of emancipation in a world where anti-Blackness is a structural necessity and a paradigmatic constant. Black Consciousness cannot restore the Black to a world predicated on his/her absence. No matter what Blacks do (fight in the realm of preconscious interest or heal disalienation in the realm of unconscious desire), Blackness cannot attain relationality. Whereas Humans are positioned on the plane of *being* and, thus, are present, alive, through struggles of/for/through/over recognition, Blacks can neither attain nor contest the plane of recognition. That is to say "Black Human" remains an oxymoron regardless of political victories in the social order or the psychic health of the mind; not because of the intransigence of White racism, or the hobble of the talking cure in the face of hallucinatory whitening, but because were there to be a place and time for Blacks, cartography and temporality would be impossible.

"My *black consciousness* is immanent in its own eyes"; but my *Black being* "has no resistance in the eyes of the White man."[48] The first clause is a central tenet in the assumptive logic of Steve Biko's Black Consciousness. It speaks to the register of preconscious interests and, perhaps, unconscious identifications. But the second clause points to a partition between how the Black *imagines* him/herself (the interests of Black Consciousness and attempts to disalienate the psyche) and how the Black is *positioned* (as a dead entity in a paradigm of living entities). My Black consciousness may well be immanent in my eyes, but my eyes are not Human eyes, they are Black, unworldly, eyes. Thus, my gaze, a blackened gaze, cannot reposition me, cannot restore me to a paradigm whose coherence—that is the integrity of Humanity at every scale: the national, the civic, the domestic, the corporeal—is predicated on the production and reproduction of my nonbeing. I am not a weak cousin, or a stepchild within the paradigm; rather I have no claims to relationality writ large.[49] And my cry to the contrary, my Black consciousness or Negritude, does not restore me to relationality; it makes me crazy, or religious, or provisionally empowered. It is an unworldly claim upon the world—a leap of faith. Through it I may find a place in heaven (or in hell) but I remain unplaced here on earth.

Biko attempted to "rescue" the Black through the rubric of Human relationality. But Human relationality is defined in absolute opposition to Blackness. For the Black to become Human, relationality itself, as defined and constituted by the march of Modernity, would have to be destroyed. Herein lies the rupture between two of Biko's objectives, the goal to disalienate and mobilize Blacks for the seizure of state power (changes at the levels of desire and interest) and the goal to bring Blackness into Humanness (a structural destruction).

Conclusion

In this essay I have distanced myself from a romantic revision of Black Consciousness as a revolutionary panacea that would have saved the liberation movement from itself and thus averted the dreadful sellout of 1994: the terms of surrender referred to first, by Mandela, as Peace and Reconciliation; and then, by Mbeki, as the African Renaissance. Some would claim that if not for the murder of Steve Biko; if not for the Soviets' and the West's unwillingness to underwrite Black Consciousness; if not for the vengeful backlash unleashed by White radicals who'd been sidelined by Black Consciousness in the 1970s, the "New" South Africa would have emerged in 1994 with uncompromising strategies for the eradication of surplus value, market relations, *as well as* anti-Blackness. This argument could not be made convincingly, in my view. It is not a foregone conclusion that had Black, African Steve Bantu Biko been sitting onstage, chairing the Rolling Mass Action Committee meeting in 1992, instead of White, Jewish Ronnie Kasrils, the affective resonance between the leaders and the led would have been free of dissonance, or that a Black structure of feeling would have enunciated a Black grammar of suffering.

But I believe that had Biko lived, and had the Black Consciousness Movement survived as a credible alternative to the ANC and the UDF, the ethical imperatives of class analysis, that were hegemonic and unchallenged within the Charterist Movement, might have experienced a distended calculus through which the grammar of suffering could be debated rather than assumed.

Steve Biko and Black Consciousness were not victims of contradictions internal to the logic of their discourse, my critique not withstanding. Black Consciousness didn't peter out, it was drummed out. Biko wasn't a victim of his thinking he was a murder victim. And given the conditions under which Black Consciousness was elaborated—between the crosshairs and without sanctuary—it's remarkable that it survived for as long as it did and that its message was potent enough to spark the 1976 uprising, replenish the rank and file of the ANC, and stiffen the ANC's resolve to fight as it had never fought before.[50] An ANC that would betray the mandate it might never have resecured were it not for Biko and Black Consciousness.

Notes

Special thanks to Janet Neary and Anita Wilkins for their research assistance.

1. Lewis Gordon, *Bad Faith and Antiblack Racism* (Atlantic Highlands, NJ: Humanities Press, 1995), 98.
2. Steve Biko, *I Write What I Like* (London: The Bowerdean Press, 1978), 63.
3. Aimé Césaire quoted in Frantz Fanon, *Black Skin, White Masks* (New York: Grove Press, 1952 and 1967), 96.
4. To my knowledge the term anti-Blackness was first named, as a structural imperative, by Lewis Gordon in *Bad Faith*.
5. David Marriott, *On Black Men* (New York: Columbia University Press, 2000), 15 and 19.
6. Gordon, *Bad Faith*, 103.
7. Ibid., 99.
8. Ibid., 100.
9. Ibid., 101.
10. Ibid., 100.
11. Ibid., 101.
12. Ibid., 100.
13. Fanon, *Black Skin*, 112.
14. I explore this assertion in more detail below.
15. David Hirschmann, "The Black Consciousness Movement in South Africa," *The Journal of Modern African Studies* 28, no. 1 (1990): 16.
16. Kogila Moodley, "The Continued Impact of Black Consciousness in South Africa," *The Journal of Modern African Studies* 29, no. 2 (1991): 246–247.
17. Quoted in Hirschmann, "The Black Consciousness Movement," 19 (my emphasis).
18. Ibid., 18.
19. Anthony W. Marx, "Race, Nation, and Class Based Ideologies in Recent Opposition in South Africa," *Comparative Politics* 23, no. 3 (1991): 317 and 319.
20. Ibid.
21. Ibid., 19.
22. Fanon, *Black Skin*, 96.
23. Marx, "Race, Nation, and Class," 320.
24. Hirschmann, "The Black Consciousness Movement," 17.
25. Fanon, *Black Skin*, 110.
26. I am thankful to Jared Sexton and Saidiya Hartman for the nomenclature that helps to clarify theses distinctions.
27. Orlando Patterson, "The Constituent Elements of Slavery," in *Slavery and Social Death: A Comparative Study* (Cambridge, MA: Harvard University Press, 1982), 10.
28. See Saidiya V. Hartman, *Scenes of Subjection: Terror, Slavery, and Self-Making in Nineteenth-Century America* (New York: Oxford University Press, 1997); Hortense J. Spillers, "Mama's Baby Papa's Maybe: An American Grammar Book," in *Black, White, and in Color: Essays on American Literature and Culture* (Chicago, IL: University of

Chicago Press, 2003), 203–229; Achille Mbembe, *On the Postcolony* (Berkeley, CA: University of California Press, 2001).
29. See Kaja Silverman, *World Spectators* (Palo Alto, CA: Stanford University Press, 2000), 66.
30. Fanon, *Black Skin*, 22.
31. Quoted in Hirschmann, "The Black Consciousness Movement," 5.
32. Biko, *I Write What I Like*, 49.
33. For lactification and hallucinatory whitening, see Fanon, *Black Skin*, 47 and 100 respectively.
34. Ibid., 100.
35. Thomas Ranuga, "Frantz Fanon and Black Consciousness in Azania (South Africa)," *Phylon* 47, no. 3 (1986): 183.
36. Biko, *I Write What I Like*, 92.
37. Fanon did not view the Oedipus complex as constituent to the structure of Black suffering: "[A] black colonized family does not mirror the colonizing nation, neuroses arise not from within the kinship group but from contact with the (white) outside world." Deborah Wyrick, *Fanon for Beginners* (New York: Writers and Readers Publishers, 1998), 43; Fanon, *Black Skin*, 142.
38. Leopoldina Fortunati, *The Arcane of Reproduction: Housework, Prostitution, Labor and Capital* (New York: Autonomedia, 1992).
39. Biko, *I Write What I Like*, 30.
40. Ibid., 46.
41. For a graphic illustration of this, see the artwork in *Fanon for Beginners*, 39–40; Fanon, *Black Skin*, 126–127.
42. Fanon, *Black Skin*, 129.
43. Jean-Paul Sartre, *Orphée Noir*, preface to *Anthologie de la nouvelle poésie nègre et malgache* (Paris: Presses Univeritaires de France: 1948), xl, ff. Quoted in Fanon, *Black Skin*, 132–133.
44. Hirschmann, "The Black Consciousness Movement," 317–318.
45. Biko, *I Write What I Like*, 89–90.
46. Fanon, *Black Skin*, 135.
47. Ibid., 110.
48. Ibid., 135 and 110 (emphasis mine).
49. Patterson, *Slavery and Social Death*, 3–15.
50. "Between October 1976 and March 1978, the ANC launched 112 attacks within South Africa... This level of activity became possible only after June 1976, with the inflow to the ANC of [Black Consciousness] students fleeing South Africa." Marx, *Race, Nation, and Class*, 326.

5

May the Black God Stand Please!: Biko's Challenge to Religion

Tinyiko Sam Maluleke

At some stage one can foresee a situation where black people will feel they have nothing to live for and will shout out unto their God: "Thy will be done." Indeed His will shall be done but it will not appeal equally to all mortals for indeed we have different versions of his will. If the white God has been doing the talking all along, at some stage the black God will have to raise his voice and make Himself heard over and above the noises from His counterpart.

(Steve Biko)

The Biko Legacy

I am not old enough to have known Biko personally and to have understood him deeply during his lifetime. Nor was I geographically advantaged to have had even a distant kind of access to him. When Biko died in September 1977, I was only half his age and just beginning high school. His influence on my thinking has however been phenomenal. I therefore think that his legacy is as much mine as it is for others who feel compelled to appropriate it. The Biko legacy has, at times, been the subject of much contestation with some political parties and Biko's contemporaries at the center of the contestations. The establishment of a nonpartisan Steve Biko Foundation has, therefore, brought a breath of fresh air to this atmosphere and hopefully it will "free the Biko legacy" from unhealthy contestations. The Biko legacy is important for South Africa and for the world at large.

As an activist social theorist, Biko stands proudly and firmly in the traditions of Frantz Fanon, Martin Luther King, Jr., and Malcolm X. In the midst of fierce contestations about the Biko legacy—many of which were but an aspect of the struggle against apartheid—it is my view that his unique contributions both to social theory and to the ethics of political activism remain grossly underestimated.

From Soweto 1976

I was an enthusiastic but naïve participant in the Soweto 1976 uprising. The full political significance of the moment was not apparent to me then. I now know that the outbreak of the Soweto uprising must have been somehow connected to the fact that since 1969 Black Consciousness had made serious inroads into student thinking. The 1976 uprising also came "within a month of Biko's giving evidence in Pretoria"[1] and may indeed have been influenced by the utterances, stance, and impressive poise of Biko at the trial.

What was very clear to me then was that the shift from "mathematics" to "wiskunde," from "history" to "geskiedenis," and from "general science" to "algemene wetenskap" was painful, annoying, inconvenient, and most unacceptable. But for Soweto students 1977 was in many ways a worse year. Although there had been some schooling during 1976, 1977 was a year in which schooling was so much a stop-start situation that for long periods there was in fact no schooling. Schools became battlefields between the police and students. Through the year, we played cat and mouse games with the police. In my recollection, very few schools actually wrote exams at the end of that year—Lamola Jubilee Secondary in Meadowlands Zone Five, where I attended, certainly did not. Then later that year came the news—thanks to newspapers such as the *Rand Daily Mail* and *The World*—that Steve Biko had died in police custody.

Student anger reached new heights and many—especially the older ones (those doing standards eight, nine, and ten) started looking for ways to "skip" the country to join the liberation movements. Indeed some of us students in Soweto, especially the senior students, had heard bits and pieces about Biko and his trial; it was through his death that many of us "discovered" Steve Biko. In this way, to borrow Biko's own words, his "method of death [was] itself a politicising thing."[2] Another consequence of the news of Biko's death was that copies of his articles and essays became most sought after and would be passed from one student to another. We were both amazed and inspired by someone who, in that atmosphere of fear and intimidation, had decided to "talk frank(ly)" about the South

African situation. It was as if a whole new world was opening up to us. For the first time, liberation and freedom felt like attainable goals to our young and angry minds.

When rereading material on and by Biko in preparation for this chapter, I was struck by a number of things. First, just how young he was both when he died and when he bequeathed us—through his writings and his initiatives—testimonies of his great intellect and his great love for this country and its people. In terms of the South African youth commission definition of a youth (i.e., up to the age of thirty-five), Steve Biko died a youth. At twenty-five years of age, he was already a banned and a restricted man. But his legacy and contribution is that of grown man way above his chronological age. Indeed, the revolution Biko led was a revolution led by people in their early twenties, most of whom were banned and restricted by the time they were barely twenty-six. I consider this a great challenge to the youth of our times.

Second, at a time when "Black resistance was fragmenting,"[3] I was struck by the fact that Steve was essentially a college student leader who used student campus politics to leverage a national political agenda. Although Steve is said to have regarded the Soweto uprisings as a complete surprise, his leadership in particular and that of the South African Students Organization (SASO) in general, appears to have inspired a symbiotic and coherent relationship between college student politics and high school student politics.[4] This was a remarkable achievement at that time and remarkable that Black Theology (BT) was born, not through the pen or mind of a solitary academic, but a product of the selfsame college student politics; inspired by SASO and born within the University Christian Movement.

Thirdly, I was struck once again by the sharpness of Biko's mind, breadth of knowledge, clarity of thought, and simplicity of expression. He was also a very well-read man. To make the same point in a slightly different manner, SASO, the Black People's Convention (BPC), and their associate organizations were not only student or community organizations, they also had an accompanying intellectual thrust. In my estimation, in his leadership and thinking, Biko ranks alongside such postcolonial thinkers as Frantz Fanon, Edward Said, Sékou Touré, Nkrumah, and others.

Fourth, I was struck both by the brutal circumstances in which Steve died[5] as well as the absence of bitterness among those closest to him. The white policemen, in whose custody Steve was during his last days, were vicious and cruel—he was battered, kept isolated, and naked for more than three weeks. In that state, he was thrown onto the cold floor of a Landrover to be driven for eleven hours, only to be dumped and left for several hours on a cell floor in Pretoria.

Biko on Culture, Christianity, and Religion: The Challenges

Black but White-led

In February 1970, Steve Biko, in his capacity as SASO president, wrote a letter[6] to SRC presidents in which he makes several notable references to the University Christian Movement (UCM), an organization from which formal BT was to emerge. Biko calls the UCM "a religious group concerning itself with ecumenical topics and modernisation of archaic Christian religious practice."[7] He noted with delight the fact that the UCM—established in 1967—had a black majority within one year of its existence. However, Biko was cautious:

> We believe to a great extent that UCM has overcome the problems of adjustment to a two-tier society like ours. However, we still feel that the fact that the blacks are in the majority in the organisation has not been sufficiently evidenced in the direction of thought and in the leadership of the organisation. We nevertheless feel that the UCM's progress is commendable in the direction of provoking meaningful thinking amongst the clergymen and its members.[8]

The concern about black majorities in the church not turning into leadership majorities was also shared by Biko with black ministers at a conference in Edendale in a talk titled, "The Church as Seen by a Young Layman": "It is a known fact that barring the Afrikaans churches, most of the churches have 70, 80 or 90% of their membership within the black world. It is also a known fact that most of the churches have 70, 80, and 90% of controlling power in White hands."[9] It can be argued that in making this observation, Biko was diagnosing in the church and church organizations the same problem he had observed in the National Union of South African Students (NUSAS). The absence of black leadership, even in an organization where they formed a majority, was a generalized social problem. The latter caused him to walk out and form SASO. Biko was unflinching in his conviction that as long as black people looked for and accepted white leadership in all spheres, including religion, they were not yet ready to take their future in their own hands. This brought into question whether the so-called black churches were really black, It is in this context that we should understand Biko's observation—in the opening quote—that "the white God has been doing the talking all along" and that the time had come when "the black God will have to raise his voice and make Himself heard over and above the noises from His counterpart." It was indeed about much more than just black leadership. It was the very content and form that the Christian faith had taken in the Black community. Black churches were therefore white led in terms of their ethos, practice, and outlook.

"God is not in the Habit…"

To conclude his address to ministers of religion in Edendale, Biko quipped "I would like to remind the black ministry and indeed all black people that God is not in the habit of coming down from heaven to solve people's problems on earth."[10] Having inherited this adage in textual form, we are unable to conclude whether it was told in all seriousness or in jest. But it was not the first time that Biko had used this statement. It was also used in an adapted form in his essay titled "We Blacks" where it was linked with the white liberal "theory of gradualism" that was meant to keep "blacks confused and always hoping that God will step down from heaven to solve their problems." It seems, therefore, that this was an earnest concern of his. It is in fact rather pithy, apt, if also a stingy adage. In the context of the Edendale talk, it meant at least two things. First, that black people had to take the initiative if ever the church was to retain relevance for fellow blacks, especially young blacks; second, that God does not do theology, human beings do and that the time had come for "our own theologians to take up the cudgels of the fight by restoring a meaning and direction in the black man's understanding of God."[11]

Furthermore, Biko rejected the tendency of making theology "a specialist job." Indeed, in his introduction to the address at Edendale, Biko had presented three main aims to his talk, namely to provide a young person's perspective, a layman's perspective, and to make common the concept of religion. His approach therefore was to foreground the problems faced by South Africa in general, and by blacks in particular, and challenge church people to use the Bible and their faith to respond in a relevant way. If they did not do anything about it, they should give up any hope on God doing it on their behalf. This was a profound critique of certain forms of religiosity that seemed to encourage an attitude in terms of which God was expected to come and intervene on behalf of blacks.

What to do with the White Man's Religion: An Agenda for Liberation in Religion

Biko's basic problem with Christianity was not so much its given content as it was the refusal of those who peddled it to adapt it to local needs and conditions. Worse still, it was used as the very instrument of deculturization and colonization. He was therefore fearful that it was fast becoming irrelevant—especially for the young.

> Whereas Christianity had gone through rigorous cultural adaptation from ancient Judea through Rome, through London, through Brussels and Lisbon, somehow when it landed in the Cape, it was made to look fairly rigid. Christianity was made the central point of a culture which brought with it new styles of clothing, new customs, new forms of etiquette, new medical approaches, and perhaps new armaments. The people among whom Christianity was spread had to cast away their indigenous clothing, their customs, and their beliefs which were all described as pagan and barbaric.[12]

It is my view that in the essay titled "We Blacks," Biko outlines the most complete list of agenda items for a Black response to Christianity—the white man's religion in South Africa. Central to such a response was the creation of a Black Theology of Liberation. Firstly, he suggests that Africans converted and practicing Christianity should consider the BT proposition and—

i. "get rid of the rotten foundation which many missionaries created when they came";
ii. move away from focussing on "moral trivialities";
iii. revise destructive concepts of sin and stop making people find fault with themselves;
iv. try being true to Jesus' radical ministry;
v. try and resolve the situation in which while blacks sing *mea culpa* the whites are singing *tua culpa*;
vi. Deal with the contradiction of a "well-meaning God who allows people to suffer continuously under an obviously immoral system";
vii. "redefine the message of the Bible...to make it relevant to the struggling masses";
viii. revisit the biblical notion that all authority is divinely instituted;
ix. make the Bible relevant to black people to keep them going in their long journey to freedom;
x. deal with the spiritual poverty of black people;
xi. adapt Christianity to local culture;
xii. stop the use of Christianity as "the ideal religion for the maintenance of the subjugation of people."

Elsewhere he calls Christianity a "cold cruel religion" whose early proponents preached "a theology of the existence of hell, scaring our fathers and mothers with stories about burning in eternal flames and gnashing of teeth and grinding of bone. This cold cruel religion was strange to us but our forefathers were sufficiently scared of the unknown impending danger to believe that it was worth a try. Down went our cultural values!"[13] For a "layman," as Biko called himself, he had a thorough and incisive understanding of the challenges facing theology in the black churches. It is perhaps for this reason that Dwight Hopkins described Biko as "a theologian from and with the masses of black people. He never became bogged down with strict doctrinal or theological categories of thought or elaborated long-winded treatises. Quite the opposite...he involved himself in theological issues pertaining to the very life and death of his community."[14]

Locating our Praxis, Religious Studies and Theology in Africa

> To take part in the African revolution, it is not enough to write a revolutionary song, you must fashion the revolution with the people. In order to achieve real action you must yourself be a living part of Africa and of her thought; you must be an element of that popular energy which is entirely called forth for the freeing, the progress and the happiness of Africa. There is no place outside that fight for the artist or for the intellectual who is not himself concerned with, and completely at one with, the people in the great battle of Africa and of suffering humanity.[15]

Through his use of the work of Touré, Fanon, Malcolm X, and Kaunda, Biko wanted to locate his thinking and nourish his intellect in Africa. His notion of Blackness was therefore one that included Africanity and African culture. His idea of BT was therefore, quite amazingly, not totally exclusive of what has come to be known as African Theology today. This is how Biko defined African religiosity, pointing out the discords with Christianity, but always holding out the hope of a fusion in the process of making Christianity relevant to black people.

> ...We did not believe that religion could be featured as a separate part of our existence on earth. It was manifest in our daily lives...We would obviously find it artificial to create separate occasions for worship. Neither did we see it logical to have a particular building in which all worship would be conducted. We believed that God was always in communication with us and therefore merited attention everywhere and anywhere. It was the missionaries who confused our people with their new religion. By some strange logic they argued that theirs was a scientific religion and ours was

mere superstition... They further went on to preach a theology of the existence of hell, scaring our fathers and mothers with stories about burning in eternal flames and gnashing of teeth and grinding of bone. This cold cruel religion was strange to us but our forefathers were sufficiently scared of the unknown impending anger to believe that it was worth a try. Down went our cultural values! Yet it is difficult to kill the African heritage.[16]

This is a thorough and devastating critique of Christianity—a religion to which Africans turned in fear rather than joy! The contrast between African religion and missionary Christianity are painted in stark terms. It is a communal religion pitted against a "cold and cruel" religion. With these words, Biko sought to challenge black Christians to begin making Christianity relevant to the people—changing it from being a "cold and cruel" religion into a warm and communal religion. To this end, Biko remained firm in his belief that although the West may excel in military hardware and technology, "in the long run, the special contribution to the world by Africa will be in this field of human relationships... giving the world a more human face."[17] These harsh words should not make us think that Biko disregarded or underestimated religion. He believed in the significance of religion, including Christianity—hence his friendship with several priests. For him "all societies and indeed all individuals, ancient or modern, young or old, identify themselves with a particular religion and when none is existent they develop one."[18] He also believed that "no nation can win a battle without faith, and if our faith in our God is spoilt by our having to see Him through the eyes of the same people we are fighting against, then there obviously begins to be something wrong in that relationship."

The Black Theology Challenge

Biko's critique of the church, especially the black church, always included an invitation and a challenge to the construction of a Black Theology of Liberation. He saw BT as the only way to salvage Christianity for the black masses. Otherwise Christianity would remain an imposed religion whose role was the maintenance of subjugation—always making blacks feel like the "unwanted step children of God." Therefore, BT was seen as "a situational interpretation of Christianity [meant to restore] meaning and direction in the black man's understanding of God." He therefore advocated waging an intellectual and theological battle within Christianity because "too many are involved in religion for the blacks to ignore... the only path open for us now is to redefine the message of the Bible and to make it relevant." Central to making the Bible relevant was the reimagination and reinterpretation of Jesus as a "fighting God"—the beginnings of a search for a Black Christology. Such were Biko's feelings on this matter that though he did not provide a complete outline of BT, he drew tantalizing and passionate anecdotes of the sorts of problems such a theology would have to confront.

> ...One notes the appalling irrelevance of the interpretation given to the scriptures. In a country teeming with injustice and fanatically committed to the practice of oppression, intolerance and blatant cruelty because of racial bigotry; in a country where all black people are made to feel the unwanted stepchildren of a God whose presence they cannot feel; in a country where father and son, mother and daughter alike develop daily into neurotics through sheer inability to relate the present to the future because of a completely engulfing sense of destitution, the church further adds to their insecurity by its inward-directed definition of the concept of sin and its encouragement of the *mea culpa* attitude. Stern-faced ministers stand on pulpits every Sunday to heap loads of blame on black people in townships for their thieving, housebreaking, stabbing, murdering, adultery, etc...No one ever attempts to relate all these vices to poverty, unemployment, overcrowding, lack of schooling and migratory labour. No one wants to completely condone abhorrent behaviour, but it frequently is necessary for us to analyse situations a little bit deeper than the surface suggests.[19]

If earlier we quoted Biko dishing out a devastating critique of missionary Christianity, his censure here is directed at the practice of the black church. It is the "stern-faced" black ministers whom Biko fingers and it is the prevailing and "inward-directed" concept of sin that he faults. He challenges black preachers to engage in deeper analysis. BT is necessary in order to change this situation. Instead of church practice adding to the burdens of the black masses, the question was how to make the black church and its praxis more supportive of the harassed black masses. The challenge was one of developing a theology that would provide better analytical tools than those that were being used at that time. These, together with the list we have constructed in section 3, was the agenda that Biko put forward for BT.

Challenges and Conclusion

The wealth of theological insights in Biko's thought is—for a layman—breathtaking. It is remarkable that more than thirty years ago he framed a theological agenda that in all honesty we have yet to exhaust. Tribute must indeed be paid to those who took up the challenge—Sabelo Ntwasa,

Mokgethi Motlhabi, Nyameko Pityana, Mpho Ntoane, Buti Tlhagale, Itumeleng Mosala, Takatso Mofokeng, Simon Maimela, Bonganjalo Goba, Lebamang Sebidi, Shaun Govender, Manas Buthelezi, Gabriel Setiloane, Allan Boesak, and others. My contention is that none of the challenges I highlight above have expired. Work remains to be done in each of them. Above all, I want to suggest in conclusion that if Biko and his generation helped us with tools with which to understand the role of religion, the psyche and consciousness in a violent colonial situation we now need similar but new tools to analyze the role of religion in the postcolony called South Africa often misnamed a young democracy. A postcolony is still a colony. We find ourselves in a situation in which the colony continues even after the colonial period. We see this in the way in which women are regarded and dealt with. The violence in which we live is postcolonizing all of us, especially women and children. Similarly the scourge of poverty in a world that has more than enough for all is another sign of the continuation of the colony. We are now faced not merely with the scourge of HIV/AIDS but with devastating consequences of the interface between HIV/AIDS and gender, between HIV/AIDS and poverty. Issues of identity and self-esteem that Biko and his colleagues occupied themselves with have returned in the form of sexuality and sexual orientation debates of our times. Indeed, I want to suggest that the very fact that our young seem to be forgetting the likes of Biko is a symptom of the problems we do not even acknowledge to have. In the atmosphere we live in, religion runs a real risk of becoming opium both for the rich and the poor. Perhaps the challenges that Biko put before Black Christianity can and should be extended to all religions and to all of Christianity today. To what extent are our religions revitalizing and equipping people rather than chopping their spirits down with false promises and blame-the-victim strategies?

Notes

1. (Lindy Wilson, 1991, 55) Biko was being subpoenaed to give evidence in the SASO-BPC trial of thirteen (Cooper, Myeza, Lekota, Mokoape, Nkomo, Nefolovhodwe, Sedibe, Hare, Moodley, Variava, Cindi, Ismael, and Sivalingum Moodley) who were arrested and charged after the 1974 Durban rally to celebrate the FRELIMO victory in Mozambique.
2. Biko in Stubbs, 173.
3. Steve Biko, "Fragmentation of the Black Resistance" in Aelred Stubbs, ed., *I Write What I Like* (London: Heinemann, 1978), 36, f.
4. "High school students and township youth groups became involved in the movement as Black Consciousness spread outside universities. Their involvement resulted in the formation of the South African Student Movement (SASM) and the National Youth Organisation (NAYO...a direct outcome of leadership training campaign by

SASO and the Black Community Programmes (BCP))." (Mamphela Ramphele, "The Dynamics of Gender within Black Consciousness Organisations: A Personal View," in Barney Pityana, Mamphela Ramphele, Malusi Mpumlwana, and Lindy Wilson, eds., *Bounds of Possibility: The legacy of Steve Biko and Black Consciousness* (Cape Town, SA: David Philip, 1991), 215.
5. Pityana, *Bounds of Possibility*, 80. "On the night of 11 September Biko, evidently a seriously ill patient, was driven to Pretoria, naked and manacled to the floor of a Landrover. Eleven hours later, he was carried into the hospital at Pretoria Central Prison and left on the floor of a cell. Several hours later, he was given an intravenous drip by a newly qualified doctor who had no information about him other than that he was refusing to eat. Sometimes during the night of 12 September Steve Biko died, unattended."
6. Biko, "Letter to SRC Presidents," 10, f.
7. Ibid., 15.
8. Ibid., 15.
9. Ibid., 62.
10. Stubbs, 65.
11. Ibid.
12. Biko, 60.
13. Biko, 49.
14. Hopkins, 1991: 195.
15. Biko quoting Toure in Stubbs, 35.
16. Biko, 49.
17. Stubbs, 51.
18. Ibid., 60.
19. Ibid., 61.

Bibliography

Biko, Steve. 1978. *I Write What I Like* (Johannesburg, SA: Macmillan).
Dube, Musa W. 2000. *Postcolonial Feminist Interpretation of the Bible* (St Louis, MO: Chalice Press).
———. 1999. "Consuming a Colonial Cultural Bomb: Translating Badimo into Demons in Setswana Bible" (Matt 8: 28–34, 15: 22, 10: 8) *Journal for the Study of the New Testament*, no. 73: 33–59.
Fanon, Frantz. 1986. *Black Skins. White Masks*. (London: Pluto Press).
———. 1967. *The Wretched of the Earth* (London: Penguin).
Kritzinger J. N. J. 1988. "Black Theology—Challenge to Mission" (Ph.D. Thesis: UNISA).
Manganyi, N. C. 1973. *Being Black in the World* (Johannesburg, SA: Sprocas).
Maunier, Rene. 1949. *The Sociology of Colonies: An Introduction to the Study of Race Contact* (London: Routledge).
Mazrui, Ali. 1990. *Cultural Forces in World Politics* (London: James Curry).
Mbembe, Achille. 2001. *On the Postcolony* (Berkeley, CA: University of California Press).
Motlhabi, Mokgethi. 1988. *Challenge to Apartheid: Toward a Moral National Resistance* (Grand Rapids, MI: Eerdmans Publishing Company).
Mudimbe, Valentin. 1994. *The Idea of Africa* (London: James Curry).
———. 1988. *The Invention of Africa. Gnosis, Philosophy and the Order of Knowledge* (Bloomington, IN: Indiana University Press).

Pityana, Barney, Mamphela Ramphele, Malusi Mpumlwana, and Lindy Wilson, eds. 1991. *Bounds of Possibility: The Legacy of Steve Biko and Black Consciousness* (Cape Town, SA: David Philip).

Said, Edward. 1994. *Representations of the Intellectual* (New York: Pantheon).

———. 1993. *Culture and Imperialism* (New York: Alfred A. Knopf).

———. 1983. *The World, the Text and the Critic* (Cambridge, MA: Harvard University Press).

———. 1978. *Orientalism* (New York: Vintage Books).

Setiloane, Gabriel M. 1976. *Concept of God among the Sotho-Tswana* (Amsterdam: Balkema).

———. 1975. "I am an African," *Risk*, vol. 27: 128–131.

Thiong'o, Ngugi wa. 1993. *Moving the Center: The Struggle for Cultural Freedoms* (London: James Curry).

———. 1986. *Decolonising the mind: The Politics of Language in African Literature* (London: James Curry).

Part 2

Contested Histories and Intellectual Trajectories

6

Black Consciousness after Biko: The Dialectics of Liberation in South Africa, 1977–1987

Nigel C. Gibson

Introduction

> It so happens that the unpreparedness of the educated classes, the lack of practical links between them and the mass of people, their laziness, and, let it be said, their cowardice at the decisive moment of the struggle will give rise to tragic mishaps.
>
> *(Frantz Fanon, "The Pitfalls of National Consciousness")*

This article was written in 1988 as an attempt to understand what had happened to Black Consciousness (BC) as an ideological force ten years after Steve Biko's death. As a young anti-Stalinist, anti-apartheid activist in London in the late 1970s I had been energized by the June 16, 1976 Soweto revolt but disgusted by the mainstream anti-apartheid movement's dismissal of Black Consciousness. At the time I was impressed by an important pamphlet written by John Alan and Lou Turner, *Frantz Fanon, Soweto and American Black Thought*,[1] which articulated the importance of Fanon to Biko's thought and considered Black Consciousness a new stage of cognition. Like Biko, they considered the Soweto revolt as a concrete expression of that new stage and underscored the importance of revolutionary humanism in Biko's and Fanon's thought.[2]

I had been particularly taken with Fanon's understanding of race and class in his critique of Sartre's conception that negritude was a "minor term" in the dialectic. Fanon reacted to Sartre as if Sartre was another white leftist telling him to "grow up." But more seriously, it showed Sartre's failure to comprehend the dialectic of negativity. Black Consciousness, Fanon insisted, was not "a passing stage" but instead had to be understood as an absolute. In other words, Fanon's conception of the dialectic of consciousness was radically different than Sartre's and replaced Sartre's abstraction with the existential concrete of the lived experience of the Black. Rather than a synthetic movement, Fanon was arguing for a more radical dialectic of negativity and indeed, therefore, a more radical notion of consciousness and revolution. This idea, I argued, had an appeal to Biko and can be seen in the centrality he placed on the "mind of the oppressed" in his conception of liberation. Taking Biko's idea of the "mind of oppressed" further meant engaging in what Fanon saw as the major obstacle to Africa's liberation movements, "the lack of ideology." However, I argued, post Biko Black Consciousness activists did not take the issue of the "lack of ideology" seriously, instead they thought they could simply touch it up. Instead of grounding their engagement with Marx's Marxism, they embraced the crude materialism that went by the name of Marxism in South Africa. Today these same "Marxists" who had derided Black Consciousness for its lack of "class analysis" and who had advocated the economism of "scientific socialism," while dismissive of the moral economy of Black Communalism, have become enforcers of the new "authoritarian economism."[3]

It is shocking to reflect on how many founding leaders of Black Consciousness (as well as, of course, the UDF, COSATU, and the ANC) have "sold out" their principles for power, privilege and money. Barney Pityana had already left Black Consciousness by the early 1980s, but it was shocking to me that Saths Cooper, whom I met in Boston in the later 1980s and felt had a more sophisticated idea of praxis, seemed to abandon these ideas soon after.[4] Today these betrayals make even clearer the need to focus on the dialectic of ideas and objective conditions and on the relationship of intellectuals and mass movements—of cognition and material life—rather than the psychobiography of individual personalities. I think that the larger issue at stake in my analysis of Black Consciousness from 1977 to 1987, therefore, was the problematic of comprehending the degeneration of Black Consciousness not only as a betrayal of principle but in terms of the logic of that betrayal.

Today one can point to the objectivity of the logic as capital—indeed feel its stifling heavy weight—as part of the reason the ANC so quickly abandoned its promises and the principles of the Freedom Charter and the

Reconstruction and Development Programme (RDP). Out of state power, (even if we emphasize the objectivity of the destabilization created by the bannings of its organizations and leaders), it is more difficult to comprehend the logic behind Black Consciousness' degeneration. In other words, trace the internal logic of its objective demise.

When Fanon had designated Black Consciousness as an absolute rather than a "passing stage," he was thinking in terms of a dialectic of experience. It did not mean that BC was not itself susceptible to dialectical negativity. Just as Fanon understood the importance of "national consciousness," he also understood that it could also ossify. Fanon's description of the "end of the dialectic" as a "motionless equilibrium" was what appeared to be happening to the Black Consciousness Movement. By the late 1980s it too was becoming "motionless"—not that it wasn't an active organization without a mass following and not that it did not experience the violence of the state, Inkatha, and from elements of the UDF but that it did not deepen its own ideas philosophically. Politically the ANC became hegemonic but as a pragmatic, multitendency organization it was at best strategic and always limiting and limited in terms of ideas and discussion. It never, in other words, matched the philosophic potential of Black Consciousness. It was never interested in a radical humanistic program based on a lively and open discussion with black South Africans but remained a pragmatic amalgam of a leftist rhetoric which dismissed BC as petit bourgeois covering a pragmatist (petit bourgeois) nationalist leadership whose ideas were determined by the immediacy of strategy and control. A new movement like Black Consciousness, on the other hand, was of great philosophical-political consequence.

I understand the Hegelian-Marxian dialectic as a progressive movement but also one that doesn't discount retrogression. This is fundamentally important methodologically and challenges the popular conception of Hegelian dialectic as a progressive system of syntheses. For example, at the end of his monograph *Hegel: Phenomenology and System*, the American Hegel scholar H.S. Harris explains: "There is nothing in [Hegel's] logical theory to warrant the belief that the motion of consciousness must always be progressive... regression is just as possible as progress."[5]

The Marxist humanist Raya Dunayevskaya emphasized this point when she spoke of the difference between Hegel and Marx's conception of dialectical movement: "Where Hegel's Absolutes are always 'syntheses,' unities... Marx's are always diremptions—absolute, irreconcilable contradictions... Where Hegel's Absolutes are always high points, Marx's are always collapses."[6] Speaking of Hegel's three Attitudes to Objectivity in Hegel's Smaller Logic, she added: "Far from expressing a sequence of never-ending progression, the Hegelian dialectic lets retrogression appear as translucent as progression and indeed makes it very nearly inevitable if one ever tries to escape it by mere faith."[7]

This last point is suggestive for post-apartheid politics where "faith" in reified forms such as The Party, The Struggle, The Leader, The Nation, The Market, Law, Culture, and so on, takes the place of critical thought and conceals the true condition of men and women suffocating what Biko called their "quest for a true humanity." For Hegel, Marx and Fanon, the dialectic moves and there is no such thing as a "stasis." If a political organization does not face contradictions openly, if it does not engage in a battle of ideas, and if it does not develop ideas in relation to concrete social movements it retrogresses and degenerates. Indeed, Fanon warned us of the consequences of such retrogression in his critique of the nationalist middle class in *The Wretched of the Earth* and we continued to experience it.

Avoiding this retrogression necessitated developing an explicit humanist program in concert with ongoing discussions with the wretched of the earth whose actions had made the destruction of the old regime possible, according to Fanon. In "Black Consciousness, 1977–87," I understood one iteration as an engagement with Marxist humanism. I attempted to develop this idea in an essay called "Fanon's Humanism and the Second Independence in Africa," which was written in 1994, the year that the ANC gained power in South Africa:

> There is a parallel between Marx's and Fanon's humanism. For Marx, the dialectic of liberation meant that communism (not the stratification of property that he called vulgar communism, which "negates the personality of human beings"), as the total freeing of all the human senses and attributes, was not the "goal" but the necessary presupposition for "positive humanism beginning from itself." For Fanon, national consciousness, not nationalism, was the presupposition for a genuine internationalism and a new humanism.

By insisting that Black self-consciousness means that Blacks not view themselves as "an extension of a broom or additional leverage to some machine," Biko had approximated Marx's critique of alienated labor under capitalism that Marx explained reduces the worker to an appendage of the machine. In Biko's terms the measure of a post-apartheid society, as not the goal but the presupposition of a truly free and human society, had to be the degree to which this material and spiritual alienation had been transcended. Fanon had also developed a series of guidelines to judge the success of the anti-colonial movement. The following (also from the 1994 article quoted above) could quite easily be applied to South Africa as a further articulation of measure of its development "post-apartheid":

> Rather than worrying about the withdrawal of capital and "output in the post-independence society," Fanon writes, "it is a very concrete question of not dragging [people] toward mutilation, of not imposing upon the brain rhythms which very quickly obliterate and wreck it." That was Fanon's vision. Labor as self-activity and humanism as self development remain tightly connected...What kind of labor [people do] and how people work becomes the "form and body" of the postcolonial society. I think this emphasis remains valid, perhaps more so in an integrated world, as the only alternative to the freedom of the free market. Fanon's goal is not the reform of society nor the takeover of existing institutions but the avoidance of another system of exploitation.[8]

Nevertheless, in 1994 the narrow and neo-liberal transition from apartheid, which would guarantee "another system of exploitation,"[9] did not dampen the excitement of Mandela's election. Yet the speed of Mandela's abandonment of the most limited socio-economic goals of the anti-apartheid movement was still a shock to even those who saw it coming; the greater tragedy was the silencing of oppositional voices (often in the name of "the struggle" as Fanon predicted). For the ANC, all roads led to global neo-liberalism. There is no alternative, as Margaret Thatcher famously put it. Today, accumulation is still the name of the game and the voluntarism of this Plan is heralded by ex-radicals huckstering, as Fanon would put it, in the national game. In this context the rhetoric of "working for the good of the nation" has moved from tragedy to farce. The crude Marxist and white liberal have become disciplinary tools to help impose the "imperialist economism"[10] of neo-liberalism. How is it possible that apparently radically opposed attitudes find an affinity? Quite simply as class attitudes toward subjectivity. The radical leaders of nationalist parties and former white Marxists start playing politics with multinational capitalist powerbrokers and stop having a dialogue with the masses.[11] This became clear during the "transition" period when Mandela and the ANC sidelined the mass movements that had help bring them to the negotiation table. Yet rather than an issue of strategy, let me return to the issue of objectivity in as far as that objectivity is understood dialectically as "objective/subjective" (or perhaps as Gramsci put it "humanly objective" or "historically subjective").[12] In other words the difference between the subject as accumulation of capital and the Black as pacified and objectified object subjected to that accumulation (an extension of a broom without a mind of her own) and an active subjectivity (in mind and body) that has absorbed objectivity and thus is a historical protagonist intent on changing the world. It is historically subjectivity in as far as it is the creativity of the masses and of an idea whose time has come and not the subjectivism of any particular leader. Black Consciousness represented such an objective/subjective moment in 1976 and thus it was a new stage and as such a challenge to work out philosophically and organizationally the expression of that idea. Though this did not happen, in today's "self-limiting" politics defined by neo-liberal "realities" it shows another "reality"—what Fanon called "the absurd and impossible"[13]—the concreteness of apparently outrageous revolutionary principles and the concreteness of ideas of freedom.

* * *

Black Consciousness After Biko

> *In the colonies the economic substructure is also superstructure. The cause is the consequence; you are rich because you are white, you are white because you are rich... The native's challenge to the colonial world is not a rational confrontation of points of view. It is not a treatise on the universal, but an untidy affirmation of an original idea propounded as an absolute.*
>
> (*Frantz Fanon,* The Wretched of the Earth)

The February 1988 ban against all anti-apartheid organizations, including AZAPO (Azanian People's Organization), AZASM (Azanian Students Movement), and the trade unions, could mark the end of a second period in the history of the Black Consciousness Movement, the first period having ended with the death of Steve Biko and the banning of 17 Black Consciousness organizations in 1977. Little scholarly attention has been paid to the development of BC since 1977. Much has been written on its birth and growth as an idea in the 1970s, especially its relation to the Soweto revolt of 1976. But today it is generally considered completely overshadowed by the ANC and UDF, which now include many of its former adherents. Those whom John Brewer calls the "radical wing of Black Consciousness," COSAS (Congress of South African Students), AZASO (Azanian Students Organization), and PEBCO (Port Elizabeth Black Civic Organization), and others, have it is argued moved to a "class analysis'" and "joined the ANC camp."[14] This essay seeks to assess BC's development over the last ten years, with special reference to its relation to Marxism, since, as will be demonstrated, both Marxist slogans and some dialogue with Marxist concepts have played an increasing role in the movement in this period.

Black Consciousness was an important part of a new stage in the South African revolt in the 1970s. Emerging out of the very colleges the government had set up to control black students' minds, BC's founders recognized the importance of the mind of the oppressed.

At its inaugural conference at Turfloop in 1969 they redefined the word "black," to mean a new sense of unity and liberation of the oppressed and dropped the term "Non-White," which they viewed as a negation of their being.[15]

Over the last ten years BC has been a recognizable force and has obviously influenced the present situation. Most radicals, leaders of trade unions, and popular organizations, even if not adherents, have roots in BC and have a relationship to its concepts and prescriptions, because BC did raise questions and did present a new concept of liberation. However it will be argued that although BC was a new philosophic point of departure for the liberation movement, its philosophic development has remained in a preliminary stage. "It remains to be seen," Lebamang Sebidi writes, "whether it was a shift at the level of principles (ideology) or merely strategy and tactics."[16] I will argue that the continual attempts to "broaden" BC by incorporating Marxism into its ideology have been a failure not because the idea is wrong but because it has taken on board very doctrinaire and narrow concepts of "scientific socialism" that go by the name of Marxism. If BC wants to continue a dialogue with Marxism, much still could come from a discussion with Marx's humanism.

Black Consciousness After 1977

After the banning in 1977, it seemed that BC had vanished into thin air. Many of its cadres who did not leave the BC camp moved away from the type of looser, decentralized organization that had characterized BC's earlier period towards a more "Leninist" type vanguard party based on the principle of "democratic centralism." These young militants started calling themselves the "vanguard of the working class." BC began to shift its emphasis with the "class question" in South Africa as its new theoretical point of departure. The leaders of this shift argued that a critique of capitalism was inherent in BC from the beginning. But for the most implacable critics, BC was a spent force, merely an expression of "cultural revolution in the minds of the subordinates... 'self-love,' 'identity,' 'cultural assertion.'"[17] Once self-awareness had been found, they argued, BC could to be disregarded for "real political action."

This duality between black self-awareness and the liberation struggle runs contrary to the ideas of the most important theoretician of BC, Steve Biko. It is worth quoting him to get a full appreciation of this idea:

> I must emphasise the cultural depth of Black Consciousness. The recognition of the death of white invincibility forces Blacks to ask the question: "Who am I?" "Who are we?" And the fundamental answer we give is: "People are people!" So "Black" Consciousness says: "Forget about colour!" But the reality we faced 10 to 15 years ago did not articulate this…One must immediately dispel the thought that Black Consciousness is merely a methodology or a means to an end.[18]

The idea is not simple opposition to white society. To understand what he means, we must turn to Frantz Fanon, with whom Biko felt a close affinity. For Fanon the black/white conflict is in a philosophic context of transcendence of contradiction and self-liberation as a cognitive development: BC is not merely a passing stage in the revolutionary process; it is an actuality in which the transformation of reality is grounded.

Biko situated BC internationally, in the movements for freedom within the black world. "The surge towards Black Consciousness is a phenomenon that has manifested itself throughout the so-called Third World." But he did not view liberation as inevitable. Two black American writers remarked, shortly after his death, "What is powerful and new about Biko's ideas is that he always centers the possibility for change within the subjectivity of the oppressed person, and not simply within the South African economy or the hierarchy of the system."[19] In recognizing that the "most potent weapon in the hands of the oppressor is the mind of the oppressed," Biko was speaking of the needed self-liberation of the black. Far from being a psychological exercise, he was speaking of the liberation of the whole person; a "quest for a new humanity," where the black would no longer be thought of as "an extension of a broom or some additional leverage to some machine." Against the force of the South African state Biko placed the force of the liberatory idea—the creative subjectivity of the black masses. This appreciation for the African masses as a revolutionary subject with a unique historical contribution to make to humanity's development was a characteristic element in the writings of many leading African intellectuals of the late 1950s and the early 1960s. It was true of Leopold Senghor who spoke of "Socialist Humanism" as well as of Fanon, who wrote passionately, "we must set afoot a new man."[20] But whereas Senghor's abstract philosophic statements gave way to disillusioning power politics, Fanon, who died a young man, remained uncompromising in his critique of the new African rulers and the nature of their relationship to the masses. Steve Biko was powerfully affected by Fanon's writings.²¹

The Black, according to Biko, "associates everything good with white... so you tend to feel there is something incomplete in your humanity, and that your humanity goes with whiteness." But opposition to white society could not become a preoccupation. As "Black Consciousness develops there is a need to work out further the quest for a new humanity... What Black Consciousness seeks to do is to produce at the end of the process real Black people who do not regard themselves as appendages of white society."²² In terms of the dialectic, the negation of white racism is black unity. But the end is not a "synthesis" of white racism and black unity but a complete transcendence where race would not be a factor. Biko is against integration if that means integration into white society with its values and codes of behavior maintained by whites. "If on the other hand by integration you mean there shall be free participation by all members of society, catering for the full expression of the self in a freely changing society dominated by the will of the people, then I am with you."²³ This assertion of the positive role of BC, emerging through its process and resistance, had a powerful impact on the youth of South Africa in the 1970s, and it is this, rather than BC as a passing phase, that could have become the ground for further theoretic development in the late 1970s and early 1980s.

Black Consciousness 1978—1983

One month after the death of Steve Biko at the hands of the security police, the government declared 17 BC organizations, including the Black People's Convention (BPC) illegal. The government was attempting to behead the movement that had come of age with the Soweto revolt of 1976–1977. Despite the banning of the movement, BC had taken root in the country, and new organizations emerged. Under the threat of new bannings, a new BC organization, the Azanian Peoples Organization (AZAPO) was formed in April 1978 in Soweto at a meeting which included Bishop Desmond Tutu. Almost immediately, before a constitution could be drafted, police detained the organizers, including the chairman, Ishmael Mkhabela, and the secretary, Lybon Mabasa, under the Terrorism Act. They were subsequently banned for three years. A year later a number of other organizations inspired by BC were formed, including COSAS and AZASO.²⁴ In October 1979 PEBCO (Port Elizabeth Black Civic Organization) was formed and grew quickly among the African townships in Port Elizabeth. Although it did not join AZAPO, it shared BC principles.²⁵

AZAPO held its inaugural conference in September 1979. But it, too, was quickly thrown into disarray both by internal strife and police repression. Its president, Curtis Nkondo, was suspended by the AZAPO executive, its leading members were arrested and victimized. In less than three years, almost the entire leadership of the founding Black Consciousness movements was wiped out. Nine SASO/BPC leaders had been jailed at the end of 1976; Biko was murdered in detention; Pityana left the country. Many dropped out of the movement. Around 5000 young BC inspired revolutionaries fled the country and joined up with the ANC (African National Congress) and PAC (Pan Africanist Congress) guerrilla units.

After Soweto, the ANC was revitalized mainly by these young BC militants who left the country. Inside the country the ANC was again becoming a significant force, attracting important figures from the Black Consciousness Movement. Botha from PEBCO and Pityana from BCMA joined the ANC in exile. Later, Nkondo from AZAPO, and the whole of AZASO, went over to the UDF (United Democratic Front). Even the militant BC Media Workers Association split over whether to join the UDF, with some branches joining and some not. In the late seventies the government was entertaining proposals to encourage a black middle class, as well as granting blacks trade union rights. Inkatha was growing, and becoming a major force, using some of the terminology of Black Consciousness. The new situation handed a challenge to BC to work out radically new concepts.

From the 1979 AZAPO conference on, there were efforts to work out the race/class question, to "fuse Black Consciousness with class consciousness."[26] But it was still sketchy. BC papers pointed to the Trade Unions as "an instrument that can bring about the re-distribution of power," but instead of worker control they envisaged a future state where "capital and profits accruing from labour shall be equitably distributed."[27] The question of the relationship between race and class has been the focus of much of BC writing. In a July 1981 AZAPO newsletter, Quraish Patel, editor of *Kwasala*, the official Media Workers newsletter, wrote: "A system of thought or an ideology is of little value if it can only be defined as a response to a particular period of historical crisis. When an ideology is able to reflect the continuous process of change and conflict, then that ideology has the potential for challenging the dominant ideas of the ruling class." Black Consciousness had to become such a reflexive ideology which asserted its humanism. For Patel BC was "a negation of while superiority, not a negation of whites as people—black consciousness is at the same time a positive assertion of our being what we want to be." He declared that BC wished to "restore our being human even if the environment is hostile and inhuman for it prepares us for participating in the historical movement towards a free society."

Yet at the same symposium where the "positive humanism" of Black Consciousness in South Africa was being discussed, AZAPO resolved to "confirm that race is a class determinant in the current South African context." At the same time there were moves to incorporate "scientific socialism."

In 1980 the external wing of BC, then chaired by one of its original founders, Barney Pityana, created a unified organization, the Black Consciousness Movement of Azania, committed to the "historical, political and organizational experience of the black working class," and adopting "the theory and practice of scientific socialism to guide it in its struggle." In October 1979, they had held an all-day symposium in London where "everybody seemed to agree that capitalism was the enemy and that the new order would have to be a socialist one."[28] Taking power, however, "could no longer be taken for granted as progressive. Onward development should not just flow but should be the result of very conscious thought."[29] Resolutions from the 1980 Conference, printed by the BCMA as "Our Urgent Tasks," show how they tried to graft Scientific Socialism onto the philosophy of Black Consciousness.[30] While they noted the "maturity of our population" and spoke of "the initiative of the masses themselves, their self-activity which is the prerequisite and precondition for self emancipation," these concepts are not the point of departure for theoretical development: Instead, "Scientific Socialism" is adopted as the "guide to the struggle" while BC would "have a mobilising role."[31]

It is surprising that by pinpointing the black working class as the major force of revolution, the BCMA felt compelled to adopt "scientific socialism," what seems to be an opposing ideology, as its guide. Were they now projecting "class" rather than "black" as the major term? There was a great deal of ambiguity as to what relationship "scientific socialism" had to the philosophy of BC. With the emphasis on "scientific socialism" as the "guide" to the struggle BC seemed an abstraction. By 1981, AZAPO saw itself as an activist organization which had "taken Black Consciousness beyond the phase of Black awareness into class struggle...[leading] the workers in their everyday struggle...[giving] clear priority to mobilising the worker not only in the factory but in the ghetto."[32]

How could the "idealism" and concreteness of BC be united with the determinism and "materialism" of scientific socialism?[33]

An attempt to move the debate past this duality was made by Buti Tlhagale, a Sowetan priest in the Black Consciousness Movement, at an address delivered in May 1978 and subsequently printed in issue number 5 of the London-based BCMA journal *Solidarity*, titled "A Further Determination Of Black Consciousness." The Black Consciousness Movement had done little "to bridge the gap between empirical consciousness of alienation and radical action to uproot the causes of alienation," he wrote. To be radical, according to Tlhagale, both economic exploitation and racial discrimination have to be addressed. "Within South Africa capital is made possible by the collective effort of black workers. It is cheap labour that keeps the capitalist monster alive." It is black labor, specifically, that can herald in a new epoch. "The mobilization of black workers [is] a radical solution," writes Tlhagale, "for it strikes at the very root of exploitation and alienation." Once black labor is recognized as a central category in the black struggle, BC ceases to be just an attitude of mind, it becomes a material weapon in the struggle, "an organizational power aimed at combatting the violence of the state."

By sharpening his critique so that it struck specifically at the alienation of labor, which results because "labour is converted into a commodity," Tlhagale searched for the principles of social reorganization which are based on the uprooting of alienated labor and give "hints as to the nature of the future state." For Tlhagale the term "proletariat" specifically referred to black workers because white workers enjoyed the protection of the state. But in elevating black labor he did not neglect the continual importance of the students who, he said, gave "rise to the Black Consciousness philosophy," spelling out the "student-worker alliance [as] part of the total modus operandi in the black liberation struggle."

The fusion of a class analysis into black consciousness received a boost under the influence of Saths Cooper's prison studies[34] and the work of Neville Alexander who introduced into BC the concept of "racial capitalism,"[35] which became part of the theoretical focus with the Hammanskraal Manifesto,[36] the draft manifesto of the National Forum.

The National Forum

In prison Saths Cooper and others in BC studied the "economic and other issues" that they had not had time to study in the preceding years. "We debated very intensely, roping in the PAC, the Unity Movement and ANC; different groups at different times would pull out, but our development continued."[37] After release from prison, they decided to create a forum where different tendencies in the liberation movement could air their views. The idea of the Forum was to narrow some of the differences between the liberation groups.

As Cooper put it: "[There has been] a tremendous degree of ideological ferment and confusion. We think we need mature, sober consideration of all the issues in the liberation struggle; and while principles should not be sacrificed, partisan approaches should take a back seat."[38]

In 1981, the Cape Action League, in which Neville Alexander is a key figure, circulated a document "Let Us Build the United Front," and in the Western Cape this was put into practice with the formation of the Disorderly Bills Action Committee against the Koornhoff Bills in 1982.[39] It included ex-Unity Movement people, BC and others. "By October 1982 we were working towards a national organization to oppose the Koornhoff Bills and the President's Council," says Alexander,

> Saths Cooper and others recently released had joined AZAPO. They came to Cape Town... Cooper agreed to be Convenor of a Conference for all "oppressed people" to organize a national agenda. At first there was a good response from all across the spectrum, including Tutu, Charterists... up to this day Boesak hasn't resigned from the NF Committee. But a month or two later, all the known Charterists withdrew. The thing was getting all the hallmarks of a large popular movement, and they [the Charterists] didn't want to let that gather behind a Black Consciousness intiative.[40]

The call for the creation of the National Forum (NF) was made at the fifth AZAPO congress in February 1983. Its rallying point was opposition to the new Constitution. In June 1983, 800 delegates representing 200 organizations met at Hammanskraal. At the end of the two-day discussion, delegates voted unanimously to adopt the Manifesto of the Azanian People, a document that identified "racial capitalism" as the enemy and was based on four basic principles: anti-racism, anti-imperialism, anti-collaboration with the ruling class, and independent working class organizations. At the July 1984 conference the Manifesto was endorsed with slight changes, the most important being that the "system of racial capitalism" was changed to "the historically evolved system of racism and capitalism," and the principle of anti-sexism was adopted. This Manifesto became the article of faith for the National Forum and AZAPO.

Saths Cooper views the National Forum as the most important political development in South Africa since the All African Congress. For AZAPO, the Manifesto supersedes the "other two historical documents, namely the Freedom Charter and 'Towards a Free Azania—Projection: Future State' of the now banned Black People's Convention."[41]

The National Forum is not a "Black Consciousness front," although it is widely perceived as being such. AZAPO is the largest political organization in the Forum yet it does not dominate it.[42] The Forum represents a wide range of opposition tendencies, from BC, to Africanism, workerists and the Unity Movement.[43] It accepts white membership but does not accept affiliate organizations made up "predominantly of the ruling class." An official National Forum publication states: "To suggest that the NF excludes whites on the basis of their 'whiteness' or any other superficial criterion is a gross misrepresentation of many NF adherents and the anti-racist project and method of struggle adopted by the NF."[44] Those involved in the National Forum see themselves as a non-sectarian tendency on the left, and do not believe in a one-party approach.

Finally the NF does not follow any existing socialist system: "We have no models, in that we do not espouse the Soviet or the Chinese or any other existing system...we see the move towards socialism as a process of dealing with specific local problems and issues on a principled basis. Because the NF is coherent as to its goal, it can tolerate differences in approach, tactics and strategy."[45] In fact Cooper sees the movement strengthened when different opinions are allowed to be aired within it and regards the National Forum as a structure that encourages dialogue.

AZAPO—1983 Onwards

BC faced two problems as the 1980s began; its image as an "intellectual" tendency with no influence in the working class; and the flow of BC people into the ANC (which claimed a monopoly of active resistance by virtue of an established military wing). By 1983 the BCM was strengthened with the release of many who had been sent to jail following the pro-Frelimo Rally.[46] Twenty Robben Island graduates were present at AZAPO's 1983 conference, and three gave keynote addresses: Muntu Myeza, former President of SASO, Saths Cooper, founder member of BPC, and Neville Alexander of the National Liberation Front. Most of the new leadership of AZAPO in the early and mid–1980s were prison "graduates," and the release of these people was a turning point for AZAPO. Cooper points out:

> Up until 1983 there really wasn't much of a development besides the race/class adoption...I think AZAPO was put on the defensive right from its initiation by other forces, particularly former BC adherents who may have adopted pro-ANC or pro-PAC positions and the organization tended to be, from 1978 to 1982, largely defending itself, defending its position, defending its right to exist.[47]

Asked how he thought things had changed since he was in prison, Cooper said, "when we left, there was a unity of purpose and a clear political direction. When we came back, we found these two elements missing."

Neville Alexander's involvement in the 1983 Conference was an important development. Only a few years earlier he had been sharply critical of BC.[48] At the Conference he read a paper on the National Situation, arguing the ruling class's alliance "with the white workers is to be downplayed in importance. Instead, the junior partners in the new alliance are to be the black middle class."[49] In the *City Press* he wrote of his new attitude to BC:

> I consider Black Consciousness an important nation building and liberatory idea based on the community of oppression of all those people in the country whom the regime classifies as "black," "coloured," and "indian." It is NOT an ethnic idea based on prejudice and division but rather a unifying solidarity of all the oppressed and exploited people of our country.[50]

In his 1983 address Cooper characterized AZAPO as "the vanguard of the people's struggle" and accused the system of attempting to buy off a section of the movement by trying to create black capitalism. In analyzing the class nature of the struggle, Cooper reemphasized that for AZAPO "the soul force of our struggle, its blackness, must be shouted from the rooftops."

The dominant attitude in BC in the early '80s was that philosophy had been formulated and political activity was all that was now needed. The theoretic void within BC on the question of labor was answered initially in an almost instantaneous manner with "Scientific Socialism."[51] For BC there has been no further development of the philosophy of Steve Biko. Nor is there evidence of a perceived need to do so. A new AZAPO journal *Frank Talk* came out in 1981. Its first issue carried two articles by Biko and summed up the years since 1977 as those in which AZAPO had "succeeded in working out the dialectic between race and class." AZAPO views "black nationalism as the driving force of the Azanian struggle," and believes that "AZAPO's coalition of the National Question and the Social Question has been thorough and cogent." This kind of assuredness seems to be the result of making class and race synonymous while adding some Marxian phraseology. It is not a very thoroughly developed framework of ideas and shows a marked preference for addressing tactical needs over the broader political questions. Another feature of the journal was its curious shift in ideology towards the narrowest nationalism.[52]

While the black nationalist tendency is dominant in *Frank Talk*, its columns also reveal the strength of certain anti-intellectual attitudes in BC. In an interview with this author, a BC unionist made this lack of debate into a virtue:

> According to our belief, we do not have to publish...we do not have to write volumes on BC. I can write what I like about BC. Anyone can claim a publication is BC, that is the danger. BC is not an ideology that you can

write down like Marxism. It is a philosophy. There is no importance in writing about philosophy.[53]

I do not assume that this is the official attitude but a philosophy, if it is vibrant and lives, must be discussed, written and argued about. Without this it becomes merely a popular ideology and an empty shell of one at that.

The major AZAPO campaigns of the 1980s include the 1981 Northern Transvaal school and bus boycott,[54] the launching of the National Forum in 1983 and the campaign against the Kennedy Tour in 1985. Under the banner "Socialist AZAPO versus Capitalist Kennedy" AZAPO showed itself as a non-collaborationist tendency mobilizing a large section of the youth outside its ranks, who did not want Kennedy to speak for them. But this was only a tactical, albeit principled, stand.[55] It gathered around it many different tendencies, outside of the UDF, who shared this non-collaborationist position. At that moment it did correspond with a broad layer of opinion in the country. It made harsh criticisms of the UDF for telling the people to boycott, rather than seeking the views of the people. But how AZAPO gauges what the "people" are thinking is unclear.

On the whole AZAPO seems to be moving more towards a black nationalist position while drawing on Marxist phrases about "class struggle," in effect, taking over the position of the earlier Pan Africanist Congress (PAC), with emphasis on the black working class. It appears that BC has moved away from the language of "consciousness" to the language of "scientific socialism."

In the September 1987 issue of *Frank Talk*, its staff writers spelled out BC as a "scientific ideology": "focuss[ing] on the material conditions in occupied Azania for the ultimate causes and directions of every event and phenomenon therein; comprehends these phenomena in their *changingness* and development and their interaction with other phenomena."[56] These phenomena, which are really the struggles of live human beings, become the objects of their "scientific" investigation. They continue by saying, "the goal of 'scientific socialism' was defined by Black Consciousness... and unambiguously asserted by AZAPO." This "science" is what they believe must be "applied towards transforming spontaneous resistance into conscious revolution." Scientific Socialism has become the code phrase for today's Black Consciousness Movement, and with it they herald the "leadership of the Black working class," maintaining that the 1970s generation who moved into the UDF "constitute a deformed BCM." But the leadership of the black working class is nothing but the "phenomena" for the "vanguard party's" leadership; the science they speak of is nothing but a rehash of the old left's "diamat,"[57] containing nothing that would stamp it as uniquely BC.

By the end of 1987 it seemed that BC as seen through AZAPO is becoming something radically different from its origins. As an idea originally situated in the subjectivity of the oppressed, which refused to comply with narrow "Marxist" applications, it is now merely the projection of another Marxist-Leninist tendency. Black is the substance rather than the subject of revolution, the "phenomena" of material conditions. As substance, AZAPO believes, the black working class needs the leadership of the "vanguard party" in order to acquire revolutionary consciousness. The fact that the "consciousness" of the worker is a mere reflection of material conditions necessitates, according to AZAPO, the "vanguard party." AZAPO has followed another "Leninist" principle with its attitude to the trade unions: "The Black working class has to transcend trade union consciousness in order to acquire revolutionary consciousness." Presumably that "revolutionary consciousness" has to be acquired from outside, from AZAPO.

What began as a very new revolutionary idea in the early 1970s seems to be little more than an application of Lenin's analysis of Russia in 1902. Even BC's earlier theoreticians did not spell out the form of organization best suited to expressing BC ideas, it was not to be a simple application of the vanguard party. They wanted more flexibility to express their ideas, to ask new questions, "encourage a new consciousness, and to suggest new forms which express it...Black Consciousness constitutes a revolution of ideas, of values and of standards." They wanted to engage black people in the emancipatory process. To cry out "to the black in the factory, at home, on the train, in the shebeen, at the playing fields, in the classroom."[58]

But the answer is not merely to oppose the earlier generation to today's. Saths Cooper, considered one of the leading intellectuals of BC in the eighties, does not think the rhetoric of Scientific Socialism has much content:

> It is quite problematic considering the BC approach. I think there are many unresolvable issues. I think Scientific Socialism is almost like a slogan without much consideration. The BCMA adopted it in 1980 and spelt it out in certain of their rhetoric but practically what that means hasn't been developed.[59]

In considering what possible direction BC might take in the future, it should be noted that much could come from its connection with Marxism. Thus far, the connection has been somewhat superficial. I have shown that the trend towards Marxist concepts flowed from the reality of South Africa, especially in view of the labor struggle. Baruch Hirson writes of young people searching for socialist literature which had been systematically banned since 1950. The Marxism they found came from old Stalinist texts.[60] It is this crude materialist, mechanical type of Marxism that appears to be the answer for some BC thinkers.[61] To consider Marx a materialist counterposed to idealism is a mark of a poor reading, but it characterizes many of the "Marxists" in South Africa.[62] Heribert Adam has written: "Marxist (materialist) interpretations of South Africa rarely go beyond the notion of base and superstructure. By mechanically relegating the realm of ideology to a mere reflection of underlying interests, Marxists usually ignore the subjective reality. A peculiar sterility—therefore—characterizes much of the recent leftist writing on South Africa."[63]

To conclude, let us turn to a consideration of a different possible future of Black Consciousness through rethinking its relation to the ideas of Biko, Fanon and Marxist-Humanism.

A Future for Black Consciousness? Biko, Fanon, and Marx's Humanism

A leading BC activist, now in the United States, Jongilizwe, appreciates the creativity of the spontaneous movements, but he also emphasizes the need for a "theoretical structure" to constantly evaluate actions. This is a very difficult thing to do, he says:

> Because every moment there is a new campaign, action or struggle that people are involved in...people have not really had the opportunity to sit back for little periods of time and assess the situation...Being in the maelstrom of activity, the question of the relationship of theory to praxis has been difficult to look at...The humanist approach to any analysis of our society...needs to be developed...Our task is to root ourselves in the people, have a relationship to material reality and begin to develop the future country we have envisioned.[64]

Biko was searching for a vision of the future when he stated that he did not want to opt for "capitalism or communism but a genuine African Communalism." He envisioned a society centered on 'man,' not only his material conditions "but just man himself with all his ramifications." Africa's gift will be "giving the world a more human face."[65]

There was much here that needed to be elaborated as Biko recognized: "There is a certain plasticity in this interpretation precisely because no one has yet made an ultimate definition of it."[66] Biko deliberately did not make an "ultimate definition" because he believed that doing so would only divide people. Many have criticized his statement that, "BPC believes in a judicious blending of private enterprise...with state participation," but have ignored the fact that Biko did not want to create a blueprint but wanted the future society determined by the oppressed themselves, however there was "recognition of the fact that a change in colour of the occupier does not necessarily change the system."[67] For Biko liberation and with it the complete transformation of the system were of paramount importance to the concept of Black Consciousness.[68] Many Marxists have been quick to call for state ownership and take it as the measure of socialist transformation. Other Marxists, especially Marxist-Humanists, not associated with a state power, have shown what was central to Marx was not the property formation as much as the actual human relations.

The question of what happens after the revolutionary party takes power is not only a philosophical question but also a practical question with life and death implications. This was evident with what happened in Ghana, which was the first African country to win independence from Britain under the leadership of Nkrumah. When a general strike broke out two years later, the leadership was surprisingly quick to put it down and arrest the worker-leaders. It was evident in Cuba where Castro had taken power and declared the revolution "humanist." After he suppressed the independent trade unions, calling their convention a "madhouse," he embraced the Communist Party to help him transform the unions into "pliant tools of the new armed state."[69] There are, admittedly, a number of analyses of what happened to the African revolutions. However, one writer, Raya Dunayevskaya, needs to be singled out for the very penetrating analysis she has made of the "tragedy of the African revolutions" which "began so soon after the revolution had succeeded because leaders were so weighted down with consciousness of technological backwardness...The isolation from the masses deepened so that the new rulers began to look at them as mere labor power."[70]

Frantz Fanon spoke out against those leaders who "want to send the people back to caves" and the party that forbids the "free flow of ideas between people and the government:

> The single party is the modern form of the dictatorship of the bourgeoisie, unmasked, unpainted, unscrupulous and cynical...The party leaders behave like common sergeant majors, frequently reminding the people of the need for "silence in the ranks"..."Leader": the word comes from the English verb "to lead," but a frequent French translation is "to drive." The driver, the shepherd of the people, no longer exists today. The people are no longer a herd; they do not need to be driven.[71]

In AZAPO the two questions of leadership and the importance of ideas have lain side by side as is exemplified in the two following quotes from Lybon Mabasa. Speaking at the fifth annual AZAPO conference he had this to say about AZAPO's role: "If the masses were a conscious mass then we would have had a revolution a long time ago...It is our duty as leaders and members of the movement to give decisive leadership...to create the momentum of a continuous offensive towards revolutionary objectives." A year later at the presidential address to AZAPO, he said:

> In our country, Black people are faced with the task of having to defeat an enemy armed to the teeth with destructive weapons of modern technology...The final outcome will not be decided by the massive accumulation of weapons, however genocidal, but by the local and historical consciousness of the masses...prov[ing] the old saying that "ideas and men are stronger than weapons."

These two concepts, voluntarism (momentum and decisive leadership) and the power of ideas (consciousness of the masses) are two elements of BC that up until now have not come into contradiction.

The power of ideas has always been a characteristic of the revolutionary movement in South Africa. As far back as 1951 I.B. Tabata spelt it out as "the weapons with which you cut your path in the barbaric jungle of South African society today. We fight ideas with ideas."[72] What was compelling Steve Biko was to develop a philosophy of liberation, what BC calls "a way of life." It is not merely a question of reading other philosophers nor his stature as an original thinker. What is unfairly passed over is the passion for total vision which pervades his writings, the standpoint which captured the attention of at least one generation of youth.

Some BC theologians have seized on an interpretation of Marxism contrary to established Marxism, emphasizing Marx's humanism. Itumeleng J. Mosala writes of Black Theology becoming a "theoretical weapon in the hands of the oppressed." "In this respect," he says, "we take our cue from the words of Marx when he says, 'To be radical is to grasp the root of the matter. But for man the root is man himself.'"[73] Biko's affinity with Marx consisted of the centrality of the human subject struggling to be free. Fanon, too, wrote, "let us work out new concepts, let us set afoot a new man..." He believed this needed a new relationship between theory and practice, a theory that is grounded both in the aspirations of the black masses as they strive for freedom and in a philosophy of revolutionary humanism. This does not mean nobody is digging into the humanism of Marx and Fanon. In an interview, Saths Cooper was very clear on his relationship to Marx, revolutionary humanism and the new society.

> I think the aspect of Marx that is often overlooked is his humanism. Many tend to cotton on to his economist concepts and exclude Marx from

Marxism, because Marxism is essentially humanist, and I'm not talking about any liberalism. I am talking about mankind, humanity having its humanity restored rather than being chattelled, being work horses in the service of capital. I am talking about living life to the full, not merely being production animals. In our country you will find that is how apartheid has been conceptualized, I think it is Verwoerd who said it, "There is no place for the Bantu above certain forms of labour." You can see the restoration of humanity to people is very very important. Fanon mentions that at the rendezvous of victory we cannot have half human beings, you cannot have Uhuru without people having had their humanity restored in the process of creating that Uhuru, otherwise you are going to have half human beings and you are going to have all these problems post Uhuru. Psychological liberation is very important. Of course we are fighting for physical liberation but what physical liberation is it where you are psychologically unprepared to handle that liberation and have full national self determination.[74]

Bonganjano Goba, another Black theologian, summing up the importance of BC philosophy, said of those who want to subsume blackness within the class question, "They tragically underestimate the uniqueness of the black situation and experience as a whole." He challenges the Black Consciousness Movement of which he feels he is a part, "to spell out what kind of society we envisage and how we will work for it, given our present political situation. For example, if we are committed to a socialist state, what do we mean by that." He sees the need for a vision, not as something abstract, but as something "that emerges within the prophetic vision of those who engage in a concrete struggle. Therefore there is a sense in which BC is part of this prophetic vision…" Goba wants to "explore the real meaning of Black Consciousness as an ideology of the black struggle."

Though Goba has a difference emphasis about Fanon than Biko did it is quite clear that he is not talking only of theology:

> We need a much more comprehensive analysis of our own situation, one that avoids ideological reductionism current in some of the vulgar materialistically orientated approaches to our situation. We need a critical perspective that will force us as black theologians to question existing categories of thought.[75]

While Goba questions existing categories of thought in the context of a philosophic framework, i.e. Black Theology, other black theologians, for example Itumeleng Mosala, have looked to Marx's Humanism for their approach:

> The weapon of criticism cannot, of course, replace the criticism of weapons; material force must be overthrown by material force; but theory

also becomes a material force as soon as it has gripped the masses...To be radical is to grasp the root of the matter. But for man the root is man himself.[76]

Mosala criticizes Black Theology for not having become a weapon in theory because it has not yet "gripped the masses." The point is not Black Theology, however important that is in the liberation movement, but "how does a philosophy 'live' with the lives of the people?" BC did grip a generation in the 1970s, but where does it stand in the 1980s? I have tried to show that BC's interest in Marx is a valid one, one that has tried to come to terms with the important workers' movement of the eighties, but their approach has often times been pragmatic and they have been happier with Marxist jargon rather than an engagement with Marx's ideas.

Mokgethi Motlhabi challenges not only all the black political organizations but also the trade union movement for its seeming "lack [of] a strong theoretical base that can enable it to analyse the situation meaningfully."[77] At the conclusion of his book he argues that to work out the relationship between economic and political change needs to be grounded in Marx's Marxism rather than any simple application of what is called Scientific Socialism. He goes on to quote Marx, "the emancipation of the workers contains universal human emancipation...because the whole of human servitude is involved in the relation of the worker to production."[78] While Motlhabi argues that black South Africans have to work out their relationship to Marx, he stresses the "contribution they can make in trying to shape their future" but the "knowledge of the situation is not sufficient to help bring about change in it." To work out a new "praxis," a new unity of theory and practice, is no easy task, it requires great labor, patience, and openness to ideas. One essential ingredient is criticism, and criticism, as Wole Soyinka put it, "begins at home." I have argued that the early expression of BC did contain a critique of capitalism, and through its encounter with the dialectic in Frantz Fanon could have found a bridge to the humanism of Marx.[79] This encounter could help work out both the race/class dialectic and the relationship between consciousness and organization.

Ironically, the critique made by those who have left the Black Consciousness Movement, that BC is just a passing stage, is one that has been taken on board by AZAPO. They believe they have passed that "earlier" stage adding to their philosophy the language of Scientific Socialism. Yet, although BC has shown seriousness in the debate of theory, whether the radicalism of BC's own concepts can be deepened remains to be seen.

Notes

This introduction was first presented at a seminar at the University of KwaZulu-Natal, Durban and published in *Centre for Civil Society Research Report No. 18* (Durban, SA: Centre for Civil Society, June 2004). This originally appeared in *Africa Today* 35, no. 1 (1988): 1–26.

1. John Alan and Lou Turner, *Frantz Fanon, Soweto and American Black Thought* (Detroit: News and Letters, 1978; Chicago: 1986). The section on Fanon was reprinted in my *Rethinking Fanon* (Amherst, NY: Humanity Books, 1999).
2. For a recent discussion of "revolutionary humanism" in Fanon's thought, see Richard Pithouse, "'That the Tool Never Possess the Man': Taking Fanon's Humanism Seriously," *Politikon* 30, no. 2 (2003): 107–131.
3. This is a term I use in "Fanon's Humanism and Africa Today," in Eileen McCarthy-Arnold, David Penna, and Joy Cruz Sobrepeña, eds., *Africa, Human Rights and the Global System: The Political Economy of Human Rights in a Changing World* (Boulder CO: Greenwood Press, 1994), 23–36.
4. Perhaps readers could inform me of the actual details. But I was astonished when he became a cofounder of a new organization with links to Inkatha and then later (like Mosala) became a corporatist university manager.
5. H. S. Harris, *Hegel: Phenomenology and System* (Indianapolis, IN: Hackett Publishing, 1995): 107.
6. Raya Dunayevskaya, *Philosophy and Revolution: From Hegel to Sartre and From Marx to Mao* (New York: Columbia University Press, 1989), 93.
7. Ibid., xliii.
8. Gibson, "Fanon's Humanism."
9. See Nigel Gibson "Transition from Apartheid," *Journal of Asian and Asian Studies* 36, no. 1 (2001): 65–85, and "The Pitfalls of South Africa's Liberation," *New Political Science* 23 (2001): 371–386.
10. Lenin criticized Bukharin's mechanistic approach to the national question in 1916 as "imperialist economism."
11. One can think of two radical anticolonialists who fit this description: Nkrumah who shocked the British, Sekou Touré who shocked the French.
12. Antonio Gramsci, *The Prison Notebooks* (New York: International Publishers, 1971), 445. It shouldn't be forgotten that Gramsci (perhaps this was a historic barrier) was unable to shed his concept of a vanguard party despite his notion of historical materialism as an "absolute humanism."
13. Frantz Fanon, *Toward the African Revolution* (New York: Grove, 1967), 181.
14. John Brewer, *After Soweto: An Unfinished Journey* (Oxford: Clarendon Press, 1986), ch. 4. This is somewhat ironic as the ANC and UDF are nationalist and populist rather than working class parties.
15. This point is made by Mbulelo Vizikhungo Mzamane in his "Steve Biko Memorial Address," printed in *Solidarity* (Official organ of the BCMA), no. 7 (1981): 8.
16. Itumeleng Mosala and Buti Tlhangle, *The Unquestionable Right to Be Free: Black Theology From South Africa* (Maryknoll, NY: Orbis Books, 1986), 13.
17. Heribert Adam, "The Rise of Black Consciousness in South Africa," *Race* 15, no. 2 (October 1973): 155.
18. Bernard Zylstra interview with Steve Biko, published in *The Reform Journal* (Michigan) December 1977 and "The Definition of Black Consciousness" in Steve Biko's *I Write What I Like* (London: Heineman, 1979), 51.

19. Alan and Turner, *Frantz Fanon*, 22.
20. Frantz Fanon, *Black Skin, White Masks* (New York: Grove Press, 1967), 7,8, and 222.
21. (Eds. Note: The following section on Fanon has been cut from the original article. Readers may want to consult Nigel C. Gibson's, *Fanon: A Postcolonial Imagination* [Polity Press, 2003]). Many have reduced Fanon to an "apostle of violent revolution." One only has to look at the writings of some of the leaders of the American Black Power movement to find this. Even Robert Fatton in *Black Consciousness in South Africa, the Dialectics of Ideological Resistance to White Supremacy* (Albany, NJ: SUNY Press, 1986) reduces Fanon to the "terrorist acts of POQO" (the Pan Africanist Congress' military wing), see 24–26. What Biko found in Fanon is never mentioned. In contrast, Sam Noluntshugu in *Changing South Africa: Political Considerations* (Manchester, UK: Manchester University Press, 1982) writes: "Although Fanon's writings were read widely and his ideas of alienation in colonial society had much influence on many theorists of black consciousness there is little evidence that his ideas on violence were much discussed."
22. Biko, *I Write What I Like*, 51.
23. Ibid.
24. AZASO is no longer in the BC camp. It defected to the Charterists in 1981 after Curtis Nkondo was suspended from his post as president of AZAPO when he tried to lead the organization in the charterist camp. In late 1986 it dropped the title "Azanian," renaming itself the South African National Students' Congress. It now views "the system of exploitation of man by man and not…whites as such" as the main "cause of black oppression in South Africa." COSAS, founded in 1979, "stood in conscious opposition to those organisations which claim to be inspired by black consciousness." (See James Leatt, Theo Kneifel, and Klaus Nurnburger, eds., *Contending Ideologies in South Africa* [Cape Town, SA: David Phillip, 1986], 116.) In 1980 COSAS declared its support for the Freedom Charter and sees its role as students "to support the struggles of workers." It is ironic that both these organizations, which identify with the black working class, should also take into their programs the Freedom Charter. The Azanian Students Movement was formed in 1982 to replace AZASO as a student organization grounded in black consciousness principles; it also sees itself as an organization linked to workers' struggles.
25. The dismissal of PEBCO's chairman, Thozamile Botha, from the Ford Motor company (allegedly because of complaints by white workers for his involvement in PEBCO) started a major strike there. On January 10, 1980, 5 of PEBCO's leaders, including Botha, were arrested and given three-year banning orders. The repression by the state essentially, temporarily, destroyed the movement. Botha fled the country and received political asylum in Lesotho.
26. *Johannesburg Star*. May 1979 (cited in *South Africa: Time is Running Out*, [Berkeley, CA: University of California Press. 1981], 200).
27. *On Policy*, AZAPO document, September 1979.
28. *Post*, October 20, 1979.
29. Ibid.
30. Scientific Socialism is a name that Engels used for "Marxism" and popularized in his *Socialism, Utopian, and Scientific*. It is the generic name for the mechanistic materialism that passes for "Orthodox Marxism."
31. "Our Urgent Tasks," *Solidarity* October 1980, no. 4 (London).
32. This was asserted in a 1981 AZAPO Conference paper, quoted in Tom Lodge, *Black Politics in South Africa Since 1945* (Essex, UK: Longman, 1983), 345.
33. Lebamang Sebidi writes in *The Unquestionable Right to be Free*: "Race analysts are strategically mind oriented, class analysts focus almost exclusively on the

material conditions of life... The Black Consciousness philosophy, particularly at the beginning, made it explicit that it would refuse to be derailed from viewing the South African problematic from the race-analysis point of departure... which led political scientists like Sam C. Noluntshugu to think that, despite some uneasiness with capitalism within the Black Consciousness philosophy... there was no systematic economic analysis of class, nor, even a political account of what the interests and roles of the various classes might be in the process of liberation... It was in the aftermath of the October 1977 bannings that objections against this idealistic approach were openly and persistently raised within black political circles, in favour of a materialist methodology. Matters have reached a stage where one is either an idealist in one's approach or a materialist." 24 and 29.
34. "Young adherents of Black Consciousness who are prisoners on Robben Island now refer to themselves as Marxists. In exile, some Black Consciousness activists who have not joined the ANC claim a more radical position by virtue of new found scientific socialism." *South Africa: Time Running Out*, 199–200.
35. This is seen most clearly in the first draft of the *Azanian Manifesto*. Put simply "racial capitalism" is a system by which the state and capital maintain their economic hegemony by means of racial oppression.
36. See, Graham Leach, *South Africa* (London: BBC Publications, 1986) and Heribert Adam and Kogila Moodley, *South Africa Without Apartheid*, (Berkeley, CA: University of California Press, 1986), 97.
37. Interview by author with Saths Cooper, New York, April 1987.
38. *Christian Science Monitor*, June 30, 1983.
39. The so-called Koornhof Bills concerned the freedom of movement of black people in South Africa.
40. Nonverbatim notes from an interview with Neville Alexander by Gail Gerhart, Cape Town, November 1985. (Followers of the Freedom Charter are referred to as charterists).
41. "For the Record," *Solidarity*, no. 11/12 (1985).
42. The major constituents of the National Forum are: AZAPO, claimed membership—110,000; AZACTU (Azanian Congress of Trade Unions, now part of the National Congress of Trade Unions, NACTU), 11 union affiliates, claimed membership—95,000; AZASM claimed membership—80,000; AZAYO (Azanian Youth Organization), claimed membership—12,000; AZANYU (Azanian Youth Unity), membership not available; CAL (Cape Action League), membership not available; CUSA (Council of Unions of South Africa, now part of NACTU), 12 union affiliates, claimed membership—180,000.
43. "Workerists" refer to those in the trade union movement who stress workers' issues in the factory over community issues and were represented especially by the Federation of South African Trade Unions (FOSATU). This term has become a little more indeterminate over the past few years, especially since 1984 when militant FOSATU unionists became more involved in community politics. However, they would emphasize the importance of worker leadership and democratic structures developed in the unions as important for community struggles. For an interesting analysis of the comparison of stayaways in the Transvaal, 1984, with Port Elizabeth-Uitenhage, 1985, and their relation to union and community politics, see Mark Swilling, "Stayaways, Urban Protest and the State," *South African Review*, 3 (Johannesburg: South Africa Research Service, 1986).
44. "Know Your Forum," a NF document, 2 (quoted in Zwakala's 1986 NF paper).
45. Ibid.

46. On September 25, 1974, SASO and BPC organized rallies to celebrate the installation of the Frelimo government in Mozambique. Despite police bans, the rallies went ahead. Nine BPC/SASO leaders were charged under the Terrorism Act and, after a seventeen month trial, were given sentences from five to ten years.
47. Interview with Saths Cooper, April 1987.
48. In his book *One Azania, One Nation*, written under the pseudonym No Sizwe (London: Zed Press, 1979).
49. AZAPO conference issue, February 1983, 18.
50. *City Press*, March 20, 1983.
51. In an interview with me in New York, February 1987, a young Black Consciousness militant asserted: "Our struggle is unfortunate that we are not afforded the opportunity of fully engaging into guerrilla warfare and labour becomes the next alternative." It seems to suggest that some reluctantly adopted labor as a force of revolution.
52. One example is the printing of an eight-page article from Louis Farrakhan, and the subsequent editorial "Israel has no Right to Exist," vol. 1, no. 5 (November/December 1984) and vol. 1, no. 6 (February/March 1985).
53. Interview with Author. Pandelani Nefolovhodwe, the coordinator of AZACTU, answering a question about the split in MAWU (Metal and Allied Workers Union) said, "The question is not white intellectuals, but intellectuals period" (See Zwakala, 15). However, he wasn't simply being anti-intellectual; he wanted to establish a new relationship between intellectuals and workers, especially in the unions. "If intellectuals won't admit that's what they are, they are gong to be useless organisers. If you truly accept what you are, you work at interacting with workers, listening and accepting. Then you can systematise and form the ideas that project working class aspirations." *Work in Progress* (WIP) 33 (Braamfontein: South African Research Service).
54. See "We Don't Need No Education" in *Solidarity*, nos. 5 and 6.
55. It should be noted that the fratricide between the ANC and AZAPO can be traced to this campaign. The government made the most of the opposing positions over Kennedy by stirring up differences.
56. *Frank Talk* (Domerton), September 2, 1987.
57. The abbreviated term used by Stalinism for "dialectical materialism."
58. Barney Pityana, quoted in Donald Woods, *Biko* (London: Paddington Press, 1978), 33, and in *Africa News* (Durham, North Carolina, June 1979).
59. Interview with Author, April 1987.
60. Baruch Hirson, *Year of Fire, Year of Ash* (London: Zed Press, 1979), 328.
61. One can see this type of thinking especially in the Black Nationalist wing of BC. See, for example, the forty-seven page critique of Mokgethi Mothabi's *Black Resistance to Apartheid*, by Matthew Nkoana, published by BCMA region, 1985.
62. See Marx, *Theses on Feuerbach* (1945) for his critique of both materialism and idealism.
63. Heribert Adam, quoted in Mosale and Tlhagale, *Unquestionable Right to be Free*, 30.
64. Jongilizwe, *News and Letters*, December 1986.
65. Steve Biko, Interview with Bernard Zylstra, 46–7.
66. Biko quoted in Woods, *Biko*, 141.
67. Biko interview with Zylstra.
68. In an interview with Gail Gerhart in 1972, he explained that the goal was deeper than getting rid of a capitalist economy: "It is not only capitalism that is involved; it is also the whole gamut of white value systems which has been adopted as standard by South Africa, both by whites and blacks so far. And that will need attention, even in a postrevolutionary society. Values relating to all the fields—education, religion, culture,

and so on. So your problems are not solved completely when you alter the economic pattern to socialist pattern. You still don't become what you ought to be. There is still a lot of dust to be swept off, you know, from the kind of slate we got from white society."
69. See Raya Dunayevaskya, "The Cuban Revolution: The Year After" in *News and Letters*, December 1960.
70. Dunayevaskya, *Philosophy and Revolution*, 218.
71. Frantz Fanon, *Wretched of the Earth* (New York: Grove Press, 1968), 165 and 183–184.
72. Tabata's opening address to the first conference of the Society of Young Africa on December 20, 1951, in *From Protest to Challenge: A Documentary History of African Politics in South Africa, 1882–1964*, ed. Thomas Karis and Gwendolen Carter (Stanford: Hoover Institution Press, 1973), document 98.
73. Mosala and Tlhagale, *Unquestionable Right to be Free*, 176.
74. Interview, April 1987.
75. Bonganjalo Goba, "The Black Consciousness Movement: Its impact on Black Theology," in Mosala and Tlhagale, *Unquestionable Right to be Free*, 69.
76. Marx quoted by Itumeleng Mosala in Mosala and Tlhagale, *Unquestionable Right to be Free*, 176.
77. Motgethi Motlhabi, *The Theory and Practice of Black Resistance to Apartheid: A Social-Ethical Analysis* (Braamfontein, SA: Skotaville Publishers, 1984), 274.
78. From Marx's Economic and Philosophic Manuscripts of 1844, quoted in ibid., 273–274.
79. Some in BC, who do not consider themselves Marxists, do appreciate that he stands for more than a photocopy theory of materialism. "We can understand," wrote a group of South African revolutionaries, quoted in Allen and Turner, *Frantz Fanon*, "why the Marxist-Humanists felt a need to call themselves not just Marxists but Marxist-Humanists, because the humanism has been removed from Marx to such an extent that people thought they could come with certain theories and ideas just from the top—the intellectuals theorizing and telling the people how to liberate themselves."

7

An Illuminating Moment: Background to the Azanian Manifesto

Neville Alexander

Salvaging Elements of Historical Truth

Any political program of principles has to be understood and assessed in the context of the times of its genesis. The terminology used, the underlying concepts or theory it expresses, as well as the strategy implicit in the formulations are all necessarily informed by the class character and the immediate and long-term objectives of the political movement or forces concerned as well as by the legal-political environment where they are operative. The Manifesto of the Azanian People is no exception. Accordingly, I want to describe and analyze as concisely as possible the social, political, and organizational background to the evolution of the Manifesto. This is especially important because of the furious but misguided attempts that were made from time to time to vilify the authors of the Manifesto and to falsify the circumstances in which the document came to be adopted in June 1983 by the National Forum (NF) as the unifying program of principles of what was intended to be a united front against the apartheid strategy of divide and rule as manifested in, among other things, P.W. Botha's tricameral constitution.

Historians and political sociologists expect that victorious movements will attempt to represent the past as a trajectory that inexorably and uninterruptedly leads to the moment of their victory, the moment of the seizure or, as in the South African case, the "transfer" of power. Even so, the rapidity and the comprehensiveness of the process of recasting and rewriting South Africa's contemporary history that began sometime before 1994 is surprising. Although a certain cavalier attitude on the part of journalists and pseudohistorians can be understood within limits, it is not acceptable that reputable historians and political and other social scientists can satisfy themselves with versions of what happened in South Africa between 1960 and 1990, more or less, that are misleading and distorting, even if only because of omission of significant moments. Although some of the earlier, near-contemporary accounts attempt to situate the NF in a more open perspective,[1] by the time we reach the late 1990s it has virtually disappeared from the historical canvas.[2] Some of the latest "historical" writings are among the worst examples of contemporary history even if one takes into account the well-known limitations of the genre.

This essay, which is consciously formulated in a quasi-anecdotal rather than a strictly analytical mode, is an attempt to put forward a set of perceptions and an account of a particularly dynamic moment in the early 1980s in South Africa that may help to correct the distorting mirror that has, by and large, been held up to the post-1994 generation hitherto. It is important, therefore, to point out that there are hundreds of people who were party or privy to the events and processes I refer to here, who will either confirm or amend the picture I paint. Some, because of the twists and turns in their lives, might deny some or even all of what I have noted here. But should this occur, future historians will have to judge the merits of the respective versions.

Black Consciousness and Socialist Influences

Without explicit reference to, but basing myself on, the numerous accounts of the origins and development of the Black Consciousness Movement (BCM) in South Africa in the late 1960s, I want to highlight a few generalizations about this development that are relevant to the subject of this essay.

To begin with, the repression of the early 1960s, which was initiated with the proliferation of banning orders served on individuals under the Suppression of Communism Act of 1950 and intensified after Sharpeville by means of the General Laws Amendment Act of 1962 and the Terrorism Act of 1967, appeared to bring down a blanket of silence and compliance on the oppressed people of the country. Of course, none of the organizations involved in and committed to the national liberation struggle abandoned that struggle, but their activities were effectively curbed and disrupted for more than a decade after 1963.

Steve Biko and his comrades were products of the apartheid university and secondary school system, notably of the network of Bush Colleges.

Some of them had direct and indirect links, sometimes no more than familial bonds, with persons who were in prison, in exile, or in the underground political structures of the national liberation movement, properly so called. It is also clear that, besides these natural influences on their thinking and their political universe, they were, albeit by way of many detours, decisively influenced by developments in the rest of the world, especially by the rise of the student movement and youth activism in Europe and in the United States of the 1960s. Through the University Christian Movement and other sources, they came into contact with the pedagogical and social conceptions of Paulo Freire and the theology of liberation, among others, and all of these influences, in the context of the repression and against the background of the mixture of Christian philanthropy and African communal life that all of us who were adults in those days had experienced in the countryside, undoubtedly contributed to their formulation and conscious promotion of a strategy that was in fact a version of Gramsci's famous "war of position." The strategy of Black Community Programmes, together with the development of a modern labor movement, which had a more differentiated but related source and a sometimes converging, sometimes diverging, trajectory, was no less than such a war of position, one that eventually brought about a change in the balance of forces and helped to reshape the political space in the worst years of the repression.

There is also no doubt that the crucial element in the expansion and deepening of the BCM was the cadre of students that was strategically distributed across the country, especially in the countryside, through the mechanism of the Bush Colleges and related institutions. These young people, intended by white supremacist rulers whose sanity was compromised because of their simplistic racist preconceptions, to become "Eiselen men" and "Eiselen women," that is, a collaborationist layer of intellectuals and professionals committed to tribal (so-called ethnic) communities became, instead, the Trojan horse of Afrikaner nationalism and the natural vanguard of this apparently reformist and, as they believed, potentially co-optable student and youth movement.

The politics of the BCM as a movement was complex and constantly changing. At first sight, it was informed by an Africanist ideology that was closer to the views of a Robert Sobukwe than those of a Nelson Mandela. The leadership tried to shape an inclusive black identity that, in ruling class South African terms, included all the oppressed people whether classified—in terms of the apartheid social categories—Bantu, Coloured, or Indian. In this respect, the BCM appeared, on the surface and in the modalities of its operations, to be closer to the Non-European Unity Movement than to the Congress Movement. Whichever way one approaches the matter, however, it is very obvious that both the leadership and the membership of the BCM were strongly influenced by *all* the different tendencies that constituted the national liberation movement. This catholicity of the movement turned out to be a great strength initially, but also held within itself the danger of political fragmentation under pressure. In retrospect, this angle on the subject makes a lot of sense in the context of the repression and the consequent potential of any radical quasi-political grouping to serve as a pole of gravitation for impressionable young students of diverse backgrounds who could not but be politically orientated.

I will not expound any further on the ideological developments and contradictions within the BCM.[3] However, in order to understand the theoretical and ideological content of the Azanian Manifesto, it is essential that I say a few words about my perception of the relationship between the BCM and socialism as an ideology as well as specific socialist currents in South Africa.

When I emerged from prison in 1974, after serving ten years on Robben Island, I was placed under house arrest in my mother's home, where I have continued to live up to the present. It soon became obvious to me and my comrades that the activists of the BCM were the main group of political people among the oppressed who were trying, overtly and covertly, to organize them, mainly at the point of reproduction. The independent trade union movement, including those unions initiated by BCM activists, was in its infancy at that time and was, naturally, focused on conditions at the point of production. Because of our reputation as members of the "National Liberation Front" and a certain measure of publicity locally and abroad, many BCM members gravitated toward us and soon we were involved with them in (illegal) study groups, in which mainly political and historical themes or developments were the subject. By way of example, I can vouch for the fact that, among other things, in our Cape Peninsula study groups we addressed the staple issues of the movement such as the land question, the national question, the language question, African culture, the economic system. Needless to say, similar patterns involving political activists and ex-Robben Islanders from different political organizations occurred throughout the country with more or less regularity and for similar reasons. It is in these study groups and, from what I was told by men such as the late Strini Moodley and Saths Cooper, among others, those that they attended on Robben Island, mainly in collaboration with Unity Movement comrades, that the BCM came, not necessarily for the first time, to engage directly and systematically with Marxist socialist thought. Up to that time, besides some reading of revolutionary socialist texts, most BCM activists were guided by the political concepts of Black Communalism that, as I understood it then, was an amalgam of notions of ubuntu and liberal-individualist democratic principles.

There was never any explicit attempt on our part to "convert" the BCM comrades to our version of socialist principles and strategy. I have no doubt that most of them would have resented and rejected any such agenda. Like us, they were interested in an exchange of ideas, knowledge, and information in order to conduct the struggle better, as they saw it. However, the levels of trust and mutual respect that were established amongst us were of great importance subsequently. One specific moment that has never been recorded adequately should be noted explicitly. I refer to the planned public protest demonstration against the granting of so-called independence to the Transkei on October 26, 1976, that, at the initiative of the BCM, we set out as a united internal movement, to organize at Hammanskraal in the Transvaal on the national scale for the day of "independence." Although none of us, whether members of underground political structures of the Pan Africanist Congress (PAC), the African National Congress (ANC), or of independent socialist groups, who were privy to this plan from its inception believed that there was any real danger of the country being partitioned by this self-delusional Act of the white South African parliament, we believed that it was essential that a public stand be taken by the oppressed people against the principle of partition and for the territorial integrity of South Africa. In addition, this was considered to be the ideal issue on which to reassert publicly the political aspirations and demands of the oppressed people and to test the resolve of the apartheid state. Committees were set up in different parts of the country in order to arrange for transport and other logistical requirements. These committees, as far as I know, involved mostly people who were or considered themselves to be members of the BCM, but they included some people from other groups, including the independent socialist network we had begun establishing almost as soon as the prison gates were shut behind us.

Whether or not this particular initiative would have succeeded without much bloodshed belongs in the realm of speculation. As is well known now, the events of June 1976 rendered everything else irrelevant and rang in a new phase of the struggle for national liberation. It is also clear that some of the preparatory work that had been occasioned by the anti-Transkei "independence" protest helped to spread the Soweto Uprising across the country much more rapidly than would otherwise have been the case. This is certainly true in respect of the Western Cape.

Also unrecorded but equally significant was the plan that we, in Cape Town, had worked out in conjunction with and at the initiative of Steve Biko and his comrades in Ginsberg to send abroad myself and Comrade Steve in order to discuss with the armed movements in exile the suggestion to constitute a single united liberation army that would be complemented and "represented" by the Black People's Convention (BPC) as the legitimate voice of the oppressed inside the country. Whether or not this exploratory talk was naïve is not the point here. It is quite possible that some of the individuals who were involved in this plan will now deny that it was ever considered. If so, they would, quite simply, be guilty of selective amnesia. It is certainly a matter of historical fact that Biko, in taking this initiative, was acting in terms of existing positions of the BPC and in line with the general political orientation and of specific discussions within the BCM after the Soweto Uprising had exploded. By way of example, I quote at some length from a "position paper" discussed at a BPC executive meeting not long after December 1976:

> Who then are the people involved in the liberation process? It is quite clear that the front line role is now played partly by the banned movements ANC, PAC, UMSA and partly by the black consciousness movement. Over and above the frontline role, there are those groups who are merely important in so far as they can form useful or destructive alliances with the frontline groups. The following features ought to be recognised in the further analysis of those involved in the liberation process:
> (a) There is a need for the resolution of conflicting interests and in pursuit of this the following options are open:
> –we can form a new front operating both internally and externally;
> –we can form a basis for future unity encompassing all liberation movements;
> –we can form an exclusive frontline alliance with one group at the expense of others;
> –we need to be ready to form alliances with non-frontline groups of particular importance to us.

The strategist who drafted this document goes on to suggest the following course of action:

> Of all the available options there is no doubt that going for amalgamation of all groups under one banner would be the best option in the interests of the struggle. It would appear though that preferable though this option might be it is full of limitations which we will impose on other groups and which they in turn would impose on us. Reluctantly therefore one is forced to suggest that for the time being the only option available to us is to be on our own both internally and externally, but all the same to maintain a positive neutrality with regard to other groups which operate outside and underground internally in the hope that in future we might be a useful unifying force.[4]

In the light of what happened subsequently but without having been privy to the relevant discussions, I can only conclude that Steve Biko and his comrades had decided (with or without mandate, I have no way of telling) to explore the "preferred option." Hence, the plans they were busy working out with our group and others. In any case, it is now a matter of history that before Biko's projected departure and by the time I managed to get to Europe in 1978–1979, he had been murdered in detention as the result of a series of catastrophic events, the definitive account of which remains outstanding. As I have noted elsewhere,[5] one of the objectives of his fateful journey to Cape Town, a few days before he was murdered in detention, was to meet with our group and others in order to discuss this plan. In Cape Town, he in fact stayed with one of our underground operatives. As recounted there, that meeting was, tragically, aborted. It is also important to record here, against the detractors of Steve Biko, that whatever one's critique of the BCM in general and of Biko in particular, he died, literally, in quest of the unification of the forces of liberation in South Africa.

The Manifesto of the Azanian People

The point of this all too brief reference to a potentially revolutionary moment in our contemporary history is to underline the fact that the BCM leadership, whatever the contradictions and disagreements in its ranks, together with other organizations, including underground socialist groups such as the one to which I belonged, was actively exploring ways and means of establishing a united political front not merely as a tactical alliance but as a long-term strategic alliance for the attainment of the overthrow of the apartheid state. Another significant step along this path was the systematic underground circulation in 1982 of "the Stuurman document," of which I myself had written the original draft and which is referred to below.[6] This well-considered move, however, was prevented from gaining momentum and actively opposed by, among others, leading members of the South African Communist Party, who spread the vicious rumor that this was a manifestation of the activities of a so-called "Third Force" that was being nurtured and funded by American imperialism.[7] This contemptible political nonsense helped to create an atmosphere of suspicion and rivalry between the BCM and many cadres of the ANC and was, without any doubt, part and parcel of the strategy of gaining for that organization the spurious United Nations Organization (UNO) and Organisation of African Unity (OAU) accredited status of "sole authentic representative" of the oppressed people of South Africa, a fashionable and patently antidemocratic "divide and weaken" tactic used by "liberal" as well as some "communist" organ grinders in order to control "their" particular monkey.

This episode does, however, provide the necessary background to understanding how the Azanian Manifesto came to be conceptualized and eventually adopted by the NF in June 1983. By the time the South African Students' Organization (SASO) trialists emerged from prison, there was a history of close cooperation between the BCM and some of the revolutionary socialist groups that were operating in the country. The early 1980s was a period of intense agitation and mobilization in the Western Cape, beginning with the 1980 Schools Boycott campaign and the establishment of the Parents Teachers Students Association (PTSA) movement, followed by the militant opposition to the "Koornhof Bills" by the ad hoc Disorderly Bills Action Committee (DBAC) that culminated in the formation of the broad united front that came to be known as the Cape Action League (CAL). In this context, the sterling political work that was being done on a countrywide basis in the diverse structures that were accountable to the South African Council on Sport (SACOS) has a place of honor. Like all the other initiatives and organizations referred to here, these structures worked on a strictly nonsectarian basis in accordance with the united front ethos that characterized this phase of struggle. It was undoubtedly this wave of militant and overt political action that attracted the Azanian People's Organisation (AZAPO) leadership to those of us who were known to be sympathetic to cooperation with the BCM. It was, moreover, in this context that the Stuurman document that, from many accounts, had an important catalytic effect, was widely disseminated in samizdat fashion. After a careful analysis of the idea of the united front, the document called on the active cadres of all the organizations of the oppressed to band together in a fighting front for liberation from racist oppression and class exploitation. It is appropriate in this context to quote the concluding paragraphs:

> The intensification of the struggle in Southern Africa and the mortal danger of disunity and civil war among the oppressed people have created a situation of urgency. Ever since the historic events of 1976 it has become clear to all serious-minded militants that we can work together and that we can have unity in action even though we have not reached full agreement on all principles.
>
> Although some recent developments appear to contradict this tendency of people's organizations to work together, it is clear that most serious militants realise that such developments would constitute a modern-day national suicide. There is great need for a national debate on the principles and practice of the united front.
>
> The time has come to combine our forces in a united front that represents the vast majority of the black workers and of the radical black middle class. The challenge to the oppressed and exploited people has never been

greater in our entire history. Against the background of the heroic events since the Soweto uprising, there is no doubt that the organizations of the people will rise to the occasion and will create through united action the instruments required to meet this challenge.

Let us make 1982 into the year of the united front and raise our struggle for liberation from apartheid and capitalism on to a higher level. Let us unite for a nonracial, democratic and undivided Azania-South Africa![8]

Informal and formal discussions with various political tendencies and groupings initiated and coordinated by the AZAPO leadership, which included well known and prominent comrades such as Lybon Mabasa, Strini Moodley, Saths Cooper, Muntu Myeza, Pandelani Nefolovhodwe, Ish Mkhabela, and Zithulele Cindi among many others, eventually led to the decision to organize the first NF. A provisional NF Committee was established that included non-AZAPO members, and, among others, Bishop Tutu, Rev. Alan Boesak, Frank van der Horst (SACOS), and myself. The decision to establish a "Forum" was calculated to appeal to the broadest possible constituency among the oppressed people as well as to individuals classified "white" but committed to the liberation of South Africa. It was in respect of this latter objective, insisted upon by groups such as ours, that contradictions arose at various times during the months preceding the conference as well as during the conference and its successive gatherings.

It is unnecessary to delve into the details of organization and mobilization of the first NF. However, a few noteworthy features of this event should be mentioned here.[9] The first is the fact of the participation of the two clerics—Bishop Tutu and Rev. Boesak—who subsequently played such a prominent role in the United Democratic Front (UDF).[10] As soon as the UDF move was initiated, Rev. Boesak abandoned ship and devoted all his time to promoting, funding, and strengthening the UDF. Bishop Tutu, to his credit, tried for a few years to straddle both formations and to get them to work together. In his trademark ironic manner, he both lauded those who had initiated the Forum and warned against the dangers of divisive, sectarian approaches and practices:

> We all know that we Blacks, as they say, are slow thinkers. We could not think for ourselves that it was high time we held such a National Forum worried as we must have been by the fragmentation of the Black community making it easier for the enemy of the struggle to apply the old ploy of divide and rule... We do their dirty work for them. We wash our dirty linen in public. What does it really matter whether you say you are an exponent of Black Consciousness and somebody else is an upholder of

the Freedom Charter, whether you are AZAPO, COSAS or Committee of Ten—isn't the most important thing the struggle itself for the total liberation of all the people of South Africa, Black and White to live where the rule of law obtains with habeas corpus holding sway, where all have full citizenship rights and obligations...[11]

Other clerics affiliated to the South African Council of Churches—with warm thoughts for Rev. Manas Buthelezi—stayed the distance until the overwhelming material and political support for the UDF eliminated the NF as a notional rival.

To come back to the Manifesto: for the historical record, it should be noted that I was given the task of preparing the draft document on the basis of the resolutions put forward for adoption at the first NF. This task was completed during the night before the final day of the Forum. Inevitably, my political background and my political stance influenced the specific formulations that now comprise that document, although it was, naturally, amended in decisive ways before it was unanimously adopted by the hundreds of Forum delegates. It is essential, if one is interested in getting a sense of the many-stranded texture of the Forum and of its social matrix, to go back to the actual resolutions that were proposed.

Lest the leadership of the Forum be accused of blatant manipulation, it ought to be stressed that this phenomenon is generic to all such gatherings. Some of the laughable strictures to which we have been subjected by Stalinist critics of the Forum over the years are disingenuous at best and downright mendacious at worst.[12] The Manifesto is usually—implicitly rather than explicitly, lest it be dignified by the very act of juxtaposition—compared to the Freedom Charter that is presented as a "sacred" text that was "written" by "the people" themselves.[13] On reflection, it is obvious that the manner in which the Freedom Charter came to be formulated is reflective of a particular historical moment in the mid-1950s before the full repressive might of the apartheid state was brought to bear on the liberation movement. It is, therefore, invidious to suggest, as Comrade Mzala does, that unless a political program has evolved in the manner of the Freedom Charter, it cannot have any validity. Besides the obvious ahistorical character of this argument, one need only apply it to a world-historic document such as the Communist Manifesto to realize how fallacious it is.

Retrospect

Today, twenty-three years after the event, with all the advantages of hindsight and of the volumes of analysis that have tried to explain the geopolitical shifts that took place in the period 1985–1989, it is easy to understand why the NF and its brave attempt at placing an overtly socialist alternative on the political agenda of the South African revolution had to fail. That is not the subject of this chapter. It is relevant, however, to conclude by referring to the contemporary analysis of the Manifesto and of the NF that I made at the second NF during the Easter weekend of 1984. In retrospect, the following judgment seems to have been as accurate as it was possible to be at the time:

> The [National Party (NA)] government's New Deal strategy, which embraces at the same time the Koornhof Acts and the relocation of the African people in Bantustan concentration camps, threatened to unleash a flood of working-class militancy and action. Since 1980, almost every significant mass action in South Africa has carried the imprint of the black working class. Socialist solutions to the system of racial capitalism were becoming common coinage among the youth and in workers' organizations. This development was and is feared by the petite bourgeoisie and by the liberal bourgeoisie.
> Liberals of all colours and shapes thus tried to ensure that the mass movement against the New Deal would not be placed under the leadership of the working class. The instrument that they chose for this purpose is the so-called United Democratic Front… [Despite] the fond illusions of some self-proclaimed leftists in the UDF, the reins of that bandwagon are firmly in the hands of middle-class leaders whose vision and practices do not extend beyond opposition to the superficial symptoms of apartheid. Men have been built up through the newspapers and by other means who can now steer the bandwagon almost in any direction they choose…[14]

In the same stocktaking, I also looked at the achievements and failures of the NF under the motto: *Tell no lies, claim no easy victories*, but still in the belief that an albeit conflictual constructive interaction between some of the UDF formations and the NF was possible and necessary. With respect to the Manifesto itself, we were still brimming with hope and did not realize that as we were speaking, developments around the ascent to power of Mikhail Gorbachev in the USSR were going to squash for a long time any hopes of successful socialist revolution anywhere in the world. So, in the light of the profound technological, economic, political, and general social changes that have occurred during these past twenty-five years, although the principles of the Manifesto remain relevant because, like similar documents that proclaimed the socialist alternative at a peculiar sociohistorical moment, new approaches to strategy and tactics are essential, indeed, a new "language" has to be forged, in order to reveal the relevance and the feasibility of realizing those principles. It is as clear now as it was then that the struggle continues. *Aluta continua!*[15]

Appendix: The Azanian Manifesto

Manifesto of the Azanian people

This historic conference of organisations of the oppressed and exploited people of Azania held at Hammanskraal on 11–12 June 1983 and convened by the National Forum Committee, having deliberated on vital questions affecting our nation and in particular having considered the implications of the Botha Government's 'new deal' strategy (the President's Council, constitutional proposals and Koornhof Bills) resolves:

1. To condemn the murder of freedom fighters by the racist minority regime.
2. To issue the following manifesto for consideration by all the organisations of the people to be reviewed at the second National Forum to be convened during the Easter Weekend of 1984.

Our struggle for national liberation is directed against the system of racial capitalism which holds the people of Azania in bondage for the benefit of the small minority of white capitalist and their allies, the white workers and the reactionary sections of the black middle class. The struggle against apartheid is no more than the point of departure for our liberation efforts. Apartheid will be eradicated with the system of racial capitalism.

The black working class inspired by revolutionary consciousness is the driving force of our struggle. They alone can end the system as it stands today because they alone have nothing at all to lose. They have a world to gain in a democratic, antiracist and socialist Azania. It is the historic task of the black working class and its organisations to mobilise the urban and the rural poor together with the radical sections of the middle classes in order to put an end to the system of oppression and exploitation by the white ruling class.

The successful conduct of the national liberation struggle depends on the firm basis of principle whereby we will ensure that the liberation struggle will not be turned against our people by a treacherous and opportunistic "leader." Of these principles, the most important are:

- Antiracism and anti-imperialism.
- Noncollaboration with the oppressor and its political instruments.
- Independent working-class organisation.
- Opposition to all alliances with ruling-class parties.

In accordance with these principles, the oppressed and exploited people of Azania demand immediately:

- The right to work.
- The right to form trade unions that will heighten revolutionary worker consciousness.
- The establishment of a democratic, antiracist worker Republic in Azania where the interests of the workers shall be paramount through worker control of the means of production, distribution and exchange.
- State provision of free and compulsory education for all and this education be geared towards liberating the Azanian people from all forms of oppression, exploitation and ignorance.
- State provision of adequate and decent housing.
- State provision of free health, legal, recreational and other community services that will respond positively to the needs of the people.
- Development of one national progressive culture in the process of struggle.
- The land and all that belongs to it shall be wholly owned and controlled by the Azanian people.
- The usage of the land and all that accrues to it shall be aimed at ending all forms and means of exploitation.

In order to bring into effect these demands of the Azanian people, we pledge ourselves to struggle tirelessly for:

- The abolition of all laws that discriminate against our people on the basis of colour, sex, class, religion or language.
- The abolition of all influx control measures and pass laws.
- The abolition of all resettlement and group areas removals.
- Reintegration of the 'bantustan' human dumping grounds into a unitary Azania.

Notes

1. See, for example, Tom Lodge and Bill Nasson, *All Here and Now: Black Politics in South Africa in the 1980s* (New York: Ford Foundation, 1991).
2. See T. H. R. Davenport and Christopher Saunders, *South Africa: A Modern History* (London: Palgrave Macmillan and New York: St. Martin's Press, 2000).
3. See Neville Alexander, "Black Consciousness: A Reactionary Tendency?" in Barney Pityana, Mamphela Ramphele, Malusi Mpumlwana, and Lindy Wilson, eds., *Bounds of Possibility: The Legacy of Steve Biko and Black Consciousness* (Cape Town, London, and New Jersey: David Philip and Zed Press, 1991), 238–252. Also see Mokgethi

Motlhabi, *The Theory and Practice of Black Resistance to Apartheid: A Social-Ethical Analysis* (Johannesburg, SA: Skotaville Publishers, 1985), especially ch. 4.
4. Readers will have to accept my word for it that this is an unaltered quote from an authentic minute of the executive meeting of the BPC, referred to in the text. I have taken it from a letter I wrote from Germany to comrades in South Africa in 1979, which is in my personal archives.
5. See Charles Villa-Vicencio, *The Spirit of Hope: Conversations on Religion, Politics and Values* (Johannesburg, SA: Skotaville Publishers, 1993), 3–4.
6. See Neville Alexander, "Let Us Unite in the Year of the United Front," in *Sow the Wind: Contemporary Speeches* (Johannesburg, SA: Skotaville Publishers, 1985).
7. In an acerbic altercation with Mac Maharaj in the London home of a mutual friend toward the end of 1978, he accused people such as Biko and myself of trying to establish a "third force" and of being either the dupes of, or willing collaborators with "American imperialism." Also see Dale T. McKinley, *The ANC and the Liberation Struggle: A Critical Political Biography* (London and Chicago: Pluto Press, 1997), 59.
8. Alexander, *Sow the Wind*, 16–17.
9. Some of the papers delivered at the Forum as well as the reports of the Commissions (large breakaway groups), the resolutions and the Manifesto itself were published in NF Committee, *National Forum* (Johannesburg, SA: National Forum Committee, 1983).
10. Rev. Boesak was actually in Scandinavia at the time of the conference but sent a telegram to convey warm greetings and full support.
11. Desmond Tutu, "Unity and Liberation," *National Forum*, 10–11. Johannesburg: National Forum Committee, 1983.
12. See, for example, Comrade Mzala, *Latest Opportunism and the Theory of the South African Revolution* (NP: African National Congress [?], 1984). To my regret, I met Comrade Mzala only briefly at Yale University in 1990 or 1991 and found him to be a very different person from the apparatchik that peers from underneath the cloak of scholarship he presents in this forgettable pamphlet.
13. See R. Suttner and J. Cronin, *30 Years of the Freedom Charter* (Johannesburg: Ravan Press, 1985), 206–208.
14. Alexander, *Sow the Wind*, 175.
15. Ibid., 178–179.

8

Critical Intellectualism: The Role of Black Consciousness in Reconfiguring the Race-Class Problematic in South Africa

Nurina Ally and Shireen Ally

Introduction

In 1968, when Steve Biko and Barney Pityana walked out of a National Union of South African Students (NUSAS) meeting, they changed the landscape of South African politics. The Black Consciousness movement inaugurated by that watershed event has been described as "the single most important development in the internal politics of South Africa in the period 1967–76."[1] But, while the impact of the Black Consciousness movement on the political landscape has been recognized, the defining role that the movement played in shaping the intellectual landscape of South Africa has remained largely unexamined. This chapter rescripts Black Consciousness into the intellectual history of South Africa by examining the dramatic role played by the movement in inspiring the most influential intellectual debate of the period following its birth—that of the analytical configuration of the relationship between race and class in explaining the sociopolitical structure of South Africa. We argue that the Black Consciousness critique on liberalism, and the alienating politics of race engendered by it, proved a pivotal determinant in the shift toward critical Marxist thought among white, English-speaking intellectuals in the 1970s. Dialogue between the dominant intellectual position among white radicals and the changing nature of Black Consciousness intersected with the politics of class in emerging labor movements to fundamentally shape reconfigurations of class and race in opposition to apartheid. That dialogue has had profound implications on the South African intellectual landscape, and it is argued that Black Consciousness must be located within that moment as a form of critical intellectualism.

"Black Man, You Are on Your Own"

Coined by Barney Pityana, popularized by Stephen Bantu Biko, and used as the rallying cry of the South African Student's Organisation (SASO), the phrase "Black Man, You Are On Your Own!" resonated in the 1970s as a hailing to (and impelled dramatic shifts among) both black and white intellectual circles. The phrase captured the liberation ideology underpinning Black Consciousness as a philosophy speaking directly and collectively to the oppressed black majority. It principally called for a "mental renaissance of black intellect,"[2] an invigoration of black agency and will.

This was the pivotal psychological dimension to Black Consciousness's "pre-figurative"[3] approach to emancipatory politics. That is, the understanding that social transformation and a true humanity could only be achieved once a counterhegemony to the dominating values and practices of the white superstructure had been prefigured in the opposition movement. Internalized acceptance of racial domination among the oppressed stemmed from low self-esteem and feelings of self-hatred, conditioned by the prevailing ideology of white superiority and black inferiority.[4] The movement's message thus called on black people to identify themselves not only as passive objects, but rather as active, "self-defining initiators."[5]

Implicit in this awakening was an indictment of dependency upon whites in the struggle, a dependency fostered by the "Black Man's" lack of recognition of self and solidarity with an oppressed collective. The slogan "Black Man, You Are On Your Own" expressed then not only the importance of the constructive exercise of self-affirmation and recognition, but also how this process was intrinsically linked to deconstructing the politics inherent in relations of dependency between blacks and whites within the liberation struggle.

These two elements to Black Consciousness philosophy are well illustrated in an address by Barney Pityana. First, quoting Fanon, he asserts: "My Negro consciousness does not hold itself out as black. It *is*. It is its own follower. This is all that we blacks are after, *to be*. We believe that we are quite different in handling our Beness and for this purpose we are self-sufficient."[6] He then goes on to explain, "The point I am trying to make here is that we shall never find our goals and aspirations as a people centered anywhere else but in *us*. This, therefore, necessitates a self-examination and a rediscovery of ourselves. Blacks can no longer afford to be led and dominated by non-Blacks."

Benny Khoapa, too, described the need for exclusive black organization using the term "regroupment,"[7] referring to a movement of "transcendent negations."[8] "Paradoxically," he writes, "a prerequisite for human solidarity is a feeling of non-solidarity with men who stand in the way of solidarity."[9]

But, of course, the distinctiveness of Black Consciousness was that it did not target direct supporters of the apartheid regime. Rather, the Black Consciousness movement was birthed in the rejection of that group of whites who purported to support the struggle for liberation, collectively identified as the "white liberal establishment." Black Consciousness saw white liberalism as the primary obstacle to independent black initiative and organization and, therefore, to black liberation. Liberalism was a shifting and changing political and intellectual movement,[10] but came to define a particular white oppositionalism coordinated within distinctive institutions, including NUSAS. It was against these oppositional whites that Black Consciousness levelled its most devastating attacks.

In the early years of its development, fears of consolidating a form of "second-class apartheid"[11] saw the movement (as embodied in SASO student politics at the time) approaching questions of exclusive black organization and separation wearily. SASO's first constitution, therefore, still recognized NUSAS as a national union and was careful in only claiming itself as an organization to "promote contact among black students."[12] However, Buthelezi notes that as the movement began to establish a more coherent political identity and ideology, its objective shifted to a more direct targeting of the political influence of white liberalism and effectively distinguishing SASO from white liberal politics.

By 1970, SASO newsletters took a clear and uncompromising stance against collaboration with white liberals who, in Biko's words, "call a few 'intelligent and articulate' blacks to 'come to around for tea at home,' where all present ask each other the same old hackneyed question 'how can we bring about change in South Africa.'"[13] In his well-known critique of white liberals, "*Black Souls in White Skins?*," Biko betrayed his indebtedness to Fanon. In it, he revealed the cultural-psychological aspect of the skepticism levelled against involvement by, and cooperation with, white sympathizers. For Black Consciousness, solidarity emerged out of the common experience of oppression, an experience of suffering that white people could never fully identify with since "sympathetic White countrymen, sincere and well-meaning though they may be, have been rendered by circumstances unable to view the problem from the Black man's viewpoint."[14]

The persistent influence of whites in the struggle under the banners of integration and bilateral approaches were also held to be deliberately responsible for preventing the black man from being "on his own," and in so doing, was a primary cause in perpetuating a cycle of dependency within the superiority-inferiority complex of racial domination. As Budlender notes, Black Consciousness pointed out that when white people proposed integration as the ideal, what was really proposed was assimilation: "The concept of integration, whose virtues are often extolled in white liberal circles, is full of unquestioned assumptions that embrace white values... It is an integration in which the black man will have to prove himself in terms of those values before meriting acceptance and ultimate assimilation..."[15]

Furthermore, integration also implied white initiative rather than grassroots direction, stemming from the embedded prejudice of "the intellectual arrogance of white people that makes them believe that white leadership is a sine qua non in this country and that whites are the divinely appointed pace-setters in progress."[16] With the rejection of NUSAS in 1971 and the resolve that "Blacks only are qualified to determine the means for change,"[17] the South African political and intellectual landscape became a minefield for white involvement.

For Black Consciousness, whites would always be beneficiaries and "part and parcel of the system of white domination,"[18] thus limiting their ability to be fully committed to the required overhaul of such a system and hence "no matter what a white man does, the colour of his skin—his passport to privilege—will always put him miles ahead of the black man."[19] White people involved in the struggle would always have some stake in reflecting power politics rather than challenging it, Biko emphasized. Motivated by "metaphysical guilt," white sympathizers were charged with failing to recognize the problem as white racism and as rather persisting in appeasing their own conscience or, in Pityana's words, "at best eager to demonstrate his identification with the black people only in so far as so doing does not sever all his ties with his relative on the other side of the colour line."[20]

Biko was unforgiving in his evaluation of the resultant involvement of whites in an oppositional politics: "Their presence among us is irksome and of nuisance value. It removes the focus of attention from essentials and shifts it to ill-defined philosophical concepts that are both irrelevant to the black man and merely a red herring across the track."[21]

In this, Biko revealed Black Consciousness's antipathy to white involvement not only on a political level, but on the intellectual terrain as well. In questioning the legitimacy of white involvement in an oppositional politics, in denouncing white intellectualism as an "irksome" diversion of attention from "essentials," and in focusing so vigorously in these early years on the analytic of race, Black Consciousness would come to distinctively participate in the intellectual landscape of South Africa for the following two decades.

The First Moment: Impelling the Shift

By the 1960s, liberal political economy was fairly established as the dominant paradigm for white liberalism as an intellectual movement, arguing that apartheid was caused by pathological racial attitudes that would be proven dysfunctional with the growth of capitalism and the extension of modernization.[22] By the mid-1970s, a different generation of white oppositional intellectuals refuted this liberal claim by arguing that race was only an ideological justification for the essentially class project of apartheid, introducing Marxism as a distinctive intellectual movement. Although only used quite late in the 1970s, the fact that its primary intellectual claim remained the characterization of South Africa as "racial capitalism" signaled that the central intellectual debate was of the shifting balance of race versus class (of oppression versus exploitation) in explaining the peculiar characteristics of apartheid. Although liberalism had only conceded the centrality of race prejudice to explaining apartheid, Marxism recoded the role of race, firmly enmeshing it with the materialism of class.

By the mid 1970s, an entire generation of scholars and activists used Marxism (in its various forms) as the preferred mode of analytic inquiry. Although a distinction could be made between the scholars trained in social science who were most forcefully in direct opposition to liberalism on the one hand, and the revisionist historians who were more concerned to unearth struggles of ordinary people in history on the other, there was nonetheless a clear commonality to their positioning as white radicals, separate from the earlier generation of white liberals. At the same time, they represented a different tradition even within the left. Rejecting the "old" left of dogmatic doctrine and elitist politics, this "new left" offered a democratic intellectualism and politics grounded in the historical and lived realities of people's and groups' agency. So influential was this generation that Nash summarizes that they came to constitute "a powerful presence in South African political and intellectual life throughout the 1980s":

> Their ideas and analyses reshaped social and political studies at South African universities, established themselves at the heart of the curriculum of many academic departments, and gave impetus to conferences, journals and other publications. They played a crucial role in guiding student, women's and civic organizations, and above all the trade union movement which they had helped to build.[23]

Although the genesis of this influential intellectual movement has been attributed to the moral certitude of the generation of young, white, English-speaking intellectuals that constituted it,[24] or the relaxation of state controls that allowed this group of oppositional whites to express their moral certitude,[25] the role of Black Consciousness in inspiring this shift has only been mutedly acknowledged. In a recent reinterpretation of the history of this shift, Shireen Ally demonstrates that Marxism among this group of white oppositional intellectuals reflected, in part, a response by this group to the challenge posed by Black Consciousness.[26]

In questioning the legitimacy of any white involvement in an oppositional politics, Black Consciousness threatened the political role of white intellectuals. For the generation of South African students located in British and other universities, and conscientized by New Left politics there, reentering South Africa with a desire to play a political role in opposition, but confronted by a radical black philosophical program that denied the same, produced a deep sense of alienation. Richard Turner, a key figure of the white radical left during this period, reflected the anxiety among white intellectuals of their irrelevance suggested by the rise of Black Consciousness: "Thus, for whites, in the face of the phenomenon of 'black consciousness,' to believe that they must now simply shut up and leave it to the blacks would be a serious mistake."[27]

For this group of white, English-speaking intellectuals, whose role in the struggle was being questioned by a movement of Blacks resolutely focused on race as the basis of a critical intellectualism and politics, the turn to Marxism was not coincidental. As Ally concludes, "Marxism offered a re-positioning of race in the explanatory equation of apartheid in ways that constructed an intellectual and political role for this group of white, English-speaking intellectuals."[28] Nash indirectly suggests this process:

> The moment of Western Marxism in South Africa began with the recognition among white radical students that they were not part of the social force which would bring about revolutionary change. Fundamental social change could not result from radical white students organizing themselves, nor could they claim to speak for the oppressed majority. The idea of organization as a catalyst in the process of transforming class consciousness was shaped by their need to define a political role in that context.[29]

The turn of white radical intellectualism to an analytic of class must therefore be understood as a political positioning, one contextually framed by the Black Consciousness movement's association of radical politics with a prioritization of race. Budlender therefore argues that "the result was that many of those who were most challenged by Black Consciousness and who were most persuaded by the force of this critique, found themselves without a direct political home. The option for most was either to drop out of political engagement or to find indirect methods of engagement which were consistent with the lessons they had learned."[30] The indirect method of engagement became a reformulation of the relationship between race and class. Glaser suggests the same: "White, Indian and Mestico leftists found in Marxism's prioritization of class over race an analysis that did not associate them indelibly with the system of oppression or exclude them from exercising active influence in radical politics."[31]

Biko reflected a definite awareness around this relationship between the marginalization of a racial analysis and a strategic positioning by white leftists:

> A number of whites in this country adopt the class analysis primarily because they want to detach us from anything relating to race in case it has a rebound effect on them because they are white...as a defence mechanism...And of course a number of them are terrible about it. They (pronounce judgments) again and again on this whole problem of black-white relationships in a court or a yard which is basically ours. They are terribly puritanical, dogmatic and very very arrogant.[32]

In attempting a response to Black Consciousness's recognition of the politics of race embedded in white radicals' critical thought, the white left insistently sought to distinguish themselves from white liberals, the main target of Black Consciousness's attack, in order to restate a claim to legitimacy. Turner insisted that Black Consciousness had "confused" "racist, liberal, and radical whites," and that the introduction of the third category established the unique differentiation of radical whites from the other targets of Black Consciousness's critique.[33] Webster attempted a similar exercise, suggesting the category of "committed radical" to differentiate white radicals from "traditional" and "despairing" liberals.[34] This proliferation of categories among oppositional whites as a defense mechanism became so common that Budlender argues those attacked by Black Consciousness "found a more skilful method of denial...[t]he obvious response was to deny that one was a liberal. And so new labels abounded: some called themselves radicals; others said that they were liberal radicals."[35] A writer, A.P., satirized this amusing multiplication of labels in *Reality* (which from November 1972 called itself a journal of liberal *and radical* opinion) as follows:

Sometimes I was a glad lib
Sometimes I was a sad lib
No more I'll be a bad lib
For now I am a rad lib.
I never was a mad rad

> *I would have made a bad rad*
> *Although I hate the glib rad*
> *Myself am now a lib rad.*[36]

Biko, in keeping with A.P.'s satire, refused to recognize these distinctions, arguing at one point that the "liberal establishment" that was the target of Black Consciousness's critique included radicals: "We now come to that group that has enjoyed the longest confidence from the black world—the liberal establishment including the radical and leftist groups. The major mistake the black world ever made was to assume that whoever opposed apartheid was an ally."[37]

Although often unacknowledged, white Marxism and Black Consciousness were clearly in dialogue with one another, albeit indirectly. In this, Black Consciousness was not only critical to the genesis of a particular landscape of intellectual engagement and debate in the 1970s, but participated in the resulting animating debate between the analytical acuity of class versus race in the explanation of apartheid.

Although Marxism organized itself clearly around a theorization of "racial capitalism," Black Consciousness shifted the terms of the debate. The philosophy of Black Consciousness clearly rested on an introspective psychological and cultural transformation in values and consciousness, with an emphasis on an identity of interests emerging out of the common experience of oppression based on color. This particular prefigurative model translated into the initial emergence of a strong theoretical and political analytic of race, and a reticence toward understanding apartheid as a class project.[38] Hirschmann does note the recognition of a relationship between class and race to some degree by Njabulo Ndebele who warned blacks to "be careful of concentrating on racial struggle to the detriment of the economic struggle, because the latter may have become more important than the former."[39] But, despite this recognition, Black Consciousness discourse remained, at this time, in opposition to theorizations of racial capitalism. Some suggest that this was to a certain degree a reflection of the academic persuasion fostered at tribal universities, either with its censoring of Marxist literature or European-oriented faculty.[40]

While the privileging of race over class may in some part be attributed to the institutional and generational ideological influences identified by some commentators, this particular formulation of the race-class analytic was also decidedly shaped by a self-conscious awareness of the relationship between the influence of white intellectuals and Marxist class rhetoric. Theorizations of racial capitalism were indeed recognized, but were consciously avoided and made explicitly secondary to a racial analysis. Moodley somewhat recognizes this by suggesting that one reason for the limited focus on class and economic forces was, in some part, based on the "rejection of Marxism as a white ideology."[41] Karis and Gerhart are more explicit: "The founders of SASO had explicitly avoided Marxist rhetoric. The know-it-all manner of white leftists in NUSAS had antagonized them."[42] Biko clearly reflected this:

> There are some white leftists who have attachment to, say, the same rough principles of post revolutionary society (as ourselves) but a lot of them are terribly cynical about for instance, the importance of the value systems which we enunciate so often, from the black consciousness angle. That it is not only capitalism that is involved; it is also the whole gamut of white value systems, which has been adopted as standard by South Africa, both whites and blacks so far...So your problems are not solved completely when you alter the economic pattern, to a socialist pattern. You still don't become what you ought to be.[43]

In this presentation, then, of race as a basis of not only political mobilization, but also as a primary and independent analytic, Black Consciousness participated in and shaped the defining intellectual debate of the 1970s. In the reformulation of the analytic primacy of class and race, the Marxist turn that was to so definitively shape the intellectual landscape of South Africa in the 1970s firmly bore the imprint of Black Consciousness' definition of the limits and possibilities of whites in radical politics. At the same time, Black Consciousness participated in the defining debate of the decade by offering an intellectually articulate alternative theorization of the relationship between race and class. As the debate progressed and mutated in the 1980s, so did Black Consciousness' involvement and intellectual program, positioning the movement differently—but still centrally—to the ongoing attempt to understand the race-class analytic, and of the limits and possibilities of that theorization in a politics of change. For white radicals, "racial capitalism" was the summative analytical program, and out of this was forged a politics committed to independent, black, working-class mobilization. It was in this political extension of white oppositional intellectualism that Black Consciousness came to dialogue with the movement it partly inspired yet again, redefining for itself the theorized intersections between race and class.

The Second Moment: Consolidating the Shift

Despite the movement's apparent marginalization of material perspectives on apartheid exploitation and Biko's caution against "white leftists" who "by dragging all sorts of red herrings across our paths...tell us that the situation is a class struggle"—earlier described as "the kind of twisted logic that the Black Consciousness approach seeks to eradicate"[44] during the 1970s—a shift toward a focus on the link and impact of capitalism and imperialism was increasingly evident in SASO.[45] At the Black Renaissance Convention, in 1974, it was clear that Black Consciousness was trying to accommodate an analysis of capitalist *exploitation* in South Africa more coherently within its framework.[46]

Explaining the radical shift within Black Consciousness, Fatton identifies the Sono affair of 1972, the Durban Strikes of 1973, massive repression against Black Consciousness advocates in 1974, the coming independence of the Transkei, the Tanzanian experiment, and the emergence of socialist-Marxist regimes in Mozambique, Angola, and Guinea-Bissau; while Karis and Gerhart also point out the increased accessibility of left-wing literature both inside and outside South Africa and the influence of former ANC-PAC members within the movement.[47] While not failing to recognize the importance of the multiplicity of factors influencing the radicalization of Black Consciousness, shifting race-class configurations were also shaped by the politics of decline affecting the Black Consciousness movement in the late 1970s.

One influential factor was the decline of the movement in the 1970s precipitated by the failure to mobilize significant grassroots support beyond the student base. Black Consciousness was charged with being a predominantly intellectual movement unable to translate consciousness into action.[48] At a meeting of the Soweto Action Committee in 1978, for instance, a critique declared:

> The major concern of the movement has been to draw all black people into the orbit of consciousness. It has been restricted to the empirical consciousness of alienation grasped in terms of racial discrimination, exploitation and systematic land spoliation. But little has been done in terms of translating black aspirations into a praxis for the black masses. Little has been done to bridge the gap between empirical consciousness of alienation and radical action to uproot the causes of alienation. Any new dimension therefore must bring along with it a qualitative difference, a promotion from empirical consciousness of the enforced process of black alienation to a creative yet radical action.[49]

By the mid-1970s, the emergence of a strong trade union movement served to further highlight this failing within Black Consciousness. No longer "the only show in town,"[50] the politics of class inspired by the influence of white radicals effectively contributed to the declining influence of Black Consciousness as a mobilizing ideology. As Hirschmann states quite clearly:

> Its [Black Consciousness'] influence also appears to have been undermined by white intellectuals and organisations...Progressive white scholars

have had a powerful influence in integrating class analysis and socialist strategies into the domestic South Africa anti-apartheid debate...White activists have also contributed to the development of the trade union movement which had arisen as a very strong competing political force, one which in general does not pay very strong heed to the BCM.[51]

Within the Black Consciousness movement, this became a confirmation of white control over black politics, but also a seemingly bitter reflection of Black Consciousness's failure to produce a more compelling politics for change:

> Indeed, the indictment against the black consciousness movement for allowing this situation to develop was a telling one. For the white university radicals not only had the energy and hard work needed to achieve what they did, but they also had endless resources at their disposal. In every aspect of the black community's life the white liberal element returned to sweet talk their way into directing our liberation struggle.[52]

The success of white progressives in mobilizing class as a theoretical and political analytic in the antiapartheid struggle motivated, by the end of the 1970s, more explicit critiques of Black Consciousness's failure to address class adequately. This critique called upon the incorporation and development of a more class-based identity of interests within Black Consciousness. As seen most clearly within AZAPO in the 1980s, a reconfiguration of the analytic of race and class was underway within the movement: "It is true that black people in South Africa are exploited and oppressed but it is not that they are exploited because they are black. To see the problem this way is to see it through the eyes of Apartheid and necessarily the solution must follow along such lines, which is an ill-conceived perception."[53] Further on, the paper continues:

> The question of colour of course cannot be ignored in South Africa given the nature of [the] racially-structured socio-economic system, but this is a *tactical and interim issue which involves modus operandi and strategy* [emphasis added], not the political and ideological direction of our liberation process, those must be cemented in the revolutionary theory of the working class party.[54]

In both its need to extend its influence to the masses and as a reaction to its own marginalization within the class discourse of the trade union movement, the movement had to reformulate the relationship of race and class in an emancipatory politics. Partly a strategic defense to maintain the numbers required of a political movement, this "shift" also clearly reflected, however, the movement's continuing internal reformulation of its ideas based on the continually changing context in which it was located. In that reformulation, Black Consciousness found itself influencing and being influenced by the intellectual terrain of South Africa. Spurring a shifting valency in its initial race-class configuration, Black Consciousness politics looked to working class mobilization and a theoretical engagement with class as the "new dimension" needed to respond to the critiques facing the movement. In one interview statement, the shift toward a reformulation of the race-class analytic is evident:

> Then 1976 posed new questions. The B.C. movements were banned. There were liberal inroads into black politics... This time B.C applied Marxian analysis—now it was no longer just black pride. Addressing itself to the situation and adapting a Marxian philosophy to the South African situation. In post-1976 B.C. says we have in South Africa the owners of the means of production and non-owners of means of production, it says further that race divides us into owners and non-owners. Race is a class determinant... Now Black Consciousness lays emphasis on Marxism.[55]

This intellectual retheorization engaged with and responded to the shifting possibilities for a politics of change in the context of the mid to late 1970s, a part of the dynamism of the movement in dialogue with an equally dynamic context of trade union mobilization among the black working classes. The increasing importance of the trade union movement (with its attendant commitment to class as a politics of change supported by white radicals) forced Black Consciousness to interrogate the limits of a politics of the self in a politics of social change, and coaxed a shift in understanding not only the basis of politics, but of the valence of race and class in theorizing apartheid's particular cocktail of oppression and exploitation. By 1978, the Soweto Action Committee was calling for an extension of the achievements of Black Consciousness through an incorporation of the labor struggle:

> The role of black labour within the black struggle introduces a definitive sense of orientation. Black Consciousness ceases to be just a pervasive philosophy of an empirical consciousness of the evil of the apartheid system. Black Consciousness ceases to be just an attitude of mind, it becomes an organizational power aimed at combating the violence of the state. With black labour as a revolutionary ferment at the heart of Black consciousness one already makes hints as to the nature of the future state... It is clear therefore that the ideological stance hitherto adhered to demands a qualitative change.[56]

This "qualitative change," then, responded to the broader intellectual and political landscape of South Africa, and was a continuation of the politics of class actually inspired by Black Consciousness in the challenges it posed for white radicals.[57] By the 1980s organizations like the Black Consciousness Movement of Azania (BCMA) and Azanian People's Organization (AZAPO) had adopted a decidedly class-based focus, with the AZAPO manifesto stating an understanding of the philosophy of Black Consciousness as "[a] philosophy that understands the position of the Black people who are de facto a race of workers and therefore an inevitable agent of change within the present political system."[58] Not only was there a direct refutation by Black Consciousness of assertions that it had no role in the true class struggle against apartheid exploitation, but an important affirmation of the repositioned politics as embedded in an intellectual engagement with the defining theoretical conversation at the time:

> The question is not to view black consciousness within the class struggle but to find out the relationship of black consciousness and the class struggle within the pattern of social transformation in the country. I suggest that Black Consciousness does not conflict with the notion of class struggle. There are in fact no practical problems in this regard. To suggest otherwise would be to imply that a black worker does not exist as "colour-blind" orthodox Marxists wish to do.[59]

Further on, it continues:

> Since black consciousness exposes the reality of life for black people, it is not a preconceived doctrine. The task of black consciousness can now be extended to articulate the problems of black workers. And what is their main problem? Exploitation of labour. The conflict between black workers and capital in South Africa is evident almost daily.[60]

With a more systematic analysis of the class basis of apartheid and the role of black labor as an agent of change, the shift from the more determinedly racial analysis of the Biko era both reflected and consolidated the radical shift among white English-speaking intellectuals. Fatton is keen to note, however, that the radicalization of Black Consciousness was not simply an adoption of class analysis to the exclusion of a racial emphasis. "Blackness," he says, "remained central to the analysis, but to it was added a materialistic conception of history purporting to explain the unity of the white ethnie, and the fragmentation of the black bloc... the class struggle existed among blacks, and among whites, but it had not yet become interracial."[61]

Indeed, a heavy emphasis on the "racial" aspect of "racial capitalism" was maintained. The consciousness of working-class struggle was framed as "merely a labour-directed view of black consciousness."[62] And the 1980 AZAPO manifesto held that "in our country, race is a class determinant."[63]

But the engagement with the intellectual terrain now dominated by Marxism was clear, and the focus on black working class consciousness eclipsed an erstwhile attempt to theorize black identity and culture.

The rallying cry, "Black Man, You Are on Your Own," so prevalent in the early part of the movement, now became less an independent political program in itself, but important in highlighting the need for independent black working class mobilization. As Moodley notes, the focus on psychological liberation and "blackness" turned more toward the framing of "socialist," "anti-capitalist" alternatives, rather than as a politics in its own right.[64] Letsatsi Mosala, national organizer of AZAPO in 1980, clearly states where the focus of the Black Consciousness Movement now lay:

> The dynamics of BC as a philosophy for liberation in SA have taken the philosophy out of its introspective phase. The introspective phase gave black people a chance to indulge in self-reflection and self-definition that resulted in self-affirmation as a people... AZAPO, the main black political organization operating above-board in SA today, has taken BC beyond the phase of black awareness into the class struggle. It has taken into cognizance the fact that black people are exploited as a nation in South Africa... Since the task of a philosophy is not merely to interpret the world but to change it, BC seeks a radical transformation of the SA situation. Transformation requires the dismantling of the unjust economic system which has reduced blacks to impoverished starving masses.[65]

At this stage, race became less an object or mode of analysis aimed at developing the common oppressed subjectivity and marginalizing white political involvement. Rather, race now developed more as a politics for rooting out white involvement within a broader class political project—a reformulation that was certainly a direct reaction to the success of white involvement in grassroots trade union politics. The influence of intellectuals in grassroots politics, especially when it came from white intellectuals, was targeted as a continuity of the meddlesome assertion of white leadership that defined the entire white liberal establishment for Black Consciousness. Mthembu in 1982, for instance, said: "White liberals manufactured a kind of compass that gives some white academics a status equal to the oppressed in the struggle. In all histories of the oppressed, the people have adopted their existential truism and analysed it scientifically and come up with an ideology suiting their struggle."[66] For Black Consciousness, the engagement with the terrain of intellectual debate was equally an engagement with the terrain of intellectuals' involvement in politics, and as Black Consciousness repositioned itself on the defining theoretical question of the moment, it remained committed to an analysis of race that understood it as potentially divisive of class solidarity, and of the stated self-serving interests of those who professed the possibilities of erasing the potency of race in politics:

> Those who hope that black and white workers will unite and fight and dream of solidarity between them do not realize that whenever white workers have struggled or supported a struggle in this country, it has not been a struggle for liberation—but a struggle to get something for themselves...The only whites who profess to want to join black workers are those who are economically most secure: university students, professionals and a handful of intellectuals—individuals who represent no significant social force.[67]

Although race was still a relevant factor in Black Consciousness intellectualism and politics by the end of the 1980s, class had emerged as an important analytic through which to understand apartheid exploitation. Hirschmann therefore concludes: "Even AZAPO and the National Forum, the declared successors of the BCM, have altered their own ideology: class has become more significant as a category of analysis than race, and capitalism has become as much the enemy as *apartheid*."[68] The theorization of class as theory and politics remained, nonetheless, distinct from competing conceptualizations, structuring a particular set of contours for the intellectual debates of the time. This radical shift from the early positioning of race and class in its initial stages was embedded in the contextual richness of both academic and political discourses and movements during the 1970s and 1980s. In this demonstration, we place Black Consciousness more centrally in the history of effervescent critical debate that defined the intellectual landscapes of the period, a role usually unacknowledged. Moreover, that particular role highlights a more critical understanding of the class analysis predominating intellectual circles from the seventies, suggesting its relationship to an alienating politics of race and the power politics inherent in such a relationship.

Conclusion

When Steve Biko and Barney Pityana walked out of the 1968 NUSAS meetings and challenged "Black Man, You Are On Your Own," they redefined the landscape of South African politics. But inasmuch as Black Consciousness fashioned dramatic shifts in the political landscape of South Africa, it also refashioned its intellectual landscapes. In the early to late 1970s, the Black Consciousness critique of white liberalism and of the role of whites in an oppositional politics contributed to the intellectual ferment that birthed white radical intellectualism. This shaped an enduring debate within Southern African studies on the balance of race and class in explaining apartheid. "Racial capitalism," the dominant analytic of the influential Marxist turn, was not only indirectly inspired by Black Consciousness, but an indirect conversation ensued that positioned Black Consciousness within this critical debate. In the 1980s, through the contextual determination of black working-class organization, itself impelled and facilitated by white radicals, the analytic of race and class morphed yet further in Black Consciousness's engagements with the ongoing theoretical and political conversation about the politics of change, establishing a dialogue that mapped the contours of the intellectual landscape of the period. By highlighting this, we rescript Black Consciousness into the history of critical intellectualism in South Africa.

Notes

1. Sam C. Nolutshungu, *Changing South Africa: Political Considerations* (Manchester, UK: Manchester University Press, 1982), 147.
2. Steve Biko, quoted in Robert Fatton, *Black Consciousness in South Africa: The Dialectics of Ideological Resistance to White Supremacy* (Albany, NY: SUNY Press, 1986), 78.
3. C. R. D. Halisi, "Biko and Black Consciousness Philosophy: An Interpretation," in N. Barney Pityana, Mamphela Ramphele, Malusi Mpumlwana, and Lindy Wilson, eds., *Bounds of Possibility: The Legacy of Steve Biko and Black Consciousness* (Cape Town, SA: David Philip, 1991), 110.
4. Steve Biko, *I Write What I Like* (London: Bowerdean, 1978).
5. Kogila Moodley, "The Continued Impact of Black Consciousness in South Africa," *The Journal of Modern African Studies* 29, no. 2 (1991): 239.
6. Barney Pityana, "Power and Social Change in SA," Abe Bailey Institute Seminar (Johannesburg, SA: University of the Witwatersrand, Karis-Gerhart Collection, A2675 Folder 245, Historical Papers, March 1971).
7. Benny Khoapa, ed., *Black Review 1972* (Durban, SA: Black Community Programmes, 1973), 63.
8. Robert Fatton, *Black Consciousness in South Africa* (New York: SUNY Press), 76.
9. Khoapa, quoted in ibid., 76.
10. Pierre L. van den Berghe, ed., *The Liberal Dilemma in South Africa* (1973; repr., London: Croom Helm, 1993); Paul B. Rich, *Hope and Despair: English-Speaking Intellectuals and South African Politics, 1896–1976* (London: British Academic Press, 1993); John Kane-Berman, *The New Liberals* (Johannesburg: SAIRR, 1994); Jill Wetzel, *The Liberal Slideaway* (Johannesburg: SAIRR, 1995); Libby Husemeyer, *Watchdogs or Hypocrites? The Amazing Debate on South African Liberals and Liberalism* (Johannesburg, SA: Friedrich-Naumann-Stiftung, 1997).
11. S. Buthelezi, "The Emergence of Black Consciousness: An Historical Appraisal," in N. Barney Pityana, Mamphela Ramphele, Malusi Mpumlwana, and Lindy Wilson, eds., *Bounds of Possibility: The Legacy of Steve Biko and Black Consciousness* (London: Zed Books, 1991): 118.
12. Ibid.

13. Steve Biko, *Black Souls in White Skins?*, South African Students' Organisation Newsletter (Johannesburg, SA: University of the Witwatersrand, Historical Papers Collection, August 1970).
14. SASO newsletter, cited in Buthelezi, "The Emergence," 119.
15. Biko, quoted in Geoff Budlender, "BC and the Liberal Tradition: Then and Now," in Pityana et al., eds., *Bounds of Possibility*, 229.
16. Ibid.
17. Pityana, *Power and Social Change*, 189.
18. Ranwedzi Nengwekhulu, *The Meaning of Black Consciousness in the Struggle for Liberation in South Africa* (Johannesburg, SA: University of the Witwatersrand, Karis-Gerhart Collection, A2675 Folder 274, Historical Papers, 1976).
19. Biko, *Black Souls*.
20. Pityana, *Power and Social Change*.
21. Biko, *Black Souls*.
22. Michael O'Dowd, "South Africa in the Light of Stages of Economic Growth," in Adrian Leftwich, ed., *South Africa: Economic Growth and Political Change* (London: Alison and Busby, 1974); Ralph Horwitz, *The Political Economy of South Africa* (London: Weidenfeld and Nicolson, 1967).
23. Andrew Nash, "The Moment of Western Marxism in South Africa," *Comparative Studies of South Asia, Africa and the Middle East* 19, no. 1 (1999): 66.
24. K. Jubber, "Sociology and its Social Context: The Case of the Rise of Marxist Sociology in South Africa," *Social Dynamics* 9, no. 2 (1983).
25. Eddie Webster, "Competing Paradigms: Towards a Critical Sociology in Southern Africa," *Social Dynamics* 11, no. 1 (1985); David Welsh, "Social Research in a Divided Society: The Case of South Africa" in John Rex, ed., *Apartheid and Social Research* (Paris: UNESCO, 1981).
26. Shireen Ally, "Oppositional Intellectualism as Reflection, not Rejection of Power: Wits Sociology, 1975–1989," *Transformation* 59 (2005): 66–97.
27. Richard Turner, "Black Consciousness and White Liberals," *Reality* 4, no. 3 (1972): 21.
28. Ally, "Oppositional Intellectualism."
29. Nash, "The Moment," 69.
30. Budlender, "BC and the Liberal Tradition," 233.
31. Daryl Glaser, "African Marxism's Moment" (Paper delivered to Department of Sociology Staff Seminar, University of the Wiwatersrand, 2005), 5.
32. Biko in interview with Gail Gerhart, quoted Nolutshungu, *Changing South Africa*, 155.
33. Turner, "Black Consciousness."
34. See Ally, "Oppositional Intellectualism."
35. Budlender, "Black Consciousness and the Liberal Tradition," 231.
36. *Reality*, January 1973.
37. Steve Biko, "White Racism and Black Consciousness', in Hendrick W. van der Merwe and David Welsh, eds., *Student Perspectives on South Africa* (Cape Town, SA: David Philip, 1972), 2.
38. Moodley, "The Continued Impact"; David Hirschmann, "The Black Consciousness Movement in South Africa," *The Journal of Modern African Studies* 28, no. 1 (March, 1990): 1–22; Fatton, "Black Consciousness in South Africa"; Neville Alexander, "*Black Consciousness: A Reactionary Tendency?*" in Pityana et al., eds., *Bounds of Possibility*.
39. Ndebele quoted by Hirschmann, "The Black Consciousness Movement," 6.
40. Halisi, "Biko and Black Consciousness"; Moodley, "The Continued Impact."
41. Moodley, "The Continued Impact," 242.

42. Thomas Karis and Gail M. Gerhart, *From Protest to Challenge: A Documentary of African Politics in South Africa , 1882–1964* (Stanford, CA: Hoover Institution Press, 1972), 147.
43. Biko in interview with Gerhart, quoted in Fatton, "Black Consciousness," 79.
44. Biko, quoted in Hirschmann, "The Black Consciousness Movement," 8.
45. Fatton, *Black Consciousness*; Karis and Gerhart, *From Protest to Challenge*.
46. Fatton, *Black Consciousness*, 88.
47. Ibid.; Karis and Gerhart, *From Protest to Challenge*.
48. Moodley, "The Continued Impact," 248; Hirschmann, "The Black Consciousness Movement," 18; Karis and Gerhart, *From Protest to Challenge*, 148.
49. Soweto Action Committee (Johannesburg, SA: University of the Witwatersrand, Karis-Gerhart Collection, Folder 251, Historical Papers, April 29–30, 1978).
50. Hirschmann, "The Black Consciousness Movement," 14.
51. Ibid., 18.
52. "What Is to Be Done—A Black Consciousness Perspective for the 80s," *Umtapo Focus* (Johannesburg, SA: University of the Witwatersrand, Karis-Gerhart Collection, A2675, Folder 257, Historical Papers, November 1987).
53. "Azanian Marxist-Leninists Respond to BCM Communiqué," *Ikwezi*, no. 13 (Durban, SA: University of KwaZulu-Natal, Digital Imaging Project of South Africa (DISA), October 1979).
54. Ibid.
55. Interview cited by Hirschmann, "The Black Consciousness Movement," 14.
56. Soweto Action Committee.
57. It is important to note here that in presenting the Black Consciousness movement's shifting valuation of race and class in a politics of change as a continuation of the politics of class initially inspired by the movement, there is a recognition that the history of the Black Consciousness movement is not one of discrete stages, but of a movement shifting in dialectical relation to a dynamic political and intellectual landscape.
58. AZAPO Manifesto (Johannesburg, SA: University of the Witwatersrand, Karis-Gerhart Collection, A2675, Folder 251, Historical Papers, 1980).
59. "Black Consciousness and the Class Struggle," *Frank Talk* 1 (February 1984): 12.
60. Ibid., 13.
61. Fatton, *Black Consciousness*, 83.
62. "Black Consciousness and the Class Struggle," 13.
63. This made the Black Consciousness movement, even in its embrace of class analysis, distinctly different from the "nonracial" Charterist traditions of the ANC and the UDF in the 1980s.
64. Moodley, "The Continued Impact," 249.
65. Letsatsi Mosala, "The Dynamics of Black Thinking in this Society," *Rand Daily Mail*, July 1, 1980.
66. Mthembu, "One People One Azania," *Pace* (Johannesburg, SA: University of the Witwatersrand, Karis-Gerhart Collection, Folder 251, A2675, Historical Papers, 1982/2009).
67. "Black Consciousness and the Class Struggle," 13.
68. Hirschmann, "The Black Consciousness Movement," 20.

Part 3

Cultural Critique and the Politics of Gender

9

The Influences and Representations of Biko and Black Consciousness in Poetry in Apartheid and Postapartheid South Africa/Azania

Mphutlane wa Bofelo

This chapter examines the influences of Stephen Bantu Biko and Black Consciousness on (Black) poetry in South Africa, focusing particularly on the points of convergence and divergence, connection and disconnection between the poetry movement of the era between the 1960s and 1980s—the so-called "Black Consciousness era"—and the post-1994 poetry resurgence. It looks at the aesthetic, stylistic, and thematic content of the works of some of the prominent "BC-era" poets (so-called Soweto Poets) and the thoughts and works of some of the current generation of South African poets. The chapter also explores the issue of the representations of Black Consciousness and Biko in the works of these poets and concludes with some thoughts on connecting the Black Consciousness era and post-1994 poetry movements.

The life and thoughts of Stephen Bantu Biko have been immortalized in various works and mediums of literary, visual, and performed arts such as songs, books, websites, theatre plays, poems, films, paintings, sculptures, clothing labels, and graffiti on the walls in various townships of South Africa declaring: ***Biko Lives!*** It is apt that literature and the arts be one of the media to serve as a tapestry for the invincibility and immortality of Steve Biko's message of self-definition, self-realization, self-love, self-respect, self-reliance, and self-expression as a potent weapon for the physical and psychological liberation of oppressed and downtrodden people. The development of Black culture and thus Black literature was one of the main tenets of the Black Consciousness Movement. Through the influence of Biko and the philosophy of Black Consciousness the poets and writers of the late 1960s and early 1970s saw themselves as spokespersons for blacks in the country, refusing to be beholden to "proper" grammar and style, searching for black aesthetics and literary values, and afro-centric artistic and cultural expressions rooted in the historical-material experiences of Black people and grounded on the socioeconomic and political realities of South Africa/Azania and the global struggles of oppressed people.

The literary revival spurred by the Black Consciousness Movement came in the aftermath of "the Drum decade," referred to as such because of the significant role played by *Drum* magazine with its publication of the expository, investigative, and sociopolitical journalistic writings of the likes of Henry Nxumalo and Nat Nakasa, short stories by writers of the caliber of Es'kia Mphahlele, and satirical pieces by the likes of Casey Motsisi. Many of the Drum decade writers exposed the brutalities and banalities of settler/colonial domination and apartheid/capitalism. The fallout from the Sharpeville massacre led to exile for many of these writers and artists. The political oppression of the resistance itself led to a new growth of Black South African literature mainly inspired by the new consciousness and new forms of struggle that emanated from the birth of the Black Consciousness Movement under the leadership of SASO-BPC and people like Stephen Bantu Biko, Mthuli Ka Shezi, Barney Pityana, Mosiuwa Patrick "Terror" Lekota, Ben Khoapa, Mualusi Mpumlwana, Winnie Motlalepule Kgware, Aubrey Nchaupe Mokoape, and Strinivasa "Strini" Raju Moodley.

The Rediscovery of the Reality of Being Black in the World

Playwright, poet, and journalist Strinivasa "Strini" Raju Moodley (also known as "Connection," the name he acquired on Robben Island) was a member of the black radical theatre group The Clan when he met Biko, and was instrumental in the formation of the first union of black theatre, the South African Black Theatre Union (SABTU), and the Theatre Council of Natal (TECON). The Clan was made popular by its satirical depiction of Black people's lives and the inequities and injustices in

South Africa in plays like "Black and White," "Resurrection," and "Africa Hurrah!"—a collaboration with the Jazz group Dashiki that fused poetry in its music. A former member of The Clan and a stalwart of the BC movement, Asha Moodley is of the view that the noticeable situation of inequality was responsible for the politicization of Black students and Black writers and the Black Community in general. She asserts that the works of writers and artists were a symbolic reflection of the rediscovery of blackness and a reflection of the general heightened state of awareness of "the reality of being Black." Asha Moodley recounts that in addition to its overtly political and revolutionary message, what was radical about their theatre at that time was its integration of drama, music, poetry, and visual art, its reliance more on improvisation than on props, and the interaction and dialogue between the audience and the performers. Moodley refers to this form of theatre as "total theatre." She mentions that the effective use of humor in the writings of Drum decade writers like Casey Motsisi appealed to them. She also cites writers and poets of the Negritude movement like Diop, Senghor, and Césaire as one of the influences in their works. Moodley indicates that they found affirmation from reading the works of black writers in *The Classic*, the earliest literary journal of the time.[1] In later years, South African literary practitioners became influenced by Black American and British poets such as Giovanni, Langston Hughes, Mutabaruka, Linton Kwesi Johnson, Gill Scott Heron, Amiri Baraka (formerly Leroi Jones) and The Last Poets—one of the earliest poetic voices of influence on hip-hop. The post-1976 era also saw writers like Gcina Mhlophe tapping into traditional African folktales and fables as a medium of popular education and alternative entertainment.

According to Moodley, The Clan's reputation led to the group being invited to perform at BC movement events, and ultimately to the participation of some of the members, including Strini Moodley and herself, in the formal structures of the movement. Although the writers and artists operated independently of the movement, the BC movement played a significant role in the development of writers by establishing journals such as *Black Perspective* and *Black Creativity and Development*, and the *Black Review*. These provided an annual review of the state of affairs in the country as seen through the eyes of Black people, and therefore countered the often jaundiced and jazzed-up view presented in the mainstream media. Moodley adds that they also organized biannual national drama festivals at Orient hall in Durban where groups like Wits Drama Society and the Serpent Players performed. *Staffrider* magazine became the dominant forum for the publication of BC-inspired and BC-oriented literature, mostly in the form of poetry and short stories. The Soweto uprising was the pinnacle point of the new consciousness and the creation of a new form of Black person—free of the mental chains and infused with a sense of dignity and pride as well as the spirit of resilience and resistance.

Sipho Sipamla, Mongane Wally Serote, Mafika Pascal Gwala, and Don Mattera paved the way and inspired a myriad of followers, most notably poet-performance artist Ingoapele Madingoane; painter and musician Matsemela Manaka; the fire-brand word-bomber Lesego Rampolokeng; and the renowned Mzwakhe Mbuli. Mzwakhe, who became closely associated with the structures of the Congress Movement and became known as the people's poet in the 1980s, popularized the idea of doing oral poetry over music.

Black Consciousness and the Resurgence of Poetry in the Late 1960s and Early 1970s

With its emphasis on psychological liberation and self-reliance, the Black Consciousness movement became a rallying point for cultural reclamation, cultural rejuvenation and artistic production. Apart from its message of political consciousness, the BC movement articulated a message of cultural and religious awakening as reflected in the questioning of mainstream Christianity and the development of Black Theology (BT) that rejected the status quo to produce a new Christian paradigm geared toward revolutionizing both the material and cultural structure of South Africa. Writers of the BC movement period were in the forefront of heeding that cultural call and poetry and plays became the major genres of that period. Couched in graphic language designed to arouse the emotions of listeners, their poems were often performed at political rallies.

The first poetry book to be published by a black poet in this era is most probably Oswald Mtshali's *The Sound of a Cowhide Drum*, which was an appeal for sympathy for the plight of poor black people. Sipho Sepamla was at first considered a "contemplative" poet, but by the time of *The Soweto I Love* (1977) his poetic persona fully identified with the oppressed. Sepamla also wrote a novel of this turbulent time, *A Ride on the Whirlwind* (1981), several other novels, and his *Selected Poems* were published in 1984. The early poems of Mongane Wally Serote published in volumes like *Yakhal'inkomo* (1972) and *Tsetlo* (1974) are short and sharp, and tackle the life and attitudes of a politically aware black person, looking at his society and its discontentment. In later volumes, Serote begins to develop an epic, incantatory voice with the long poems of *Behold Mama, Flowers* (1978) and *Come and Hope with Me* (1994), winner of the Noma Award for Publishing in Africa. Don Mattera's poems in the poetry anthology

Azanian Love Song became anthems of the struggle, recording the pain and anguish of the oppressed and the injustices of the system, but also infusing the spirit of hope and resistance in the oppressed black majority. The volume also includes beautiful love poems as well as poems simply celebrating the beauty of humanity. Although writers like Es'kia Mphahlele have attributed the drastic shift toward poetry among those South African writers who lived and worked inside South Africa in the 1960s to the fact that the immediacy of the political realities demanded poetry which did not need the long, consistent work of prose, Nadine Gordimer and others have argued that the poetic form was simply less obvious and would bypass government censorship.

However, poetry did get banned; the first collection of poems banned under the Publication Act was *Cry Rage* by James Mathews and Gladys Thomas. Subsequent poetry books suffered the same fate. According to Amatoritsero,[2] this was probably because poets, particularly the poets of the Black Consciousness period, were too emotionally close to the subject and not subtle but rather explicit in their choice of diction and imagery. Amatoritsero asserts that perhaps one good reason for the persistence of poetry, apart from the fact that the government tolerated it more readily since they assumed it reached a smaller audience, was the performance culture that began to emerge in the face of ironclad control and the lack of adequate publication outlets. He reminds us that literature anywhere in Africa was actually "orature" in several forms like parables, fables, work songs, praise songs, lullabies, genealogy chants, the folk ballad, the dirge, the abuse, and stories—all verbally transferred generation to generation. In many ways, the advent of performance poetry (now popularly known as the spoken word scene, and tapping the slam poetry and hip-hop traditions) could be seen as poetry returning to its oral roots in the form of readings and performances, in the absence of traditional mediums of orature.

The Thematic and Aesthetic Concerns of Post-1976 Poetry

The stylistic, aesthetic, and thematic concerns of the Black Consciousness poets were based in the idea of a complete break with the economic base and sociocultural superstructure of settler/colonial capitalism and aimed at recreating political and cultural expression of the South African reality, rooted in historical-material experiences of Black People and defined by the concrete and tangible conditions of the black majority. This meant confronting the white power structure and providing inspiration for black solidarity as an instrument of Black Power, as well as destroying the complex of inferiority and the culture of subservience—and on their ashes building a culture of resilience and resistance. Although the stylistic and aesthetic part of this project meant breaking with Eurocentric conventions of literature—which included deliberately breaking the English language, mixing it with indigenous African languages, township slang, and fusing the literary genres—the thematic part meant engaging and disengaging every aspect and apparatus of the system and putting together the building blocks for the creation of a new society. Peter Horn observes:

> To the black poet, as to any black, the white power structure is visible in very concrete terms; just as the American negro "in the ghetto sees his white landlord come only to collect exorbitant rents and fail to make necessary repairs...sees the white policeman on the corner brutally manhandle the black drunkard in a doorway, and at the same time accept a pay-off from one of the white-controlled rackets...sees the streets in the ghetto lined with uncollected garbage, and he knows that the powers which could send trucks in to collect that garbage are white."[3]

In confronting state control over South African black life, the poetry raged against constant supervision by the white government and by white employers, and therefore poured scorn and ridicule upon the main tool of this constant surveillance of black people's every move—the "pass," a document which determined where one was allowed to live, work and travel. In a satirical poem, "To Whom it May Concern," Sipho Sepamla expounds the absurdities of this instrument of white power. Mafika Pascal Gwala gave poetic voice to the cries of black people whose loss of the *dompass* (or forgetting it at home) earned them a "Kwela Ride"—a ride in the police van—to the next jail, which, as described in a poem by Oswald Mtshali, could easily become a "Ride upon the Death Chariot."

This poetry did not just record the injustices but exposed the fact that the power structures perpetuated and entrenched the master-servant, rich-poor relations between white and black South Africa because of the necessary relationship between white privilege and black poverty. *Speak* magazine argued:

> That standards of whites are high because those of the black are low, and that the total machinery of the state, all its apartheid laws, are necessary to protect this privilege against the demands of the black worker. If the white can benefit from plentiful and undemanding labour, it is because the blacks can be exploited at will and are not protected by the laws of the

country; if he can easily obtain positions of power and influence, it is because they are reserved for him and others are excluded from them."[4]

Black Consciousness-inspired poetry portrayed the reality of the underprivileged and exposed the hollowness of attempts to justify oppression on the basis of the fallacious notion that black people cannot rule themselves and should be under the tutelage of white people. It also dealt with the reality that white supremacy thrived on a black inferiority complex and internalized sense of submissiveness, and the realization that psychological emancipation of Black people required new political strategies and a new consciousness that would combat the realities of racist society effectively. The greatest obstacle to this spirit of self-assertion was that centuries of colonial and imperialist domination, and decades of apartheid capitalism, had imposed on black people a "rigid discipline" of unconditional submission, an innate sense of inferiority and paralyzing fear of the white man and the power structures of white supremacism. Mongane Wally Serote's "Anonymous Throbs + A Dream" is a poetic articulation of the break with the culture of submissiveness and of a search for a new consciousness and for forms of struggle other than nonviolent, passive resistance:

> I did this world great wrong
> with my kindness of a dog
> my heart like a dog's tongue
> licking too many hands, boots and bums.

Although many critics have dismissed the BC-era poets as protest poets, many of the poems, like Serote's "Sunset," moved beyond lamenting the conditions of oppression and looked forward to the triumph of the forces of liberation, and also painted a vision of the kind of society a liberated Azania would be. The certainty of a utopian tomorrow is significantly symbolized by black night and not white day, yet there is also an expression of the poet's fear of terror, even necessary terror: The humanistic ethos of the poetry is expressed by the articulation of a black poet's fear that he may become as brutal, as insensitive, and as callous as the white oppressor, and in doing what is needed he might lose his essential humanity. Serote's poetic contemplation of the dialectics of violence and counterviolence, inhumanity and arising counterinhumanity, best expressed this fear.

Horn observes that the theme of the cleansing power of rain and storm, of the rebirth of the barren and drought-stricken field by water, is a common theme in South African poetry, denoting (in the case of black poets) the total upheaval to restore the life of humanity of African society, the destruction of "white lies" by "black truth," as in Stanley Motjuwadi's poem, "White Lies."[5]

The Relationship Between the Poets and the Political Structures of the BC Movement

Apparently, the Black Consciousness influence was the result of general political education and mass conscientization efforts of the BC movement rather than a product of an attempt to recruit writers and artists into the fold of the BC movement. Though almost every poet wrote politically-inspired and socially-engaged poetry with clear indication of the BC influence, not all poets operated within the formal structures of the BC movement. Some writers eventually joined the BC movement formally while other writers and groups simply operated autonomously and independently but with some link with and support from the Black Consciousness movement, which helped to organize venues for performances and provided them with platforms at rallies. This interdependent relationship between the BC movement and the writers and artists is confirmed by Lefifi Tladi's account:

> Dashiki became a very important group because we were fusing music and poetry and our music was more towards malopo, this traditional music. The poetry was socially committed...Dashiki worked within the political structure [of] Black Consciousness with absolute independence. The BC movement used to book places where we could perform, whatever we wanted. That was one of the best outreach programmes. From there we started organising other groups like Batsumi, Medumo, ya bo Bra Paul Motaung, the late. And other groups like Medupe. We went into universities broadening the consciousness of students, and organising exhibitions...Dashiki was an important band of that era.[6]

According to Mzi Mahola, theatre performers like John Kani, Malefetse Bogolane, George Luse, Nomhle Nkonyeni, Winston Ntshona of the Serpent Players, and Mzwandile Maqhina of the Black Slaves and others like Khaya Mqhayisa were members of the BC movement but were not directed or mandated by the BC movement. Mahola is of the view that although the BC movement did not necessarily recruit writers to join it, writers were drawn into the movement by the platform and the opportunity to be heard as well as the chance for growth. Mzi Mahola, who experimented with poetry writing when he was doing Matric in 1969 and joined the BC movement in 1970, says his writing was encouraged in the BC movement where he was told to write in English because black people did not have to be told that they were suffering; that it was white people who caused our suffering and, therefore, should be told. However, it is apparent that there was a voice within the movement for writing in African languages.[7]

Rismathi Mathonsi recounts that at one of the writers' meetings, discussions centered on the use of English and African languages, and that people like Sipho Sipamla and himself advocated for more writings in African languages.[8] Though he does not have any work published in an African language, Sipamla is renowned for writing in a mix of English, Afrikaans, and isiXhosa and was a major influence on the writers of the 1980s like Ike Muila, who only writes in Iscamtho, the South African township-born slang—so-called *tsotsi taal*. Poet, jazz artist, and painter Lefifi Tladi—who was a leading member of Dashiki—writes most of his poems in Setswana and experiments with proverbial and idiomatic expressions. He says this is his way of highlighting the richness and depth of African languages:

> I was telling my young students that we need a new generation that is going to write poetry that draws from African proverbs, and which is able to translate to our contemporary setting. I used as an example these few lines of a poem: "Gophuthulla metsweditswedi ya hlago, kego ngatholla masedi a sedimosang ditoro" which means something like "Unfolding the oasis of nature is to share the light that makes dreams visible." The beauty and depth of this is that for any person to see anything, you need light, but what kind of light is it that makes dreams visible? This shows you how much we can go into our languages. Our languages are fantastic! There are so many ways to say things; I find my language more sophisticated. Our linguists actually need to invent new symbols to express some of this wealth... when it comes to ways of thinking for example, African languages have no "he" or "she." So they suggest no gender "hierarchy."[9]

The presence of writers of the era who wrote in African languages and their commitment to the development of indigenous African languages, as captured in Tladi's words, indicates that the BC movement did not impose rigid and fixed rules and/or prescriptions on writers and artists in as far as the choice of language is concerned. Actually, many writers have observed the fact that many musical groups and artists started writing in their own languages more in the 1970s. Mzi Mahola traces his journey into the BC movement to listening to Biko give a public address at Fort Hare in 1968 when he was doing matric at Lovedale. He declares that the BC movement inculcated in the individual a sense of being, pride, dignity, and self-confidence. "It changed people's passive and negative attitude of viewing themselves as inferior and made them feel equal with whites. Its ideology was premised on the legitimization of blackness."[10]

Mahola also mentions that his writing matured from the influence, advice, and evaluation of BC movement members like Barney Pityana and John Kani. "Either you had talent or there was no platform for your poor work. There was a program of encouraging and stimulating cultural awareness in black people. Individuals were encouraged to read and write and to express themselves in crafts and visual arts," says Mahola, lamenting that culture has vanished. He says the lack of interest in reading has resulted in the loss of the love of languages. And hence the poor quality of the manuscripts that many of the current generation of writers produce. However, Mahola is quick to add that though the Black Consciousness era produced inspiring cultural expressions, the repressive conditions and police brutality served to demoralize and demotivate writers. For example, Mahola's first poetry manuscript was confiscated by the police in August 1975, and this devastated him so much that he spent the next fourteen years without writing a single line of poetry.

Perhaps such repression, complemented by the dictates of market forces and the trappings of capital in the mainstream entertainment industry, played a major role in some of the poets, playwrights, and artists toning down their political messages later in their careers. However, poets like Mzwakhe Mbuli maintained the culture of social commentary poetry in the 1980s and inspired many in the younger generation of writers.

The Response of Poetry to Global Capitalism and Neoliberalism

With the advent and euphoria of a democratic South Africa, the huge political audiences waned and less attention was paid to poetry as compared to other literary genres in as far as government and corporate funding and prominence in academia and the media was concerned. Poetry continued to be housed mainly in small journals, websites, and café venues, and prose remained the medium that commanded more publicity and commentary in academia, with attention and discussions centered on established names like Coetzee and Gordimer, along with a number of emerging voices such as Zakes Mda, Ivan Vladislavic and Sindiwe Magona. Kelwyn Sole observes that the prose writers in the first decade of democracy have tended to concentrate their attention on themes that resonate with and seem to offer space for representation of a number of social issues that have been widely discussed in public life and in the media since 1994.[11] He asserts that perhaps most academic attention has been focused in the direction of prose because most novels and short stories are impregnated with narratives of reconciliation, multiculturalism, examination of memory, and the redefinition of identity. However, Sole argues that such themes are not absent in poetry, and that in actual fact the younger generation of poets seems prepared to both expand its social purview and experiment with form. Although heeding the post-apartheid mood of exploring human life more multidimensionally rather than merely through political narratives, many of these poets continued to lay emphasis on and put into practice the notion that poets also have roles of social responsibility and political commentary. The political developments post-1994 helped to ferment and sustain sociopolitical commentary poetry. The shift of the ANC in power—from its previous position of "national democracy plus economic egalitarianism" to unbridled capitalism/free-marketism—unsettled popular expectations of an equitable distribution of wealth and resources and the opening of doors to education, health, and other social services in a new dispensation.

The most significant element of this shift was the adoption of the Growth Employment and Redistribution (GEAR) policy, effectively meaning the adoption of an orthodox neoliberal framework as both a policy and vision of the government, and therefore the erosion of the relatively welfare-oriented principles of the Reconstruction and Development Program (RDP). At the local level the implementation of neoliberal policies resulted in the poorest of the poor being victims of massive retrenchments and escalating levels of unemployment, electricity and water cutoffs, evictions, and outbreaks of cholera, typhoid, and klepsella. Although ordinary people are the ones who feel the squeeze of neoliberal capitalist policies the most, and therefore have a much clearer perception of the barbarism and corruption of global capitalism, they seldom speak out and they are rarely listened to. Kelwyn Sole is of the view that literature can act as a vehicle for such ordinary views and that poetry has done this in an eloquent fashion in South Africa. He cites the critical voices of poets like Mxolisi Nyezwa, Nkwapa Moloto, Sphokazi Mthathi, Vonani Bila, Phedi Tlhobolo and even members of the ruling party like Mongane Wally Serote and Jeremy Cronin. Their works frankly question the meaning of freedom in the new South Africa and highlight the contradictions of the new dispensation, the vagaries of the market, the enormous chasm between the quality of the lives of the poor and the rich, the corruption of power, the pomp and decadence of the emergent black bourgeoisie and the mediocrity of "parrot poetry." However, there is no homogeneity with regard to the relationship of poets/poetry with the political elite and corporate capital, or as far as poetry's response to the seductions of power and the vicissitudes of the market.

Ever since Zolani Mkiva rose to prominence in 1990 by praising Nelson Mandela and later becoming ordained *Imbongi Yesizwe*, poet to the nation, and the president's poet laureate, a number of oral poets see their task as the public praising of leaders and their policies, curtain-raising for every state function or corporate event. The most well-known poet of the 1983–1990 era of political turbulence, Mzwakhe Mbuli, even performed praises on television advertisements for commercial products and parastatals, such as Cremora Coffee Creamer and Spoornet (South Africa Rail).

Spoken Word and Social Activism Post–1994

The era of political independence, with its emphasis on freedom of expression and the opening of access to information, saw many young people getting interested in poetry. Many of these young people were influenced by hip-hop and the slam poetry phenomenon. Only a few remnants of the BC generation of writers are still active today and, according to Mzi Mahola, "one can surmise that the negation of literature in the class and disappearance of the culture of reading brings about *the demise of BC socially engaging poetry*" (my own emphasis). Mahola attributes this to the fact that the Censorship Board of the Nationalist government had cleaned the shelves of all relevant literature, and periodically banned certain publications and journals like *Time Magazine* and *South African Outlook* which played major roles in inspiring and informing communities, and to the current absence of projects similar to the tertiary programs run by the BC movement. He explains:

> At tertiary institutions the BC movement had programs of developing and encouraging public speaking where popular guest speakers were invited to deliver speeches; debates formed part of the program as well as mock trials for law students. It was varsity culture and norms to come across public debates where students would be analyzing topical issues in public places. Alternative media and popular journals encouraged people to read so as to empower and broaden their minds. All that is history now. Today one does not see the role of literature in developing writers and educating our people because it has been neglected from lower levels. In certain schools and provinces literature has become anathema to learners.[12]

Mahola sees the slam poets as filling the vacuum that was left behind after the gradual exit of the socially-engaging BC protest poetry of the pre-1994 era. He explains that the present generation has other problems to deal with. However, Mahola laments that the expression of their problems tends to take the form of an articulation of personal frustrations. He says, "The BC poetry was meant to conscientize, mobilize, moralize, politicize, inspire and motivate. It sought to spread and promote BC philosophy and ideas. Spoken word seems to attract youth only and it does not carry any particular message or philosophy espoused by the community. The stage is for individualism where DJs battle. Unlike BC poetry, spoken word relies on musical backing, rhyming, repetition, and weird language which are meant to entertain. Spoken word is not meant to be analyzed and understood but to entertain."[13]

This sweeping generalization about spoken word and slam poetry ignores the plurality and diversity of voices within the spoken word scene. The label "slam poet" is misleading when applied to many of the poets who also write so-called "page poetry," essays, and drama, but who use the spoken word/slam poetry platform to reach out to a wider audience, and also to free poetry from the elitist enclave of "high art." Unfortunately, the media and academia (preoccupied by labels) impose the slam poetry / hip-hop label on any young poet or any poet who also uses the stage as a platform of sharing his poetry. Hence Lebo Mashile's poetic combat of this stereotype: "Shake off the dust of 'slam poetry' expectations / And relieve the green words / where the world is no obstacle to my desire."

In Durban, cultural workers, social activists, poets, MCs, and hip-hop activists within *Izimbongi Zesimanje*/Nowadays Poets, Slam Poetry Operation Team (SPOT), the Ghetto Prophecy Movement (GPM), and Young Basadzi Projects (YPB) are at the forefront of attempts to use art as a platform and medium of popular education, political conscientization, social development, and economic empowerment. One significant program is the Ghetto Kids project initiated by the GPM band led by Sandile Sibiya. This project imparted life-skills education to displaced children (so-called "street kids") through the vehicles of hip-hop, break-dance, graffiti, gumboots, creative writing and disc-jockeying. According to MC and hip-hop activist Bullet, the aim of the project was to move beyond pity and sympathy to embrace the displaced children as a part of the broader Ghetto Prophecy Movement, which included GPM, its fan-base, and all the artists, groups, and social activists participating in the project. The key aspect of the project was to give the children a sense of being and belonging, and to unlock their hidden potentialities, capacities, and talents and help them to use these for their own empowerment. Miracle (Sphephelo Mbhele), who joined the movement in 2001, recounts: "Ghetto Kids became something else. It grew and embraced kids from all over. We had 'white' kids breaking with 'street' kids. We had parents initially dropping off kids but now staying through the whole show. Ghetto Kids had rules like no smoking or drinking of alcohol during the session, none of the older cats were allowed to perform, etc."[14] Miracle and Zorro (Lwazi Xaba) have initiated *Izwi* poetry nights, a series of collaborative performances between poets and jazz bands at the Zulu Lounge, inaugurated with a performance on February 1, 2007. SPOT, headed by DJ Cool-fire (Eric Nkosinathi Hadebe), conducts creative writing workshops and slamjams in high schools and also uses

Slam Showcases to address issues like HIV/AIDS, poverty, and homelessness. Members of the Nowadays Poets have participated in programs such as the Fatherhood Project and were also commissioned by the eThekwini Municipality to run the Creative Ink project, a part of the Urban Renewal Programme in the Inanda, Ntuzuma Kwamashu (INK) area. The Young Basadzi Project has run several creative writing workshops in high schools and has collaborated with various NGOs in community outreach projects. In 2006, the YBP published a collection of poetry and prose by young South African women.

Undertones of BC in Current Works of Black Poets

A careful look at the performed poetry/spoken word/slam poetry scene and some of the recently published poetry books would reveal that there are a variety of voices with a socially-engaging message inspired by the ethos of Black Consciousness, Afrocentricity, and Pan-Africanism as well as anticapitalist, feminist and/or womanist, and environmental concerns. Among these voices one can include Kgafela Oa Magogodi (*Thy Condom Come, I Mike What I Like*), Vonani Bila (*Magicstan Fires, In the Name of Amandla*), Lebogang Mashile (*In a Ribbon of Rhythm*), Mzi Mahola—one of the few BC-era poets still active on the literary scene—(*Dancing in the Rain*), Myesha Jenkins (*Breaking Surface*), and Bandile Gumbi (*Pangs of Initiation*).

A typical example of a satirical take on the corrupting effect of power and the lures of capital on leaders is found in Magogodi's poem "No More Carrots," which shows how the system dangles material wealth and offers of high offices like a carrot to co-opt and corrupt conscientious people. In his debut poetry CD, Magogodi paraphrases Biko's famous signature, "I write what I like" into *I Mike What I Like*. The title-poem is a poetic testament of the poet's resolve not to be a parrot poet and his refusal to let his literary expression be dictated by political correctness. Anticapitalist activist, poet, and publisher Vonani Bila's poetry is marked by its expression of sympathy and empathy for the most marginalized and underground sections of society. Another important feature of Bila's poetry is its narratives of village anecdotes and legends that capture everyday life experience in rural Limpopo, particularly Elim Village, as well as its tributes to celebrated and unsung practitioners of the literary, visual, and performing arts—Jackson Hlungwani, Lucy Shivambu, Noria Mabasa, John Baloyi, Willi Mangayi, Obed Ngubeni, and Elias Baloyi—mostly from the Limpopo Province.

Bila is also renowned for his poetic critique of neoliberal capitalism and the Washington consensus agenda, particularly the squeeze of neoliberal policies on the poorest of the poor in South Africa and the world: "In the name of Amandla / tell me what has changed in this village / the tap is dry/ coughs hot air/the pump is off/granny has no cash to buy diesel/she walks distances to draw dirty water/in the still pool/ in the poisoned dam / where people share water with animals."[15] Bila's boldness comes out in a critical look at freedom struggle heroes who are regarded as holy cows by many African poets. He asks Mandela troubling questions in "Mandela Have You Ever Wondered," and is very frank with Mugabe in "Dear Gabriel":

> I don't care
> how many tobacco & flower white farmers
> the war vet-chefs ambushed & butchered last night
> nor how many shops were torched
> not even the rise & fall of Hitler hunzwi bothers me
> nor the aborted & bogus Lancaster house agreement
> nor how many foreigners & funders have fled the country
> I care about men and women by the roadside
> liberated vagabonds
> who walk from Harare to Johannesburg on foot
> swimming across the crocodile infested limpopo
> braving the mewing wild cats
> & the pecking vultures
> victims of the roving green fly.

Bila's poem "Mr President, Let the Babies Die" has effectively become an anthem within the circles of the anticapitalist social movements. It was performed at the World Social Forum in Brazil and is quoted in full at the end of Patrick Bond's critique of South Africa's neoliberal trajectory, *Talk Left, Walk Right*:

> This is the millennium plan
> followed by declarations and slogans
> poor men and women goaded by the western whip
> dawn of a new century
> money talks
> the rich get richer
> we can only sell our breasts and thighs for a living
> I'm scared of urban beasts
> their tongues are too sharp
> in the meantime
> ghetto babies die in public toilets.[16]

Mahola's is a patriotic voice but outspoken in its criticism of the leadership and populace. He tackles themes such as corruption, moral degeneration, talk of an African renaissance, the aloofness of the erstwhile freedom fighters from the masses, and the lack of accountability. The latter is aptly captured in the poem "Impassable Bridge":

> I phoned for an MP
> A former bosom friend
> His secretary asked
> In connection with what
> It punctured my ego
> *I felt my manhood shrinking.*[17]

In "In a Ribbon of Rhythm," television personality and poet Lebo Mashile articulates the joys and sorrows of being a (black)woman in a patriarchal and male-centric world, celebrates the beauty, resilience, and resourcefulness of women, and gives voice to the stories and songs/cries of ordinary women. She calls on women to "tell your story / let it nourish you / sustain you / and claim you / tell your story / let it twist and remix your shattered heart / tell your story / until your past stops tearing your present apart." Her call is for every child to know she is "wrapped in a ribbon of rhythm" and her mission is "to show pretty black girls / how to look at their hearts / with eyes blaring full blast / the way you did / together we can build a bridge / to the promises in their faces / and pull them towards poems / by pretty black girls / wearing the crown of change."[18]

Lebogang Mashile's colleague in the Feela Sister Spoken Word Collective, Myesha Jenkins, breaks the private/public, personal/social dichotomy, articulating and capturing the human side of social issues like women abuse, the disempowerment of women, and patriarchal and sexist practices and stereotypes. She celebrates the connectedness of the black experience and the resilient spirit of black people in "Diaspora," rages against war in "Fighting men," and declares her love for revolutionary women (Dora Maria Tellez, Nora Astorga, Haydee Santamaria, Asanta Aguilar, Nguyen Thi Binh, Laila Khalid, Thenjiwe Mthintso, Sheila Weinberg) in "Revolutionary Woman."[19]

Bandile Gumbi describes herself as a guerrilla poet and defines her poetry as "conversations with myself." In the poetry collection *Pangs of Initiation*, Gumbi addresses the politics and complexity of identity, interrogates art, poetry, and freedom, and highlights the contradictions of the new South Africa and the dangers of assimilation: "We are definitely stuck / between the s's / of assimilation / *a banana is an exotic fruit in africa / when chasing / coconut dreams.*"[20] The poem "After the Fact" evokes the spirit of Biko to triumph above the commodification and commercialization of his name on the alter of "bumper sticker consciousness." Here the poet rages against the transformation of former freedom fighters into corporate fat cats and laments the demise of the struggle: "Someone seems to be shouting / Biko is in parliament / driving a Yengeni / living in yuppiedom / these are definitely post times /vibrations: struggle my life! / burned with the 80s / but the phoenix is yet to rise from the ashes." For Gumbi, the hopeless and desperate characteristics of black people's lives in the new South Africa marks "the death of Black Consciousness": He lap-danced / To the jukebox tunes / Home of the brave / With his head buried in sand dune / BC, He! Bantu! / Ngiyamgcoba!

Post-Struggle Praise-Singing and Performance Poetry

In post-1994 South Africa, the praise poetry genre was repopularized with the huge prospects for government and corporate funding and the lucrative chances of being praise-singers for the president, premiers, mayors, and ministers, and official advertisers/ambassadors of particular corporate products/companies. The mass media, with its proclivity to promote mediocrity and to churn out instant celebrities, plays a critical role in promoting poetry for its own sake as opposed to the poetry of commitment. Although many of these poets raise contemporary issues like HIV/AIDS, sexist and patriarchal practices, gender-based violence, and poverty and inequality, a lot of them are either courtier clowns and praise poets or simply escape into the world of neoromanticism away from socioeconomic and political issues emanating from the neocolonial, neoliberal capitalist dispensation. The mainstream corporate world and government and civil society organizations have all recognized the power of the spoken word/performed poetry and traditional African oral poetry as mediums of communication. Therefore, there is an increase in the use of poetry and hip-hop and kwaito music for advertising and public relations. Performance poets are increasingly being commissioned by corporations or the government to write or perform their works to advance one cause or the other. This adds another dimension where the lure of quick bucks and celebrity status as well as awards, honors, and titles like poet laureate or the prospects of being the official *imbongi* of a high-powered political individual or office, threatens the dedication and commitment of the poets to poetry as an art form and to the poetry of conscience and, therefore, threatens the literary quality of the works produced. The competitive aspect of the slam poetry scene in particular, along with rampant commercialization, has led to more individualistic rather than communitarian tendencies.

In this regard, the instructive observations of freelance journalist and poet Goodenough Mashego deserve some lengthy quotation:

> The spoken word scene is abuzz with talented souls who are mostly BC, or anti-establishment. The problem is that the scene is only exclusively an urban phenomenon. Jo'burg has got its people who walk around with groupies who will ululate even when they fart. I have a feeling it has developed elitist tendencies which are going to kill it and the message... You have "celebrated" slam poets who will come at book launches and never recite, only to distribute flyers about where their next paid gig will be. That's the undoing. One is left wondering how they can claim Bohemia while their attitude smirks of Utopia... Money can buy anything. I never believed it until I saw some BC heavy-hitters who are appointed to head state institutions toning down on their rhetoric. I think most of them who are now mainstream cannot write hard-hitting commentaries or poetry while they know they might be called to present their works in front of the President and his side-kicks. You can't label Zuma corrupt when he is paying your bills, you can't quiz the destructive nature of the arms industry when DENEL has invited you to a luncheon. That poem that you have that says "Mandela is a blunder/ leading the nation asunder" will die a natural death when you have to perform for Oprah during the Nelson Mandela Children's Fund gala dinner. Sometimes they just make you mainstream to steal you from the people to whom you really matter.[21]

Lefifi Tladi is of the view that the mediocrity and lack of direction prevalent in artistic and literary circles reflects the general crisis of identity in a postindependence, neocolonial dispensation characterized by amnesia and the assault of eurocentricism and Western hegemony on the mindset of South Africans. "The problem today is that the issues now have changed because it is not an issue of black people or white people. We don't have focus. Artists are on their own, and the direction is not defined. So we are improvising most of the time. That's why it's easy to be an artist because there are no guidelines... We have an identity crisis. Everything is wishy-washy... We are all part of this confusion where we are trying to define what is South African."[22]

The Misappropriation of Biko/BC

Mashego argues that the dictates of capital are one of the major reasons for the lack of a Black Consciousness-oriented popular theatre and spoken word: "Poets like Kgafela (oa Magogodi), Vonani (Bila), Mpho (Ramaano), and a few outspoken individuals do still talk from the heart. But at the end of the day even artists get hungry and have to eat, and it's the ruthless capitalists who have the money. They are the ones who run the State Theatre, Polokwane Auditorium and other venues where you need approval to utilize. Connections between the arts, spoken or written, and BC still exist. One needs to read the text because I think that's where honesty lies. Performance is another thing, the audience dictates the direction. Post-'94 one looks at the audience and sees the Mayor and tones down on the venom. I'm not saying BC artists sell out, I'm just saying they need to eat, and that's the consideration." Mahola posits that another reason for a lack of connectivity between BC-era poetry and the current poetry resurgence is the censorship and systematic purging of BC-oriented materials and works by writers like Fanon and Cabral off library bookshelves.

Mashego's account of the difficulty he experienced when trying to access books by the likes of Césaire and Ngugi wa Thiong'o, as part of an initiative to establish the first African Library, somewhat supports Mahola's assertion. "We faxed the list to embassies of all the countries that once colonized a certain part of Africa to search for the books through their cultural desks and donate them to us. Something like, 'give us back our wisdom.' Nothing was happening and we were only exhausting money calling these embassies and one day I met Mama Miriam [Tlali] at the same event where I met the late Phaswane Mpe and we started talking. Tlali said, 'o ka se di thole ngwanake. Ke nahana hore ba di rekile tso tsohle ba di tshuma ka mollo.' [I think they bought all BC literature and burned it.] Now you see, the colonizers or racists had a SWAT team that was out to make sure that any literature that sympathized with BC got destroyed. They had a plan to separate oral and literature from a BC agenda because they knew African people are artistic people who sing and dance when happy, sad and celebrating. What needs to be done now is to make a call to our government, 'please, give us back our wisdom, even if it's on paperback.'"

This view is supported by Asha Moodley who says that, among other things, the fact that a great deal of time in the SASO-BPC trial was taken on interrogating the writings of BC leaders like Strini Moodley and Stephen Bantu Biko, shows that there was a constant and concerted attack on Black creativity. She also highlights the fact that in addition to the murder of prominent BC leaders like Mthuli Ka Shezi, Mapetla Mohapi, Onkgopotse Tiro, and Steve Biko by the apartheid regime in the 1970s, thousands of Black Consciousness adherents were killed for their political beliefs between 1983 and 1990. Moodley goes further to suggest that there is currently a systematic attempt to gloss over—or obliterate from the memory of South Africans—the era between 1960 and 1980 in narrating the history of the struggle for liberation in South Africa, and to appropriate Stephen Bantu Biko by political forces that have always been detractors and critics of Biko and the philosophy of Black Consciousness. She says it is not unusual for corporate capital and the political establishment to appropriate the message of revolution and change and utilize it for their own interests. Part of this, argues Moodley, is the commodification of martyrs and heroes of the struggle as exemplified by the designer clothes bearing the names of Biko and Che Guevara. Mashego is more scathing in his attack on the misrepresentation and abuse of Biko's name: "True, Biko is becoming the new media agenda, thanks to people like Xolela Mangcu, the Steve Biko Foundation, Writes Associates and Nkosinathi Biko. But he is being commercialized like Che Guevara. Biko is now a screensaver on a 14 year old's cellphone and a Ventersdorp farmer's desktop. But, who is Biko?; ask any of the people who are wearing his T-shirt while holding a can of Black Label and soliciting sex without a condom from a 15-year-old girl. The media is prostituting Biko instead of representing him."

Some Proposals on Connecting the "BC Era" and Post-1994 Poets and Writers

Splits and lack of unity and cooperation among the three political parties that claim Black Consciousness have left South Africa with no visible and audible party-political force articulating a Black Consciousness perspective at the macro level of parliamentary politics. The general state of disorganization and dysfunctionality within these parties makes it difficult for them to connect with the resurgent literary and cultural movement that carries some resonance of Black Consciousness. The few community-based organizations and cultural organizations with some affinity to Black Consciousness operate in isolation from each other with no efforts to synergize and consolidate their works. The need to solicit corporate funding forces many organizations to lie low as far as a more pronounced commitment to Black Consciousness is concerned. The silence and/or marginalization of many BC-era writers and the cooption of a handful of them (either into the corporate world or the structures of government) make it difficult for the younger generation of writers and poets to connect with their literary predecessors. What is missing is a conscious and well-coordinated program to link up the present literary and cultural movement with the past and to educate the current crop of poets and cultural activists about their predecessors.

In spite of this lack of awareness about Black Consciousness-oriented writers and the actual contributions of the BC movement in pushing literature and the arts in South Africa forward, Biko and Black Consciousness continue to be points of reference (or at least a source of inspiration) for writers, including the slam poets and hip hop artists. Bullet indicates that the philosophy of Black Consciousness, with its emphasis on self-reliance, serves as an inspiration to the artists and groups that do community development work. But they prefer to be nonaligned when it comes to party politics, and nonsectarian in their dealings with communities and organizations. Attributing his political consciousness to his mother's account of how his grandfather was dispossessed of his plot of land and how many African families and communities were displaced by forced removals, Bullet declares that parents and the older generation have a responsibility to teach the younger generation their history and to raise their awareness about cultural, social, economic, and political issues affecting their communities.[23]

Mashego suggests the way forward: "The same way the current US hip-hop practitioners are linking to Ray Charles, Billie Holiday, Stevie Wonder, and others, the old generation must not hold on to their masters as if they were their hearts. They should let the young generation exploit that. If there is a book entitled *This Way I Salute You*, it shouldn't be a matter of a thousand lawyers converging around a copy of the Copyright Act before a young spoken word artist can be allowed to use that as a title of his hip-hop or spoken word album." Asha Moodley suggests that one way of doing this is to create a platform where the BC-era poets and other artists of that era share the stage with the current crop of writers and artists in concerts, festivals, seminars, workshops, and exchange programs. She also calls for a drastic change in the school curriculum to ensure that African literature and writings by Black writers take center stage in languages, literature, and moral and cultural studies from primary to tertiary education. Mashego also proposes that the politics of ethnicity and tribalism need to be exposed and combated through the vehicles of drama, theatre, writing and poetry. These works should point out the weakness of such thinking, with Black Consciousness as the point of departure.

Notes

1. Interview with Asha Moodley, January 19, 2007.
2. Amatoritsero Godwin Ede. BC movement South African Literature: (www.nigeriansin.america.com/articles/26/1/theblackconsciousnessmovement-in-south-african-literature).
3. Peter Horn, "When it Rains: U.S, BC and Lyric Poetry in South Africa," *Speak*, Cape Town 1, no.1 (October–November 1978).
4. *Speak*, Cape Town, 1. no.1 (October–November 1978).
5. Ibid.

6. "Hidden Treasures: Lefifi Tladi." *Pulse* (www.news.com/citypress/entertainment/ 0, 7515, 186-16982018078, 00html).
7. Interview with Mzi Mahola, January 8, 2007.
8. Interview with Rismathi Mathonsi.
9. "Hidden Treasures: Lefifi Tladi." *Pulse* (www.news.com/citypress/entertainment/ 0, 7515, 186-16982018078, 00html).
10. Interview with Mahola.
11. Kelwyn Sole, "The Witness of Poetry (Economic Calculation, Civil Society and the Limits of Everyday Experience in Liberated South Africa)" in Botsotso, *Contemporary South African Culture* 13.
12. Interview with Mahola.
13. Ibid.
14. Interview with Sphephelo Mbhele aka Miracle.
15. Vonani Bila, *Magicstan Fires* (Elim Hospital: Timbila Poetry Project, 2006).
16. Vonani Bila, *In the Name of Amandla* (Elim Hospital: Timbila Poetry Project, 2004).
17. Mzi Mahola, *Dancing in the Rain* (Scottsville: UKZN Press, 2006).
18. Lebogang Mashile, *In a Ribbon of Rhythm* (Capetown, SA: Oshun Books, 2005).
19. Myesha Jenkins, *Breaking the Surface* (Elim Hospital: Timbila Poetry Project, 2005).
20. Bandile Gumbi, *Pangs of Initiation* (Somerset west: H.A Hodgie, 2004).
21. Pulse; Hidden Treasures; Lefifi Tladi: (www.news.com/citypress/entertainment/ 0, 7515, 186-16982018078, 00html).
22. Interview with Goodenough Mashego, January 8, 2007.
23. Interview with Bullet, December 2, 2006.

10

A Human Face: Biko's Conceptions of African Culture and Humanism

Andries Oliphant

A culture is essentially the society's composite answer to the varied problems of life.

(Steve Biko)

* * *

The world knows that at the age of 30, Stephen Bantu Biko died in police custody on September 12, 1977. This essay, written in early September 2007, coincided with the 30th anniversary of his death. Given the brutality of his death, writing about him is always profoundly distressing for me. This is so in light of the fact that although the circumstances of his murder and the identities of his killers and others complicit in this crime have been public knowledge since the late 1970s, to date, no one has been brought to justice. The recent deaths of the two security policemen who assaulted him have, it seems, foreclosed all prospects of ever attaining any justice in this matter.

This essay, however, is not directed toward the history of Biko's brutal death at the hands of the agents of the apartheid state. It is concerned with his humanist legacy and its inscription that are his writings. Invariably, however, the chilling facts of the inhuman treatment he was subjected to and that resulted in his death are a spectre that haunts anyone who invokes his name.

Thirty-four years ago in his essay "Black Consciousness and the Quest for a True Humanity," first published in England in 1973, and subsequently collected by Aelred Stubbs in the volume of essays, *I Write What I Like* (1979), Biko concludes what is considered by many as his most eloquent and moving exposition on the nature and imperatives of Black Consciousness with the following three sentences:

> We have set out on a quest for true humanity, and somewhere on the distant horizon we can see the glittering prize. Let us march forth with courage and determination drawing strength from our common plight and our brotherhood. In time we shall be in a position to bestow upon South Africa the greatest possible gift—a more human face.

When read in relation to everything he wrote, these three sentences encapsulated his vision. Often cited at the end of the account of his life and ideas, these pronouncements serve to accentuate the tragedy of his death. In this essay, they are given prominence because they clearly represent the daunting challenge Biko set for himself, for the movement he initiated and guided, and for all South Africans. Elsewhere, he sets a challenge to the world.

Read closely and in relation to the essay as a whole, to his other writings and to the context of their enunciation, these three sentences, not in the least speculative, are both programmatic exhortations and commitments to a radical task. Using the collective pronoun "we," they serve to mobilize the oppressed at the height of apartheid to pursue the historical task of national liberation with valor and resolve. Most significantly, the reward for this is not something that the oppressed will receive upon the attainment of liberation, but something the liberated will give to or "bestow upon" the country of their birth. This "glittering prize" that becomes "a gift" is not something to receive but something to give. In fact, it is referred to as "the greatest possible gift," not only for freedom from oppression, which it no doubt includes, but also for "a more human face," meaning a greater humanization of South Africa.

This pronouncement is an extraordinary exhortation insofar as the sentences that constitute it are not formulated in the hoary lexicon or style of conventional political exhortations that predictably draw their rhetorical force from vitriolic denunciations of adversaries. In mobilizing the oppressed, Biko's exhortation draws its energy from the positive potential of the oppressed not only to liberate themselves but also to effect a fundamental transformation in the world in which they live. Revolutionary, the exhortation is not cast in negative form but as a positive alternative to the then status quo of racial domination.

The centrality of the concept of humanity to the three sentences, I think, signifies that the struggle for national liberation, in Black Consciousness terms, is conceived as a quest by the formerly oppressed to humanize South Africa by liberating it from the inhuman social system of racial prejudice, human oppression, and exploitation, and replacing it with a new order of human equality.

This vision of the future humanization of South Africa is echoed in the essay "Some African Cultural Concepts" where it is given global dimensions. In this instance Biko observes: "The great powers of the world may have done wonders in giving the world a military and industrial look, but the great gift still has to come from Africa—giving the world a more human face." In this phrase it becomes clear that the metaphorical "human face" Biko had in mind was African.[1] In other words, the future humanization of the world will take on an African quality. The same applies to South Africa.

As cited above, it emerges that a central aspect of Biko's political philosophy is based on a culturally specific humanist concept. This can be described as a form of African humanism. This essay, consequently, undertakes a textual exploration of the three sentences quoted above with the view of establishing their relationship to Biko's conception of humanism and its embeddedness in his theory of African culture. It seeks to show that Biko's ideas on African culture directly inform his concept of African humanism.

* * *

In approaching Biko's ideas on African culture and humanism, it is essential to broadly note that the advent of colonization in South Africa resulted in the violent subjugation of Africans over a period of four centuries. Biko points out that colonialism is not complete, or satisfied, with just military and political conquest.[2] For it to succeed in the long term, it must erode and destroy the culture of the colonized. This included distorting the history of the colonized. In this, Biko draws directly on Fanon's essay "On National Culture."[3] He does so without naming Fanon or the text, doubtless due to the risk of censorship. Accordingly, Biko emphasizes: "Whenever colonialism sets in with its dominant culture, it devours the native culture and leaves behind a bastardized culture that can only thrive at the rate and pace allowed it by the dominant culture."[4] Given this, all struggles for national liberation necessarily involve a cultural dimension.

If, however, society is understood as an irreducible cultural formation (i.e., as a specific and spatially localized product of a distinctive group of people developed over time in accordance with their values), one could assert, as Amilcar Cabral does, that all anticolonial struggles are basically "acts of culture."[5] This is so since, if they are thoroughgoing anticolonial campaigns, they will be aimed at overthrowing the political, economic, and social order; in other words, the entire colonial dispensation, its material foundations, and the cultural edifice imposed on colonized societies by the colonial invaders. Culture, then, is not just a matter of language, religion, forms of art, and customs, but the totality of a specific social formation. As defined by Biko: "Culture is a society's composite answer to the varied problems of life."[6] It is, therefore, not possible to merely strip away culture as a thin layer of paint from an object, since both the object and the layer of paint are irreducibly cultural.

In writing about African culture, Biko observes that in the wake of colonialism African culture was not only denigrated and displaced by colonial culture but also appropriated as an object of knowledge by colonial ethnographers. This was carried out to such an extent that the colonizers took it upon themselves to instruct Africans on the nature of African culture. Biko muses ironically:

> One of the most difficult things to do these days is to speak with authority on anything to do with African culture. Somehow Africans are not expected to have any deep understanding of their own culture or even of themselves. Other people have become authorities on all aspects of African life or, to be more accurate, on BANTU life. Thus we have the thickest of volumes on some of the strangest subjects—even "the feeding habits of the Urban Africans," a publication by a fairly "liberal" group, Institute of Race Relations.[7]

He observes that since the permanent settlement of Europeans in South Africa in 1652, Africans have been subjected to a one-sided process of acculturation. This emphasized Anglo-Boer culture, through the use of military force and force-fed education by missionaries, as an advanced, more sophisticated, and superior culture relative to African culture, which was considered elementary, backward, and primitive and, therefore, "simple and inferior." The upshot of this was that the Africans themselves were considered uncivilized and inferior to the European settlers. Hence, colonial discourse furnished the requisite justification for the colonial invaders to impose colonial culture on Africans. In a staggeringly patronizing gesture, this was pronounced to the world as a benevolent act aimed at civilizing barbaric Africans. This resulted in the systematic suppression and denigration of African culture and the administration of Anglo-Boer culture to Africans with the promise that once they convert to Christianity and denounce their heathen beliefs and practices, they would be admitted to the kingdom of humanity where the colonizers were guardians.

Duped by this promise of equality, the first few Africans who entered mission schools, most often the children of the defeated African aristocracy, were psychologically torn from their cultural traditions and from African society. With a modicum of literacy and a new religion, they came to despise those who clung to African culture. As Kunene puts it, the new converts, initially all men, couldn't but come to the conclusion that their "people were living in a state of darkness" from which only Western culture could deliver them.[8] In the long run this uncritical supplication to Western culture by the new African converts would not endure. The litany of broken promises to Africans, the main one consisting of the ruse that Africans' adoption of European culture would qualify them to become members of civilized humanity (which never materialized), triggered a new wave of dissent and revolt.

Nevertheless, Biko observes African culture, however denigrated, suppressed, and displaced by colonial discourse, policies, and practice, as not completely vanquished.[9] Biko has a dynamic conception of culture. He accepts that having survived the violent contact with colonial cultures, African culture changed over time in response to changing circumstances while still retaining some of its "fundamental aspects." In other words, it is not a static African culture frozen in the past that summons Biko's attention; rather, he is concerned with identifying the residue of traditional African culture in contemporary or "modern African culture." His approach is not the descriptive ethnocultural exercise associated with colonial ethnography, which conventionally has as its object the culture of this or that ethnic community. It is an attempt to construct a theory of African culture by identifying the distinctive principles that regulate the content and practices of African culture as a whole. As such, it is a theorization of African culture.

An attentive reading of Biko's essay, "Some Aspects of African Culture," enables one to draw a list of the main, or what he calls, the "fundamental aspects" that constitute African culture. These are: Human-centeredness; intimacy; trust; belief in the inherent goodness of human beings; communalism and cooperativeness; caring and sharing; collective ownership; a monotheistic religion with a benevolent God and ancestral deities; a situation-experiencing mind-set; communicativeness; and a closeness to nature. In a nutshell, this is Biko's theory of African culture.

Listed thus, these aspects may strike readers familiar with ethnography as a typical typology of cultural traits widely used by the early colonial ethnographers. For example, in 1653, Jodocus Hondius published a monograph called *A Clear Description of the Cape of Good Hope* in Amsterdam in which he describes the KhoiKhoi in terms of a list of categories ranging from their physical appearance, their dress, and diet to their religion, language, and character.[10]

Coetzee explains that the template that organizes the study of the KhoiKhoi by Hondius was used as a handy conceptual scheme by all colonial ethnographers.[11] Although it served to organize data, it also regulated perceptions according to a standard schema. It structured the observations and interpretations of colonial ethnographers to conform to the demands of colonial discourse and its political agenda—namely to provide information, listed and organized as scientific evidence of the cultural inferiority of the colonized. The function of the template was to exclude anything that contradicted colonial discourse—where it could be excluded—to distort it to meet the injunctions of this discourse that presented itself as the Science of Man. Like much of the literature on Africa produced by Europeans for over five centuries, these ethnographic studies were primarily concerned with refuting the fact that Africans were human, and if they were, then, relative to Europeans, they belonged to a lower form of humanity.

Biko's discourse, being an anticolonial discourse on African culture, operates in the silences, omissions, and willed areas of blindness of colonial discourse on African culture. Although the list of aspects given above seem to approximate the typology of colonial ethnography, Biko's elaboration of what he considers the "fundamental aspects of African culture" is not a pseudoscientific case study of an ethnic group, but a theoretical intervention governed by a triple strategy. Firstly, to formulate a theory of African culture that will restore the intrinsic value of African culture to Africans; secondly, to present it as a basis for inter-African solidarity; thirdly, to critically unmask the pretensions of colonial culture. As we shall see, this is a complex task not without pitfalls.

The tenor of the essay on African culture, like everything Biko penned, is frank and directed both inward and outward. It is simultaneously a remorseless self-examination directed at "we blacks" and a visceral critique of the "westerner." He takes great care to emphasize that his enunciations issue from within a collective African experience and are presented, not on behalf of himself to unspecified readers, but on behalf of Africans to fellow Africans. Because of this, he frequently mentions that Black Consciousness should not unnecessarily preoccupy itself with the colonizer, yet he is fully aware of the complex dialectics that his double critique entails.

Beginning his characterization of African culture, Biko states: "One of the most fundamental aspects of African culture is the importance we attach to Man. Ours has always been a Man-centred society."[12] Expressed in the language of prepolitical correctness, with the "m" of "man" printed in capital, we however know that "Man" here refers to humanity and that what Biko asserts is that African culture is human-centered. It is a society by and for human beings and not a formation in the service of an economic idea or some other nonhuman goal.

This seems tautologous. After all, what is a human society, if not a human-centered settlement? To understand what Biko has in mind, it is necessary to place his assertion in historical perspective. Prior to European colonization of Africa, African society, as Biko conceives of it, consisted of relatively small hunting and gathering groups and large farming villages:

> Everybody here knows, African society had the village community as it basis. Africans always believed in having many villages with a controllable number in each. This obviously was a requirement to suit the community-based and man-centred society.[13]

This is in implicit contrast to the patterns of western and colonial urbanization: the European and colonial city, with its large concentration of people in a confined geographical area that escalated with the rapid industrialization of South Africa in the late nineteenth and twentieth centuries. This brought with it new forms of social organization, hierarchical and depersonalized. These mammoth agglomerations pushed small-scale rural communities, and the close association between people that they made possible, to the periphery of society. The new centers, designed to serve the needs of an industrial culture, subordinated human beings to depersonalized production-centered imperatives in which human beings, alienated from each other, are treated as nothing more than disposable labor resources by the captains and managers of industry.

The human-centeredness of African village communities, on the other hand, is manifest in the bonds of kinship and forms of social interaction not exclusively governed by economic interests or any other forms of exploitive instrumentality. For Biko, the inherent value accorded to every person in African society engenders an intimacy or closeness between people who are not necessarily friends or family members, but merely members of a community. Biko avers that where *intimacy* in modern Western culture is associated with "two friends," African communities extend the reach of this concept to include larger groups of people where a person had something in common, either through related tasks, age groups, or the mere fact of the locality where people resided. This is a communal definition of intimacy.[14] It is invoked as a counter to the bourgeois application of the term that restricts intimacy to the domestic sphere and the monogamous nuclear family, or to a limited number of close friends. Biko explains:

> In fact in the traditional African culture, there is no such thing as two friends. Conversation groups are more or less naturally determined by age and division of labour. Thus one would find all boys whose job it was to look after cattle periodically meeting at popular spots to engage in

conversation about their cattle, girlfriends, parents, heroes, etc. No one felt unnecessarily an intruder into some one else's business. The curiosity manifested was welcomed. It came out of a desire to share. This pattern one would find in all age groups. House visiting was always a feature of the elderly folk's way of life. No reason was needed as a basis for the visits. It was all part of our deep concern for each other.

This human-centeredness and intimacy characterizes African culture in a fundamental way. According to Biko this was "never done in the Westerner's culture."[15] Western culture sees and treats people, not as human beings worthy and meaningful in and of themselves, but as mere "agents for some particular function either to one's advantage or disadvantage." If human-centeredness and collective intimacy are alien to Western culture, then conversely, the reduction of human beings to agents or objects in an exploitative calculation is alien to traditional African culture. Because of the instrumentality, interpersonal relations in Western culture are haunted by mistrust and ceaseless competition between individuals. Concerning Africans, Biko tells us: "We are not a suspicious race. We believe in the inherent goodness of man. We enjoy man for himself."[16] African culture therefore eschews "using people as stepping stones."

In placing human beings at the center of African culture and valuing them in and of themselves, African life is based on cooperation and joint human action. This applied to farming, hunting, and all other tasks and activities. Biko expresses it thus:

> We regard our living together not as an unfortunate mishap but as a deliberate act of God to make us a community of brothers and sisters jointly involved in the quest for a composite answer to the various problems of life. Hence in all we do we place Man first and hence all our action is usually joint community oriented action rather than the individualism which is the hallmark of the capitalist approach.[17]

This communal ethos, according to Biko, engenders an eagerness among Africans to spontaneously communicate with each other in every way possible. It is expressed in what Biko calls the African "love for song and rhythm."[18] Music and movement are not practiced as special autonomous art forms divorced from everyday life. They are integral to all facets of life, including work, war, suffering, and celebrations. This music also expresses collective as opposed to individual experience. Biko writes:

> The major thing to note about our songs is that they were never songs for individuals. All African songs are group songs. Though many have words, this is not the important thing about them. Tunes were adapted to suit the

occasion and had the wonderful effect of making everybody read the same things from the common experience.[19]

This African communalism, in which the collective absorbs the individual without denying anyone's self, also finds expression in its traditions of ownership. As a human-centered and community-based social formation, the idea of private ownership, we read, is considered alien to African culture. Hence Biko emphasizes that "most things were jointly owned by the group, for instance there was no individual ownership. The land belonged to the people and was merely under the control of the chief on behalf of the people."[20]

This collective ownership coupled with the human-centeredness fosters an ethos of caring in African culture. It ensured that the community never hesitated to come to the assistance of anyone experiencing material or other problems. Consequently, Biko remarks: "It was never considered repugnant to ask one's neighbour for help if one was struggling. In almost all instances there was help between individual, tribe and tribe, chief and chief etc, even in spite of war." Hence, persistent and dire poverty afflicting one section of society, except in times of famine when everyone is in need, was unknown to African society.

Most of the aspects pertaining to African culture discussed thus far relate to flow and express one of the distinctive features of traditional African society, namely its communal or collective nature. This feature has been evoked by both Africans and non-Africans who sought to define African society as they knew or encountered it. They include African writers, philosophers, and political leaders such as Nkrumah[21], Senghor[22], Kenyatta[23], Nyerere[24], Kaunda[25], and Mbiti[26], to mention only some of the most prominent. Non-Africans such as Temples[27], Dickson[28], and Bohannan and Curtin[29] also insist on the communal, communitarian, or communalist nature of social relations in traditional African society. African society, however, is not programmatically anti-individualist in the sense that it ritually denounces and suppresses individualism in an orchestrated and systematic manner. Rather, its very communal nature renders it nonindividualistic insofar as it places emphasis on the well-being of the community as a whole as opposed to that of the individual, as is the case in capitalist societies.

Having sketched the communal nature of African society, Biko's essay proceeds to deal with two other aspects of African culture: African thought and African religion. Although the aspects dealt with thus far are concerned with the political, social, interpersonal, economic, and artistic values of African society that have some material basis, African thought and religion, which Biko also deals with, are concerned with cognitive and spiritual matters. His approach to these matters is threefold: it seeks to define and characterize the nature of African thought and religion; to establish their roles in dealing with problems presented by life; and to explain their relationships to and roles in African culture as a whole.

Africans thought, Biko suggests, that the mental disposition of Africans differs from that of westerners. He draws on Kenneth Kaunda's characterization of Africans as a "pre-scientific people."[30] Unlike westerners, with their aggressive mentality relying on logic and intolerance for contradiction, Africans, Kaunda and Biko claim, do not differentiate between the natural and supernatural worlds because they are open to both rational and nonrational forces. Biko states:

> Another important aspect of African culture is our mental attitude to problems presented by life in general. Whereas the Westerner is geared to use a problem-solving approach following very trenchant analyses, our approach is that of situation experiencing.[31]

According to Kaunda, Africans "experience the situation rather than face the problem."[32] In not facing the problem, "They allow both the natural and the supernatural to make an impact on them. And any response they may take could be described more as a response of the total personality to the situation rather then the result of some mental exercise."

This is a rather startling characterization of African thinking advanced by Kaunda, and endorsed by Biko, who considers it the most "apt analysis of the essential difference in the approach to life of these two groups." However Biko does not refer to Africans in the third person "they" as Kaunda does. To avoid the impression that he is not part of the people he is discussing, Biko uses the first person collective pronoun "we." Although he supports Kaunda's "analyses," he declares his personal "belief in the strong need for scientific experimentation." Biko writes:

> We as a community are prepared to accept that nature will have its enigmas which are beyond our powers to resolve. Many people have interpreted this as a lack of initiative and drive and yet in spite of my belief in the strong need for scientific experimentation I cannot help feeling more time also should be spent in teaching man and man to live together and that perhaps the African personality with its attitude of laying less stress on power and more stress on man is well on the way to solving our confrontation problems.[33]

An inner tension is detectable in Biko's exposition of African thought. At one level he seems to identify with the long dubious history of the colonial and postcolonial tradition that attributes to Africans a special type of thinking and personality. This is a scandalous claim that Africans have a reduced capacity for scientific thinking and logic. It is something that is also found in Senghor's theory of African sensibilities. Senghor pronounces: "Classical European thinking is analytical and makes use of the object. African reason is intuitive and participates in the object."[34] Senghor goes so far as to claim that: "Emotion is African as Reason is Hellenic."

This, to say the least, is highly problematic. It seems to uncritically reproduce an outrageous and discredited Western stereotype about Africans, namely that Africans are inferior to Europeans due to the putative lack in Africans of the mental capacity for abstract and analytical thought. This white myth has been in circulation since the earliest recorded contact between Africans and Europeans and it became especially pervasive during the successive eras of modern colonialism. So pervasive was it that even thinkers of the European Enlightenment such as Hegel, Locke, Hume, and even Marx and Engels were, as Soyinka writes, "unabashed theorists of racial superiority and the denigrators of African history and being."[35]

Any suggestion that Africans are incapable of logical thought and scientific enquiry is obviously false as it dangerously suggests that analytical reasoning is the monopoly of Western culture. Hence Biko's cautionary comment that he believes "in the strong need for scientific experimentation." With this caveat, however muted, he refutes and distances himself from claims that the African mentality is merely emotive, nonrational and intuitive. His qualification indicates he knew better and that rational capacities as well as nonrational elements are to be found in all human beings irrespective of their cultures, "race," or ethnicity. It is conceivable that at a particular point in time one culture may lay more emphasis on this or that capacity, but that this is not a fixed and immutable condition that renders one culture permanently rational and another mired forever in irrationality.

That said, if, however, we study the ideas in Biko's essay closely and relate them to those of Senghor, it emerges that, despite the rigid contrast that both seem to draw between African and Western culture and the mentalities each culture fosters, there is something critical at work in their ideas. What Senghor calls the "participation in the object" has affinities with Biko's "situation-experiencing," which he takes from Kaunda. Both concepts suggest a mental immersion in and exposure to all aspects of reality rather than a limited exposure filtered by one mental faculty, namely reason (as they claim is the case with Western thought). The resulting response to reality by Africans, it implies, is not just through one part of the person's mental faculties but by his or her "total personality."

As mentioned, in its totality the personality may and does consist of both rational and nonrational elements. If both are appropriately brought into play, the possibility of grasping and rendering the world, things, and experiences more comprehensively, is enhanced. Furthermore, by recognizing a wider range of mental dispositions, they seem to engage in an effort to give a positive value to the very things that colonial discourse enlisted in its denigration of Africans. Hence Biko's conviction that the potential for African culture to humanize the world is greater since it is aware of and sensitive to this fuller understanding and appreciation of human beings. This, however, if expressed the way that Senghor did in his early writings, is counterproductive and open to gross misreading.

Likewise, of the assertion that Africans are close to nature, Biko writes: "Thus in its entirety the African Culture spells us out as a people particularly close to nature."[36] As with the myth of Africa's mind-set, this claim of the closeness of Africans to nature has also been invoked in colonial discourse where it served to signify the primitiveness of Africans. Biko, however, sees this differently. The removal of people from nature in Western culture, as the consequence of industrial development and the construction of settlements cutoff from the countryside, produced a reliance upon artificial accoutrements fuelled by crass materialism and capitalist values. As Marx diagnosed, it alienates people from the natural environment, from their inner spiritual dimensions, from other people, and stunts their capacity to empathize with their fellow human beings. For Biko, African culture's "close proximity to Nature enables the emotional component in us to be much richer in that it makes it possible for us, without any apparent difficulty to feel for people and to easily identify with them in any emotional situation arising out of suffering." Biko sees the closeness of African culture to nature as a positive, even ideal form of existence. It grasps, as all the finest traditions of humanism do, the irrefutable fact that human beings are part of nature and dependent for their existence on it.

The other distinctive cognitive aspect of African culture is its religion. African religion, according to Biko is monotheistic, consisting of a single God where the living communicate through their ancestors, who after their lifetime join the spirit world to assume the role of interceding divinities.[37] In contradistinction to Christianity, the African Deity or Supreme Being is not a wrathful God; no hell exists in African religions; the ancestors assume the identity of saints in the afterlife. Furthermore, African religion was not something separated from everyday life. Where Christian worship is reserved for special sacred days and practiced in buildings set aside for this, African religion, according to Biko, is based on the belief "that God was always in communication with us and merited attention everywhere and anywhere."[38] African religion, like everything else in African culture, however, was undermined by colonial agents and missionaries who considered Africans either as heathens or superstitious pagans while presenting Christianity as the only true religion.

Biko's approach in defining African culture is consistently presented in a comparative form. He acknowledges this comparative strategy when he notes that "in taking a look at cultural aspects of African people one inevitably finds himself having to compare."[39] This inevitability arises from what he calls "the contempt" that colonial culture exhibited toward African culture. His strategy is thus intent on reversing the hierarchy of cultural value introduced by colonialism. Where colonialists sought to depict African culture as inferior and backward and Western culture as the epitome of civilization and humanness, Biko seeks to argue for the exact opposite.

As we have seen in his discourse, African culture is presented as the embodiment of respect for humanity while Western culture entails a violation and debasement of humanity. Accordingly, Biko exposes Western culture as a self-serving sham that cannot survive critical scrutiny. Proclaiming itself as the expression of human refinement, Western culture, in its colonial and capitalist guises, turns out to be little more than an apparatus designed to serve, maintain, and justify social relations based on the exploitation and oppression of human beings.

Anglo-Boer culture, as he refers to it, results in the remorseless dehumanization of people. Dehumanization occurs on differential lines with regard to the colonized and the colonizer. It places the colonized in a position of privilege and power over the colonized. The effect of this is that the colonial subject is completely drained of its humanity and treated as nothing but an object of use to the colonizers in economic terms. However, as a culture of reductive instrumentality, it is a double-edged sword: The colonizer, despite his power and privilege, is also afflicted by the scourge of dehumanization. It is a toxic and terminal state from which the colonizer cannot extricate himself, given the grip of the dehumanizing culture in which it is embedded.

A final observation, and perhaps the most important to be made with regard to Biko's ideas as outlined above, is that Biko, invoking as he does traditional African culture, writes, at least in the first part of his essay, of it as something of the past. If not quite of precolonial times then of something that once existed. This reference to the past is marked by his consistent use of the past tense. This is so even where the music is used by industrial workers to bind themselves together and lend some rhythm to repetitive and backbreaking labor or with regard to collective ownership of land and property. Everything in African society was based on a philosophy and culture that places a supreme value on human cooperation for the collective good.

Biko's discourse on African culture is an attempt at the recuperation and restoration of African culture. The central tenet of Black Consciousness is to affirm Africans and reverse the human negations of colonial domination. However submerged, displaced, and denigrated, the core or fundamental aspects of African culture, Biko believes, have not been completely destroyed and much of them can still be rescued from oblivion even under the condition of colonial domination.

In his recuperative discourse, Biko seems to bear striking resemblance to Fanon's anticolonial intellectual who rejects Western culture and "relentlessly determines to renew contact once more with the oldest and most pre-colonial springs" of indigenous culture.[40] Biko, however, asserts in his essay that his concern is not with pre-Van Riebeeck African culture but with aspects of African culture discernable in contemporary African society. Biko writes:

> Our culture must be defined in concrete terms. We must relate the past to the present and demonstrate a historical evolution of the black man. There is a tendency to think our culture is a static culture that was arrested in 1652 and never developed since. The "return to the bush" concept suggests that we have nothing to boast about except, lions, sex and drink. We accept that when colonialism sets in it devours the indigenous culture and leaves behind a bastard culture that may thrive at the pace allowed it by the dominant culture. But we also realise that the basic tenets of our culture have largely succeeded in withstanding the process of bastardization and that even at this moment we can still demonstrate that we appreciate a man for himself. Ours is a true man-centred society. We must reject, as we have been doing, the individualistic cold approach to life that is the cornerstone of Anglo-Boer culture. We must seek to restore in the black man the great importance we used to give to human relations, the high regard for people and their property and for life in general; to reduce the triumph of technology over man and the materialistic element that is slowly creeping into our society.[41]

The above citation enables us to see that Biko's concept of African culture and his humanist ideas are intertwined. In other words, his concept of humanity is a cultural construct and is conceptualized in terms of the following postulates:

1. In African culture, humans are social beings endowed with an inherent value, that is, human beings have value in and of themselves.
2. This inherent value of human beings is not automatically guaranteed but is dependent on a culture that understands respects, upholds, and safeguards this value.
3. As such, the inherent value of humans cannot be actualized and honored independent from and in isolation from other humans beings and, thus, outside of human society.

4. Hence the appropriate social conditions for recognition, respect, protection, and actualization of the inherent value of human beings is the existence of a human-centered culture.
5. Such a human-centered culture, which does not consider or treat human beings as a means to an end but as an end in itself, exists in African culture.
6. It is therefore incumbent on Africans to draw on this human-centered culture in their struggle for liberation from colonialism, inequality, and oppression.
7. In due course, this human-centered African culture will triumph over colonial culture and, in a postcolonial context, play a role in humanizing South Africa and those parts of world where dehumanizing cultures prevail.

It should not come as any surprise that the above conception resembles the African philosophy of *ubuntu*. As theorized by Ramose[42], Khoza[43], and Nkondo[44], among others, *ubuntu*'s principle concept of a common being, shared by all humans without having to forfeit their individual identities, informs its humanist and communal social principles. Belonging together in a community where the being and the well-being of each is dependent on and related to the well-being of all, a person is a person because of other persons. This interdependent and reciprocal relation, in which individual difference is not a source of conflict but the basis of the inherent value of each person that makes up and informs the humanist culture of the society as a whole, is distinctively African. It is a collectivist and not an individualistic worldview.

The emphasis on the collective in African culture, as Biko conceives it, differs from the arguments of individualist conceptions of society. For instance, Rawls posits that "individual difference is the basis of a social contract" in liberal democracies.[45] This social contract is an agreement to regard the "random and uneven distribution of natural talents" in society "as a common asset." That is, as assets which may belong to specific individuals but that are nevertheless at the disposal of the rest of society. In this way, individual assets turn out to be the "collective assets" of society. Individual assets become the basis for a form of collective individualism held together by institutions that regulate the rights of all individuals on the basis of equality. With respect to Gyekye, he infers a convergence between African communalism, humanism, and liberal humanism.[46] What he overlooks is the emphasis on tangible and intangible "assets" or property that defines the relationships of individuals to each other in liberal democracies. The cutthroat competition, social disproportions, hierarchies, and human discards that result from these are of course not considered by individualist theories such as the one put forward by Rawls.

For Biko, on the other hand, it is sufficient to set out from the principle that all human beings, their differences included, have the same inherent value. This value is not conceived in terms of asset, that is, in terms of tangible or intangible commodity, but as a right. The human-centered collective and communal culture of African society is based on the right of everyone to be treated equally within a framework of sharing that does not entail systematic exploitation. However, African collectivist discourse, which is invoked under colonial conditions, is basically a response to and a rejection of the individualist discourses. Frequently, African communal discourse imposes a willed blindness to its own history of contradictions and human violations, including intra-African conquest, slavery, and gender inequality. As a counter-discourse it attributes all inhuman acts to its ideological adversary.

Such oversights, omissions, and denials are predictable when discourses are pitted against each other as colonial and anticolonial discourses have been in South Africa for centuries. This adversarial relationship continues in postcolonial South Africa largely because the restoration of African culture that Biko envisaged has not materialized. In fact, in the context of globalization and the spread of Western culture via the new information and communication technology and the absence of an African-oriented cultural program in South Africa, the marginalization of African culture continues.

Biko was apprehensive of such an eventuality. Courageous and fearless, he has made a historic contribution to African humanism by channeling his "immeasurable rage" into critical analysis and the formulation of radical alternatives to white supremacy in South Africa. Like Fanon and Cabral, he understood the psycho-political importance of reasserting the significance, value, and dignity of African culture.

The central tenant of Black Consciousness, as everyone knows, is to oppose, reverse, and undo the long history of the dehumanization and emptying of being of Africans. Thus, the focus on African culture is not a nostalgic longing for something that no longer exists. Rather, it is a deliberate decision aimed at reinstilling a sense of African pride and an African consciousness in the colonized world by recuperating the suppressed culture of Africans. For Biko:

> The first step therefore is to make the black man come to himself: to pump back life into his empty shell; to infuse him with pride and dignity, to remind him of his complicity in the crime to allow himself to be misused and thereby letting evil rule supreme in the country of his birth. This is what we mean by an inward-looking process. This is the definition of Black Consciousness.[47]

This inward focus, which involves a critical self-examination, was not conceived as a continuation of the negation of African culture in the terms proposed by colonial discourse and practices. It was a form of introspection that was directed toward bringing into full consciousness the extent of the colonial ravages. By facing up to the cold truth, the arduous task of reconstituting African society necessarily required a rediscovery of African heritage and culture as a necessary condition for the liberation of Africans. This served to ignite a popular insurrection in the 1970s from which the colonial state never recovered.

However, this discourse on African culture and humanism, for all its radicalism, Biko knew, would be ineffective and meaningless if it were not part of a larger political philosophy and program of action. Thus, like so many African leaders, Biko was of the view that since colonialism set out to destroy the communalist social fabric of African society, a postcolonial social and economic order would have to be based on what he called a "non-racial" and "egalitarian society" based on some form of socialism. He envisaged the reorganization of the colonial economic dispensation through a "judicious blend of private enterprise... and state participation in industry and commerce."[48]

With this, he predicted the situation where the wealth of South Africa would remain concentrated in the hands of the small white minority, now coined as minority Africans, while the majority blacks would remain poor. This, he argued, would perpetuate the human inequalities of colonialism.

* * *

Biko confirms, "We have set out," signifying a collective departure on a historical challenge defined as "the quest for true humanity." This humanity, a true and authentic humanity, is something, somewhere, on the distant horizon to which the collective is marching with "courage and determination" sustained by a shared suffering and fraternal solidarity.

This prize is far-off in the future, but it is "glittering." It can nevertheless be seen from a position in the then present, the early 1970s. Although far-off and in the future, the quest for this prize, which is the attainment of "true humanity," is not some visual mirage or illusion. It is not even spectral. It is something manifest to vision. It can be seen and is thus knowable. This true humanity is a human-centered, caring society of nonracialism and equality that will change the lives of all South Africans, especially the lives of the colonized. This is the human face Steve Biko fought to bring into being. Thirty years after his death, it remains an unfinished work.

Notes

1. Steve Biko, *I Write What I Like* (London, Ibadan, and Nairobi: Heinemann, 1979), 47.
2. Ibid., 95.
3. Frantz Fanon, *The Wretched of the Earth*, trans. C. Farrington (Harmondsworth, UK: Penguin Books, 1967), 169.
4. Biko, *I Write What I Like*, 46.
5. Amilcar Cabral, *Unity and Struggle: Speeches and Writings* (London: Heinemann, 1980), 138–154.
6. Biko, *I Write What I Like*, 79.
7. Ibid., 40.
8. Daniel Kunene, *Thomas Mofolo and the Emergence of Written Sesotho Prose* (Johannesburg: Ravan Press, 1989), 8.
9. Biko, *I Write What I Like*, 41, 97.
10. Jodocus Hondius, *A Clear Description of the Cape of Good Hope*, trans. L. C. van Oordt (Cape Town, SA: Van Riebeeck Festival Book Exhibition Committee, 1952).
11. J. M. Coetzee, *White Writing: On the Culture of Letters in South Africa* (Sandton, SA: Radix, 1988), 14.
12. Biko, *I Write What I Like*, 41.
13. Ibid., 43.
14. Ibid., 41–40.
15. Ibid., 42.
16. Ibid., 47, 1877.
17. Ibid., 42.
18. Ibid.
19. Ibid., 43.
20. Ibid.
21. Kwame Nkrumah, *Africa Must Unite* (London: Heinemann, 1963).
22. Leopold Senghor, *On African Socialism*, trans. Mercer Cook (New York: Praeger Books, 1964).
23. Jomo Kenyatta, *Facing Mount Kenya* (New York: Vintage Books, 1965).
24. Julius Nyerere, *Freedom and Socialism; Uhuru ba Ujamah* (Oxford: Oxford University Press, 1968).
25. Kenneth Kaunda, *A Humanist in Africa* (London: Camelot Press, 1966).
26. John Mbiti, *African Religions and Philosophy* (New York: Doubleday, 1970).
27. P. Temples, *Bantu Philosophy*, trans. C. King (Paris: Présence Africaine, 1959).
28. Kwesi Dickson, *Aspects of Religion and Life in Africa* (Accra: Ghana Academy of Arts and Science, 1977).
29. Paul Bohannan and Philip Curtin, *Africa and Africans* (Garden City, NY: Natural History Press, 1973).
30. Kaunda, *A Humanist in Africa*.
31. Biko, *I Write What I Like*, 44.

32. Kenneth Kaunda, cited in Steve Biko, *I write what I Like* (London, Ibadan, and Nairobi: Heinemann, 1979), 44.
33. Biko, *I Write What I Like*, 44.
34. Leopold Senghor, *Prose and Poetry*, trans. Clive Wake (London: Oxford University Press, 1965), 33.
35. Wole Soyinka, "This Past must Address its Present." *Staffrider* 2, vol. 7 (1988): 59.
36. Biko, *I Write What I Like*, 45.
37. Ibid., 44.
38. Ibid.
39. Ibid., 41.
40. Fanon, *The Wretched of the Earth*, 175.
41. Biko, *I Write What I Like*, 95.
42. Mogobe Ramose, "The Philosophy of *Ubuntu* and *Ubuntu* as a Philosophy," in *Philosophy from Africa: A Text with Readings*, ed. P. H. Coetzee and A. P. J. Le Roux (Oxford: Oxford University Press, 2004).
43. R. Khoza, *Let Africa Lead: African Transformational Leadership for 21st Century Business* (Johannesburg, SA: Vezubuntu Publishing, 2006).
44. Gessler Muxo Nkondo, "Ubuntu as National Policy in South Africa: A Conceptual Framework," *International Journal of African Renaissance Studies* 1, vol. 2 (2007).
45. J. A. Rawls, *Theory of Justice* (Cambridge, MA: Harvard University Press, 1971), 102, 179.
46. Kwame Gyekye, "Person and Community in African Thought," in *Philosophy from Africa: A Text with Readings*, ed. P. H. Coetzee and A. P. J. Le Roux (Oxford: Oxford University Press, 2002), 309.
47. Biko, *I Write What I Like*, 29.
48. Ibid., 149.

Bibliography

Biko, Steve. 1979. *I Write What I Like* (London, Ibadan, and Nairobi: Heinemann).
Bohannan, Paul and Philip Curtin. 1973. *Africa and Africans* (Garden City, NY: Natural History Press).
Cabral, Amilcar. 1980. *Unity and Struggle: Speeches and Writings* (London: Heinemann).
Coetzee, J. M. 1988. *White Writing: On the Culture of Letters in South Africa* (Sandton, SA: Radix).
Dickson, Kwesi. 1977. *Aspects of Religion and Life in Africa* (Accra: Ghana Academy of Arts and Science).
Fanon, Frantz. 1967. *The Wretched of the Earth*, trans. C. Farrington (Harmondsworth, UK: Penguin Books).
Gyekye, Kwame. 2002. "Person and Community in African Thought," in *Philosophy from Africa: A Text with Readings*, ed. P. H. Coetzee and A. P. J. Le Roux (Oxford: Oxford University Press).
Hondius, Jodocus. 1952. *A Clear Description of the Cape of Good Hope*, trans. L. C. van Oordt (Cape Town, SA: Van Riebeeck Festival Book Exhibition Committee).
Kaunda, Kenneth. 1966. *A Humanist in Africa* (London: Camelot Press).

Kaunda, Kenneth cited in Biko, Steve. 1979. *I write what I Like* (London, Ibadan, and Nairobi: Heinemann).
Kenyatta, Jomo. 1965. *Facing Mount Kenya* (New York: Vintage Books).
Khoza, R. 2006. *Let Africa Lead: African Transformational Leadership for 21st Century Business* (Johannesburg, SA: Vezubuntu Publishing).
Kunene, Daniel 1989. *Thomas Mofolo and the Emergence of Written Sesotho Prose*. Johannesburg: Ravan Press.
Magubane, Bernard. 2007. *The Road to Democracy*, vol. 2 (1970–1980) (Cape Town, SA: Unisa Press), 206.
Mbiti, John. 1970. *African Religions and Philosophy* (New York: Doubleday).
Nkondo, Gessler Muxo. 2007. "Ubuntu as National Policy in South Africa: A Conceptual Framework," *International Journal of African Renaissance Studies* 1, vol. 2.
Nkrumah, Kwame. 1961. *I Speak of Freedom* (London: Heinemann).
———. 1963. *Africa Must Unite* (London: Heinemann).
Nyerere, Julius. 1968. *Freedom and Socialism; Uhuru ba Ujamah* (Oxford: Oxford University Press).
Ramose, Mogobe R. 2004. "The Philosophy of *Ubuntu* and *Ubuntu* as a Philosophy," in *Philosophy from Africa: A Text with Readings*, ed. P. H. Coetzee and A. P. J. Le Roux (Oxford: Oxford University Press).
Rawls, J. A. 1971. *Theory of Justice* (Cambridge, MA: Harvard University Press).
Senghor, Leopold. 1964. *On African Socialism*, trans. Mercer Cook (New York: Praeger Books).
———. 1965. *Prose and Poetry*, trans. Clive Wake (London: Oxford University Press).
Soyinka, Wole. 1988. "This Past must Address its Present." *Staffrider* 2, vol. 7.
Temples, P. 1959. *Bantu Philosophy*, trans. C. King (Paris: Présence Africaine).

11

Remembering Biko for the Here and Now

Ahmed Veriava and Prishani Naidoo

"Biko," four letters rich in signification, gathering the labor of a generation in struggle—a veritable treasure chest bringing out the usual looters.

Haunting

A man's life, it has been said, is always "more than a paradigm and something other than a symbol," and this is what a proper name should name.[1] But Steve knew, perhaps better than any of us, that the "method" of death could itself be a "politicising thing."[2] In the thirty years that have gone past since he was *killed*—after (real and reenacted) inquests, dozens of essays and books, a few commissions and court cases, Hollywood movies and chart busting hits—the most important statement on the death of Biko is still the haunting last chapter of *I Write What I Like*.[3] In his characteristically easy style, fixed in the rhythms of the everyday, Steve explains the philosophical paradox that black South Africans were forced to confront: Learning to live often means settling the argument with death. And for Steve, "you were either alive and proud or you were dead."[4] In the chilling account that follows—as much a statement on political courage as personal ethics—Steve explains his attitude toward the men who would finally kill him:

> I was talking to this policeman, and I told him, "if you want us to make any progress, the best thing is for us to talk. Don't try any of that rough stuff, because it just won't work"…"If you guys want to do this your way, you

have got to handcuff me and bind my feet together, so that I can't respond. If you allow me to respond, I'm certainly going to respond. And I'm afraid you may have to kill me in the process even if it's not your intention."[5]

Reading the short piece, we are left with little doubt as to the "method" of his death. He died as he lived, refusing to allow power to set the terms of the discussion, living proudly even in the face of death. Ultimately, Steve died because he refused to surrender what was not theirs to take, our dignity born of the labor of struggle. If we invoke the name "Biko," in making a "politics of memory, inheritance and generations," it is as much for unity between his style of life and way of dying as the many ways he helps us learn to live in the here and now. And if Steve's life—his easy manner, bold writings, and cutting political interventions—marked out a political imagination for our parents' generation, his death would do so for our own. In the millions of acts of everyday rebellion that invoked this style of life—against both this and the previous order—the proper name Biko was made common, the bearer of a rich and enduring legacy. A legacy steeped in struggle.

But the name made common brings new dangers, making our task of remembering Biko all the more urgent. For the name, Biko—the marker of a seditious style of life—has been made fashionable. Literally. Take a walk through the Zone in Rosebank and peek through one of the shop windows. You might be surprised to find Biko's face staring back at you from a T-shirt selling for over R300. Sit down at one of the posh coffee shops and try to listen in on the conversation at the next table. Try not to act confused if you hear some black economic empowerment (BEE) executive expound on "Corporate Black Consciousness" and the importance of black pride. Biko is "big" in Rosebank. So "big," in fact, that one can't help but be reminded of Walter Benjamin's warning: "*not even the dead will be safe if the enemy wins. And the enemy has not ceased to be victorious.*"[6] In the name we discover a struggle; our debt will not be settled cheaply, and our struggle must be to claim Biko against those who would reduce his legacy to an affirmation of our neoliberal present, a Biko reduced to a footnote in the speech of the magnum leader and proudly worn by the kids of the rich. Benjamin tells us that to articulate the past historically "means to seize hold of a memory as it flashes up in a moment of danger."[7] This is the spirit of our remembering of Biko—a Biko that begins with the scream and the labor of struggle.

To read anything of Biko's writing is to become immediately aware of this labor of struggle. It is political writing made from *political readings*. For Harry Cleaver, in his excellent book on Marx's capital, a political reading "self-consciously and unilaterally structures its approach to determine the meaning and relevance of every concept to the immediate development of working-class struggle. It is a reading which eschews all detached interpretation and abstract theorising in favour of grasping concepts only within that concrete totality of struggle whose determinations they designate."[8] In Biko, this is a reading in search of "weapons" and writing to reshape them and forge new ones; a writing where the accounts of the quotidian frustrations of delivery truck drivers and electricians, the hopes and complaints of people standing in queues, or the rebellious spirit of township youth, pass smoothly between the hardened politics of Fanon, Frederick Douglass, Stokely Charmichael, the radical poetry of Césaire, even the heady philosophy of Marx and Hegel, and probably many others whom we didn't recognize.[9] It is perhaps this that makes impossible any easy treatment of Biko's work mapped along the traditional academic coordinates of "influence," "authorial development," or even "political tradition." The rigor of the text is given not in its adherence to the conventions of academic writing but, instead, in the urgency of its political task. Made out of readings in search of weapons, it is a writing to shape and forge new ones. This writing, fashioned off the living force of struggle, the labor of the scream, is the haunting presence that threatens to rise up against the present so that we may see ourselves living differently in the here and now—to see ourselves otherwise.

This is what is often missed in so many of the contemporary mobilizations of the name Biko. Whether nationalist or socialist, the rhetorical trick is often the same, and apprehending Biko's legacy becomes a simple matter of following the paths of "Biko's development" through the respective nationalist or socialist writer's own political history. "If he lived, this is what Biko would have been," they tell us. Their Biko, reduced to a hypothetical mutation in the present and only able to choose, had he lived, between one or other of the embattled factions of the left, has nothing left to say. Nothing, that is, apart from what the respective nationalist's or socialist's party is already saying. For these theorists of the "what if Biko," there is always something insufficient about the Biko of *I Write What I Like*, something lacking that only the respective author's political trajectory could provide. In a swift political gesture, Biko is assigned "his" place in space and time. This Biko, given over to the time of the clock and calendar—a homogeneous open time filled in by the endless procession of power as one conqueror shifts to make room for the next—is damned to only ever hypothetically enter the present.

For us there is nothing lacking in Biko, nothing insufficient about the rich legacy of struggle that, like a chest of weapons, we carry *with* us into the present. Although much still remains to be discovered, and still more to be developed, this Biko—who knew that we inhabit a "larger world than the sophisticated westerner"[10]—still has a lot to say. This Biko belongs to a different order of time, heterogeneous and dense, where the dead still live with us,[11] and past and present are reconfigured in the instantaneous time of the here and now. This Biko is the ghostly presence that haunts the transition and threatens to rise up in the rebellions of the everyday and the force of ordinary people as they claim their dignity against the violence of history and power.

The Scream

If the destiny of Biko's generation—their political task and its philosophical environment—had been mapped out by the terms of debate set by the previous generation, then the great force of originality and innovation in Biko was to have never been satisfied with these terms. It is often remarked that many of the concepts and themes that appear in Biko were not his own. What is less obvious, however, is how these concepts and themes take on a new life under Biko's grip, and are constantly reinvented as he shapes them into weapons for the immediate struggle. Unfettered by narrow notions of tradition, free of allegiance to one or other "school of thought," Biko steals from everyone but bows to no one. And if the terms are not always his own, their life in the debate always is. Even Fanon, with whom—as many have recognized[12]—Biko had a strong affinity, is no exception. This spirit in Biko's writing, to be always shifting beyond the inherited terms of debate, is what has often been ignored by those who see in Biko less than an original thinker. It is, therefore, unfortunate that the rich tradition of academic writing in postcolonial theory has seen Biko feature as a relatively minor term. The editors, for instance, of the influential reader *Colonial Discourse And Post-Colonial Theory*—which begins with the important debate between Senghor and Fanon—might have done well to read *I Write What I Like*. Had they done so, they might have discovered a third moment that for all its shortcomings was already looking beyond the terms given by either.

Noting their importance as founding moments of important trajectories in cultural theory and African philosophy more generally, the reader begins with Leopold Senghor's *Negritude: A Humanism Of The Twentieth Century*, and is followed by an abridged version of the chapter "On National Culture" from Fanon's now classic *The Wretched Of The Earth*. However, beyond the purely philosophical or academic significance of this debate, the tension between these two moments of anticolonial theory is worth considering since their trajectories colored debates within liberation movements across the continent, including the Black Consciousness (BC) tradition.[13] In Biko, this was the tension between a Negritude centered on the African past and Fanon's dialectic of experience.[14] But if the former has always seemed to us a weakness in Biko, especially in his essay "Some African Cultural Concepts," the tension is also immediately productive and perhaps allows Biko to see even further than Fanon would.

For Senghor, Negritude was the logical expression of a movement attempting to "give expression to our black personality."[15] But what set it apart from others who had begun to walk these paths was the manner in which they—Senghor and others associated with the development of Negritude as a movement—were to develop "it as a weapon, an instrument of liberation and as a contribution to the humanism of the 20th century."[16] Situating Negritude within the "revolution" that begins with the publication of Bergson's *Time and Free Will* in 1889, Senghor begins to build a picture of a Europe struggling to find itself in the face of a crisis: The "new found" realization that "facts and matter, which are objects of discursive reason, were only the outer surface that had to be transcended by intuition in order to achieve a vision of reality."[17] Shifting through art, literature, even science, this humanist spirit would crystallize into an ontological position that sees consciousness "make itself: that is realise itself, by means of—yet transcending material well-being through an increase of spiritual life... [in developing] in a harmonious fashion the two complementary elements of the soul: the heart and mind."[18] The apparent paradox, however, in locating Negritude within a European humanist movement is, for Senghor, dissipated by the fact that such an ontological position is already confirmed by the African world view that, according to Senghor, has "always and everywhere presented a concept of the world which is diametrically opposed to the traditional philosophy of Europe":

> The latter is essentially static, objective, dichromatic; it is in fact dualistic, in that it makes an absolute distinction between body and soul, matter and spirit. It is founded on separation and opposition: on analysis and conflict. The African, on the other hand, conceives the world, beyond the diversity of its forms, as a fundamentally mobile, yet unique, reality that seeks synthesis.[19]

Senghor's African is, therefore, "fundamentally ethical," since "*his*" ethics are "derived from his conception of the world—his ontology."[20] Arguing that such an approach is validated by an analysis of precolonial African culture and society, which—from its art and theatre to its forms of social organization—was expressive of such a philosophical position, Senghor draws from across the entire continent examples of this conception of the world. This worldview, the profound unity between body and soul, matter and spirit—as the crucible of African experience—is not only Negritude's contribution to European humanism, but the means through which we reinforce ourselves against the violence of European domination.

Although Fanon is obviously sympathetic to the spirit of Senghor's humanism, in a compellingly dialectical exposition, he locates this attitude within the evolving consciousness of the native intellectual animated by the struggle for national liberation. Presented with the problem of legitimacy of the claims of the nation, Fanon describes how, within the parties for national liberation and the political world that surrounds them, there emerges a layer of "cultured individuals" for whom "the demand for a national culture and the affirmation of the existence of such a culture represent a special battle field."[21] For Fanon the dialectical significance that battle takes on is given in the fact that:

> [C]olonialism was never satisfied merely with hiding a people in its grip and emptying the native's brain of all form of content. By a kind of perverted logic it turns to the past of the oppressed people, and distorts, disfigures and destroys it.[22]

Confronted with the violent force of Western culture, the native intellectual searches for a "beautiful and splendid era whose existence rehabilitates us both in regard to ourselves and in regard to others" and with "the greatest delight...discovered that there was nothing to be ashamed of in the past, but rather dignity, glory and solemnity."[23] Against the force of a (European) culture that so violently distorts the African's sense of self, "the claims of the native intellectual," the affirmation of the dignity of the African past, "are no luxury but a necessity in any coherent programme."[24] But if Fanon was able to recognize the (dialectical) importance of this moment in the unfolding experience of the native intellectual, he is equally quick to point to the "pitfalls" of such an attitude.

The fact that colonialism, lofty and totalizing, "did not dream of wasting time in denying the existence of one national culture after another," means that the native intellectual who "decides to give battle to colonial lies fights on the field of the whole continent."[25] For Fanon, such an attitude is "logically inscribed from the same point of view as that of colonialism."[26] Since its condemnation of the African past was continental in scope, Negro-ism (and it is clear that here he is referring to, amongst others, Senghor's Negritude) as the "emotional if not logical antithesis of that insult that the white man flung at humanity,"[27] works to affirm African culture as a whole: "The unconditional affirmation of African culture has succeeded the unconditional affirmation of European culture."[28]

For Fanon, however, the tendency of the native intellectuals to speak "more of African culture than of national culture will tend to lead them up a blind alley."[29] These intellectuals, as they try to forge a political project beyond the nation, discover that their "objective problems are fundamentally heterogeneous" and realize that "culture is first and foremost national."[30] For Fanon, the proof of "a wonderful Songhai civilization" will not change the fact that "today the Songhais are under-fed and illiterate, thrown between sky and water with empty heads and empty eyes."[31] The problem of legitimacy to claims to the nation cannot be resolved in the past, but can ultimately only be settled in struggle for (national) liberation. There is, for Fanon, "no other fight for culture which can develop apart from the popular struggle."[32] It is this struggle that the intellectual must give himself over to, to take as the source that animates his activity in art, literature, or politics. Then, and only then, can we begin to speak of a national literature, art or culture:

> It is not to try to get back to the people in that past out of which they have already emerged; rather we must join them in the fluctuating movement, which they are just giving shape to, and which, as soon as it started, will be the signal for everything to be called into question. Let there be no mistake about it; it is to this zone of occult instability where the people dwell that we must come; and it is there that our souls are crystallised and our perceptions and our lives transfused with light.[33]

Fanon's critique, devastatingly effective in its task, has great merit. He correctly sees in Negritude a homogenizing trajectory that is content to merely invert the terms of the colonial strategy of self. And in its uncritical celebration and essentialist invocation of African culture, Fanon correctly points out that Negritude simply ignores the real circumstances of different national cultures struggling to give expression to themselves in the struggle for (national) liberation. But where does Biko, whose own position seems so intimately shaped by each of these trajectories in anticolonial theory, stand? His essay entitled "Some African Cultural Concepts" shows the extent that Biko, as early as 1971, was already wrestling with these problems. But unlike Senghor, or even Fanon, Biko's intervention is immediately inserted into a definite political context that, it seems clear, shaped the tenor and emphasis of his argument.[34] But even here, in a Biko thoroughly inserted into the Negritudinal worldview, the force of his method, and his starting point shines through.

Biko, as he often does, begins with a paradox—that of talking about African culture. Bombarded with authoritative pronouncements, weighed down by the "thickest volumes" of academic writing on African life—often "*coloured*" by intensely racist tropes and themes[35]—Biko saw that Africans themselves were "not expected to have any deep understanding of their own culture or even themselves."[36] Against the violence of white narrative, Biko, like Senghor, raises the mantle of an "authentic" culture to give back the dignity of African cultural life. But where the latter had taken white society as his audience, Biko, speaking intimately to a gathering of black cultural and social activists, is immediately inserted into the politics of the here:

> [O]ne realises that there is so much confusion sown, not only amongst casual non-African readers, but even amongst Africans themselves, that perhaps a sincere attempt should be made at emphasizing the authentic cultural aspects of African people by Africans themselves.[37]

But if Biko follows a similar path to that of Senghor, like Fanon—profoundly aware of the dialectical significance of recovering the dignity of African culture—he also recognized that this project could not be founded in the past alone. Instead, Biko locates his argument within a cultural context that, since 1652, has been experiencing a process of "acculturation." But rather than the indifferent mingling of different cultures, this process is for Biko a violent, one-sided affair. Confronted with the objectifying force of Anglo-Boer culture—a culture with all "the trappings of colonialist culture" and fully "equipped for conquest"[38]—"the African began to lose a grip on himself and his surroundings."[39] But Biko, never content to surrender any weapon into the hands of the oppressor, would still recognize an African culture that resists the obliteration of all threads that tie it to the precolonial African experience: "Obviously the African culture has had to sustain severe blows and may have been battered nearly out of shape by the belligerent culture it collided with, yet in essence even today one can easily find the fundamental aspects of the pure African culture in the present day African."[40]

As if borrowing a leaf from Negritude's book, Biko goes on to cite many of the same features of "African culture" that are emphasized by Senghor, often with the latter's homogenizing and essentialist trajectory. And like Senghor, Biko would discover in those aspects of African culture that belong to the precolonial experience a radically oppositional world view "to that of the sophisticated westerner," expressed in an ontological position that is, in Biko, centered on the community and the unity between the individual and the collective:

> Attitudes of Africans to property again show just how unindividualistic the African is. As everybody here knows, African society has the village community as its basis. Africans always believed in many villages with

a controllable number of people in each rather then the reverse. This obviously was a requirement to suit the needs of a community-based and man-centred society. Hence most things were jointly owned by the group, for instance there was no such thing as individual land ownership. The land belonged to the people and it was merely under the control of the local chief on behalf of the people.[41]

What is so striking about this and similar passages, whether related to poverty or song, beyond their obvious essentialist romanticization of the African past, is how Biko's African culture is made to speak to the strategic questions confronted by his generation. African culture is here immediately politicized, opened up to the search for "new" weapons for the present struggle. If Senghor's Negritude was an "emotional response" to that "insult that the white man flung at humanity" as Fanon suggests,[42] Biko's journey along the same path is a practical, if not opportunistic, attempt to define the poles across which a "new humanity" would have to be forged.

But if Biko's "new humanity" refused to surrender the lines running into the past, its force would be made in the present. Biko saw that even the violence of colonialism—the unity of the sword and the torch—was insufficient in completely obliterating African culture. However, for modern African culture—refigured and "bastardized" in the encounter with European colonialism and apartheid—the objects that would intimately shape its present were given in the first instance by a "common experience of oppression."[43] What survived of precolonial culture was, for Biko, not some cozy cocoon to which we could retreat, but instead weapons to be reshaped for the battle in the "now":

> Thus we see that in music the African still expresses himself with conviction...when soul struck with its all-engulfing rhythm it immediately caught on and set hundreds of millions of black bodies in gyration throughout the world. These were people reading in soul the real meaning—the defiant message "say it loud! I'm black and I'm proud." This is fast becoming our modern culture. A culture of defiance, self-assertion and group pride and solidarity. This is a culture that emanates from a situation of common experience of oppression...This is the modern black culture to which we have given a major contribution. This is the modern black culture that is responsible for the restoration of our faith in ourselves and therefore offers a hope in the direction we are taking from here.[44]

In this piece, Biko seems to seamlessly shift through different moments in the evolving consciousness of Fanon's native intellectual to arrive back at the contribution "we have made" (i.e., black consciousness) to this new black culture in the immediate struggle for national liberation. Thus, where Fanon would emphasize a culture situated on the national terrain,[45] Biko—who had drawn from across the whole continent and beyond in making a politics for his generation—would see a mutual reinforcing of struggles of the oppressed as they shifted to confront their immediate and respective enemies. Where the dialectical frame for Fanon's approach would tie him to a linear, progressive ideal for the evolution of political solidarities across national boundaries, Biko's method styled off the heterogeneous rhythms of the here and now, imagined a radical and immediate productive simultaneity in oppression and struggle whose boundaries were given, not in time nor space, but in subjectivity. This new culture, never simply national, but not yet global, would be the terrain upon which Africa's contribution to the work of "giving the world a more human face"[46] would be made.

What perhaps allows Biko to go beyond the tension between these two moments of thought is the extent to which he had been firmly grounded in a politics of the everyday, the extent to which he attempted to make a politics that begins with the scream: "I'm black and I'm proud."

On Black

> In the beginning is the scream. We scream. When we write or when we read, it is easy to forget that the beginning is not the word, but the scream. Faced with the mutilation of human lives by capitalism, a scream of sadness, a scream of horror, a scream of anger, a scream of refusal: NO.[47]

In the words "I'm black and I'm proud," resonating in the beats and rhythms of soul music, Biko apprehends the scream, the scream of millions of oppressed people refusing to be contained, shaped, and made by power. Beginning with the scream, Biko makes the starting point of his politics and philosophy the everyday, the ordinary, the spaces in which each of us is made to scream in different ways by the forces of our oppression. For it is in these spaces that Biko discovers (and not to engender or to create) the "protest talk" or "political consciousness" desiring of something other than apartheid capitalist society. During his cross-examination at the trial, that had the stated aim of finding out more about "conscientisation,"[48] Biko describes an approach to research undertaken by himself together with Barney Pityana and Jerry Modisane for a literacy project run by the South African Students Organization (SASO) in 1972, which involved listening to ordinary people in ordinary situations—on buses, in sports fields and queues, even shebeens. He goes on to explain how they discovered a common and widespread "protest talk," characterized by "a round condemnation" of white society and the oppression that it inflicted on black people.[49] Responding to further questioning about how conscientization related to this process of listening, Biko says the following about Black Consciousness:

> ...We do make reference to the conditions of the black man and the conditions in which the black man lives. We try to get blacks in conscientisation to grapple realistically with their problems, to attempt to find solutions to their problems, to develop what one might call an awareness, a physical awareness of their situation, to be able to analyse it, *and to provide answers for themselves*. The purpose behind it really being to provide some kind of hope; I think the central theme about black society is that it has got elements of a defeated society, people often look like they have given up the struggle. Like the man who was telling me that he now lives to work, he has given himself to the idea. Now this sense of defeat is basically what we are fighting against; people must not just give in to the hardship of life, people must develop a hope, people must develop some form of security to be together to look at their problems, and people must in this way build up their humanity. This is the point about conscientisation and Black Consciousness.[50] (Our emphasis)

Rooted in a process of listening, Biko's notion of conscientization is understood, then, as an open process, a manner of self-realization, itself determined in a fractured process of struggle over meaning among oppressed people.[51]

This approach to conscientization resonates today with the understanding of struggle against neoliberalism enunciated by the Zapatistas who in very simple ways have shaped a rebellion around "quite ordinary women and men, children and old people, that is, rebellious, non-conformist, uncomfortable, dreamers."[52] In a well-known story, John Holloway describes how the idea that "ordinary people are rebels" has come to lie at the heart of Zapatista politics. He tells of how the group of revolutionaries led by Subcomandante Marcos set out to "tell the people of the Selva Lacandona about capitalism and oppression and revolution," but instead learned to listen and "discovered that the people were already rebels."[53] Through this simple story, the Zapatistas relate a politics immanent to the everyday lives of ordinary people, to the spirit and potential of refusal, defiance, rebellion, and antagonism flowing from these insurgent subjectivities and their everyday acts of rebellion.

For Holloway, any theoretical reflection begins with opposition and struggle—"The starting point of theoretical reflection is opposition, negativity, struggle. It is from rage that thought is born, not from the prose of reason."⁵⁴ Holloway sees oppression (or exploitation) and struggle against it in a constant dialectical relationship that is constitutive of the scream. "The scream implies a tension between that which exists and that which might conceivably exist, between the indicative (that which is) and the subjunctive (that which might be). We live in an unjust society but we wish it were not so: the two parts of the sentence are inseparable and exist in constant tension with each other."⁵⁵ The "ordinary rebel" embodies, for Holloway, this dialectical tension between a self caught in its production by capital yet holding the potential to recognize and rebel against this production.

We see specters of Biko in Holloway too... In making the lives of ordinary people the starting point for his development of Black Consciousness, as we have argued, Biko too begins with the scream. However, his enunciation of a politics of "coming into consciousness" through a realization of the self as "Black," offers us something different to Holloway's notion of the dialectical tension between the indicative and the subjunctive. If his (listening) research in 1972 had yielded widespread "protest talk," it would not only be the force of negativity that was emphasized by Biko, but the creative force of self-valorization creeping up beside it as well. In making "I'm black and I'm proud" the starting point of our "coming into consciousness," in Biko, the indicative, "I'm black"—a statement carrying within it the marks of dehumanization and oppression—becomes temporally conjoined with the subjunctive here "and I'm proud." The scandal, "I'm black," is affirmed outside of white society, and against it. It is significant that Biko self-consciously develops the concept of black in contradistinction from the term nonwhite,⁵⁶ such that, rather than being the antithesis of white, the concept of black mobilizes the powers of positive self-definition against white supremacy and apartheid capitalism. For Biko, "black" as a "mental attitude" and "not a matter of pigmentation," was as much about a (seditious) style of life as it was about a political subject. In beginning to define oneself as black, for Biko, "you have started on a road to emancipation, you have committed yourself to fight against all forces that seek to use your blackness as a stamp that marks you out as a subservient being."⁵⁷ With this understanding of "Black," both as a positive state of being and an alternative way of seeing the world and one's relation to it, "I'm black and I'm proud" becomes a political statement founded not on any essentialist notions of blackness, but on the resonance of struggle and defiance among the oppressed, those who acknowledge their oppression based on the color of their skin and those who fight to live outside of the roles and identities assigned them by the system. Thus, rather than purely the force of negativity, the scream is in Biko more profoundly the affirmation of difference.⁵⁸

Method

For those who would assign Biko "his rightful place" in history, finding his value and limit in a "fixation on race," the Biko of *I Write What I Like* has little to offer in making a politics for the now. But what such readings of Biko miss are both the persistence of struggles around race as well as the way in which Biko's notion of "Black" works to signify the complexity of oppression in apartheid South Africa—an oppression based on racial, class and gender differences. What they miss is the Biko that begins with the scream. In response to cross-examination during his trial Biko says:

> I think the black man is subjected to two forces in this country. He is first of all oppressed by an external world through institutionalized machinery, through laws that restrict him from doing certain things, through heavy work conditions, through poor pay, through very difficult living conditions, through poor education, these are all external to him, and secondly, and this we regard as the most important, the black man in himself has developed a certain state of alienation, he rejects himself, precisely because he attaches the meaning white to all that is good, in other words he associates good and he equates good with white.[59]

Although it might be easy to caricature Biko by ignoring his unique definition and use of the concept "Black," it is a little more difficult to ignore the many references in Biko to the close relationship between apartheid and capitalism, and the ways where racial oppression is closely tied to economic oppression, making his writings as much anticapitalist as they have been read as being antiracist. In response to a question in an interview probing his views on socialism, Biko had the following to say:

> I think there is no running away from the fact that now in South Africa there is such an ill distribution of wealth that any form of political freedom which does not touch on the proper distribution of wealth will be meaningless. The whites have locked up within a small minority of themselves the greater proportion of the country's wealth. If we have a mere change of face of those in governing positions what is likely to happen is that black people will continue to be poor, and you will see a few blacks filtering through into the so-called bourgeoisie. Our society will be run almost as of yesterday. So for meaningful change to appear there needs to be an attempt at reorganising the whole economic pattern and economic policies within this particular country.[60]

As we shift to make a politics of the now, for a society "run almost as of yesterday," we remember Biko not only for the prophetic force of writings on the problem of integration or the pitfalls of postapartheid South Africa, but the efficacy of the weapons he brings into the here and now—the power of his method. Exploring how colonialism and apartheid worked to subjugate black people through common forms of exploitation and oppression, Biko produces a philosophy of struggle that enunciates both a politics and a way of being that sees as its "battleground" the everyday lives of the oppressed, lives where Black Consciousness seeks to facilitate the realization and apprehension of both these common forms of oppression, as well as the spirit and rhythms of "defiance, self-assertion, group pride and solidarity." In this, the individual is understood as "coming into consciousness,"[61] that is, realizing his/her oppression, its causes, and his/her own potential to defy the system and to produce other ways of being and living, through a process of lived experiences and exchanges with others, oppressed and oppressor. And here, acts of everyday rebellion are woven between the narratives and stories of black people retold in positive and creative ways, to produce a matrix that allows for the imagination of the black self positively, and the production of communities that are able to resist and produce wor(l)ds against the exploitative and oppressive system of apartheid and capitalism. Although Black Consciousness offers a means of understanding and approaching the world through an understanding of the self, it is not, then, a static model for changing the world on a global scale. Instead, it allows for the changing, lived experiences of people to shape and determine its own use and evolution. Signaling the need to realize the potential for revolution that lies within each of the oppressed and among the oppressed as a group, Black Consciousness roots the shaping of these revolutions in the everyday lives (or subjectivity) of the oppressed. It is this that allows us to mobilize Biko's words in our struggles in the here and now. Woven in subjectivity and fashioned in rebellion, this politics—resonating in the struggles of today's everyday insurgents—is what allows us to invoke that common voice in struggle identified by Biko in the words "I'm black and I'm proud" for the "here and now."

In the Here and Now

Although Biko might be an icon of today's burgeoning South African black middle class, his elaboration of the theory of "being black" that was based on a nonessentialist and open-ended understanding of struggle rooted in the common experience of oppression, that sought not to mimic white society, but to inaugurate something completely different, speaks against current mobilizations of his memory in support of black economic empowerment (BEE) and the like. *I Write What I Like* is peppered with passages that betray Biko's contempt for the attitude that desires nothing more than the "integration" of blacks into white society and its values:

> The concept of integration, whose virtues are often extolled in white liberal circles, is full of unquestioned assumptions that embrace white values. It is a concept long defined by whites and never examined by blacks. It is based on the assumption that all is well with the system apart from some degree of mismanagement by irrational conservatives at the top. Even the people who argue for integration often forget to veil it in its supposedly beautiful covering. They tell each other that, were it not for job reservation, there would be a beautiful market to exploit. They forget they are talking about people. They see blacks as additional levers to some complicated industrial machines. This is white man's integration based on exploitative values. It is an integration in which black will compete with black, using each other as rungs up a stepladder leading them to white values. It is an integration in which the black man will have to prove himself in terms of these values before meriting acceptance and ultimate assimilation, and in which the poor will grow poorer and the rich richer in a country where the poor have always been black.[62]

Words today, prophetic rather than cautionary, as the mantra that there is no alternative to capitalist society is preached by a democratically elected government, and the black middle class ascends with increasing mobility into white society and the assumption of its values. At a time in our history when black people are being told by black leaders to become responsible citizens contributing to the productivity of a South Africa where little has changed in the "material circumstances" of the vast majority of (black) people, this being-with-Biko[63]—as the invocation of the scream and the seditious powers of self-valorization—is what allows us to see ourselves living differently in the here and now. Some of our struggles are new, many are not. As we shift to confront our (new and old) enemies, whether embodied in lofty concepts like neoliberalism or threaded through "the relations in the home," we invoke a "method" in Biko's name. A method that allows us to bring together past and future in making a politics for the here and now, that seeks not to preach or teach, but to listen and to bring into being a consciousness rooted in struggle and rebellion and the belief that we can be 'what we like' in spite of power's persistent attempts to tell us otherwise. It is a "method" that begins with the scream, not the word; a "method" that lets subjectivity shape our "political programs" and takes as its battlefield the everyday lives of ordinary rebels.

Although the death of Black is signaled in every BEE deal, in every jingle using "black soul" to sell the latest commodities, and in every T-shirt rendering our heroes to the march of capital's time, Black is also alive—in every refusal to pay for water or electricity, in every land occupation, in every march and everyday act of resistance against today's logic of neoliberalism and the rule of the market. It is alive in the spirit of resistance and refusal, the spirit of rebellion against that which we are taught to believe is natural and unchangeable.

We re-member Biko for this world where we are told that there is no alternative, and that this time and place is all there is—all there ever will be. Work hard, they say... accumulate if you can (it will make you happy)—just don't forget to vote. They teach us to be patient, to trust our leaders and their assurances that things are getting better, however slow the pace might seem. History might as well be over and all that came before no more than the making of this present, all still to come nothing but the eternal repetition of the day before. Time is marked out into empty units to be filled in like the squares on a calendar. And they tell us this is what freedom means. We re-member Biko as a force for something else.

Notes

1. Derrida's important book on Marx begins with a dedication to Chris Hani. Here, Derrida notes that if the proper name, "Hani"—"more than a paradigm and something other than symbol"—has come to be indelibly tied to the practice of critique we call communism, it is because we recognize that he was killed for being a communist... by assassins who "themselves proclaimed that they were out to get a communist." Jacques Derrida, *Specters Of Marx*, trans. Peggy Kamuf (London and New York: Routledge, 1994), xix.
2. Steve Biko, *I Write What I Like* (Johannesburg, SA: Picador Africa, 2004), 173.
3. The short piece, entitled "On Death," is an extract from an interview Steve did with an American businessman some months before his death. Ibid., 173–175.
4. Ibid., 173.
5. Ibid., 174.
6. Walter Benjamin, *Illuminations*, trans. Harry Zohn (London: Fontana Press, 1992), 247.
7. Ibid.
8. Harry Cleaver, *Reading Capital Politically* (1979; repr., Leeds, England: Anti-Thesis, 2000), 30.
9. The writers and militants who live in Biko's work seldom do so in name. Instead, they rise up in a concept and theme, in a particular style of argument, or even a quote bent to fit the purpose Biko sets it. Biko's relationship to those he invokes is never straightforward. It seems clear, for instance, that Biko had not read much Marx or Hegel by the time the concept "dialectical materialism" first appears in his writing. In a clumsy mistake, perhaps mitigated by the nature of propagandist summaries of the dialectic (popular in the student movement at the time), Hegel becomes a materialist and Marx's innovation is forgotten. But, if Biko makes mistakes, misunderstands concepts, or glosses over important debates, these nevertheless remain productive. Like Deleuze's Kafka, Biko's writing is shot through with impossibility. The impossibility

of writing as a black man in South Africa, (systematically) insulated from the canon of radical thought, and with only "rumors" of a local political tradition to draw on; the impossibility of writing in a time and place where narrative itself was made into something "white." The impossibility of not writing as a black man in South Africa, living the anger of generations of the oppressed calling out for expression, and confronted by the violence of white narrative that systematically erodes our relationship to self. The impossibility of writing otherwise except with what is close at hand, since ultimately "black man you are on your own." It is in going through this impossibility that everything in Biko is made immediately productive.
10. Biko, *I Write What I Like*, 51.
11. Derrida's exordium to *Specters of Marx* begins with a paradox: Learning to live, as "ethics itself," is "done alone, from one self by oneself." But "to live, by definition is not something one learns. Not from oneself, it is not learned from life, taught by life. Only from the other and by death. In any case from the other at the edge of life." Thus, to learn to live (better) is to settle the argument ("come to terms") with death—to learn to live with ghosts. This being with ghosts is the "respect for those others who are no longer or for those who are not yet there, presently living, whether already dead or not yet born." For Derrida this, as "politics of memory, of inheritance, and of generation," is a condition of Justice. "No justice...seems possible or thinkable without the principle of some responsibility, beyond all living present, within that which disjoins the living present, before the ghosts of those who are not yet born or who are already dead, be they victims of wars, political or other kinds of violence, nationalist, racist, colonialist, sexist, or other kinds of exterminations, victims of oppressions of capitalist imperialism or any of the forms totalitarianism. Without this non-contemporaneity with itself of the living present, without that which secretly unhinges it, without the responsibility and this respect for justice concerning those who are not there, of those who are no longer or who are not present and living, what sense would there to ask the question 'where?' 'where tomorrow?' 'whither?'" (xix).
12. See, for instance, "Black Consciousness 1977–1987: The Dialectics Of Liberation In South Africa," *Centre for Civil Society Research Report*, no. 18 (2004), in which Nigel Gibson develops an argument around the strong resonance of Fanon in Biko's work in attempting to clarify the spirit of radical humanism in the latter's writing.
13. As we have already noted, Biko had a strong affinity for Fanon. On the other hand, the adoption of the Mafikeng Declaration by the Black People's Convention (BPC), which spoke of African communalism, shows the extent to which the early history of BC had been shaped by Negritude and a politics centered on an image of the precolonial African past. African communalism would later be replaced by "scientific socialism" as the strategic program for the BC movement without either ever having been theoretically clarified for the South African context.
14. It should be noted that our usage of the term "Negritude" in this essay refers explicitly to the movement with which Leopold Senghor was associated, not the more generic connotation of the term translating loosely as "blackness."
15. Leopold Senghor, "Negritude: A Humanism Of The Twentieth Century," in L. Chrisman and P. Williams, eds., *Colonial Discourse and Post-Colonial Theory* (New York: Columbia University Press, 1994), 27.
16. Ibid.
17. Ibid., 28.
18. Ibid., 30.
19. Ibid.
20. Ibid., 31.

21. Frantz Fanon, "On National Culture" in Chrisman and Williams, eds., *Colonial Discourse*, 36.
22. Ibid., 37.
23. Ibid.
24. Ibid.
25. Ibid., 38.
26. Ibid., 38.
27. Ibid.
28. Ibid.
29. Ibid., 39.
30. Ibid., 40.
31. Ibid., 37.
32. Ibid., 40.
33. Ibid., 43.
34. According to the short preface to the piece, it had originally been presented at a conference called by the Interdenominational Association of African Ministers of Religion and the Association for the Educational and Cultural Development of the African People to "draw together a number of black organisations who might be interested in closer association" (Biko, *I Write What I Like*, 44). It's clear that Steve was there to do politics, and as the editor of *I Write What I Like* notes, the conference "proved to be a staging post on the way to the formation the Black Peoples' Convention" (Ibid.) later that year.
35. An example of a theme, cited by Biko, is "the feeding habits of urban Africans" by the Institute for Race Relations (Ibid.).
36. Ibid.
37. Ibid.
38. Like Edward Said's Conrad (see *Culture and Imperialism* [New York: Knopf, 1994]), Biko is keenly aware of the "mutual reinforcing of the sword and the torch...where it was impossible to convert, firearms were readily available and used to advantage" (Ibid., 45).
39. Ibid., 45.
40. Ibid., 43–46.
41. Ibid., 47.
42. Biko, *I Write What I Like*, 38.
43. Ibid, 50.
44. Ibid.
45. This is a question of emphasis. In Fanon, national culture is a condition for true internationalism.
46. Ibid., 51.
47. J. Holloway, *Change the World Without Taking Power: The Meaning of Revolution Today* (London, Pluto Press, 2002), 1.
48. Judge Soggot, quoted in Biko, *I Write What I Like*, 124.
49. Biko, *I Write What I Like*, 125.
50. Ibid.
51. This seems to speak against vanguardist approaches to struggle that prioritize the importance of fixed bodies of theory in shaping and determining the actions of individuals and groups in struggle, and that "bring consciousness to people" rather than facilitating our "coming into consciousness." Although Biko has come to serve the interests of several vanguards over time, each claiming to know "what Biko really meant," it is ironic that his own method was a preference to listen rather than to tell,

and to allow for consciousness to be shaped through a process of engagement and interaction amongst and between people experiencing apartheid and capitalism as a common form of oppression. Although some may argue that Biko contradicts this by arguing for the development of a "vanguard political movement," (Biko, *I Write What I Like*, 170), we could argue that the manner in which Biko understands the elaboration of this vanguard political movement is very different from traditional notions of vanguard political parties and groups. In Biko's understanding, his vanguard could not function as a political elite separate from an organically driven process, but as a growing movement of activists, rooted in community work, taking as its starting point the views, needs, beliefs, and desires of ordinary people. In this way, Biko's vanguard movement would itself be shaped and directed by the needs of ordinary people.
52. Subcomandante Marcos, quoted in John Holloway, "Ordinary People Are Rebels," (unpublished transcript of speech, 2001), 1.
53. Holloway, "Ordinary People," 1.
54. Holloway, *Change the World*, 1.
55. Ibid., 4.
56. For "nonwhites" were those who continued to see themselves as subservient to white society, defining themselves in relation to white society. As Gibson notes, activists in the BC tradition shunned the term "non-white" as a mark of their "negation." Blacks for Biko were those "who can manage to hold their heads high rather than willingly surrender their souls to the white man" (Biko, *I Write What I Like*, 52). That is, they who understand their oppression and their negation by white society, and choose to fight against it and define themselves positively outside of white society.
57. Ibid.
58. Biko's relationship to the dialectic is an important and underdeveloped area of research. Although many have seen in Biko a shrewd dialectician (see Gibson), as we have already noted, in spite of the concept appearing a number of times in the text of *I Write What I Like*, it is unclear how well-versed Biko would have been with either Hegel's or Marx's writing on the subject. Although Biko obviously had an excellent teacher for the dialectical method in Fanon, his own usage of the term is often secondary to the principle lines of his argument or invoked to clarify the strategic differences between the vision of BC and that of the canon of left writing on race at the time (within the latter's preferred terms). Our own thoughts, preliminary and still evolving, are offered in the hope of stimulating debate and research in this area.
59. Ibid., 111.
60. Ibid., 169.
61. Ibid., 105.
62. Ibid., 101.
63. In the spirit of Derrida's "being-with-ghosts."

12

The Black Consciousness Philosophy and the Woman's Question in South Africa: 1970–1980

M. J. Oshadi Mangena

Introduction

Philosophy is born out of the living experience of a people. It is out of the living experience of the conquered, dispossessed, oppressed, and exploited peoples of South Africa that the Black Consciousness philosophy was born.[1] The philosophy took cognizance of the historical experience of conquest in the unjust wars of the colonization of South Africa. It recognized that "the Khoisan did not willingly submit to their systematic incorporation into foreign, white rule...The indigenous people were dispossessed, sometimes by violent force of arms, at other times by sheer 'non-violent' chicanery...When they lost the land, they lost their independence and the ability to shape and determine their destiny."[2] Thus the systematic dispossession of the conquered peoples of the country was questioned.

The philosophy recognized that the daughters and sons born of the sexual union between conqueror and conquered were described and defined in ways that denigrated their dignity as human beings. Ideology and legislation often prevented them from experiencing family life— living together with both biological parents coming from different cultural backgrounds. The philosophy also acknowledged that in 1860 British colonialism forced Indians out of India to come and work in South Africa as laborers in the sugar plantations. According to the Black Consciousness philosophy, being-black-in-the-world was an existential pointer to the historically diverse experiences of conquest in the unjust wars of colonization, dispossession, oppression, and callous exploitation. Thus, skin pigmentation was neither the primary nor the decisive factor in the definition of blackness. Instead, blackness referred to the already mentioned historically diverse experiences. These experiences were understood to be a compelling invitation summoning the various peoples to come together and fight for freedom. As Magobe Ramose writes, "The definition of the term 'black' to include Africans, Indians and Coloureds was crucial in the development of the movement. It is worth noting here that neither the ANC nor the PAC had at this time arrived at such a precise and strategic definition that embraced all the oppressed and sought to unite them within a single ideological discourse. Even in SASO ranks, the debate about the wisdom of including Coloureds and Indians in the organization was by no means over."[3] The imperative to fight collectively and in solidarity with one another for freedom defined the meaning of the term Black in the Black Consciousness philosophy.

Philosophy is indeed born out of the living experience of a people. Once a philosophy is translated into practice it might have to be modified and adjusted according to the demands of experience.[4] This was true of the Black Consciousness philosophy as well. In practice, it crystalized into a number of organizations.[5] It is this particular feature of the philosophy that gave rise to the name, the Black Consciousness movement. The Black Consciousness movement of South Africa emerged in the late 1960s and reached its peak in the mid-1970s. Here the focus on the movement, with particular reference to the woman's question, shall cover only one decade, namely, from 1970 until 1980.

I argue that by recognizing that women could be at an equal footing with men as leaders in the public sphere, South African Students Organization (SASO)—and, by extension the Black Consciousness philosophy—inadvertently and tacitly endorsed the legitimacy of "gender" as an issue in the terrain of social and political power relations between men and women. In this sense the Black Consciousness philosophy was ahead of its time with regard to the problematic of "gender."

Right from the very beginning—from the earliest days in SASO—there was a tacit recognition and acceptance of the idea that women could be leaders in their own right. Gail Gerhart writes about these early days:

> When the [inaugural SASO] conference met at Turfloop in July 1969, Biko was named president. Other leading figures *from the beginning* in SASO were Barney Pityana,... Harry Nengwekhulu, Hendrik Musi, Petrus Machaka, and *Manana Kgware* of Turfloop, Aubrey Mokoape,...and J. Goolam and Strini Moodley...[6] (Italics added)

If there were not a tacit acceptance of the full participation of women, it is difficult to explain why Manana Kgware was among the leading figures of SASO right from its very inception. No doubt the acknowledgement of women as leaders was then not predicated on "gender" as experience and concept. As Mamphela Ramphele put it, "Gender as a political issue was not raised at all" within Black Consciousness organizations and, "There is no evidence to suggest that the BWF [Black Women's Federation] was concerned with the special problems women experienced as a result of sexism both in the private and in the public sphere."[7] Though gender was not an organizing principle of the movement, I argue that gender concerns were tacitly endorsed.

The Definition of Gender

The idea of "gender" is defined here as the social construction of concepts that define manhood and womanhood (or maleness and femaleness) *as mutually exclusive beings opposed to each other*. Such beings have their labor (productive, reproductive, mental, and emotional) loaded with values that get measured in terms of superior and inferior. Superior values are always associated with the labor of the male person while that of the female person is associated with inferior values. This determines the unequal relations between men and women in social organization and development. The labor of the female person gets subordinated to that of the male person in various aspects of life, in the sense that the male person is uplifted to a superior position of power while the female is relegated to an inferior position relative to the male. Such positions go with corresponding roles that become stereotypes in the long term.

Although we acknowledge that there may be other ways of defining gender, experience and research shows that whatever definition one chooses the common point in such definitions is that "gender" is conceived as a *social construction*. As such, it is not a natural datum permitting talk of "human nature" or even "male" and "female nature." The rejection of the concept of "human nature" is consistent with Jean-Paul Sartre's existentialist phenomenology declaring that the human being is "condemned to be free." Gender, as defined here, means that social relations are in the first place changeable and, secondly, challengeable. Gender then focuses primarily upon the power relations between men and women.

The core argument of this essay is that in the Black Consciousness movement "gender," as defined above, was absent from the minds but not the activity of its members. The presence of "gender," in the activities of the members, was not the result of an active intention. The activities of the members manifested the implementation of a passive intention as well as the tacit recognition of "gender" as a critical category in the understanding and analysis of male and female power relations. The purpose of the argument is (i) to show that in the history of the Black Consciousness movement we discover the rudiments of the "woman's question";[8] (ii) to show that by taking the history of the Black Consciousness movement seriously some important lessons may be learnt on how to deal with the question of "gender" in contemporary South Africa. The focus on post-1994 South Africa contains within it an implicit question that must be made explicit because of its importance to the liberation of women in the first instance and men as well.

In the critique of the now bygone socialism in the former Eastern Bloc countries, Mihailo Markovic considers the "liberation" of women in that context as a far cry from the authentic liberation of women. The argument advanced by Markovic is that the authentic liberation of women cannot be attained without the contemporaneous liberation of men as well. Thus the liberation of women is tied to the liberation of the entire human race. In the words of Markovic:

> It turns out that in most contemporary societies equality with men in work is only equality in wasting one's best potential capacities. And even within the family, equality with men is a problem of only a superficial sort. A deeper problem is that even if there were equality within the family, both husband and wife would continue to be alienated, and in many different senses... The problem of women's emancipation is a general human problem—how to liberate one individual *from* the other by liberating both *to* a richer, more meaningful existence, how to maximize our power over the conditions of our life, how to get control over institutions that at present still so efficiently imprison us, how to create such relationships with other human beings in which our own full self-expression and self-realization would coincide with the satisfaction of the genuine needs of others.[9]

The question of the link between women's emancipation and human liberation may therefore be posed thus: Does the transition to the "new" South Africa warrant "gender" acquiescence to patriarchal capitalism? It is in pursuit of the two purposes and the specific question just raised that the topic of the "woman's question" within the Black Consciousness movement was chosen.

"Black Man, You Are on Your Own"

Within Black Consciousness circles, a special language evolved. For example, some people were referred to as "nonwhites." But this appellation did not have the same meaning as the official ones referring—in the different historical contexts of continuing oppression—to the "natives," the "non-Europeans," the "Africans, Coloureds and Indians" as a collective, and the "Bantu" (not to forget the "plurals" that epitomized the oppressor's obsession with the logic of negative discrimination). On the contrary, "nonwhite" in Black Consciousness language referred to someone mentally enslaved by the ideology and values of the oppressor: A human being in need of freedom from mental colonization. No doubt this freedom could hardly be meaningfully and fully realized without the breaking of the physical chains of oppression and exploitation. Within this language one often found the expression that someone was "relevant." Even in initial encounters with one another it was not unusual to be asked: Is she "relevant?" An affirmative answer to the question was understood to mean that the person could be accepted as having already had "political baptism" qualifying her or him to be involved in the activities of the Black Consciousness movement. Also, the expression, "ke system" (he/she is the system) meant that the person referred to was actually an informer for the government of the day.

As with "nonwhite," "ke system," and "relevant" so it was with "Black man, you are on your own" attributed to Steve Biko. Indeed some other leading figures of the Black Consciousness movement such as Mosibudi Mangena reaffirmed this saying through his book, *On Your Own*. For him and, many other Black Consciousness activists, the last words of the saying must be understood in the light of the full statement, "Black man, you are on your own." Did "man" in this context refer exclusively to men to the disadvantage of women? Was the Black Consciousness philosophy gender blind? The SASO "Black Students' Manifesto" is an appropriate document for analysis aimed at answering these questions. Here, only the opening statement of the manifesto shall be cited. It reads as follows: "We, the Black Students of South Africa, believing that the Black Man can no longer allow definitions that have been imposed upon him by an arrogant White world concerning his Being and his destiny and that the Black Student has a moral obligation to articulate the needs and aspirations of the Black Community hereby declare that…"[10]

The manifesto is written in English, a language in which it is not a grammatical necessity to write substantives in capital letters wherever they may occur in a sentence. It is therefore necessary to question why "Black Man," "White world" and "Being" are written in capital letters when they do not occur at the beginning of the sentence. It may well be that the intention is to emphasize that the substantives in the upper case are the key terms of the declaration. One need not quarrel with this since even names of people or book titles are ordinarily written in the upper case when they appear anywhere in a sentence. But it is so that one must take issue with "Man," "him," and "his" in this opening statement. The reason is that in this usage the male is somewhat privileged, as is the case in Aristotle's famous "man is a rational animal." Whether fairly or unfairly, depending on one's understanding of the original Greek term used by Aristotle, Western feminism has indeed taken issue with Aristotle's definition arguing that the exclusion of the woman from the human species is the reason for the woman's oppression. The questioning is legitimate to the extent that it argued that even if the original Greek term used by Aristotle may be neutral and even inclusive of male and female, his philosophy has however been shown to uphold the view that the woman is ontologically inferior to the man. Does this apply to the use of "Man" in the manifesto?

Apart from the fact that one may not quarrel with the authors' intention to identify and emphasize key terms, it is also the case that the writers were the victims of convention and not the champions of African philosophy. For a long time convention held that the use of the term "man" was sufficient since it referred to both male and female. Feminist critique showed that this convention was questionable and argued for freedom from sexist language. It is clear that in adopting such usage the Black Consciousness philosophy at the time was insensitive to the gender problematic. However, the result might be somewhat different if the term is examined in terms of African languages. In the Bantu languages spoken in South Africa the term for human being is "motho" or "umuntu" and this refers directly to either a female or a male. In both the Sotho and Nguni languages, the third person reference to both male and female is "*o*" (Sotho) "*u*," or "*yena*" (Sotho and Nguni). As it stands, there is neither social hierarchy nor sex differentiation in this usage. In order to show sex difference one has to add to the prefix the word *mama* or *baba*, thus having *umama* and *ubaba*, the first indicating the female while the second refers to the male. Furthermore, there is overwhelming anthropological evidence to suggest that the father's "sister" and the mother's "brother" had equal but differentiated voice in the conduct of family affairs. Accordingly, in the traditional "communal" context, the black woman had a voice and power. This aspect was manifested more in the practice of the Black Consciousness philosophy, but not at all in active theoretical exposition. Thus, within the Black Consciousness movement the term "man" was, at the time, used completely outside "gender" as experience and concept. There was no proximate or remote connection between this usage at the time and "gender." Feminism progressed gradually. However, identification and naming of the specific experience as "gender" occurred during the late 1970s into the early 1980s. From the point of view of intertemporal interpretation, it is questionable to extrapolate "gender" retroactively into "man" that in this context was used before the emergence of a live and active gender consciousness both within the Black Consciousness movement and globally.

The language of the Black Consciousness philosophy opened itself up to the "gender" challenge. One of the problems about this challenge is that it overlooks the fact that in practice the Black Consciousness philosophy did not problematize "gender." Instead, its conduct manifested a tacit and, perhaps, inadvertent understanding of "gender." If this were not so there must be a satisfactory explanation for the fact that "where women of ability made themselves available for leadership and other meaningful roles, they made important contributions and were accepted *fully* as colleagues by men. For, example, Mrs. M. Kgware, the first president of the Black People's Convention (BPC), was treated with respect by all. Her maturity and ability to reach out to both young and old were particularly appreciated."[11] (Italics added). Far from recognizing women as "honorary men" the Black Consciousness movement leadership acknowledged that "a greater effort needed to be made to mobilize women's active participation." This led to the "launching of the Black Women's Federation (BWF) in Durban in December 1975. The BWF acted as a national umbrella body for organizations of women from all walks of life. A total of 210 women attended the launching conference. People such as Fatima Meer, Winnie Mandela, Deborah Matshoba, Nomsisi Kraai, Oshadi Phakathi, Jeanne Noel, and other prominent mature women from established groups such as YWCA, Zanele, and church bodies were key participants in this conference."[12] Thus the Black Consciousness philosophy recognized women as equal participants and "colleagues," but not on the basis of "gender" considerations. In the light of the foregoing, it is more than odd to claim that:

> Steve Biko's work was cited as the clearest expression of black social and political experience in South Africa, and it was used as a basis for critical reflection on masculinity. Kopano argued that Biko's indictment of apartheid strongly expressed rage about a loss of black manhood. The nostalgia for a lost masculinity was seen as a major obstacle in addressing the freedom of both black men and women. Activating discussion around reconstructions of black manhood was seen as crucial in the face of the increase of GBV [gender-based violence] in South Africa. Kopano argued that scholars have a responsibility to transcend the thinking about race, freedom and manhood associated with Biko in the '60s and '70s, and to explore forms of consciousness-raising that are key to transforming all power relations.[13]

This claim is hardly sustainable since it (i) ignores the intertemporality; (ii) it attributes to Biko what can be "associated" with him only by resort to far-fetched reasoning; (iii) it reveals ignorance of the actual practice of the Black Consciousness movement, with particular reference to the participation of women in social and political life. It is thus worth reminding the author that the Black Consciousness movement was far ahead of its time in South Africa when "Mrs. Motlalepula Kgware emerged as president of BPC at its December 1973 conference, thus becoming the first black woman to head a national political organization." Seen from this perspective, contemporary debate on whether or not South Africa deserves a woman president is neither necessary nor urgent in terms of the Black Consciousness philosophy.

Progress in Feminist Thought

It was only toward the end of the 1970s and during the early 1980s when, in search of explanations for the failure of the first strategy of "integrating women into development" (the 'Women In Development' [WID] strategy), feminist perspectives informed the United Nations (UN) of the specific experience that was defined, described, and named "gender." It was then said that women could not be "integrated into development" because of "gender" as a specific phenomenon prevailing in society. It was only since then that international development policy was modified to become "gender sensitive." This reaffirmed the demand for substantive rights and opportunities such as "gender equality," "gender equity," and "gender mainstreaming." These continue to inform capitalist development policy even at the present period. However, it is true that there has been a constant conflicting discourse both with the UN and within the international feminist movement concerning various conceptions demanding the emancipation of women in society. The debate on the question of women's emancipation from the "gender" perspective clearly solidified and intensified in the 1970s and 1980s. This was precisely the time of the burgeoning of the Black Consciousness movement, still focused primarily on the liberation of Black people whether or not they were male or female. It is this primacy of liberation that contributed to the movement's insensitivity to gender. For the Black Consciousness movement, gender was blurred and dissolved into the larger and deeper struggle for the liberation of the Black people.

The Conflicting Discourse within the United Nations Debates

The various United Nations World Conferences on Women were characterized by a conflicting discourse between the countries of the North—in particular Western capitalist members states—and the countries of the South—postcolonial states. The countries of the South repeatedly argued that they were confronted by "general poverty" in their respective countries and not only by poverty among women. Poverty was lived and continues to be lived as an existential condition of both men and women in the former colonial countries. This in itself questions the perception of the Western capitalist countries with regard to the condition of poverty among women of the world relative to men. Accordingly, the woman's question cannot be dealt with from the assumption that the experiences of women around the world are the same. Nor can it be treated by the same means in the endeavor to provide remedies.

Naomi Black informs us that at the first Mexico World Conference on Women in 1975 there was no unanimity with respect to the policy of "integrating women into development." For instance, the then Soviet Union did not agree to the idea that women in their countries had been left outside development in the "backward sector." New Zealand and Australian delegates wanted to know why it was specifically women *as women* who were left out. They argued that women were discriminated against on the basis of *sexism* more than simply "left outside development." Western governments, including the United States, were inclined to the view that development had not reached maturity and was therefore not distributed to all peoples of the world. The implication here was that when capitalist development reached maturity all peoples would be "fully integrated" into development, whatever sector they participate in. In the meantime, it was acceptable for the West that women would remain in the private sphere or the sphere of subsistence production and reproduction. The problem with this argument is that it takes lightly the fact that women experience extreme poverty here and now. Also, it effectively refuted the position of the countries of the South that poverty was an existential condition lived by men and women. In view of this, the conference resolved that each member state could participate in the idea of "integrating women into development" according to how the authorities understood the problem.[14]

At the 1980 second UN Conference on Women that reviewed the five year minimum achievements of the 1975 Plan of Action, the conference recognized that signs of disparity were beginning to emerge between rights secured and women's ability to exercise these rights. The Conference pinpointed three areas where specific, highly focused action was essential. These three areas were equal access to education, employment opportunities, and adequate health services.[15] Countries of the South, in particular, again argued that they could not cope with the three areas. For this reason, "the deliberations at the Copenhagen Conference took place in the shadow of political tensions, some of which were carried over from the (first) Mexico City Conference" of 1975.[16] "Nevertheless, the Conference came to a close with the adoption of a Programme of Action, albeit not by consensus," which cited a variety of factors for the discrepancy between legal rights and women's ability to exercise these rights.[17]

The Conflicting Discourse within the Feminist Movement

In a similar manner, instead of feminism coming up with representative epistemology for all women of the world we had, right through the process, two different modes of thought and action. We had on the one hand a fragmentary mode of thought and action representing the North and white women in particular and on the other, we had a holistically oriented way of thinking and acting characteristic of the South and black women specifically. Issuing out of that is an antithesis instead of a synthesis in the name of "Black Feminist Thought, which arose when black women found that feminism that originated in the North among white women did not apply to their specific experiences *as* black women. Rather, it was a philosophy that catered for white middle class women in the main."[18] Furthermore, within the international women's movement, black women were often treated with racism by white women.[19] By the late 1970s, African American women in particular had begun to systematize Black Feminist Thought, "feeding" from the long standing conceptions of previous black feminists of the 19th century American experience. They systematically made a problem of the term "woman," arguing that the term was a "socially constructed concept" that needed to be "deconstructed" to come up with the philosophy of "womanism."[20] This was based upon the experience that although the struggle was about the oppressive condition of women, black women find their specific experiences not considered in that struggle. In fact, black women remained invisible to the extent that the term "black" was seen to refer to "black men" while the term "woman" was seen to refer to "white women." Hull et al.'s book *All Women are White, All the Blacks are Men, But Some of Us Are Brave* takes its title from this very invisibility of black women in the American reality.[21]

African women have had difficulty with this perspective from a different standpoint. For instance, the Association of African Women for Research and Development (AAWORD) argued that in the capitalist system, not only are women subordinated for superexploitation, but the African mode of production and African men are also subjugated and exploited. AAWORD published a report of the survey that the Association carried out among African women in the 1970s in which African women are reported to have said that they cannot associate themselves with the idea of sexism because they have lived for centuries as mothers, wives, daughters, and sisters of slaves. According to AAWORD, the subjugation of African modes of life to facilitate the establishment of the capitalist system in Africa implied that African women would be systematically relegated to work in subsistence production and reproduction to see to the survival of African families while African men were suffering extreme exploitation under the hands of their white male counterparts. It would, therefore, be a misreading of the objective situation to charge their men with sexism. Furthermore, by their role in subsistence production and reproduction, African women supplement the income of their male relatives. By supplementing the income, women subsidize the cost of production in the capitalist enterprises. African women have in this sense endured superexploitation for centuries. They do not accept the logic of sharing "paid" and "unpaid" work because by that very fact they would be accepting injustice. Thus, at the 1995 Beijing World Women's Forum that informs the UN Conference on Women, a member of Akina Mama Wa Afrika told the plenary session of the NGO Forum that the position of African women is that their labor in subsistence production and reproduction must be valued (paid). She said that the message of African women to their governments is that their governments "must not leave *Beijing* without pledging to meet this demand" to the UN Conference. Nothing could better underline the fact that patriarchal capitalism under the control of the Europeans victimized to differing degrees both the male and female indigenous Africans.[22]

In an issue of the journal *Development Dialogue* devoted to AAWORD, African men are called upon to "refuse to be dehumanized by today's form of industry." AAWORD has called upon men to join hands with women in the struggle to rid humanity in general of all categories of oppression.[23] This means that African women do not see their men as only part of the problem without being part of the solution.

Naomi Black also tells us that at the first International Women's Forum of the United Nations World Conference on Women, as European women were busy espousing the idea of sexism through which they sought independence in order to fight for power sharing with men in the male dominated system of life, black women were busy referring to themselves in terms that locate them into their families as integral parts of the whole. African women were here even refusing to use the term "feminism" in order to disassociate themselves from the idea of sexism.[24]

When Ellen Kuzwayo (commonly referred to in South Africa as "Mama K" and "Mother of Soweto") was in the Netherlands to receive the Dutch translation of her book *Call Me Woman*, she was asked why she gave her book that title. Her response was that she "feared" to be associated with the European notions of individualistic feminism and all that it entails because she was an "African woman" who did not share the "individualistic culture" of Europe.[25] In a similar manner, African American woman bell hooks wrote in her book *Ain't I a Woman: Black Women and Feminism* that when black women in the United States were asked whether they wanted to be equal to men they said that they did not want to be equal to their men because their men occupy low positions in the American public sphere. When they were asked whether they wanted to be restricted to the domestic (private) sphere with its corresponding roles their response was that in their own domestic sphere of "extended families" they found much more support and security than when they entered the American individualistic, subordinating, exploitative, and oppressive public sphere where they are defined by class-race-sex-ethnicity to be relegated to the lowest level of society.[26]

Battering the Male Paradigm

The above discourses and debates on the woman's question reveal that to a very large extent, Western feminism in particular persists in battering the male epistemological paradigm governing social and political relations. The battering has yielded some results because it is now no longer odd to have women at the apex of political leadership in the state; to have women as pilots and colleagues in space exploration; to have women in professions that formerly used to be the exclusive preserve of men. Even in sports women now play football as the South African *Banyana-Banyana* team testifies. But it is curious that they play as women against women and not as women against men. It seems fair to surmise that despite the heavy beating the male paradigm continues to suffer as a result of continual battering by women, patriarchy still survives. In the wider social and political context, patriarchy survives because it has retained the power to tantalize and assimilate women into the world of men precisely under the guise of "equality," "equal opportunities," and "nondiscrimination." But the emancipation of women from the yoke of patriarchy cannot be achieved simply by fixating on what is more often formal equality at the expense of substantive equality. Short of the abolition of patriarchy, women's emancipation cannot attain the ideal of human liberation: The liberation of women and men from oppressive ideologies and institutions.

The transition to the "new" South Africa came about at a time when the Western epistemological paradigm, including patriarchy, was and continues to be dominant. Feminism in South Africa was therefore bound to be tainted with the discourses and debates mentioned above in the international context. It follows, then, that true to its heritage of epistemological subservience, the "new" South Africa is suffused with these controversies. It is yet to emerge as the champion of human liberation precisely through the medium of the woman's question. Such a task could not conceivably and historically be the burden of the Black Consciousness movement in the decade discussed here.

Conclusion

It has been argued above that the question of gender was only passively present in the philosophy of Black Consciousness. However, in practice, the philosophy was inadvertently and tacitly gender sensitive. This was crowned by the election of Motlalepula Kgware as the first woman president of the Black People's Convention: a fact that made the Black Consciousness movement the harbinger of the tidings that a black woman president for South Africa is just a matter of time but not a question of principle. It has also been submitted that to argue that the Black Consciousness philosophy ought to have been gender sensitive from its inception and during the decade discussed here is simply to take an ahistorical view of the matter ignoring the importance of intertemporality in historical interpretation. Furthermore, it has been shown that the gender problematic in our time is, in reality, a call to deeper and greater emancipation, namely, the liberation of humanity—men and women—from oppressive ideologies and institutions. It is simply unfair to assign such a task to a single organization, let alone the Black Consciousness movement in the 1970s and 1980s.

Notes

1. Leonard Harris, ed., *Philosophy Born of Struggle: from 1917* (Dubuque: Iowa: Kendall/ Hunt Publishing Company, 1983).
2. Sebidi, "The Dynamics of the Black Struggle and its Implications for Black Theology," in Itumeleng Mosala and Buti Tlhagale, eds., *The Unquestionable Right to be Free: Essays in Black Theology* (Braamfontein, SA: Stockville Publishers, 1986).
3. Mogobe B. Ramose, "The Struggle for Reason in Africa," in P. H. Coetzee and A. P. J. Roux, eds., *Philosophy from Africa: A Text with Reading* (South Africa: Oxford University Press, 2002).
4. Harris, *Philosophy*.
5. Ibid.
6. Gail Gerhart, *Black Power in South Africa: The Evolution of an Ideology* (Los Angeles, CA: University of California Press, 1979), 261.
7. Mamphela Ramphele, *A Life* (Cape Town, SA: David Philip, 1995).

8. "The Women's Question" is one of the early concepts that was engaged, particularly by women in the organizations of the left, to take issue with the idea that even in these organizations that were fighting to transform the capitalist order women were still believed to be unfit to participate in the public sphere as this sphere was seen to be the exclusive preserve of the male person.
9. Mihailo Markovic, "Women's Liberation and Human Emancipation," in C. Gould and Marx W. Wartofsky, eds., *Women and Philosophy: Towards a Theory of Liberation* (New York: Schocken Books, 1976): 152.
10. The SASO Black Students Policy Manifesto, 1971.
11. Ramphele, *A Life*.
12. Ibid.
13. Kopano, in the report of the workshop on GWS (www.gwsafrica.org/about/gws%20 sept%20final.htm).
14. The United Nations, 1980. *Forum 1980*, United Nations, New York. Naomi Black and Anna Baker Cottrell, *Women and Change, Equity Issues in Development* (London: Sage Publications, 1980), 275.
15. The United Nations, 1980.
16. Ibid.
17. Ibid.
18. Patricia Hill Collins, *Black Feminist Thought: Knowledge, Consciousness and the Politics of Empowerment* (New York: Routledge, Chapman and Hall, Inc. 1990).
19. Ibid.
20. Gloria T. Hull, Patricia Bell Scott, and Barbara Smith, eds., *All the Women are White and All the Blacks are Men, But Some of Us Are Brave, Black Women's Studies* (Old Westbury, New York: The Feminist Press, 1990).
21. Hull et al., 1982.
22. Oshadi Mangena, "Perspectives on Feminist Epistemology and the Evolution of Black Feminist Thought," in Sir. Marie Pauline Eboh, ed., *Philosophical Criticisms: Anthology of Gender Issues* (Port Harcourt, Nigeria: Pearl Publishers, 2000), 188.
23. Association of African Women for Research and Development (AAWORD), "The Experience of the Association of African Women for Research and Development (AAWORD)" in *Development Dialogue: A Journal of International Development Cooperation* (Upsala: Dag Hammarksjold Foundation, 1982), 1–2.
24. Black and Cottrell, *Women and Change*; Mangena, "Perspectives," 188.
25. I was invited by Ellen Kuzwayo for the occasion where she received the Dutch translation of her book. I was in fact consulted about the accuracy of the translation by the translator of the book, Dr. Philomena Essed, a black woman living in the Netherlands. The Dutch organization that offered to translate the book asked Dr. Philomena Essed, being a black woman, to do the translation in order to be "politically correct."
26. bell hooks. *Ain't I a Woman: Black Women and Feminism* (Boston: South End Press, 1981), and Mangena, "Perspectives."

13

Interview with Strini Moodley

Naomi Klein, Ashwin Desai, and Avi Lewis

In June 2005 Naomi Klein and Avi Lewis went to Durban as part of a research project on South Africa's transition. They interviewed Strini Moodley, in conversation with Ashwin Desai, in what turned out to be Moodley's last interview. The interview has never been published. The following transcription has been edited for clarity.

Strini Moodley: When you make an analysis, always begin at the beginning. You can't make an analysis of Mandela's thinking when he goes to prison after [the] Rivonia [trial]—you've got to take Mandela way back. And even beyond Mandela, way back to the origins of the ANC. I mean, the origins of the ANC are not even the African National Congress. It's the South African Native National Congress. Made up of chiefs who go to the King of England to beg for inclusion. Not to go to war for liberation—to beg for inclusion. And today, the ANC is included.

But that is also linked to what is today called the South African Communist Party. It used to be the Communist Party of South Africa. And the Communist Party of South Africa began with the slogan "White workers of the world unite for a white South Africa"—the 1922 Rand strike. That's the Communist Party of South Africa. Then you get to 1990 and you get Joe Slovo talking about a sunset clause.

No, no. Basically in the '60s we looked at the ANC, we looked at the PAC, we looked at the Unity Movement, we looked at all of them, and we said, these guys have all got a wrong program. Because the program has to be based primarily on—and we made it a slogan: oppression is based on the fact that 70 percent of it is fixed mentally in the oppressed. So that you have to devise a philosophy that can break the chains of that psychological oppression. You've got to first free them. You've got to reintroduce into them the fact that they are human beings. And a lot of people don't understand this, but you can see it everyday of the week, wherever you go. It's still—and that psychological oppression remains up until today.

Developing Black Consciousness in Durban and Surviving Prison

SM: Basically, I think we were able to survive on Robben Island for several reasons. One, we had a couple of older men and women who actually supported us—you know, Steve [Biko], myself—and were able to tell us stories. That this is going to happen to you, they're going to make you stand on two bricks, they're going to take all your clothes off, they're going to make you stand there, they're going to do this to you, are you prepared for that? Can you handle that? So from there, already, psychologically, we were being prepared to deal with torture.

I mean, people ask me, "why are all your teeth gone?" I say, "because I got fucked up." I mean, when you get smashed in your mouth and your—fortunately, I got a very strong nose. That's the only thing that didn't break. But, everything else broke. I mean, my leg was broken on both sides. A whole lot of things. The one thing we knew—that we could take all that. I mean, physical pain is one thing. If you're mentally prepared for that, you can handle it. Three and a half months in solitary, beaten up almost every day. For three and a half months.

Primarily I survived because I had a belief in a fact that we as black people can deal with anything. We can deal with anything. And that's based on the fact that when you look back into the history, of whether it's Ashwin's mother and father, or mine, or our grandparents, and where we come from, and where everybody else comes from, we've gone through the most tremendous hardships.

Ashwin Desai: Strini's grandfather loved a woman, but when they disembarked from the ship the colonial masters separated them. And one day he just walked off the sugar plantation.

SM: To go hunt for her, my grandmother.

AD: And hunted for her, and found her. It is a very unique experience of resistance during that period, because people were doing more sly things. He just walked off and found her. And it was either they be deported or killed or be allowed to co-habitate.

SM: But not only that. My father was heavily involved in politics. He was into all the trade unions, the tin union, the tea union, that union, the other union. I was still a kid. But subconsciously, when everybody was coming to my house to sit and talk to my father about all these things, I was already learning it. So that for me, my growing up period was very significant in creating in me the understanding that if you're concerned about people, you have to do something. You can't just sit on the sidelines and watch. You have to get into the game.

And the worst thing that ever happened to me was when I was about 12 years old. My kid brother, who was an asthma sufferer, gets sick. And the doctor came, and he needed to have treatment. So I had to go to a chemist. And the only chemist that I knew was in Berea Road. And that was the day when the women were marching from Cato Manor and marching down Berea Road [the 1959 march]. And I had to get to the chemist. And here's the march going on. And I had to find a way. And what I discover is blood on the street. And Indian corporation workers scrubbing the blood. Even up until today it's still vivid in my mind. So that's what I grew up with. So when you ask me that question, Robben Island was a walk in the park. We fought with prison warders all that time. How that happened I have no damn idea. But I think we grew up as post-war babies, after 1945. We grew up with the belief that we were no different from anybody else, and therefore we had the right to demand our right to be human beings. That's all it is. And once you understand that, in yourself, it's not about Marx, or Lenin, or—it's about you. That's the starting point. So now you get to Robben Island, and you meet all these ANC guys, all they can do is quote Marx and quote Lenin, but they know fuck all about life. Now for me, Marx and Lenin and all of them are contributors to us being able to make decisions. Marx, Engels, Lenin, supplied us with tools. So I don't imitate Marx, I don't imitate Lenin, I don't imitate Engels. I learned their tools. I read *Das Kapital* when I was 18 years old. The point is what can I get out of it that we can use to our advantage? And if you go and listen to all the SACP guys, all they can do is repeat. They can't analyze.

In terms of the torture in prison, strategically what we did is, you have at least about 72 hours, in which you say nothing, you do nothing. After the 72 hours you speak only about yourself. You speak about nobody else. If they ask you about other people you say, "I don't know." That's your only answer. And so you get beaten up and you get beaten up and you continue to say, "I don't know."

What gave me the strength was belief in myself. Belief in myself that I had to protect something that I considered very sacred. And that was the struggle for revolution, for change. And once you can fix your mind on protecting the struggle for change, nobody can do anything to you.

Nobody. I don't care how big he is, I don't care how many guns he's carrying, I don't care what. Because primarily the struggle is about what's happening inside our heads. Now, I see all these movies—white people can't handle closed spaces, they can't handle this, they can't handle that, they fuckin' start talking gibberish, you know, after two days in a confined space. And I'm serious here. That is because they come out of a different environment. We come out of an, absolutely, I mean, I know what it is, I grew up on the streets, I grew up with gangsters.

AD: That's true. That's one thing the BC movement did. The BC movement said, "Come." Every gang in the city would go to their rally. It's like a convention of gangs, that's why the police were there. We were like, "who's this fuckin' FRELIMO?" I followed a notorious gang to the rally. We arrived, but we didn't like the police attention. But when they brought out the dogs and all that, we *loved* it. That was the best night of our lives. I was 14. [Laughter]

SM: The night before the FRELIMO rally at Curries Fountain, I was sitting in a gutter in Carlyle Street, with about 20 gangsters, and they said to me, we're going to soccer training at Curries Fountain tomorrow. I said, "No, tomorrow there's no soccer training. Tomorrow there's a big war with the cops." And you tell those guys there's a war with the cops. They were going to be there. They wanted to fight cops.

So you had all these gangs, and Steve and I were the head of the Black Power Gang. We were called the Black Power Gang. And we were the only gang, because the security police were around our offices, right in the heart of gangster land.

So when you ask me that question about going to prison, it's the continuation of what was happening in [in the streets]—because one of the things we said when we went to prison, was that you guys, you must not think that this prison you're in is not related to the bigger prison which all our people are in. So for ANC guys, if you're on Robben Island, the war is over. For us, the war—*a luta continua.*

Prison Culture & the ANC

SM: Prison culture is whatever you make of it. You can either subject yourself to the demands and the orders of your warders, or you can challenge it.

The ANC's history is known. In 1914, they sent a delegation to King of England to say, "please include us in the Union of South Africa." You know, all they wanted was to become a part of an existing system. For us, in the

Black Consciousness movement, you have to destroy that system in order to create a new system. And that was the difference between the ANC and the Black Consciousness movement.

The ANC's got no ideology. What ideology has the ANC got? You can see it happening today. No, it's always *been* like that. The Freedom Charter's a sell-out document, it's a liberal document. It doesn't take care of the interests of the majority of the people.

[ANC leaders tried to convince me that] "your place is with the ANC and with the SACP," and I told [them], I'm in the Black Consciousness movement, and this is our policy. And I wrote this whole policy document and I sent it to [them]. And in it I said, "As far as we're concerned, NUSAS [National Union of South African Students], the Liberal Party, Alan Paton, and all those white people are enemies of the black people." [They] write back to me and say, "The enemy of the NUSAS, and the enemy of the Liberal Party and Alan Paton is an enemy of the ANC." And that's when we realized, these guys are going to sell us out. And the big sell out came in 1990.

The consequence of the release—Kempton Park—was the biggest sellout. In 1990, we wanted to have a patriotic front of the ANC, the PAC, and ourselves. [ANC leaders] reject it and say if you want to have a patriotic front, it's got to include the PFP. The Progressive Federal Party, and the Transkei, and the Mongopes [Bantustan leaders], and all of them. And we wrote to [them] and we said, that's bullshit. When you negotiate it's a two-sided table: you have the enemy on one side and you have the liberation movement on the other side. [They] wanted everybody at the same table. And we said that that will never work. Because at the end of the day you're going to end up with the people that you say are on our side will actually sell us out.

Nelson Mandela walks out [of prison] in 1990 and he talks about nationalization. Two weeks later he says, "No, no nationalization." Go back even to that speech he made before he was sentenced. Listen to it carefully. Just analyze that. It started right then. I'm telling you.

In 1978, after he had murdered Biko, Jimmy Kruger comes to Robben Island—I'm there. And I'm in the same section, the B-section, with Mandela. Mandela used to be across—you know, my cell is here, his cell is there. When the warders are coming to open up, Mandela used to be screaming across, screaming, "Wake up! Wake up! Stand to attention!" I tell him, "Fuck you, I'm sleeping, man, I'm tired." And this one day they come to us and they tell us, "there's a very important person coming here, all of you," and you know what they used to do to us—"you have to have your spoon and your fork in your top pocket, hold your prison card, put on your jacket, and stand to attention." And we said, "No, fuck you, we're not going to do that." And on this day—I went to one of the warders there and I said, "Who the fuck is coming here?" And he said [whispering] "No, it's the Minister of Justice, Kruger." I went and told the guys, "Hey, Kruger is coming." So we decided to, fuck him—I went, I lay on the bed, I opened my *National Geographic*, and I was busy reading it. So I was lying on the bed and I'm reading my *National Geographic*, and Kruger came. This is a year after Biko's death. I mean, shit, if I had a gun I would have shot him that day. I just lay on the bed, and Kruger says to the commanding officer, "What's wrong with that guy?" "No, don't worry about him, he's a stone-thrower." We were called *klip gooiers* [Afrikaans phrase: stone-throwers], you know, from 1976. So he goes past, and he goes to Mandela's cell. Now I'm also a curious journalist. I get up, after he's passed my cell, he goes to Mandela, and there's Mandela saluting him. And *all* of the ANC guys, down the row, salute Kruger. Afterwards I go to them, I say, "What the fuck, you're saluting that man? He's killed my best comrade." [They answered:] "You're in the enemy camp you must respect the enemy." I say, what the fuck. I promise you. And I will tell it to them in their face. And I've told it to them in their face.

So now you get today—take a simple thing, like he's now doing 4-6-6-64. These concerts for HIV/AIDS. You know what 4-6-6-64 means? That's his prison number. So he was the 466th prisoner in 1964. Before him there were 465 other prisoners, and nobody talks about that. *Nobody*. Nobody has the guts to stand up and say, "Mandela, you are the 466th, in 1964, there were 465 before you." And the whole world thinks he was the first. That was all planned. It was all designed. As far as I'm concerned it was long planned. We're gonna keep this guy on ice. Because when we need him, he's the man who is going to make sure that the capital stays with us, that the money stays with us, that control stays with us.

I don't know whether he knew it or not. I think he knows it now. That's why he has these occasional outbursts. He's beginning to realize that he was duped. But you know, in older age all men do that.

Naomi Klein: When you left prison, and you knew this about the ANC, was it possible to even fight this sort of hegemonic power that they had? Did you try?

SM: We were being interviewed by every government in the world. I mean, I was going around the world, meeting governments. And one of the things I discovered, because I used to collect all the information, bring it back, and we'd analyze it. And we discovered that what actually is happening is that they are now trying to eliminate the *real* threat. And part of the biggest program they did was to eliminate us. Because we were the biggest threat. And the best kind of scenario for them was to actually have the ANC win. And that is why with the collapse of the Soviet Union, the ANC is now in America, it's in Canada, I mean, before that, they were saying, we are with the Soviet Union, we are Communists, we are this, we are that. And suddenly they end up with offices all over the damn world.

You see, the ANC had a program, together with the SACP, that there is a two-stage revolution. The first stage is to capture capitalism, and the next stage is then to transform it. Now that's a bullshit argument. It defies logic. Because once you're involved in state power without changing the economy, you're fucked. Because now you've become a part of the program.

AD: But Strini, I always wanted to ask you this. You looked into the eye of power, on both sides. Then how do you dig into your resources, psychological resources, when all the things you've fought for have been rolled back? You know, we're now into the ANC—Zulu-ism is good, Indian-ism is good, you know, all that kind of stuff. Then you're also battling to survive literally. Because we've both been down that road, right? We don't have five cents in our pocket, right? And then the people we opposed are now, even within the Indian community, the MECs [Member of Executive Council]. I mean, how do you get up in the morning? Given the esteem many held for you in the ANC, the possibility of you getting a top post in Mandela's government was high. Yet you chose not only to turn away from power but also to confront it. This threatened your ability to make a living, you can't even pay for your daughter's school fees, and we're hustling a drink at a bar. How do you deal with that? I mean, like all your best friends now, what have they got in this mad world? I don't want to name them, but they've all now gone crazy, right? The BC guys, the big guns have gone nuts, right? I mean, what makes you soldier on, what is it?

SM: The only thing I've learned is—today I say, "let them go on, let them fuck themselves." What is going to happen, and I will tell you this—there is going to be an implosion in this country which is going to give birth to a new revolution. There is. There is. I'm telling you, there is. I'm telling you there is. All you have to do is identify the signals that are there. The signals to you may be unimportant, but check them out. Check them out. I promise you, there's going to be an implosion in this country. And when that implosion occurs, you're either going to get swept away by the tide of revolution, or you are going to be with it. It's going to be the nastiest of the lot. And Thabo [Mbeki] and them know it. Deep down inside them, they know it. Thabo knows it.

AD: It's already an Armageddon. But Strini, wasn't there just a twinge, like say, 1996—about "fuck, I'm fucking down and out, I've fucked up my whole life, the society will probably regard me as a failure, I could cash in my struggle credentials, I could personally change *my* life"—

SM: I've been approached a thousand and one times. I looked it in the eye—and said, fuck you. I went through bad patches. Everybody goes through that. And I think this is where, for all of us—if you're involved in revolutionary struggle, it's basically about mental strength. I mean, I went through bad patches. And I said to myself at the end of the day, ok, I'm down and out but I'm going to pick myself up by my fuckin' bootstraps and I'm going to make it happen. It's taken me a long time. It's taken me a long time but now I'm doing it. I mean, my kids have no worries. I'm paying for myself. I've not taken a bribe from nobody. I've done nothing. I employ a lot of people here [in this bar]. I pay them the best salaries. I mean, people are dying to come and work with me. And then, at the same time what I'm doing is, I'm recreating the groundwork. But it's going to happen. I know it's going to happen.

And this is what I'm saying. It's like I'm reliving the ANC request to get Mandela released to the Transkei. But this time I'm not going to go to the ANC and say, "Guys, be careful, you're in trouble now, you've got to rethink your strategy." I'll say, "ANC, go ahead and do the fuck what you want to." Bring it on.

The one thing nobody wants to appreciate is that human beings have the capacity to decide what they want to do, when they want to do it. The problem we've had is that everybody seems to think that they know how to control people. All I'm saying is that if you are brave enough, and I think that counts a lot—if you're brave enough—but also, if you sit down and plan properly, you can translate anything into a success.

The point about it is we have hooked ourselves for so long into texts that try to design for us how a revolution occurs. And every revolution that has occurred, the people who won wrote it the way *they* wanted to write it. Whether it was in the Soviet Union with the Communist Party, they wrote it the way they wanted to write it. It actually might not have happened that way. The ANC has rewritten the whole struggle of this country the way they want it to happen. And the point about it is you go anywhere in the world and you'll see it like that.

From my point of view it's good BC has been written out of the struggle. Because if it was written in then we're part of the problem. Now we're still part of the solution.

14

Interview with Deborah Matshoba

Amanda Alexander and Andile Mngxitama

In January 2007 Amanda Alexander and Andile Mngxitama interviewed Deborah Matshoba in Braamfontein, Johannesburg about her experiences in the Black Consciousness movement. The following transcription has been edited for clarity.

BC on the Street

The hair had to be a natty afro, you know. The dashiki shirts—with those prints, *shweshwe*, and so on. There was a marked difference [between BC women and others not in the movement]. Take the masses for instance, the student masses. They straightened their hair, using Ambi skin lighteners. Lots of lipsticks. And we were not really supposed to use that. We could have but we didn't want to use that because we wanted to look real black.

We had to walk rough. Not like ladies. We would go and buy pap and nyama there by West Street. Bokwe Mafuna used to like going with the girls, Nomsisi Kraai, myself. He'd say, "See this *mlungu* [white person] that's coming? We don't move! We walk straight into him! Straight into him, he must know that this is your country. You must *gila* him you know! Don't even look back!" And oh, he would be so intimidated. It was good just to go into town—"Let's go downtown to Eloff Street to harass them"—it would be the project of the day. We leave whatever in the office, on Jorissen Street, and move in town. And being harassed by women, being a white man—it was something else. And we'd get such satisfaction. Or Harry [Nengwekhulu] would be driving in this Peugeot. We would be driving in this Peugeot and we'd just stop it somewhere in town. At the robot [stop light] or stop sign we'd say, "Baas! Baas! Are you afraid to die? Are you afraid to die?!" And Harry had that look! That look and the hair and the yellow teeth from the pipe that he was smoking. "Are you afraid to die?" [laughs] "Are you afraid to *die*?" And the robot goes and then we move on. Eh! And it would be fun! This is '72, especially when it was escalating and we were angry about what had happened—being chased out of college. And we basically didn't know what we were going to do.

Student Organizing

Let me say I met Steve in 1972, even though in my high school days he was my senior. But this was St. Francis College at Marianhill, the girls were not allowed to speak to the boys, especially when they were the matriculants and we were these scruffy little things. He was a good debater and I know all these girls in matric really hero-worshipped him. And then he went to Wentworth. So later I went to Inanda seminary also in Durban, and associated more with UCM, the University Christian Movement. And I knew about Steve, that students had broken away from NUSAS, and I followed that very closely. So I completed my [courses], worked for about a year, and went back to university. And he was SRC president at UNB [University of Natal Black Section] like Mthuli [Mthuli ka Shezi was SRC president at the University of Zululand] and so on. And I was a delegate to the GSC (General Students Council), the deciding body of SASO, at Hammanskraal, even though I was a freshman. And that's the year when we expelled Themba Sono.

And the delegations [to the GSC]! Fort Hare—these are angry students! And we were also angry. So Keith Mokoape was in the delegation from Wentworth. Keith Mokoape is Aubrey Mokoape's younger brother. So Keith comes with an explosive thing that "Ya! Actually these universities must shut down." He writes a motion with these other fiery guys. "These universities must shut down and we must all go to exile!" Eh! But this is open session! So Steve goes to talk to Patrick Laurence, a journalist, and says "You must go, Patrick." So Patrick obliges, and goes out with his bag and all that. Steve says "before we decide and discuss this motion, all observers out. Only delegates must remain." And we are all for this thing by Keith—"Ya, we are going to exile. And the universities must shut down, everybody must leave." But some people are scared [by this suggestion by Mokoape]—third-year students, final-year students. So Keith's argument, ay, we were all for it and then Steve stood up and said, "People, I have been failed twice now at Wentworth, University of Natal. And this year they are obviously going to fail me again. And you know the regulations. If you fail thrice, you are out. So I am not going to vote for this motion, me, personally, Steve, on those grounds that I am going to be excluded anyway. Those who want to continue, it's their business. Those who feel morally obliged to move out should do so." Eh! I could see that this man was making sense. So unselfish, that was the first picture that I captured of Steve. And after that obviously Mthuli said, "We are voting the counter-motion!" And Keith was outvoted, but then Keith and his combo walked out of GSC. They left. And before GSC was over—because it took a whole week or so—we heard that Keith had already crossed the border and they were in Botswana. But how unsafe it was! It was not safe for them because there were sellouts in our midst.

Q: *Who did they [Keith Mokoape and others] join when they went into exile?*

They stayed stagnant for sometime and Bokwe Mafuna followed later, '73 or so. And everybody was confused because the PAC, the Unity Movement and the ANC were confusing them and they didn't want to be divided. Eventually Keith joined the ANC, and Velile and Tiro died before he could return.

Q: *Tell us more about Mthuli ka Shezi.*

Mthuli was this short guy, but with a gigantic mind. Very religious, Catholic. He used to command a lot of support. And during this particular time of Tiro, Mthuli comes and says: "There's a telegram! There's a telegram!" And it was lunchtime—no faxes or anything, we communicated by telegram. "Tiro has been expelled! This and that has happened at Turfloop. So solidarity, they're calling for solidarity." And so we had our placards around the campus—"Reinstate Tiro!"

And we were on our own, but these telegrams moved around. There were six bush colleges: Western Cape for Coloureds; Fort Hare for Xhosas; Wentworth, UNB (University of Natal Black Section) for Coloureds, Indians, and Africans; Durban Westville for Indians; Turfloop for Sotho, Venda, and Tsongas, it was called "Sovenga"; and Zululand. So Mthuli managed to unify all the students. Even those who were opposed to SASO.

Mthuli was a very dynamic person. Not talking too much, not robust. What I liked about him was that administrators, they really listened to him, they feared him. And they [the administrators] were telling him that they were not going to expel any students, students were going to write their exams, but then he said that it was a trick because they just wanted to see who had been marching. They'd been watching, obviously. And he left university, he was the first one to leave, he was not expelled. He said, "Guys, me and my conscience—Tiro is my fellow SRC president." Steve and them they had all decided to leave. After leaving Mthuli decided to write a play—it was called "Shanti." I was going to get the leading role but my father refused. I had a very strict father. But Mthuli managed to have Shanti staged. It was one of the first plays written by a student to be banned. And he was already under a microscope by the system.

In December he came from the East Rand, Thembisa. He had been defending the dignity of women who were being harassed by a white security man on the railway. He [the security officer] was pouring them with water, always pouring them with water. The following day Mthuli went to work and he intervened. And the next day as well. The next day Mthuli went to Jo'burg, and when he came back this guy knew that he was going to wait for this train. As soon as the train was approaching he pushed Mthuli onto the railway line. And he was overridden by the train. He didn't die on the spot. He was taken to Thembisa Hospital. We all went and Mamphela [Ramphele] was trying to save him. Mthuli was bleeding profusely. We had to take sheets from other volunteering patients to try and—Mamphela had to try to stop this bleeding. And she was only an intern, Mamphela, and not in that hospital. So we went to bury Mthuli, conscientizing. These guys were not banned yet—Steve and Barney Pityana and so on were all there. And a few months later we laid a tombstone, managed to raise funds. It was a big fist! And we had a service and memorial service. The next day it was shattered, broken down. That was the last time I went to that area and that is how much Mthuli is neglected.

I remember in '72 Steve said at the GSC, "It's not that the students who have been exiled from university are going to idle. I've come up with a solution for the whole mass of them... So those that want to remain in university must remain in university." And then he came with a program called the Free University Scheme—we called it FUS. Steve said, "I'm going to get funds! And if UNISA refuses to register us, I've already worked out a plan. My contacts have spoken to Uganda, the University of Makerere. And then we are all going to register with the University of Makerere!" So we developed a concept: The Standard is Makerere! It was one of the best universities in Africa. So he had worked out a scheme. That was just before he was going to be banned. "If UNISA doesn't take us, we're studying through Makerere." But there was also a question—they had to make sure that our scripts and things were not tapped. Because there was also a danger of parcel bombs now, letter bombs. What postage are we going to use and so on. But UNISA did not discriminate, UNISA took us. And those who couldn't afford were funded. We never bothered to ask [where the money came from]. There was always the belief : "Don't ask each other." There was always this Father Stubbs. And whenever we saw this Father [Aelred] Stubbs we knew that eh! Money was coming. For starters we'd have a little gumba [dance party] but then you'd see machines coming: "You are going to start sewing projects."

"The machines are going to be coming and building material is coming, people are going to build."

I remember June 16, 1976, because we were telling these kids on the 15th, don't do that, let's wait for the 26th of June, then we do Azikwelwa— that's the ANC's don't-go-to-work type of thing. The 26th used to be an Azikwelwa day here before the ANC was banned. So we said, let's resuscitate this. They [the students] have been talking about Afrikaans, right, but let's make it one thing. We are busy with the workers. In my SASO programme, literacy, we are busy with the workers, so let's all make it the 26th. We are going to barricade the streets and call to the people not to go to work, while the students would be doing their thing. But these youngsters, ay, they are going ahead! So on that day we are still busy doing pamphlets for Azikwelwa for the 26th when they started shooting on the 16th. Ah! They ran out of the hostel mad, shouting, "They are killing these kids!"

It's a pity the system destroyed most of our memories. Because I remember one— Mapetla Mphapi and maLucia on top of the roof, having finished a house. And we had a big gumba that night. Because there was always a gumba to say thank you. They had finished several houses. And the following day more houses. And the community was involved with us. And we had to conscientize the community. "You see what the government has done. They've thrown you here in Winterveldt. And they tell you that Mangope[1] is your leader. But your leaders are on Robben Island. Your leader is Sobukwe. Your leader is Mandela. And your leaders are in exile, Tambo." That's why when Winterveldt was explosive in the '80s, I thought, "The seed has been sowing. I'm far from them, not associated with what they are doing, but the seeds have been sown."

The Role of Women in the Black Consciousness Movement

I would safely say these guys [in the BC movement] really felt that we are one. Because I remember when we suggested that we need to form a woman's organization." I remember we came with a name, made a proposal. We called it WSO—Women's Students Organization. They said down with WSO, they voted us down. And Steve blamed me and said "Debs, you're coming with your YWCA mentality." I worked at the YWCA office which was downstairs and the SASO office was upstairs. So we said, "No! We're forming WSO. These guys are undermining us." They said, "But then it means if you are WSO you are not SASO—you are not South African students—so now you are going to have two roles."

Q: Did you envision WSO being a separate thing or a branch within SASO?

It would become a branch within. No, we were played down. "You guys have to admit you are very powerful,"—that's how Steve would put it. "You are very powerful." And we asserted ourselves in the organization. We started smoking like them. And especially to make this "gumba material" [non-BC women] feel out of place. Smoking, and we wore our hot pants. We spoke loud! We would get food and we would insist that they [the men] should go and wash their hands so that we could all eat together. They wanted to take big portions for themselves. We'd say, "No, anybody who wants to eat, eats." Just like that. I remember one time Steve slaughtered a sheep at Zanemphilo. I went en route, I was going to work in Ginsburg so I was sleeping at Ginsburg, Zanemphilo. There was the sheep and they started saving the head for the men and I said no, I also want to eat this. Not that I was going to enjoy it, but I just wanted to show them that we were also part of this. We insisted that we were also eating the head of the sheep.

I remember one time from Zanemphilo, we had just come back from a literacy thing and in the morning I needed some asthma tablets which they did not have at Zanemphilo. So Steve said, "There's a chemist in town, let's go." And I wore my stilettos, platform shoes. Steve said, "You are wearing those shoes?!" Me: "I'm very comfortable with these things." Then we walked into town, we get to this fruit and vegetable shop. Oh! And I tripped, sprained my ankle, and he laughed! He burst out laughing—I'll never forget it, I wanted to hit him because it was so painful. [Laughing] He laughed! How can you be so cruel! And there I am already wobbling and it's seriously getting swollen and Mamphela, the doctor, says "Eh, this is serious, it's getting swollen. She needs treatment." And Steve said, "I'm so sorry!" But it was fashion! We wore them so high, with hot pants! Bare midriffs and walked with stilettos—we called them "dangerous weapon." We called them dangerous weapon because if we get attacked by these cops then we are armed.

I had been extremely involved in the YWCA. In 1971 I had represented the YWCA of South Africa in Ghana. My mentors being Ellen Kuzwayo, Joyce Seroke, and so on. So I had to represent the youth, that was before I became a SASO member. So when I came to SASO I had already met the YWCA women from all over the world at this YWCA conference in Ghana. So when I came into campus politics they really had a lot of respect for me, like "Eh, this one has had a lot of exposure." Now unfortunately when I came back the system took my passport. Because I spoke quite a lot that side [in Ghana]. They were already watching me. So I was in safe hands in the YWCA office.

The YWCA sent me to Durban to mobilize young girls and recruit for the Y teens. And then the SASO guys would say unkind things to me, that you are a bourgeois, that you're used to eating biscuits and tea in meetings and you want to influence others—"Here we buy bunny chow and we all eat bunny chow." Daphne Khoza worked closely with Steve there on black community programs, and Daphne would dodge and come to this YWCA office for biscuits and then Ben Khoapa started buying biscuits. [Laughs]. Steve said, "Ben, you are being influenced by this YWCA woman." And saying it jokingly, though. And I knew they were just saying it jokingly. So I was always "YWCA woman."

We were in a way feminists. For instance we believed in Angela Davis. We believed in her and we admired the way she was going on with the Jacksons and what have you. And active in the Black Panther movement. And I think because this concept was sort of drawn from the Black Panthers, their behavior, hence their walking in the streets and what have you. Wanting to start warfare in the streets. They really admired that, but I think African men are different, they are protective in their own special way. They were being very protective. That's why Steve could not allow me to go alone in a train to Kroonstad, to Bloemfontein, to do work. But on the other hand, he also had confidence in us.

In Prison, and Learning of Steve's Death

In 1977 when Steve died I was in prison, under the most gruesome sectors of detention, which were section six of the Terrorism Act. I got released on December 28, 1976 from Number Four, with Winnie Mandela, Oshadi Mangena. And then six weeks later, beginning of February, Mosibudi sends a message saying "People are leaving. I need help, I'm alone in the office." In the Durban office, which was our head office. We got Motlana to hire a car for us. And on the way there was a roadblock and I was arrested. So they took me to Pietermaritzburg and I was away for a long time—until 1978. I went away for a long time, so even when the organizations were banned, was it October '77?, I was in the dark.

The most painful moment was when and how I discovered that Steve had been murdered. There was this friend of mine and colleague in SASO, Zola Jongwe. She was already a doctor and I knew that she was in Edendale Hospital in Pietermaritzburg. So one day I smuggled a note to make her aware that I am in Pietermaritzburg. And she said she had been trying to look for me in the prisons. One day, I think it was about ten months later, October or November 1977, I shammed a pain to this prison doctor. I said to her I have an IUD [intrauterine device], which I did. The doctor said nope, we can't remove it here, I must send you to hospital. So I went to hospital. Ah! When I got to hospital I said to this nurse, "I am looking for Zola Jongwe, is she still here?" "Yes," she said, "but she works at night." I said, "Get her and tell her it's Debs Matshoba. Please get Zola." And this nurse acted fast. Zola came flying in her pajamas and her gown. "Debs! Debs!" I said. "Well, *ntombi*, I am still here. And I've just told them a lie that my loop [IUD] is hurting so we have to take time and talk." And Zola said, "No, I'll have to write that you'll come tomorrow. You know, then we can continue talking. Eh! *Ntombi*, things are so bad!" She told me they had killed Steve. And I got scared now. If they can kill Steve, it means they are going to kill all of us who are still in prison. "Zola, you are right I must come tomorrow." And I've told myself, "Tomorrow I'm going to escape. I'm going to hit the road!" So the nurse tells them that I have to come tomorrow because I have to see the doctor. But they say no, not back to this hospital. And they come in the morning to fetch me, the system, from the cell. I see they are driving in a different direction—to Howick! There's a white policeman already waiting for us there and he goes inside with me to the doctor consulting rooms. And the doctor indeed removes this IUD, which was not being used anyway. Removes this IUD and says, "Ya, *is erenstig, is erenstig*." "It's genuine. She's telling the truth, she had an IUD here which needed to be removed." So then the system trusted me a bit but they were not sure. They must have remembered that there's a doctor that's been coming to look for me. But then Zola still insisted on coming to see me. But they wouldn't let her in, instead they allowed me the privilege of receiving food parcels from Zola, as long as it's dry things—chocolate, and roll-on. Eh! It was so nice to smell nice! They took me to Middelburg hospital for the next eight months. And then transferred me back to Number Four. Two years nine months without trial.

So that's how I learnt about Steve's death and I was very angry. I was very bitter. Because he was my leader. And once you've finished something like eight months in solitary confinement, you know that there's nothing they're going to do to you, they couldn't find anybody to help them lay charges against you. So I was always thinking of "Oh! When I come out of here I'm going to tell Steve of how they tortured me and you know." That's how we looked up to him, to be honest. He was always with us in the gumba situations. Yes! He danced—when we were dancing we'd say "dim lights!." Or switch off the lights and then we would start. Eh! [Laughs] That was the Steve that I knew.

30 Years Later

I'm not happy about how Steve is being acknowledged. Ok, there was that statue in the Eastern Cape and so on. A lot of recognition goes to people who actually do not know what Steve went through and what he did. Steve believed in the grassroots. He believed in the grassroots. And we had a term for it, "community development." When the system arrests you and asks you, "What are you doing? What are you talking about there?'" "We're talking community development," that's all you tell them. "Com Dev." We used to call it Com Dev. "So what are we going to do today, you, for Com Dev?" "I'll be tackling student education, adult education." "We'll be tackling arts and culture." "We'll be tackling women, you have to talk to our women." So, it was all community development, Com Dev. We would go around communities identifying community leaders, *abafundisi*, teachers, ministers. I used to be a Sunday school teacher, teaching these women how to teach Sunday school, but using vocabulary that was relevant. So what is going on now, I don't think there is enough interaction with the grassroots. Steve would have insisted, I don't think he would have wanted to be in parliament, I don't know, things would have changed. But he would have wanted to be more involved with community organizations. At the time of his death, I don't know if he had already registered for his law degree because he intended studying law. He used to get very disturbed when people got arrested. And especially when it was women. Steve would have wanted to see himself working together with any progressive attitudes, supporting any progressive attitudes. Be it from the ANC, well, I don't think there's a PAC anymore. Remember at this time of his arrest he was going to seek to meet older leaders from the Unity Movement, from the PAC, from the ANC, so that he could unify them.

Black Consciousness should not be lost, it should still be instilled within the community. A lot of people still have not gained their self-awareness and a lot of black people are still psychologically oppressed, not talking even about economically oppressed. We all are still struggling and still battling.

Some of us are involved in ANC programs but it doesn't mean that we must forget where we come from. I always say to these people, why be ashamed? Others will say, "When you were involved in SASO you were underground." You were not underground! In fact we did not even talk the name "underground." It was just Black Consciousness—conscientize, conscientize all the way. Now all of a sudden because you have these high positions in the ANC you think you should forget. If you don't forget it must be whisper, whisper, whisper.

Note

1. Lucas Mangope was appointed by the apartheid government as president of the "homeland" Bophuthatswana.

Notes on Contributors

Amanda Alexander is a doctoral student in African history at Columbia University and a Visiting Researcher at the Centre for Civil Society, University of KwaZulu-Natal. Her research focuses on transnational social movements, land struggles, and racial politics. An associate producer of Pacifica Radio's *Wake Up Call*, her writing has appeared in the *Journal of Asian and African Studies, Feminist Africa, We Write, Mail & Guardian, Pambazuka News*, and several edited volumes.

Neville Alexander is director of the Project for the Study of Alternative Education in South Africa (PRAESA) at the University of Cape Town. After serving ten years on Robben Island (1964–1974) for alleged conspiracy to commit sabotage, he served a further five years under house arrest. Beginning in 1979, when he could operate "legally" again, he was involved in most of the left-wing antiapartheid social and political movements, and played a leading role in the National Forum.

Nurina Ally, BA (Wits), is a Masters student at the University of Edinburgh, currently working on a critical analysis of the conceptualization of citizenship within South African education.

Shireen Ally, PhD (University of Wisconsin, Madison), is currently a lecturer in the Department of Sociology at the University of the Witwatersrand. She has published on the history and politics of South African social science, and her current research examines paid domestic work in South Africa.

Mphutlane wa Bofelo is a Black Consciousness activist, writer, poet, and sociopolitical commentator, currently based in Durban. He writes for *Al-Qalam* newspaper and is a columnist for *Islamic Focus*, a monthly published by the Center for International Politics at the University of Pretoria. His published literary works include *The Heart's Interpreter, The Journey Within: Reflections in Ramadaan, Remembrance and Salutations*, and a contribution to the anthology *5-poetry* (edited by Allan Kolski Horwitz).

NOTES ON CONTRIBUTORS

Ashwin Desai holds a doctorate from Michigan State University and is currently affiliated with the Centre for Civil Society at the University of KwaZulu-Natal. One of South Africa's foremost social commentators, his work, including *We are the Poors: Community Struggles in Post-Apartheid South Africa*, is internationally celebrated for its courage and clarity of vision and for its focus on the lived experience of oppression and resistance.

Gail M. Gerhart is the author of *Black Power in South Africa: The Evolution of an Ideology* and coeditor of the series *From Protest to Challenge: A Documentary History of African Politics in South Africa, 1882–1990*.

Nigel C. Gibson is director of the Honors Program at Emerson College. He is the author of *Fanon: The Postcolonial Imagination* and the editor of a number of books including, most recently, *Challenging Hegemony: Social Movements and the Quest for a New Humanism in Post-Apartheid South Africa*. He is the editor of the *Journal of Asian and African Studies*.

Lewis R. Gordon is the Laura H. Carnell Professor of Philosophy, Religion, and Judaic Studies, and Director of the Institute for the Study of Race and Social Thought and the Center for Afro-Jewish Studies at Temple University, and President of the Caribbean Philosophical Association. He is the author of many books, including, most recently, *Disciplinary Decadence: Living Thought in Trying Times* (Paradigm Publishers), *An Introduction to Africana Philosophy* (Cambridge University Press) and, with Jane Anna Gordon, *Of Divine Warning: Reading Disaster in the Modern Age* (Paradigm Publishers).

Naomi Klein is the award-winning author of the international bestseller, *No Logo: Taking Aim at the Brand Bullies*. Translated into twenty-eight languages and with more than a million copies in print, *The New York Times* called *No Logo* "a movement bible." She writes an internationally syndicated column for *The Nation* magazine and *The Guardian* newspaper. Her latest book, *The Shock Doctrine: The Rise of Disaster Capitalism*, was published worldwide in September 2007.

Avi Lewis is one of Canada's most controversial and eloquent media personalities. His new television series, *On the Map with Avi Lewis*, a daily half hour of international news analysis debuted in June 2007 on CBC Newsworld. In 2004, he directed his first feature documentary, *The Take*, which follows Argentina's new movement of worker-run businesses. An emotional story of hope and resistance in the global economy, *The New York Times* called it "a stirring, idealistic documentary."

NOTES ON CONTRIBUTORS 287

Tinyiko Sam Maluleke is professor of Black and African Theology at the University of South Africa in Pretoria. He has published more than sixty scientific articles in the subjects of Black Theology, African Theology, African Philosophy, and African Studies. He has written several pieces on the South African Truth and Reconciliation process and is one of the most published scholars on religion since 1994. He currently serves as the Executive Director for Research at the University of South Africa.

M. J. Oshadi Mangena holds a doctorate from the University of Amsterdam and has published on feminist epistemology, black feminist thought, and women's movements in southern Africa. She was active in the Pretoria Students Organisation (PRESO), a regional branch of the South African Students Organisation (SASO), and joined the Black Peoples Convention in 1973. She also served as National President of the World Affiliated Young Women's Christian Association of South Africa (1974). She is currently a consultant on gender and development studies for the Umtapo Centre, Durban.

Deborah Matshoba is a former SASO executive member. She was arrested and tortured under the Terrorism Act in 1976. After serving her sentence, she was served with banning orders that confined her to the Krugersdorp Magisterial District that prevented her from attending her own wedding. Her wedding dress is displayed at the former women's jail as part of a permanent exhibition of women political prisoners in Johannesburg.

Strini Moodley was one of the founders of the Black Consciousness movement, along with his close friend, Steve Biko. A playwright and journalist, he played a key role in publishing SASO newsletters and other publications. Moodley was one of nine activists convicted on terrorism charges in 1976, for which he served a six-year prison sentence at Robben Island. After his release, Moodley became a member of the Azanian People's Organisation (AZAPO), and went on to work for the *Natal Witness*. He also served as a member of the National Executive Committee of the Media Workers Association. He passed away in April 2006.

Mabogo P. More is a former professor of philosophy at the University of KwaZulu-Natal. He is now a Senior Research Fellow at the same university and has, over the years, published extensively in African and Africana existential philosophy.

Andile Mngxitama is a doctoral student at the University of Witwatersrand and an activist in South Africa's Landless People's Movement. He was national president of the Azanian Students Movement, a Black Consciousness student formation. A founding coeditor of *We Write* journal, he is currently working on the reconceptualization of race theory in South Africa. He is also a columnist for *City Press*.

Andries Oliphant is a writer, critic, and lecturer in the Department of Theory of Literature at the University of South Africa. A former editor of *Staffrider* magazine, he has also chaired the Arts and Culture Trust of the President. He is a recipient of, among others, the Thomas Pringle Award for Short Stories and the 1998 Book Journalist of the Year Award.

Prishani Naidoo is a writer and researcher who lives and works in Johannesburg.

Lou Turner is currently a professor in African American studies at the University of Illinois at Urbana-Champaign, and research and public policy director for a community organization on the far south side of Chicago. With John Alan, they coauthored *Frantz Fanon, Soweto and American Black Thought*, one of the first works by American radicals to bring the thought of Steve Biko to an American audience.

Ahmed Veriava is a writer and researcher who lives and works in Johannesburg.

Frank B. Wilderson, III is an assistant professor in the Program in African American Studies and the Department of Drama at the University of California. From 1991 to 1996 he lived in Johannesburg where he taught at Wits, Vista, and Khanya College, and served as an elected official in the ANC. His forthcoming books include a memoir, *Incognegro* (South End Press), and *Red, White, & Black: Cinema and the Structure of U.S. Antagonisms* (Duke University Press).

As well as the contributors, the editors would like to thank Pumla Gqola, Kgafela oa Magogodi, Mandla Seleoane, and Veronique Tadjo for their support; Alf Kumalo for permission to use his wonderful photograph of Biko; Jonelle Lonergan for her work on the index, and Christopher Chappell for shepherding the book through at Palgrave Macmillan.

Index

72 hour law 22, 23

African National Congress (ANC) 2, 3, 4, 7, 20, 21, 26, 27, 32, 33, 40, 58, 72, 75, 77, 95, 96, 99, 100, 112, 113, 130, 130–134, 138, 140, 142, 161–163, 201, 252, 267, 270–274, 277
African Native National Council 267
African Students Association (ASA) 8, 240, 252, 285
Africana Philosophy 46–47, 49, 63, 92, 284
Afrocentricity 204
Aguilar, Asanta 206
Alan, John 11, 48, 78, 129
Alexander, Amanda 7, 275–284
Alexander, Neville 8–9, 140, 141, 142, 157–170
Ally, Nurina 6, 9, 171–189
Ally, Shireen 6, 9, 171–189
Anglo-Boer culture 216, 225, 240
Anti-blackness 97, 100, 102, 111, 112, 113
apartheid 2, 3, 4, 5, 6–8, 9, 10, 12, 13, 15, 16, 17, 18, 25, 39, 41, 51, 54, 55, 57, 70, 71, 72–74, 80, 83, 88, 104, 133, 149, 157, 158, 159, 167, 168, 173, 175, 178, 182, 183, 185, 191–212, 209, 213, 214, 245, 246, 249
Appiah, Kwame Anthony 45, 56, 67
Association of African Women for Research and Development (AAWORD) 260–261, 264
Astorga, Nora 206
Azania 144, 168, 183, 192, 197
Azanian Manifesto 9, 153, 160, 164, 168–170
Azanian People's Organization (AZAPO) 7, 9, 134, 137–139, 141, 142–145, 147–148, 150, 152, 153, 154, 164–166, 181, 183–185
Azanian Student's Movement (AZASM) 134, 153
Azikwelwa 279

Baldwin, James 54, 67
Baloyi, Elias 204
Baloyi, John 204
Baraka, Amiri 58, 67, 193

Beijing World Women's Forum (1995) 263
Berea Road march (1959) 269
Bergson, Henri 237
  Time and Free Will 237
Bernasconi, Robert 63
Biko, Bantu Stephen (Steve) 21–42
  arrest of 70
  banning of 117
  and Black Consciousness 2, 3, 21, 46, 48–49, 52, 56, 83, 90, 91, 107, 111, 136, 174, 244
  "Black Consciousness and the Quest for a True Humanity" 10, 48, 213
  "Black Souls in White Skins?" 48, 77, 173
  death of 2, 10, 116, 117, 134, 138, 163, 213, 231, 281
  detention of 70, 117
  as icon 18, 112, 191, 192, 210, 234
  and racism 54–56, 59–61
  and religion 118–122
  as student 22, 26, 31, 158, 276–278
  "Some African Cultural Concepts" 215, 237
  I Write What I Like 9, 48, 90, 204, 214, 231, 235, 236, 245, 247
  "We Blacks" 77, 119, 120
  "White Racism and Black Consciousness" 3, 48, 187
  and women 257, 277–278, 281
Biko, Nkosinathi 210
Bila, Vonani 19, 201, 204–205, 208
  "Mr. President, Let the babies die" 205
  Dear Gabriel 205
  Mandela Have you ever Wondered 205
Black Absence 97, 99, 100
Black Christology 123
black communalism 3, 12–13, 130
Black Community Programmes (BCP) 159, 279, 281
Black Consciousness (BC) 1, 2, 4–8, 10–15, 48, 49, 71, 72–81, 85, 87, 89–91, 100, 101, 103–104, 106, 108–112, 116, 129–150, 214, 218, 225, 228, 234, 243, 244, 253–254, 255, 258–260, 283
"Black Man You Are On Your Own" 13, 172, 184, 247, 255

INDEX

Black Consciousness—*continued*
and black communalism 3
corporate 18, 232
and humanism 11, 132, 138, 146, 148
and Marxism 6, 9, 104, 106, 130, 134, 135, 145–146, 148, 178–179, 182, 184
origins of 4–7, 21–24, 268–269
and racism 52, 54, 55–56, 255
and socialism 158–160
and white liberalism 171–186
Black Consciousness Movement of Azania (BCMA) 138–139, 145, 151, 154, 183
Black Creativity and Development 193
Black Economic Empowerment (BEE) 10, 16, 232, 234, 247
Black Feminist Thought 262, 266
black liberation 2, 4, 17, 18, 53, 57–59, 64, 77, 83, 140, 173
Black Panther Party 281
Black People's Convention (BPC) 29, 31, 32, 117, 137, 138, 142, 146, 161, 162, 192, 209, 259, 260
Black Perspective 193
Black Power Gang 270
Black Renaissance Convention (1974) 180
Black Review 193
Black Theology (BT) 24, 77, 117, 148, 149, 150, 194
Black Women's Federation 15, 255, 259
Black, Naomi 261, 263
blackness 2, 13, 32, 55, 56, 60–61, 79, 80, 84–85, 91, 97, 98, 100, 102, 103, 105, 111, 121, 149, 183, 184, 244, 254
black-on-black violence 62
Boeke, Julius 73, 74
Boesak, Rev. Alan 124, 141, 165
Bofelo, Mphutlane Wa 10, 13, 191–212
Bogolane, Malefetse 198
Boipatong massacre 96
Bond, Patrick 205
"Talk Left, Walk Right" 205
Bongmba, Elias 91
Brown, James 13
Buccus, Imraan 18
Bullet 203, 210, 211
Bunting, S. P. 27
Bush Colleges 158, 159, 277
Buthelezi, Gatsha 25, 124, 166, 173

Cabral, Amilcar 12, 209, 215, 228
Cape Action League 141, 153, 164
Cape Town 141, 161, 163
Carmichael, Stokely 24, 50, 51
Cassirer, Ernst 87
Césaire, Aimé 193, 209
Children's Revolution (1976) 100

Christianity 13, 21, 77, 118–124, 194, 216, 224, 225
churches 13, 15, 118, 119, 121, 122, 123, 166, 257
Cindi, Absolom Zithulele 124, 165
Clan, the 192, 193
Cleaver, Harry 232
colonialism 2, 15, 16, 19, 47, 51, 61, 75, 76, 89, 215, 216, 223, 225–227, 229, 238, 241, 246
Coloured Representative Council (CRC) 30
Comfortable politics 29
Communist Bloc (CB) 101
Communist Party 21, 33, 147, 265, 272
Cone, James 2, 20, 24
Congress of South African Students (COSAS) 134, 137, 152, 166
Congress of South African Trade Unions (COSATU) 96, 101, 130
Cooper, Sathasivan (Saths) 32, 38, 130, 140, 141, 142, 145, 148, 160, 165
Cox, Oliver Cromwell 73
Creative Ink project 204
Cronin, Jeremy 201

Dashiki (cultural group) 193, 198, 199
Davis, Angela 279
de Beauvoir, Simone 81
The Second Sex 81
de Covarrubias, Sebastian 85, 92
democratic centralism 135
Desai, Ashwin 89, 265–272
Development Dialogue 261
dialectic 3, 10, 11, 13, 29, 52, 56, 57, 59, 72, 75, 77, 78, 79, 80, 81, 85, 86, 108, 109, 111, 129–150, 237, 238, 259
see also Hegelian dialectic
Disorderly Bills Action Committee 141, 164
DJ Cool-fire (Hadebe, Eric Nkosinathi) 203
Drum decade, the 192, 193
Dunayevskaya, Raya 75, 78, 131, 147
Durban 15, 32, 36, 38, 180, 193, 203, 259, 267, 268, 276, 281
strikes (1973) 180

education 4, 7, 12, 16, 34, 35, 41, 61, 154, 169, 193, 198, 201, 203, 211, 216, 245, 250, 261, 283
eThekwini Municipality 204
Eiselen men/women 159

Fanon, Frantz 3, 10, 11–13, 19, 23, 48–49, 50, 52, 61, 70, 76–81, 86, 87, 88, 89, 97, 102–110, 117, 121, 129–134, 136, 137, 148, 149, 150, 173, 215, 226, 228, 236–242
"On National Culture" 215, 236, 250
Black Skin, White Masks 48, 78, 79, 86, 97, 103, 106, 107

INDEX 291

The Wretched of the Earth 48, 86, 132, 134, 236
Fawkes, Richard 45, 46
Feela Sister Spoken Word Collective 206
feminism 204, 258, 262–264, 281
First Congress of Negro Writers and Artists (1956) 76
Formation school 35
Fortunati, Leopoldina 107, 114
Frank Talk 1, 77, 143, 144
Free University Scheme 278
Freedom Charter (1955) 4, 7, 20, 130, 141, 152, 153, 166, 170, 271
Friere, Paulo 2, 10
Furnivall, John 73–74

gender 13–15, 107, 108, 199, 254–260
General Laws Amendment Act (1962) 158
General Students Council (GSC) 276–278
Gerhart, Gail 2, 8, 16, 21–43, 48, 75, 179, 180, 254
Ghetto Kids project 203
Ghetto Prophecy Movement (GPM) 203
Gibson, Nigel C. 9, 12, 63, 89, 129–156
Giovanni, Nikki 193
Goldberg, David Theo 51, 63
Gordon, Lewis R. 3, 9, 10, 11, 13, 46, 47, 48, 49, 50, 53, 58, 59, 60, 97, 98, 105
Gordon, Milton 73
Government of National Unity 108
Gqola, Pumla Dineo 14, 20
Gqozo, General Joshua Oupa 96
Gramsci, Antonio 103, 133, 151, 159
Grobbelaar, Arthur 31
Growth Employment and Redistribution (GEAR) 201
Guevera, Che 209, 210
Gumbi, Bandile 204, 206
 "After the Fact" 206
 Pangs of Imitation 204, 206
Gwala, Mafika Pascal 194, 196
 "Kwela Ride" 196
Gyekye, Kwame 91, 93

Hadebe, Eric Nkosinathi ("DJ Cool-fire") 203
Hamilton, Charles 24
Hammanskraal Manifesto 140, 141, 168
health 18, 71, 111, 169, 201, 261
Hegel, Georg Wilhelm Friedrich 10, 11, 78, 79–81, 83, 86, 109, 131–132
 Phenomenology of Spirit 78, 84
 Philosophy of Right 84
Hegelian dialectic 78, 80, 110, 131, 132
hegemony 70, 80, 99, 101, 103, 112, 131, 153, 172, 208, 272
Heidegger, Martin 62, 66, 68

Heron, Gill Scott 193
Hirschmann, David 101, 110
Hirson, Baruch 145, 154
HIV/AIDS 71, 103, 124, 204, 207, 272
Hlungwani, Jackson 204
Holloway, John 241, 242
"homelands" 4, 12, 96, 99, 283
Hondius, Jodocus 217, 218
 A Clear Description of the Cape of Good Hope 217
Honnekom, Derrick 100
hooks, bell 262
 Ain't I a Woman 262
Hughes, Langston 193
Humanism
 see African humanism
 see liberal humanism
 see Marxist humanism
 see socialist humanism
humanity 9, 11, 16, 19, 49, 52, 59, 60, 76–78, 104, 105, 108, 132, 149, 197, 214–218, 225, 226, 229

Imbongi Yesizwe 201, 207
imperialist economism 133, 151
Industrial and Commercial Workers' Union (ICU) 27
integration 17, 57–59, 73, 137, 174, 244, 245
International Women's Movement 262, 263
Izimbongi Zesimanje 203

Jenkins, Myesha 206
 "Revolutionary Woman" 206
 Diaspora 206
 Fighting men 206
Johannesburg x, 21, 96, 205, 275
Johannesburg Stock Exchange 2
Johnson, Linton Kwesi 193
Jones, William R. 55
Jongilizwe
 see Cooper, Saths
Jongwe, Zola 281, 282

ka Shezi, Mthuli 7, 192, 209, 274
Kabwe Congress (1985) 7
Kallen, Horace 73
Kani, John 198, 199
Karenga, Moulana 58, 67
Kasrils, Ronnie 96–97, 99, 100, 103, 112
Kaunda, Kenneth 109, 121, 221–223
ke system 257
Kempton Park 271
Kgware, Manana 254, 255
Kgware, Motlalepula 192, 260, 265
Kgware, Winnie 14
Khalid, Laila 206
Khoapa, Benny 172, 192, 281

INDEX

Khoza, Daphne 281
Klein, Naomi 267–274
Koornhoff Bills 141, 153, 164, 167, 168
Kraai, Nomsisi 15, 259, 275
Kruger, Jimmy 271, 272
Kuzwayo, Ellen 263, 265, 280
  Call Me Woman 263

labor 6, 11, 30, 54, 72, 74, 78, 79, 99, 103, 104, 108, 132, 133, 140, 143, 145, 147, 150, 154, 159, 172, 182, 183, 219, 225, 233, 234, 235, 253, 255, 263
land 2, 3, 19, 55, 103, 160, 169, 180, 211, 221, 225, 241, 248, 253
Last Poets, The 193
Laurence, Patrick 274
Lekota, Mosiuwa Patrick ("Terror") 124, 192
Lewis, Avi 267–274
Lewis, Desiree 13
liberal humanism 11, 12, 227
Liberal Party 22, 269
liberalism 3, 25, 81, 83, 89, 90, 91, 102, 149, 171, 173, 175, 186
  see also white liberalism
  see also neoliberalism
Limpopo Province 204
Luse, George 198
Luxemburg, Rosa 15

Mabasa, Lybon 7, 137, 147, 165
Mabasa, Noria 204
Madingoane, Ingoapele 194
Mafuna, Bokwe 275, 277
Magogodi, Kgafela Oa 204
  I Mike What I Like 204
Magona, Sindiwe 200
Mahola, Mzi 198, 199, 200, 292, 204, 205, 209
Makerere, University of 278
Maluleke, Tinyiko Sam 12, 115–127
Mamdani, Mahmood 88, 91, 93
Manaka, Matsemela 194
Mandela, Nelson 5, 6, 13, 33, 45, 95, 112, 133, 159, 201, 205, 208, 267, 271–274, 279
Mandela, Winnie 15, 259, 281
Mangayi, Willi 204
Mangcu, Xolela 210
Mangena, M. J. Oshadi 14, 15, 253–266, 281
Maqhina, Mzwandile 198
Marable, Manning 51
Markovic, Mihailo 264
Marx, Karl 78, 82, 103, 104, 107, 132, 146, 148, 150, 223, 224, 233, 248, 269
  Das Kapital 269
  Economic and Philosophic Manuscripts of 1844 155

Marxism 6, 9, 13, 104, 106, 130, 134–135, 144, 145, 146, 148, 152, 175–179, 182, 184
Marxist humanism 132
Mashego, Goodenough 207, 208, 209, 211
Mashile, Lebogang 204, 206
  "In a Ribbon of Rhythms" 204
Mashinini, Tsietsi 7
Mathews, James 195
  Cry Rage 195
Mathonsi, Rismathi 199
Matshoba, Deborah 7, 10, 14, 15, 259, 275–283
Mattera, Don 194
  Azanian love song 194
Mbeki, Moeletsi 16, 20, 112
Mbhele, Sphephelo ("Miracle") 203
Mbuli, Mzwakhe 194, 200, 202
McGary, Howard 58, 67
Mda, Zakes 200
Mead, Margaret 54
Meer, Fatima 15, 257
Merleau-Ponty, Maurice 87
Mhlophe, Gcina 193
Mkhabela, Ishmael 137, 165
Mkiva, Zolani 201
Mngxitama, Andile 7, 19, 20, 275–283
modernity 74, 92, 93, 102, 105, 112
Mohapi, Mapetla 7, 209
Mokoape, Aubrey Nchaupe 192, 254
Mokoape, Keith 276
Moloto, Nkwapa 201
Moodley, Asha 193, 209, 211
Moodley, Strinivasa Raju ("Strini") 6, 10, 19, 38, 146, 160, 165, 178, 184, 192, 193, 209, 254, 267–274
More, Mabogo P. 10, 45–68, 83
Mosala, Itumeleng 124, 148, 149, 151, 265
Mosala, Letsatsi 184
Motjuwadi, Stanley 197
  "White Lies" 197
Motlhabi, Mokgethi 124, 150
Motsisi, Casey 192, 193
Mphahele, Eskia 64, 192, 195
Mphapi, Mapleta 279
Mpumlwana, Mualusi 192
Mqhayisa, Khaya 198
Mthathi, Sphokazi 201
Mthintso, Thenjiwe 206
Mtshali, Oswald 194, 196
  The Sound of a Cowhide Drum 194
Mugabe, Robert 205
Mutabaruka 193
Myeza, Muntu 142, 165

Naidoo, Prishani 8, 13, 18, 231–250
Nakasa, Nat 192
Natal Indian Congress (NIC) 31

National Executive Committee (NEC)   95, 96
National Forum   9, 140–142, 144, 153, 157, 168, 170
National Union of South African Students (NUSAS)   22, 26, 118, 171, 173, 179, 185, 271, 276
   conference (1968)   185
   conference (1971)   174
Nationalist Party   133
Ndamse, Curnick   32
Ndebele, Njabulo   178
Nefolovhodwe, Pandelani   124, 154, 165
Negritude   12, 13, 52–53, 64, 69, 108–111, 130, 193, 236, 237–241
Nengwekhulu, Harry   187, 254, 275
neoliberalism   9, 19, 20, 89, 133, 200, 243, 247
Ngubeni, Obed   204
Nkonyeni, Nomhle   198
Nkrumah, Kwame   35, 45, 63, 75, 117, 147, 151, 221
Nkrumahism   75
Noel, Jeanne   15, 257
Non-European Unity Movement (NEUM)   159
Nowadays Poets   203, 204
Ntshona, Winston   198
Nxumalo, Henry   192
Nyezwa, Mxolisi   201

Oliphant, Andries   12, 213–232
ontology   49, 98, 107, 110, 237
Organisation of African Unity (OAU)   163
Oruka, Odera   45, 50
Outlaw, Lucius   46, 47, 59

Pan Africanist Congress (PAC)   4, 26, 27, 33, 40, 72, 75, 77, 138, 140, 142, 144, 161, 180, 254, 267, 271, 277, 283
Parents Teachers Students Association (PTSA)   164
parrot poetry   201
Patel, Quraish   138
Paton, Alan   34, 271
Patterson, Orlando   104, 105
   Slavery and Social Death   104
Phakathi, Oshadi   15, 257
Phenomenology   66, 77, 83, 89, 90, 255
Pithouse, Richard   89
Pityana, Barney   13, 48, 106, 130, 138, 139, 171, 172, 174, 185, 192, 199, 242, 254, 278
pluralism   72–75, 81
poetry   191–212
   hip-hop   195, 202, 203, 207, 211
   spoken word   195, 202, 203, 204, 206, 207, 208, 211
Port Elizabeth   8, 137, 153

Port Elizabeth Black Civic Organization (PEBCO)   134, 137–138, 152
positive humanism   139
Progressive Federal Party   271
Progressive Party   22, 41

racial capitalism   9, 25, 140, 141, 153, 167, 168, 175, 178, 179, 183, 186
Ramphele, Mamphela   14, 20, 65, 255
Rampolokeng, Lesego   194
Reality   177
Reconstruction and Development Program (RDP)   18, 131
Rivonia trial   265
Robben Island   5, 6, 20, 31, 142, 153, 160, 167, 192, 266, 270, 271, 279
Rolling Mass Action Committee   96, 112

Sachs, Albie   100
Said, Edward   117, 250
Santamaria, Haydee   206
Sartre, Jean-Paul   10, 11, 48–49, 50, 52–53, 55, 58–63, 66, 81, 82, 83, 92, 99, 108–111, 114, 130, 255
   Anti-Semite and Jew   81, 110
   bad faith   47, 49, 59, 60
   "Black Orpheus"   52, 53, 66–68
   Being and Nothingness   81
   Portrait of the Anti-Semite   58
Schools Boycott (1980)   164
scientific socialism   130, 135, 139, 143–145, 150
Senghor, Leopold   2, 13, 23, 48, 64, 136, 193, 221, 223–224, 236–241
   Negritude: A Humanism Of The Twentieth Century   236
Sepamla, Sipho   194, 196
   A Ride on the Whirlwind   194
   The Soweto I Love   194
   "To Whom it May Concern"   196
Serote, Mongane Wally   194, 197, 201
   "Anonymous Throbs + A Dream"   197
   Behold Mama, Flowers   194
   Come and Hope with Me   194
   Sunset   197
   Tsetlo   194
   Yakhal'inkomo   194
Serpent Players   193, 198
sexism   13–15, 206, 207, 255, 258, 261
   see also gender
sexuality   84, 124
Sharpeville Massacre (1960)   4, 192
Shivambu, Lucy   204
slam poetry   195, 202–204, 207, 208, 210
Slam Poetry Operation Team (SPOT)   203

294 INDEX

slavery   viii, ix, 47, 48, 61, 63, 75, 78–79, 80, 86, 99, 103, 104–105, 106, 113, 114, 198, 228, 257, 263
Slovo, Joe   267
Sobukwe, Robert   32, 33, 159, 279
Socialist Humanism   136
Sole, Kelwyn   200–201
Songhai   237
Sono affair (1972)   180
Sono, Themba   46, 274
South African Black Theatre Union (SABTU)   192
South African Communist Party (SACP)   3, 9, 11, 20, 99, 269, 271, 273
South African Council of Churches   166
South African Council on Sport (SACOS)   164
South African Outlook   202
South African Students Organization (SASO)   8, 14, 21, 25, 26–29, 31–39, 53, 66, 72, 73, 75, 117, 118, 124, 172, 173, 179, 180, 242, 254, 255, 257, 266, 276, 277, 279–281, 287
Soweto Action Committee   180, 182
Soweto rebellion (1976)   7, 71, 77, 129, 134
Staffrider   193
Stubbs, Aelred   214, 278
Student Nonviolent Coordinating Committee (SNCC)   24
Study Project of Christianity in Apartheid Society (SPRO-CAS)   21
Suppression of Communism Act   158
Suzman, Helen   39

Tabata, I.B.   148
Tellez, Dora Maria   206
Terrorism Act   5, 70, 137, 154, 158, 281, 287
Thatcher, Margaret   133
Theatre Council of Natal (TECON)   192
Thi Binh, Nguyen   206
Third Force   163, 170
Thomas, Gladys   195
   Cry Rage   195
Time Magazine   202
Tiro, Onkgopotse Abraham   6–7, 209, 277
   Turfloop University speech (1970)   6
Tladi, Lefifi   198–199, 208, 209
Tleane, Console   4
Tlhagale, Buti   124, 139, 140
Tlhobolo, Phedi   201
Transkei   27, 30, 161, 180, 271, 274
Triparite Alliance   96, 97
Truth and Reconciliation Commission (TRC)   7, 18
Turfloop   6, 26, 38, 135, 254, 277

Turner, Lou   11, 48, 69–82
Turner, Nat   75
Turner, Richard   176–177
Tutu, Desmond   92, 137, 141, 165

ubuntu   160, 227
United Democratic Front (UDF)   6, 7, 9, 99, 101–102, 112, 130, 131, 134, 138, 144, 151, 165–167
United Nations (UN)   258, 259, 261
United Nations Organization   163
United Nations World Conferences on Women   258, 261
   Copenhagen Conference (1980)   259
   Mexico City Conference (1975)   259
   Plan of Action (1975)   259
Unity Movement   140, 141, 159, 160, 267, 277, 283
University Christian Movement (UCM)   37, 118, 276
University of Natal Black Section (UNB)   276, 277

van der Horst, Frank   165
Veriava, Ahmed   8, 13, 18, 233–252
Verwoerd, Hendrik   51, 52, 149
village communities   219
Vladislavic, Ivan   200

Weinberg, Sheila   206
Westville   38, 275
white liberalism   2, 3, 72, 173, 175, 185
white Marxism   178
Wilderson, Frank B. III   6, 10, 11, 13, 95–114
Winterveldt   279
Wits Drama Society   193
womanism   204, 262
Women in Development (WID)   260
Women's Students Organization (WSO)   14, 277, 278
Wright, Richard   63

X, Malcolm   ix, 2, 116, 121
Xaba, Lwazi ("Zorro")   203

Young Basadzi Projects (YPB)   203–204
Young Progressives   22
Young Women's Christian Association (YWCA)   14, 15, 259, 279, 280, 281

Zapatistas   3, 243
Zimbabwe   55, 205
Zizek, Slavoj   72, 82